Thinking About Schools

New Theories and Innovative Practice

Thinking About Schools

New Theories and Innovative Practice

Aimee Howley
Craig Howley
Ohio University

2007

LAWRENCE ERLBAUM ASSOCIATES, PUBLISHERS

Mahwah, New Jersey   London

Lawrence Erlbaum Associates, Inc., Publishers
10 Industrial Avenue
Mahwah, New Jersey 07430
www.erlbaum.com

Cover design by Kathryn Houghtaling Lacey

Library of Congress Cataloging-in-Publication Data

Howley, Aimee
     Thinking about schools : new theories and innovative practice / by Aimee
     Howley, Craig B. Howley.
            p.   cm.
     Includes index.
     ISBN 0-8058-5194-1 (pbk.: alk. paper)
     ISBN 1-4106-1463-8 (E book)
     1. School management and organization—United States.   2. Educational
     leadership—United States. 3. School principles—United States. I. Howley,
     Craig B. II. Title.
     LB2801.A2H69   2006
     371.200973—dc22

                                                                2006002685
                                                                CIP

Books published by Lawrence Erlbaum Associates are printed on acid-free paper, and their bindings are chosen for strength and durability.

Printed in the United States of America
10 9 8 7 6 5 4 3 2 1

Contents

Preface

This book hopes to occupy the middle ground between practice and theory, where educators think about their work. Actually getting to that ground represents a challenge for people who write about educational administration, although getting there is frequently their goal. The effort falters, too often, because the middle ground is hard to find. Two very predictable detours lead many writers astray.

First is the impulse to be practical. Writers about educational administration recognize the pressures confronting school administrators, and in an effort to be sympathetic and helpful, some try to translate theory directly into advice. Theory, however, is both more and less useful than advice. Its subtlety and complexity make it richer than advice, but its abstraction makes it less immediate. In fact, theory is the foundation from which practitioners formulate advice *by themselves* and *for themselves*. And arguably, for each of us, taking our own good advice is what wise practice is all about.

A second impulse is to fall in love with theory. After all, theory deals with the big ideas; it's heady and challenging. In fact, the complexity and subtlety of theory make it difficult to write about. As a result, many writers begin to focus primarily on the features of theories rather than on their applicability. And they come to see their task as one of explaining theoretical ideas with precision rather than of demonstrating the ways in which clearly formulated theories can help school administrators think about schools. In the end, these writers mistake clarity for practicality, leaving their readers in a bind. After all, readers of clear explanations understand the ideas, but their understanding does not necessarily provide them with a reason to (or ways to) apply the ideas.

Interestingly, the need for a middle ground between theory and practice prompted a large number of sociological theorists in the mid-20th century to set off in search of what they called midrange theory. For a variety of reasons—several of which we discuss in chapter 2—their approach did not work out as well as they had hoped. And in the end, their approach proved inadequate because they created theories that were neither very powerful nor very practical. Midrange theories were supposed to explain how practice did and should work everywhere, for everyone; but reality has turned out to be much messier.

From our perspective, the middle ground does not reside within theories but belongs to those directly involved with practical reality. For school administrators, the process of using theory—of translating ideas into actions and also of translating actions into ideas—is what opens up the middle ground, enabling administrators to give good advice to themselves—and to one another. In a sense then, the theory-to-practice translation itself *creates* the middle ground. Readers have to be the ones to make the translation.

Why school administrators would want to bother with such translations, and how they might approach the work of translation, are matters we discuss in chapter one. There we champion theory in a big way. We talk about theory as explanation and theory as the basis for "visioning," and then we talk about the connection between the two. Of course, our arguments may fail to persuade, in which case we hope you'll blame our ineptitude rather than blaming theory. After all, the ongoing work of school administration is to connect the little pieces to the bigger picture—and that's possible only through careful reflection about both. As chapter one demonstrates, various bodies of theory provide crucial intellectual tools to enable reflection.

In this book, we offer theory as a way to examine practice, both the routine events taking place at a particular school or district and the wider political events that shape school routines. But, as we explain in chapter 2, just any old theory will not do. In fact, we find only some theories relevant to the project of examining practice because these theories recognize the social world—and schools as part of that social world—as contingent, complex, and subject to interpretation. These conditions of the social world map to three old adages that we see as helpful "rules of thumb" for reflection about practice: (1) "All is *not* what it seems," (2) "there is *more* than meets the eye," and (3) "*beauty* is in the eye of the beholder."

- "All is not what it seems." Despite what we believe to be adequate explanations of events that take place in schools, there are often deeper explanations. And certain theories focus on these, revealing hidden mechanisms that often have a profound influence. In important ways, what happens in a school or other organization depends on where it stands with regard to these hidden mechanisms. Three of the theoretical threads considered in this book pay particular attention to such hidden mechanisms, although they construe them differently. Dynamic systems theory (chap. 4) considers how underlying processes such as feedback and self-organization influence what happens. Critical theory (chap. 9) explores the implications for social relations of inevitable conflict between social classes. Although the conflict sometimes rises to the surface, it often proceeds covertly through practices embedded in everyday life. Drawing on the insights of critical theory, theories of globalization (chap. 11) look beneath the optimistic claims about the global economy to examine some of the more disturbing ramifications for schools and communities.

• "There is more than meets the eye." Not only are there hidden mechanisms that influence the social world to which schools belong, but that world reflects and contributes to human diversity. Unlike older theories that ignored diversity or tried to suppress it, some contemporary theories recognize its value and the complexity to which it contributes. Theories that focus on diversity from various perspectives are considered in chapters on the cultural bases of leadership (chap. 6), comparative and international contexts (chap. 7), and theories of gender and sexual orientation (chap. 8).

• "Beauty is in the eye of the beholder." Here we're stretching the old adage a bit to suggest that what's *valued* depends on who is doing the valuing. Theories that explore this insight build on understandings about social diversity, by focusing particularly on their philosophical implications. Whereas communitarian theories (chap. 5) primarily consider the moral and ethical implications of the differing values that are sustained through diverse communities, postmodern theories (chap. 10) primarily consider the implications for what's valued as "real" (ontology) and what's valued as "knowable" (epistemology). Looking at how social reality is made and then understood, postmodern theories explore the three conditions of the social world—contingency, complexity, and contestedness—all at once. In a sense, because this book tries to do the same thing, it represents a "postmodern" conception.

As these brief descriptions suggest, the rules of thumb are very different from those that imagine social life and school practice in terms of "one best way," and with which school administration has been most concerned since 1945 or so. Most of the book (the eight chapters just identified) explores those theories and suggests connections to everyday dilemmas that administrators confront.

But before getting underway, we consider (in chap. 3) practical justifications for the choice to address these theories. What's the rationale? It's a response to what our careers have suggested is the impracticality and arrogance of efforts to find "the one best way." The conditions of society and schooling demand the response, in our view. It's overdue. And the explorations are not just academic exercises. Each alternative theoretical approach offers a rich set of possibilities for thinking about schools. In particular, we hope that readers will draw on these possibilities (and others that they continue to learn about) as they struggle to connect what happens day-to-day in schools and what those schools will or might become.

Acknowledgments

This book has been a longer journey than most we have taken creating one. It began life in 1999, according to our records, with a publisher to whom, in course of time, the manuscript appeared to be a poor fit. The manuscript's trials in that quarter, however, yielded benefits that well-seasoned authors might predict: improved focus, clarified aims, and even stylistic insights. We're now done: So thanks go to the anonymous predecessor of the book's actual publisher; the frustration was small, the improvements substantive, and the eventual home a happy one. In particular, then, we especially thank Lawrence Erlbaum Associates and its editors and advisors for helping to voice a perspective very long overdue in school administration.

Aimee gives special thanks to Megan Rhodes, her graduate assistant and doctoral student, for happily embracing the drudgery of proofreading and checking references. Such work comes with the turf of scholarship, and is a very important part of a dissertation. And she thanks her secret correspondents—unidentified librarians who help with reference checks via IM (virtually) night and day. Aimee also expresses her gratitude to Ohio University for providing her first-ever, 10-week sabbatical, which was nicely extended by the university's 6-week winter break. That space around the completion of the manuscript was a welcome relief. We'll write another one on the same terms, immediately. Just say the word, OU. We are your humble servants.

Craig and Aimee thank Jerry Johnson (chaps. 6, 8, and 9) and Jim Williams (chap. 7) for agreeing to play in this sandbox. Both weathered the original debacle and then had to endure some, even considerable, violence to their chapter drafts. Jerry's a former student and Jim's a former Ohio faculty member. They knew what to expect: Thanks so much guys. Craig also thanks all his colleagues, every one of them, and all the students, in ACCLAIM, the Appalachian Collaborative Center for Learning, Assessment, and Instruction in Mathematics. What they contributed to this book for him was more than an organizational home, it was genuine common purpose. That's inspiration and motive.

Penultimately, Aimee and Craig together want to thank some sacred places: Roane County, West Virginia, particularly Seaman Fork Road, Rt. 1, Box 56, Liverpool, where we lived and raised our kids from 1973 to 1983; "the Palace," aka 102 Hickory Heights, in Scott Depot, West Virginia, where we completed our child-rearing and unfolded careers we couldn't have earlier imagined; and Vinton County, Ohio, particularly Lively Ridge Road, our current place and farm. To the skeptics of thanking places, we also affirm cosmopolitan homes in New York City and Philadelphia. They gave us secular purpose and a critical disposition.

Finally, we'd like to dedicate this book, once again, to family. This time to Hugh and Sabine Weiss, and to Marion and Christophe and Sara, more family, who live in Paris, France. Hugh and Sabine have lived in large measure what they imagine in times good and bad. They have work to prove it. This book may not be a worthy gift to you, nos camarades, but it's a lot like what we do.

—*Aimee & Craig Howley*

1

Using Theory
to Think About Schools

Among many contemporary educators, there seems to have developed a misguided belief about the antagonism between theory and practice. We sometimes hear our students—practicing principals and superintendents—say, "what you're teaching us here at the university is ok, but it's just theory. It won't work in the real world."

This common response to theory baffles us, as well, because theory, as we view it, involves propositions about the way the world does or should work. It isn't a prescription for what to do, but it's useless to us if it doesn't help us make sense of the real world and take effective action (in the real world) on behalf of what we value (see e.g., Mungazi, 1999).

But theory can help us do more than that. It can help us imagine alternatives by supporting useful visions of what the world might become. And it is critical that school leaders be able to do this. Equally important, theory, in its broadest sense, guides dialog about school practice, whether that dialog involves colleagues in the teachers' lounge or representatives from the many groups with a stake in what schools do and how they are run.

THEORIES THAT EXPLAIN WHAT'S GOING ON

Derived either from personal experience or from systematic study of some set of causes and effects, many theories strive to offer explanations of why things happen (see, e.g., Argyris & Schon, 1974). Unlike some explanations, however, theories attempt to provide *general principles* explaining why things typically happen. For example, contrast the following explanations:

- The teacher gave candy to the students because they were well behaved.
- The fourth-grade reading test scores improved because students had daily practice in phonics.

The first statement offers an explanation of a particular event. The statement may be perfectly true, but it does not help anyone understand how the world works. Unlike this arbitrary association of one event with another, the association between events in the second statement implies a systematic (and perhaps even a causal) relationship. If we are willing to limit our "world" to the fourth-grade classes referenced in the statement, we can formulate the second statement as a principle about how the world works: "Teaching phonics improves achievement in reading." The second statement, then, may properly be classified as a theory.

In education, we use and develop many theories of this second type. In fact, almost every feature of school life—from the association between teaching and learning to the behavior of school boards—has been theorized in this way. Sidebar 1-1 presents a list of some of these theories. You will notice in several cases that different (and even conflicting) theories purport to explain the same outcome (e.g., reading achievement or teacher motivation).

Sidebar 1-1: Theories About Why Certain Things Happen in Schools

Student Achievement

1. Achievement increases when students are taught via direct instructional methods.
2. Achievement increases when students see the meaningfulness of what they're learning.
3. Students' achievement is strongly associated with their socio-economic status.

Teachers' Job Satisfaction

1. Teachers' job satisfaction increases when they are given control over school-wide decisions.
2. Teachers' job satisfaction increases when they feel they can control what goes on in their individual classrooms.

3. Teachers' job satisfaction increases when they are treated like professionals.

School Effectiveness

1. School effectiveness improves when the professionals—teachers and administrators—are responsible for school governance.
2. School effectiveness improves when the entire community—educators, parents, and citizens—are responsible for school governance.
3. Effectiveness increases when schools are governed by strong instructional leaders.

Theoretical Systems

Often, propositions about how the world works are organized into coherent systems. In fact, when people use the word "theory" they often mean "theoretical system." For example, we may talk about "critical theory" or about "compliance theory." Each of these so-called "theories" incorporates many propositions about how the world works, not just one. This perspective of theory is what Gutek (1988) was talking about when he wrote:

> Theory refers to a grouping or clustering of general ideas or propositions that explain the operations of an institution, such as a school, or a situation, such as teaching or learning; moreover, these ideas and propositions are sufficiently abstract or general that they can be transferred and applied to situations other than those in which they are directly developed. (p. 250)

Not only do alternative theoretical systems offer different explanations of how the world works, but also, within some theoretical systems, different versions of the theory are put forth by different theorists. In dynamic systems theory, for instance, the claims made by Peter Senge differ from the claims made by Margaret Wheatley. Both versions clearly belong to dynamic systems theory, but they also show marked differences.

Another use of the word "theory" denotes an entire branch of theoretical work. For example, when we talk about "leadership theory," we are not speaking about one proposition about how the world works, nor are we speaking about one coherent set of propositions about how leadership works in the world. Instead, we are talking about a scholarly tradition devoted to explaining about leadership. Quite different, even contradictory, theoretical systems can be categorized under a heading such as "leadership theory." In Sidebar 1-2, we list several theoretical systems that pertain in some way to school leadership. We categorize these theoretical systems on the basis of the scholarly traditions to which they belong; and, for each of the theoretical systems, we provide examples of theorists who share fundamental theoretical assumptions but who offer different versions of the theory.

Sidebar 1-2: Theoretical Traditions, Systems, and Versions of Systems

Tradition 1: Leadership Theory

System 1: Contingency Theories
> Version 1: House's path-goal theory
> Version 2: Fiedler's contingency theory

System 2: Transformational Leadership Theories
> Version 1: Burn's theory of transactional and transformational leaders
> Version 2: Fullan's theory of educational change agents

Traditional 2: Organizational Theory

System 1: Theories of Bureaucracy
> Version 1: Weber's theory of the ideal bureaucracy
> Version 2: Barnard's theory of the functions of the executive

System 2: Theories of Organizational Culture
> Version 1: Schon's theory of organizational culture
> Version 2: Sergiovanni's theory of the life-world and systems-world

Tradition 3: Learning Theory

System 1: Behaviorist Theories
> Version 1: Skinner's theory of operant conditioning
> Version 2: Gagne's theory of task analysis

System 2: Constructivist Theory
> Version 1: Vygotsky's theory of social constructionism
> Version 2: Posner's conceptual change theory

Theories of Action

One important category of explanatory theory encompasses "theories of action." These theories—however derived—incorporate propositions about the means and ends (or causes and effects) of action (Argyris & Schon, 1974). For example, a school principal may act on the basis of the following theory of action: "If you want students to respect the rules, you must involve students in setting the rules." Another principal might hold a rather different theory of action: "If you want students to respect the rules, you must apply the rules firmly and consistently." These theories of action guide how each of the principals acts, and, to some extent, they may also condition the way students react.

Moreover, the fact that people hold theories of action also enables us to understand why they do what they do. Indeed, the set of propositions related to theories of action themselves constitute a theory (Argyris & Schon, 1974; Argyris, Putnam, & Smith, 1985). In other words, one theory about how people function in the world is that they develop theories and act on them. Accepting this theory means that we maintain the belief that, in order to understand a person's or a group's actions, it is necessary to understand the theories on which those actions are based.

For example, let's say we want to understand why a particular set of dynamics—interactions and relationships among people—is at play in a particular school. One place to start would be to examine the theories of action held by those who are exercising power within the school. Take, for instance, a principal who believes that, if given the chance, students will misbehave. This principal is likely to set up school structures and procedures that influence students' behavior in certain ways. Perhaps those structures and procedures will even predispose students to misbehave, contrary to the principal's theory of action (McCadden, 1998).

Our understanding of the situation, however, needs to account for greater complexity than this simple hypothetical cause and effect relationship. We must remember, after all, that not only the principal but also the students, teachers, and parents are taking actions on the basis of the theories they hold. And all of these theory-based actions are interacting in very complex ways. To understand the dynamics of a disciplinary incident or the complexities of the establishment of a school's discipline policy—or any other event, for that matter—we need first to understand how the various participants used action to produce effects on the external world (including other people). Then we need to analyze the moves and countermoves made by the participants as their different theory-based actions collided, merged, diverged, and conflicted. In such encounters, each participant's actions are likely to shift from their original course, and, in the process, their theories of action may end up being altered.

Theories-In-Use.   Explicitly stated theories of action (sometimes referred to as "espoused theories") are not always the theories on which people base their actions. Whereas sometimes people's theories-in-use are congruent with their espoused theories, often people act in ways that seem to contradict their explicitly stated theories of action (Argyris & Schon, 1974; Argyris et al., 1985). For example, we have all heard about the professor of pedagogy who lectures day after day about the importance of using active methods of teaching. The professor's theory of action (i.e., that active methods of teaching are better than passive methods of teaching for promoting students' learning) does not influence the professor's own actions. Rather, the professor operates on the basis of a tacit "theory-in-use."

According to Argyris and Schon (1974), "Theories-in-use are means for getting what we want. They specify strategies for resolving conflicts, making a living, closing a deal, organizing a neighborhood—indeed, for every kind of intended consequence" (p. 15). Professionals, such as school administrators, develop many theories-in-use in response to the conditions of their work. These theories, in fact, enable them to perform their jobs on a day-to-day basis. Without such theories, administrators would have to ponder every action they were going to take—an impossibility given the fast-paced nature of their jobs. Tacitly held theories, then, clearly enable school leaders to cope with the daily necessities of their work. At the same time, tacitly held theories can cause difficulties. In particular, because theories-in-use often embed unexamined assumptions, they can color our understanding of what's happening and thereby restrict our potential to respond flexibly to new circumstances. Tacitly held theories determine (and, as a result, limit) how we see the world. And such limitations are often opaque to us because we rarely stop to examine our unexamined assumptions! All of us are subject to this difficulty, and a better appreciation of theory and theory-making can help.

THEORIES THAT PRESENT ALTERNATIVES

Rather than describing how the world works, some theories present visions of how the world *might* work better. The visions put forward by these theories offer an ideal (or normative) view of the world or some part of it. Of course, different theorists view "the ideal" quite differently. And your views of "the ideal" might not match the views of any of the theorists.

The following example shows what we mean. Max Weber (1947) developed a theory of the "ideal bureaucracy" in which he outlined the way in which a bureaucracy might work under the best of circumstances. To Weber, bureaucracy was an innovation. It offered an objective basis for running organizations and a corrective to the arbitrary and capricious ways that 19th century and early 20th century industrialists often managed their corporations. To us today, though, bureaucracy may seem like a bad idea. When we think of bureaucracy, we usually think of huge and complicated organizations, of "red tape," and of doing things "by the book." The word "bureaucracy" does not conjure up images of fairness and job opportunity. Rather, the word suggests impersonal treatment and limitations of possibilities for employee growth. Why does this mismatch exist? Why do we see as dysfunctional what Weber imagined as an improvement?

Something like what our students complain about happened. Theories about what might, or should be are often subject to real-world testing. Bureaucracy was put to the test, but the field-testing of bureaucracy was not an intentional experiment. It just happened. As modern organizations became larger, and as managers sought ways to handle the size and complexity of these enterprises, they created rules and regulations, established hierarchies, and specialized tasks and roles, and only partly because Weber had described it all. Indeed, models had already existed for most of these things (especially in 18th and 19th century government).

Our criticisms of bureaucracy, however, stem from our experiences with these actual bureaucracies. Most of us, after all, are unaware of Weber's scholarship. We have a basis for faulting Weber in that his "ideal" version of bureaucracy did not take into account its possible dysfunctions.

Our criticisms, of course, do not address the question of whether or not bureaucracies turned out to be more fair or to offer more opportunities for advancement than the organizational arrangements that preceded them. Rather, we tend to base our criticisms on a different vision—our own personal vision—of the ideal organization. We express concerns about bureaucracies because they are not sufficiently democratic or not sufficiently attentive to the human side of organizational life. Bureaucracies, then, often fail to match up with our personal vision of "the ideal" organization. Note, however, that in order to do such a matching up, we must hold—perhaps without acknowledging so explicitly—particular theories about what constitute good (or effective) organizations. Furthermore, our views about good organizations tend to reflect our more general views about which goals and actions are "good" and which are not. Most of us, by the way, could not do a very good job of describing in detail our own vision of the ideal organization. That's another reason to study theory: to help us describe in some detail what we think—both in the mode of description and in the mode of what might be.

The Connection Between Theories and Philosophies

Philosophies are coherent and comprehensive bodies of speculative thought about the nature of the world and human beings' place within it (see, e.g., Gutek, 1988). Because they are speculative, however, philosophical systems cannot be shown to be "true" or "false" in the commonsense way that we use those terms (Perkinson, 1971). Different philosophies, instead, offer alternative perspectives on the world. Moreover, these perspectives guide the *types* of theories human beings derive about how the world *ought* to work. In particular, ethical philosophies offer visions of "the good" and principles for doing "what's right."

Our ideas about what goes into making an organization good, for example, derive from our philosophical views about "the good" in general. If we believe that caring is a fundamental good (e.g., Noddings, 1984), then we will judge organizations to be good insofar as they offer opportunities for people to care for one another. This particular philosophical perspective disposes us, for instance, to favor schools that promote nurture of children, collaboration, and parent involvement. If, by contrast, we believe that acting on the basis of rationally derived principles is a fundamental good, we might prefer schools with a clear and narrowly defined mission and with policies and procedures that justly promote that mission.

Our ethical beliefs also provide constraints—both explicit and implicit—on our theories of action. For example, empirical research studies might compel us to accept as true the finding that giving mild electric shocks to students with severe behavior disorders decreases these students' undesirable behaviors. Our ethical belief in the importance of caring, however, might keep us from acting on the basis of this knowledge. In this case, our philosophical belief intervenes overtly in our process of translating theory into practice.

Often, however, our philosophical beliefs function under the surface to keep us from asking particular questions, producing certain kinds of knowledge, or deriving particular theories. For instance, an ethical belief in the sanctity of human life might constrain some researchers from theorizing about the benefits to families of "letting nature take its course" with severely handicapped children. Or an ethical belief in the fairness of providing equal opportunity might keep educators from examining the academic improvements that might be gained by providing low income students with greater than equal opportunities (e.g., affirmitive action).

Our underlying philosophies may also guide our thinking about the nature of reality, the character of human existence and selfhood, and the properties of knowledge. Philosophical beliefs in these domains predispose us to view education in particular ways. For example, if we hold certain beliefs (e.g., existentialist beliefs) about human experience, we will tend to view education as an individual quest for self-knowledge and self-fulfillment. Or, if we hold realist beliefs about the nature of knowledge, we will most likely want education to expose students to the truth about the natural world (e.g., evolution over "intelligent design"). Philosophies and theories have immediate, unavoidable implications in the real world for everyone—and studying theory can help us influence and even control those implications.

The Language of Possibility

As we previously indicated, theories that support alternative visions of schooling often depict an ideal view of the world. Theorists who develop such visions, however, ground them, in part, in critical analyses of the way schools actually are. Each of these theories tends to couple a view of what's wrong with real schools with a vision of what schools might become. For theorists who put forth such views, the first step in changing what schools are like is to change how we think and talk about them. Nevertheless, when long-standing structures sustain the current reality of schools, we may find it hard to believe that changes in language and thinking can have much of an effect.

We provide two brief examples of theories of this type and some structural conditions that might keep such theories from serving as blueprints for real schools. It is important to note, however, that theorists who offer alternative views of schooling through "the language of possibility" (Giroux, 1988b) do not typically expect that their ideas will be put into practice wholesale. Instead, they hope that educators will put these ideas into practice to whatever extent possible given the constraints of existing social, political, and economic structures. From the perspective of these theorists, partial or incomplete implementation of worthy alternative approaches—a practice often referred to as "resistance"—sows the seeds of change (see e.g., Giroux, 1983, 1988a). Ultimately, they imagine or hope such change will profoundly alter the underlying structures of society that condition how schools work and what they can accomplish.

The Life-World of Schools. Building on the philosophical legacy of Alfred Schutz and Jürgen Habermas, Thomas Sergiovanni (2000) discussed schools in relationship to local communities (i.e., the life-world) and remote structures of governance (i.e., the systems-world). From Sergiovanni's perspective, the systems-world exerts too much influence over local schools. In his view, contemporary schools are in trouble because they are overly responsive to the systems-world while not being adequately rooted in the life-world. From this critique of current schools, Sergiovanni derived recommendations for shifting the balance. He argued that schools will be more effective once they are more closely aligned with the meanings and values inherent in the life-worlds of local communities.

Aligning schools with communities, however, may be difficult in contemporary society. Fewer and fewer traditional communities exist even in rural locales (Wilkinson, 1991). Moreover, among parents whose children attend the same school, especially in cities and suburbs, there may be little agreement on key issues such as what aims schooling ought to accomplish and which content ought to be taught. Furthermore, the power of educational bureaucracies (e.g., legislatures and state education agencies) appears to be increasing, not diminishing (e.g., Spillane, 1996). Reducing the influence of the systems-world, then, may turn out to be an uphill battle.

Feminist Pedagogy.   Numerous feminists (e.g., Brady, 1995; Mayberry, 1999; Weiler, 1988) believe that schooling ought to offer possibilities for liberation by engaging students in critical explorations of power, knowledge, and identity construction. From the vantage of many feminist educators, students' personal experiences ought to form the starting point for such explorations. In particular, examining one's own subjective position within a complex social network can help a student come to understand the way patriarchal power functions to confer privilege, including the privilege to define what counts as important knowledge. These theorists claim that through such critical interrogations, students, particularly female students and students of color, learn to value and give voice to the knowledge produced out of their own experiences.

In practice, however, teachers—even feminist teachers—encounter state and district expectations for what ought to be taught in schools (e.g., Strachan, 1997). Furthermore, overt efforts are often made to suppress oppositional approaches to teaching (e.g., Morton, 1992). Generally speaking, in fact, teachers do not believe that they have the power to make decisions about curriculum content, although they do believe they have the power to make decisions about teaching methods (Anderson, 1995). To the extent, then, that feminist pedagogy implicates teaching methods without substantially altering curriculum, teachers may be able to adapt some of its tenets even in public school classrooms (see e.g., Hauser & Jipson, 1998; Ng, Staton, & Scane, 1995).

USING THEORY TO PROMOTE DIALOG

Because theories concern the way the world does and ought to work, they are closely bound up with our determinations of what's going on around us and our decisions about what actions to take. In schools (and, we would argue, probably everywhere else as well), these determinations and decisions do not take place in isolation. Rather, they are a product of the social interaction that occurs within a particular context (e.g., Berger & Luckmann, 1966). In other words, the students, teachers, administrators, and parents who participate in the life of a school shape *collective* understandings about what's going on there.

Decision making, moreover, depends on and extends those understandings. We rest our decisions—about how to teach, how to supervise teachers, how to respond to parents' concerns—on our beliefs. And the actions we decide to take produce effects that give us a basis for reflecting on and reevaluating our original understandings and the beliefs on which they are founded. For this process to work well, however, we must be open to multiple points of view. Examining issues from a variety of perspectives improves our decision making and enriches our reflections.

When we are making a decision, our own interpretations may be so narrow that they constrain us from taking the important risks required for doing our work well. For example, a principal might believe that teachers will participate in a curriculum project only if they receive extra pay. This belief rests on a theory about what motivates teachers. Unless that principal hears different views about the issue, he or she might never ask teachers to participate in the project, but might instead select a packaged curriculum. Dialog about the issue—perhaps with some teachers, other principals, the superintendent, or parents—might expose the principal to other theories about what motivates teachers. And with that broader set of theories in mind, the principal might choose to take the risk of asking teachers to participate. If some teachers then did agree to become involved, the principal might come to revise his or her beliefs about what motivates teachers.

Reflection on past action and planning for future action are also made more meaningful and more productive when we examine our experiences and objectives from a variety of points of view. By considering multiple perspectives, we give ourselves access to more than one interpretation of past events. For example, many teachers have had the experience of explaining a student's low achievement first in one way (as a lack of effort, perhaps) and then finding out information about the student that leads to a different interpretation (e.g., that a learning disability keeps the student from performing well on certain kinds of tasks). In response to new information or to the views of others, educators frequently revise their interpretations of events and circumstances in their classrooms and schools.

Less often, however, do teachers and school leaders have the experience of engaging in planning that is informed by multiple perspectives. This approach to planning, however, is recommended in the literature on strategic thinking (e.g., Senge, 1990). By using a technique called "scenario planning," leaders are able to imagine different ways that events might play out in the future (e.g., Tucker, 1999). This type of forecasting allows leaders to account for complexity when they seek to determine the actions with the greatest chance of producing desired future outcomes.

Although an individual leader can often imagine some alternative futures, dialog among several knowledgeable practitioners can greatly increase the scope and complexity of the imagined scenarios, thereby increasing the likelihood that the strategic decisions made as a result of the exercise will position the organization to succeed (Senge, 1990). Some authors urge educational leaders (especially college and university leaders) to use this type of approach when they undertake strategic planning (e.g., Rieley, 1997). But others ignore this approach, instead favoring strategic planning approaches grounded in stakeholders' prior beliefs and values or on a shared vision of an "ideal" future (Kaufman, 1995). We suggest that all of these sources have a place in assisting schools to set a wise course of action for the future. Moreover, scenario planning has the advantage of embedding what participants think (that is, their theoretical assertions) about the relationship between particular means and particular ends. Studying theory can prepare a principal to describe these embedded beliefs, in order to make them obvious to participants, who would not otherwise be clear about their beliefs. It improves a principal's capacity to lead.

Revealing Theories Through Dialog

Although there are clear organizational benefits resulting from a consideration of multiple explanations and perspectives, most organizational cultures—including school cultures—actually discourage employees, clients, and stakeholders from honestly disclosing their points of view (Simmons, 1999). As a consequence, school leaders who wish to create theory-rich environments must take action to encourage and sustain dialog. They must establish structures in which dialog can take place and provide opportunities for participants to engage in dialog. Furthermore, they must work to keep dialog from becoming an occasion for participants to exert influence on behalf of well-established or self-interested positions (Senge, 1990).

Unlike discussion or debate, dialog requires an honest exchange of ideas in consideration of the underlying theories that support them. To Simmons (1999), this means that individuals who participate in a dialog must "tell the truth" as they see it about the organization. School teachers and administrators who participate in a dialog, therefore, must honestly disclose their personal "truths" and openly entertain other people's truths about their school and district. Once a variety of "truths" are put forth and examined, participants can shape a "dialogic agreement," that is, they can "assent to a unified truth which includes the partial truths of each point of view, but is greater than any one of them taken by itself" (Schultz, 1990, p. 145).

In many cases dialogic agreement is impossible. This outcome, however, does not demonstrate that a dialog has itself been unsuccessful. Agreement is not the only benefit of dialog. Clarification of one's own theories and deeper understanding of other people's theories are two additional and equally important outcomes of dialog. These clarifications and understandings enable school leaders to engage in careful thinking about past events and to accommodate complexity in framing plans for future action.

USING THEORY TO EXPLORE PRACTICE: CASE STUDY

In this final section of the chapter, we present a case study, examining it in light of the three uses of theory discussed in the previous sections, namely: (1) using theory to describe things, (2) using theory to improve things, and (3) using theory to promote dialog. This case study is a bit different from the ones in subsequent chapters. Most of those chapters consider a single theory, and they present stories about how principals used those theories to solve problems. Here, at the start, we want to show you how using theory in general is a very practical matter in the real world, and the story is about a principal who unwittingly creates a problem. This happens a lot in the real world. The point of the story is how to deal with this common, unpleasant, event—not merely how to avoid it.

We consider the uses of theory by posing three questions. To focus discussion on the way theory can help us understand what's going on, we ask, "How can the events be explained?" To draw attention to theories that present alternative views of how schools might work, we ask, "How can the situation be improved?" And to engage discussion about the use of theoretical dialog to improve decision-making and planning, we ask, "What perspectives help us make sense of the situation?"

Angry Parents at Lakewood Elementary

Lakewood Elementary is a school of 700 children in Grades K–6. Located in an industrial town about 25 miles from a large northeastern metropolis, the school enrolls students from a variety of backgrounds. A majority of the students are from families in which at least one parent is employed in a blue- or white-collar job in one of the local factories. The racial and ethnic mix of the school is 62% white, 26% black, 7% Hispanic, and 5% other.

Previously a veteran teacher from a nearby suburban district, Bill Ellis is now employed as the principal at Lakewood. Although Bill had no prior experience as a school administrator, the board hired him on the understanding that his major objective would be to improve students' scores on state tests of academic achievement. For the previous 3 years, Lakewood has scored below the state criterion for "an improving school" on all of the state's tests of achievement; and Lakewood's math scores have been even lower in most years, falling below the criterion for "schools at risk."

With academic improvement in view, one of Bill's first acts as principal was to organize a school improvement council with representatives from the teaching staff, the central office, and the community. The council met once a week during the months of November, January, and February; and in March, the group issued a set of recommendations. Among these was a request that all teachers of Grades 2–6 assign homework.

Bill brought these recommendations to a meeting of the teaching staff, and the teachers showed overwhelming support for the idea of increasing emphasis on homework. Bill then wrote a note to all parents, explaining the new homework policy. In the first week of April, the teachers in Grades 2–6 began to assign daily homework and to count homework grades in the calculation of students' report card grades.

Beginning in about the second week of April, Bill began to get calls from parents about the new homework policy. Some parents even stopped by the office to talk about the policy. The parents who contacted the school all seemed to oppose the policy, although their reasons differed. When Bill explained that parents had been represented on the school improvement council, the group responsible for generating the policy, parents argued that those few parents did not really represent their interests. They wanted to know why Bill had not aired the policy in a public forum.

Concerned to hear all voices, Bill decided to schedule a public forum on the question. In the end-of-year rush of school and community activities, however, the date had to be set for mid-May.

Prior to the May meeting, the teachers met to discuss their "position." They were pleased with the homework policy. It gave them a way to monitor students' levels of effort, and, from their perspective, grading effort was an important way to improve achievement.

The date in May arrived, and teachers and parents turned out in force. Unfortunately, everyone seemed to be in a "fighting mood." Parents spoke vehemently against the policy; teachers spoke strongly and at great length in favor of the policy. Fearing the worst, Bill stopped the discussion before it devolved into name calling. Before the crowd dispersed, he asked for volunteers to serve on a panel to evaluate how the policy was being implemented, and he explained that the evaluation would be conducted over the course of the next school year. Then he called the meeting to a close. The parents, however, did not leave. Instead, they began to discuss ways to protest. They were not satisfied with the plan to test the policy over the course of a full school year. As many of the parents argued, the policy was already interfering with family time and with community activities. They wanted to put an end to the homework policy right away.

Although the teachers left the school quickly, they were no happier than the parents about the outcome of the meeting. As one teacher put it, "Who's side is he on anyway. Next thing you know we'll be having parents conducting our performance evaluations."

How Can the Events Be Explained?   Like most problems and controversies that arise in schools, the problem at Lakewood Elementary has complicated origins. However, several "theories" might help explain what is going on:

- Because many of the parents have limited educational backgrounds, they may feel intimidated by the requirement, implicit in the homework policy, that they help their children with learning tasks (see, e.g., Hoover-Dempsey, Bassler, & Burow, 1995). Unsure of their own skills and knowledge, parents may feel uncomfortable about revealing their limitations to their children.
- Parents may believe that, because the new principal is an outsider, he is unsympathetic to community concerns. Already partially disengaged from the school, they may feel even further distanced by a principal who does not allow their perspectives to have an important influence on school policies and practices (see, e.g., Porter, 1995; Sokolof, 1996).
- Perhaps the principal took action too quickly, without have a clear understanding of the culture of the school and its surrounding community (Harvey, 1991). Without understanding previous relationships between teachers and parents, his approach may have served to bring covert animosities to the surface.

In order to remedy the situation, Bill Ellis will need to evaluate these and other theories and "test them" against the available evidence. Once he identifies one or more theories that correspond well to the evidence, he will have a better idea of what's going on. This understanding may also help him decide what to do next.

How Can the Situation Be Improved?   Bill's underlying theories about what makes a "good school" will help him decide on what actions to take to assist the school community in understanding, recovering from, and moving beyond this difficult situation. Whether or not he shares his vision of "the good school" with the school community, the theories on which his vision rests will inform and justify the actions he eventually takes.

For example, if Bill believes that "good schools" ought to be responsive to community concerns (e.g., Sergiovanni, 2000), he will do everything in his power to allow community members to express their views about the proposed homework policy. Moreover, he will work to make sure that these views play an important role in shaping the eventual policy that is adopted.

In contrast, if Bill believes that "good schools" ought to be governed by a professional cadre of teachers (e.g., Lieberman, 1988, 1995), he will call the teachers together to reiterate his support for their position. At the same time, he may also cultivate groups of influential parents in an effort to convince the community that Lakewood's teachers are well-trained professionals, capable of deciding the strategies most likely to promote their children's learning.

Alternately, if Bills holds the view that "good schools" are those governed by strong instructional leaders (e.g., Smith & Andrews, 1989), he may decide to call together a public meeting of teachers and community members in order to share his vision of school improvement. Without disrespecting the opinions of parents and teachers, Bill will nevertheless convey the message that his view of school improvement is the one that will ultimately guide schoolwide policies and practices.

Interestingly, the theories Bill holds about what makes a school "good" reflect a range of other—perhaps more deeply embedded—theories about how the world of human beings ought to work. These theories may cover a wide range of experiences, but they may not all work together to articulate a coherent view of the social world. Nevertheless, Bill's theories about such matters as what ought to motivate social participation, how leaders ought to act, and what sorts of power are legitimate, among many others, guide his more focused theories about such matters as what constitutes effective teaching, who should make decisions about school governance, and what role a principal should play in resolving school conflicts.

What Perspectives Can Help Make Sense of the Situation?   Unless Bill is an extreme authoritarian, he will likely understand that his theories are not the only important ones to consider. The theories held by teachers, other district administrators, parents, and students also provide valuable interpretations of the events that transpired and suggest alternative strategies for remedying the situation.

If Bill were able to poll representatives from all these groups, he might hear the following explanations of the events.

- From students: Parents got mad because they are too tired in the evening to help with homework; they were upset because homework interferes with after-school activities in the community; no one likes homework.
- From parents: We expressed our distress because the school didn't involve us in decision making in a meaningful way; the teachers were ganging up on us because they don't think we set high enough expectations for our kids.
- From teachers: The parents were expressing their long-term disapproval of the way teachers enforce policies at this school; the parents were upset with the board's choice of a new principal.
- From other administrators: The parents sensed that the new principal was vulnerable to pressure; the parents don't understand what it takes to improve students' achievement test scores; historically, the teachers at Lakewood Elementary have ignored or downplayed parents' concerns.

By accepting the possible validity of all of these interpretations, Bill will achieve broad understanding of the complexities of the issue. Moreover, he will now have a much more extensive set of theories to deploy in attempting to make sense of the event.

A person's role (i.e., student, parent, teacher, administrator), however, is just one characteristic that may influence views about the situation. Along with explanations associated with individuals' roles, Bill might also be interested in interpretations reflecting different orientations toward political and economic issues. For example, he might want to hear the perspectives offered by communitarians, feminists, or critical theorists. By enlarging the discussion of the event to include politicians, university faculty, and community leaders, he might bring more generalized theories to bear on the immediate problem. (Of course, he has to "hear" these perspectives in his mind's eye, based on reading.)

A feminist, for example, might suggest that mothers' negative reactions to the homework policy could reflect their stress over the extensive demands associated with the combined roles of homemaker, mother, and wage earner. A critical theorist might offer an interpretation related to the power differential between teachers and parents, and a communitarian might explain that a focus on individual children's achievement could be functioning to undermine school–community relations.

Because of the numerous credible theories that claim to describe the event, the issues at play may be more complicated than Bill first imagined. Perhaps the unpleasant meeting about the homework policy was merely a symptom of a problem deeper and more extensive than the one that meets the eye. Given this possibility, all of the stakeholders might benefit from participation in a dialog about what's been going on. Even if it does not result in a clear resolution of the problem, a dialog widely accessible to all stakeholders will enable participants to arrive at a fuller and more sympathetic understanding of the perspectives fueling conflict over the issue.

CHAPTER SUMMARY

This chapter discusses three ways that school leaders use theory. In addition, through the examination of a case study, it provides an illustration of the three uses of theory.

One way that school leaders use theory is to explain or describe events in the social world. Explanations, moreover, are often combined to produce coherent theoretical systems. Theories of organizational culture and of dynamic systems exemplify such approaches. Explanatory theories often map directly to action. When such theories explicitly link particular ends with particular means, they constitute "theories of action." Explicitly stated theories of action do not always guide the way people act, though. Very often, individuals espouse one theory but act in a quite different way. The theories underlying the way people *really* act are called theories-in-use.

Another use of theory is to present possibilities: how people *ought* to treat one another, what schools *ought* to be like, how benefits *ought* to be distributed. These theories enable school leaders to imagine a world of schooling that is quite different from what is actually confronting them. By imagining alternatives, school leaders can formulate plans directed toward the betterment of their schools and communities.

Finally, school leaders can promote greater understanding of important issues by enabling multiple perspectives to inform reflection and decision making. Strategic use of dialog fosters understanding of school dilemmas that is deeper, richer, and more tolerant than that produced by conventional approaches to decision making.

2

Traditional Theories

Effective prediction and control are as central to the task of management as they are to the task of engineering or medicine.... Human behavior is predictable, but, as in physical science, accurate prediction hinges on the correctness of underlying theoretical assumptions. There is, in fact, no prediction without theory.
—(McGregor, 1960, p. 11)

From the moment schools were organized into systems, educational administration came into being. And the decisions made about schools, about how they should be structured and provisioned in order to achieve valued ends, depended on theories. Theories guiding the administration of early schools, of course, usually were tacit and informal. With the advent of scientific management in the early 20th century, however, educators began to write down theories of administration. Early articles on school administration reveal that the theories recommended to practicing and prospective administrators came from two sources: the work experiences of seasoned principals and superintendents, and the results of studies conducted by a group of social psychologists sometimes referred to as "efficiency experts" (Callahan, 1962).

Scientific management and associated theories of organizational efficiency were part of a broader movement of social engineering, which constituted the foundation for social science disciplines such as economics, psychology, and sociology (e.g., Brown, 1989). As these disciplines emerged from their early grounding in philosophy, they sought to become more like the natural sciences, using methods purported to reveal objective knowledge about the social world. Social scientists believed that such knowledge would give technicians (e.g., factory managers, educational administrators, clinical psychologists) a neutral basis for manipulating the social world. And the purpose of such manipulation was improvement (Willower, 1996).

Of course, the ideal of objectivity and its related ethical position, neutrality, is difficult, impossible according to some observers, to realize in studies of the social world, and arguably in studies of the natural world as well (Brown, 1989). Human beings come to the scientific enterprise with prior beliefs and commitments that influence the direction of the science they perform. This circumstance explains why it is possible for so-called *objective* social science to make competing and sometimes "undecidable" claims. And certainly the prior commitments of varied theorists and researchers lead them to view improvement quite differently from one another (Rule, 1997).

For example, the efficiency experts believed that improvement was equivalent to improved productivity, irrespective of the costs to the human dignity of workers. Although they did not abandon the goal of productivity, later theorists focused on the alignment of organizational productivity with the personal satisfaction of workers (e.g., McGregor, 1960). "Improvement," defined by each set of theorists, turned out to look quite different. And, not surprisingly, these differences had an influence on the "facts" that were discovered by researchers subscribing to each of these theoretical perspectives.

POSITIVISM AS A LEADING THEORETICAL FAMILY

Despite differences in how they construed "improvement," how they studied social phenomena, and the "truths" they discovered about the social world, most 20th-century theorists and researchers shared a common view of what social science was all about (Brown, 1989). In the second half of the 20th century, however, increasing numbers of social scientists became disenchanted with the consensus view. In subsequent chapters, we consider the theories arising from their discontent, but here, the discussion focuses on the commonalities of the theories and the research supported by the dominant paradigm.

As the discussion shows, even though the dominant paradigm (often called "positivism") rests on a set of shared assumptions about the nature of the world, it also has supported a rich variety of theories and empirical claims. Much of what we think about as educators and much of what we do routinely in our practice is grounded in positivist theories and the findings of research grounded in those theories. In Sidebar 2-1, we provide examples of some of the positivist theories that have had the greatest impact on today's schools.

Sidebar 2-1

Positivist Theories That Impact Schools

- Many schools use discipline approaches, such as "assertive discipline" (Canter & Canter, 1992) that are grounded in behaviorist theories of learning. Behaviorism is also the basis for incentive systems that reward students for attendance, compliance, or achievement.

- Methods of direct instruction (e.g., Hunter, 1982) that rely on drill and practice are also grounded in behaviorism.

- Schools use psychometric theories of intelligence (e.g., Terman, 1919) to determine students' eligibility for special education and gifted education services.

- Large schools and districts, in particular, are organized as bureaucracies (e.g., Weber, 1924/1968).

- Efforts to improve school climate and culture draw on theories of organizational culture (e.g., Schein, 1992).

- State accountability systems (with their view that schools need to be punished and rewarded in order to improve) fit well with early 20th-century theories of scientific management (e.g., Taylor, 1911).

Positivism in Research and Practice

In the previous discussion, the word "positivism" refers to the views embedded in the dominant approach to theorizing and research in the social sciences. We might also have used the term "functionalism," although there are slight differences in meaning. To distinguish one from the other, it is useful to think of positivism as a way of viewing the world and functionalism as a way of studying the world from the perspective of positivism. Here are some of the important assumptions underlying the positivist view:

- There is a social reality that exists apart from our observation of it (e.g., Brown, 1989).
- By using objective techniques of observation, we can represent the real social world accurately. We might call our representations "facts" or "truths" (e.g., Lincoln & Guba, 2000).
- The truths discovered through the use of objective methods ought to form the basis for improving the social world (e.g., Brown, 1989).

- Such improvements will result in progress toward more rational social arrangements (e.g., Saul, 1992).

Later in the chapter, we devote attention to the various ways in which theories grounded in positivism affect current thinking about educational organizations and leadership of such organizations. But here, for the purpose of illustration, are just a few. First, there's the belief that school achievement can be adequately represented by test scores. Such scores purportedly tell the "truth" about a student, a school, or a district. Second is the idea (put forward strongly in the "No Child Left Behind" Act) that students' achievement will increase if teachers use practices that have been proven effective in experimental studies. In addition, there's the belief that principals' leadership has a direct effect on school culture, which, in turn, has a direct effect on student outcomes.

Readers of this book might at this point be shaking their heads in agreement with each of these statements. That's because positivism is still the dominant way of thinking about learning, teaching, and leading. Nevertheless, as we'll begin to see in this chapter and the next, positivism has limits, and it introduces blinders that can keep those of us who lead schools from seeing other possibilities.

From outside the dominant perspective, positivism seems to impose too many constraints to be helpful to most educational administrators. Why? Practical experience suggests to many educators that (a) social reality is influenced by the character of the observer and the nature of the observation; (b) findings from empirical studies of the social world are merely provisional, not definitive; (c) ideas about "improvement" are debatable (you might regard my "improvement" as making things worse); (d) even when everyone agrees on a definition of improvement, numerous approaches—not just one—can turn out to be effective; (e) context is an extremely important mediator of the relationship between means and ends; and (f) what's called "progress" might not be all that it's cracked up to be.

Let's look briefly at each of these claims.

Even if everyone agrees that there really is a real physical world with properties that we can discover in systematic ways (some people don't believe this), many of us would still acknowledge that the social world is somehow different. Human beings both make the social world, and they live in it (Berger & Luckmann, 1966). It is hard, in fact, to imagine human beings existing outside of the social world. To make matters even more complex, human beings are the ones who study the social world that they help to construct and in which they live. This causes problems that the study of planets, of rocks, and of plants and animals doesn't confront.

Social science theories that do not take into account the social construction, and therefore the dynamism of the social world cannot hope to explain it faithfully. Nevertheless, research grounded in positivism makes the attempt to do just that by purporting to derive law-like generalizations about human behavior and social interaction from supposedly objective observations of those phenomena (Brown, 1989). One way to understand the limits of this approach is to look at theories from the human sciences that have become outdated. Sidebar 2-2 provides some illustrative theories with implications for education.

Sidebar 2-2

Outmoded Theories

- In the early parts of the 20th century, educators believed that left-handedness created learning problems. As a result, they tried to train left-handed students to write with their right hand (Costas, 1996).

- Throughout most of the 20th century, educators put forth the view that bigger schools were better. Research since that time has demonstrated, however, that smaller schools tend to cultivate higher student achievement, especially among low-SES students (e.g., Howley & Howley, 2004).

- When personal computers first were being used in schools, researchers claimed that computer-mediated instruction would be much more effective than traditional teacher-mediated instruction. Over the years, however, the accumulating body of evidence suggests that computer-mediated instruction is no more effective—and sometimes is less effective—than teacher-mediated instruction (see, e.g., Lowe, 2002).

- Autism used to be considered a form of schizophrenia, resulting from a mother's coldness toward her child (e.g., Axline, 1964). Now it is thought to be a developmental disability, possibly a severe learning disability (e.g., O'Brien & Pearson, 2004), and some studies have attempted to identify its genetic basis (e.g., Castermans et al., 2004).

Not only do the techniques for improving schools change as a result of emerging theories and empirical findings, the fundamental character of improvement is something that is subject to debate. For example, whereas state policymakers seem to believe that raising standardized test scores ought to be how improvement is defined, many educators and parents disagree, seeing the cultivation of responsible behavior or the development of citizenship skills and attitudes as more important reforms. Even among the teachers in a school, there is often disagreement about what changes would represent improvements. From a leadership perspective, in fact, the school leader plays a critical role in structuring activities that work to create consensus among members of the school community with respect to the meaning of "improvement." Principals exert a lot of influence in this way.

Once consensus (or provisional consensus) about the aims of an improvement effort has been reached, the educators in a school usually begin to think about ways to address those aims. Fortunately for the students we work with, there are many instructional and organizational approaches that can be deployed. Despite much rhetoric about "best practice," no convincing body of evidence gives educators a clear basis for knowing which method will be most effective with a particular student or group of students. Moreover, efforts to find the "one best way" are arguably misguided and damaging because teaching and learning are (some believe) inventive and synergistic processes. If this is so, the rigid adherence to a set of prescribed ("best") practices can lead teachers to lose interest in their work. Uninterested teachers are not effective at motivating students.

Even if educational science were to become better at identifying the practices that, on average, result in better outcomes, those practices would not work well with some groups or in certain contexts. In some cases, long-standing cultural assumptions will limit the effectiveness of particular instructional practices with certain groups of children. For example, although direct and frequent questioning of individuals has generally been shown to promote learning, children from some cultural groups see such an approach as culturally dissonant. For such children, questions are more acceptable if they are directed to the class as a whole or embedded in group projects.

Individual learning preferences also influence the extent to which particular instructional approaches will be successful. Efforts to define which approaches work best with which students have been undertaken from time to time (e.g., attribute-treatment-interaction research and learning-styles research), but the results of such efforts are far from conclusive. In the absence of convincing evidence that particular methods "work" in particular circumstances whereas other methods "work" in other circumstances, teachers tend to adopt a trial-and-error approach to figuring out "what works" (Howley & Spatig, 1998).

One final concern about the application of a positivist perspective to educational practice is the faith that positivism places in "progress." For instance, while many of us enjoy the freedom of movement made possible by automobiles, we also regret the environmental degradation resulting from the emissions produced by internal combustion engines. And an examination of history certainly shows that some groups benefit far more than other groups when progress is made. Some groups may not even believe that the particular progress made has improved their lives. Furthermore, ordinary people seem to have little influence over the direction that progress takes. Even if we resent the abridgement of privacy that comes with the existence of large, interconnecting electronic data bases, for example, we understand that we have no voice in the decisions governing their development and use (Mander & Goldsmith, 1996). The overall value for humankind of positivism's ultimate quarry, progress, is uncertain at best. The idea of progress is at least regarded by some thoughtful observers as a very mixed blessing.

Functionalist Research

A positivist worldview leads to research that treats human interactions as if they were predictable functions. In its simplest form, this research paradigm, often called functionalism, assumes that certain conditions inevitably produce certain effects. As educators, we are likely both to wish that such predictability really existed and to recall a host of experiences showing just how elusive such predictability actually is. The hypothesis itself (that human behavior is predictable) is reasonable; the greatest difficulty is the *application* of research findings from functionalist research.

Preparing school administrators would, of course, be much easier if preparation programs could simply train educators in the leadership methods known to work all the time. If the world of schools were predictable, then new administrators would simply use the methods they learned in their preparation programs to accomplish the ends they desired. But such assurance not only is seldom justified, it appears more often to be wishful thinking. Leadership is simply risky business, as subsequent chapters show.

Nevertheless, functionalist research has made important contributions to our understanding of the way schooling processes work. Focusing on probability, rather than certainty, however, provides a cushion for the findings from many functionalist studies. Certainty still remains the "gold standard" in many circles, so methods that purport to approximate certainty are often valued more highly than those acknowledging the relatively high levels of uncertainty in human endeavors.

To get a sense of what's at stake here, compare the theory of gravity with the theory of constructivist pedagogy. We could hardly live in a world in which gravity operated probabilistically. Imagine if the force of gravity worked with 95% certainty (a probability level often used in social science research). On 5 out of 100 days, perhaps, we'd wake up to find that gravity wasn't going to be working.

Or perhaps gravity would work for only 95 out of 100 people. These possibilities are absurd, of course. But equally absurd is the idea that constructivist pedagogy will work more effectively than other approaches with all students and types of curriculum content. Everyday experience of the world tells us that gravity works every day, but that constructivist pedagogy works some of the time—with some teachers, under some conditions, and with some students better than others. There are many threats to certainty in the social sciences.

Despite the probabilistic character of many findings about human behavior and interactions, the value of these findings is nevertheless evident. If we knew, for example, that constructivist pedagogy worked better than rote memorization for 8 out of 10 students, we could adjust our teaching practices accordingly. We might want to find ways to figure out which students were likely to benefit from which approach or which content worked best with which approach. But we'd still know that if we had to choose between using one or the other, our overall effectiveness would improve if we selected the constructivist approach.

Unfortunately, there do not seem to be very many educational interventions or leadership approaches that have effectiveness levels nearly so high as the one used in this example. So the connection of theory to practice in teaching and in educational leadership almost always embeds a large measure of hopefulness in a slim margin of certainty.

Social Engineering

As the previous discussion suggests, functionalist research is arguably not an adequate basis for deciding how social life ought to be arranged. Questions of "ought," in fact, call on value positions, not knowledge claims, although knowledge can certainly help us achieve what we value, once we decide what that is. Because of their stance on ethical "neutrality," however, positivists make it seem as if knowledge by itself tells people what they ought to do. In education, as in other realms of social life, this presumption encourages participants (e.g., principals, teachers, parents) to overlook critical ethical issues in favor of scientifically based prescriptions. The problem is that these prescriptions carry with them a set of hidden values.

For example, accepting behaviorist research showing that extrinsic rewards (e.g., candy, toys, money) improve children's behavior, many educators in the 1970s and 1980s chose to make use of reward systems to promote compliant behaviors (many still do). Although this approach worked, it is said to have done so at a price: Children learned to respond to adult manipulation, and they failed to learn how and why to act responsibly (Kohn, 1993). If the value position (i.e., that cultivating responsibility among children is what schools ought to do) had been identified first, then the educators might have chosen different methods for handling behavior issues in classrooms and schools—they would have at least had that option. Despite the fact that reward systems worked, some educators would have avoided this technique because it promoted values they did not endorse.

This example, which focuses on an everyday experience in classrooms, is hardly the only circumstance in which social engineering based on functionalist research has been used to alter educational practice in ways that work counter to the value positions of many educators and parents. Some other examples are:

- School consolidation for the supposed purpose of improving student achievement.
- Lock-step organizational schemes (e.g., age–grade placement, Carnegie units).
- High-school curriculum tracking.
- Direct instruction.

Social engineering, of course, has affected all social institutions, not just schools. Moreover, in cases where we agree to some extent with its direction, we may be less likely to scrutinize its methods. For example, policies requiring school desegregation came about in response to research showing that African American children needed to be educated with White children in order to learn better. Mandated busing for the purpose of integrating schools, however, almost always brought African American children into White schools, not White children into African American schools (hooks, 1996). Moreover, desegregation resulted in the loss of jobs for many African American educators (Hudson & Holmes, 1994).

In this case, well-meaning policymakers overlooked possible limitations of the applicable research, and they supported particular approaches to desegregation that had unintended but nonetheless negative consequences (Wilkinson, 1996). Research conducted later on, during less tumultuous times, revealed a more complicated picture. For example, some studies revealed the extraordinary performance of certain all-Black schools in the South (e.g., Savage, 2001; Siddle Walker, 1996), and some showed that desegregation at the district or school level often failed to translate into desegregation at the classroom level (e.g., Baker, 2001). Findings from some recent studies suggest that African American students generally perform better when they are taught by African American teachers (e.g., Dee, 2001). And some evidence demonstrates benefits for segregated Afrocentric education (Majors, 2001). Whereas this research hardly supports school segregation as a universal policy, it does introduce doubt about the wisdom of simplistic schemes. Improvement efforts that focus too narrowly on one feature of schooling may overlook the complex and contingent linkages among educational practices and desired outcomes.

TRADITIONAL THEORIES: THE TWO SIDES OF A COIN

Two bodies of positivist literature coming from the disciplines of organizational sociology and social psychology have had important influences on school organization and management. One focuses on the nature, operation, and change of organizations; the other focuses on leadership. Despite the fact that real-world leadership takes place in organizations, the academic study of leadership and organizational behavior has, until quite recently, proceeded along separate lines. With few exceptions, those people who theorized about organizations did not consult those who theorized about leadership, and vice versa. More recent positivist literature, such as what's been written about *total quality management*, however, has begun to attend to the important connection between leadership and organizational behavior (Bass & Avolio, 1994).

This section of the chapter considers illustrative theories of organizations and leadership. Both bodies of positivist literature are extensive, and a short discussion like this cannot possibly do justice to them. Our discussion, therefore, focuses not on the details of different theories but on the fundamental concepts that distinguish theoretical traditions such as scientific management, institutional theory, and contingency theories of leadership. For an excellent overview of organizational theories that apply to school administration, we recommend Hoy and Miskel's (1996) well-respected text, and for an overview of leadership theories, we find Yukl's (2006) text inclusive and accessible.

Illustrative Theories of Organization

Beginning with proponents of scientific management, theorists and researchers have offered explanations of how organizations actually work (i.e., descriptive or empirical theories of organizations) and prescriptions about how organizations ought to work (i.e., normative or prescriptive theories). Major traditions in the study of organizations can be categorized as relating to: (a) the rational features of organizations (incorporating theories of scientific management and bureaucracy), (b) the affective and social features of organizations (incorporating human relations and human resource theories), (c) the political dimensions of organizations (incorporating institutional and political theories), and (d) the cultural dimensions of organizations (incorporating theories of organizational culture and symbols).

This categorization closely parallels the approach used by Bolman and Deal (2003) in their discussion of different ways of viewing or "framing" what goes on in organizations. Interestingly, these four frames or categories also offer a chronology of the concerns of organizational theorists over time. Early classical theorists (i.e., theorists of scientific management and bureaucracy) were concerned with the structural features of organizations. They were followed by theorists who were more concerned with relationships among the people in organizations. Later theorists considered those relationships in terms of systemwide relations of power, and still later theorists devoted attention to the cultural and symbolic features of organizations. In Bolman and Deal's approach, these features of organizations are at play all at once. Over the course of the 20th century, however, theorists tended to pay attention to each feature in turn.

As we undertake our historical tour of these theories, the discussion focuses on the explicit linkages between means and ends. In other words, we focus on what each theory claims will work in organizations in order to accomplish maximum productivity.

Bureaucracy.   When we hear the word "bureaucracy," we often think about a large and impersonal system characterized by procedural "red tape" and staffed with insensitive, and even hostile and rude, functionaries. This stereotype of bureaucracy—grounded in all-too familiar experiences with large corporate and government offices—focuses on the defects of an organizational arrangement that is pervasive in contemporary society. And the stereotype makes it hard for us to imagine bureaucracy as an innovation designed to improve the rationality and the ethical conduct of business in the private and public sectors (du Gay, 2000).

Nevertheless, improvement of both efficiency and effectiveness is exactly what Max Weber (1924/1968) had in mind when he proposed a system for structuring large organizations so that authority would be vested in those with the greatest expertise, communication channels would be easily identified and used, and technical and social processes would be governed by explicit rules rather than by tradition. One way to see the sense in which such arrangements represent an improvement is to contrast a school organization dominated by prebureaucratic authority with one dominated by bureaucratic authority.

Tradition High School has served the town of Tradition for 100 years. Like many towns, Tradition has an elite group of citizens who control most of what goes on. The school board in Tradition is made up of members of the elite, and they employ teachers based on the families they come from and their loyalty to those in power. Unfortunately, these teachers are not always competent to work with children, and most do not have degrees in disciplines that match up with their teaching fields. The principal is a young educator from a prominent family. He does not know much about teaching or about the way the school has functioned in the past. As a result, older teachers have the greatest influence on school operations. Nevertheless, when faced with a decision, he does take action, "shooting from the hip" rather than consulting those with relevant knowledge and experience. His decisions tend to be arbitrary and to exhibit favoritism toward some members of the staff. But his decisions are often overturned because, whenever older teachers or influential parents want to exert authority over what goes on at Tradition High School, they go directly to a member of the board of education. Often the squabbles that result from these power dynamics throw the whole school community into turmoil. (This may sound familiar to some readers.)

Bureaucrat High School has also served its town for a long time, but at Bureaucrat, board members and educators do things "by the book." Teachers are employed based on their credentials and experience, and the principal was a veteran teacher who worked his way up the ranks. Furthermore, all members of the Bureaucrat community are treated equally. When an issue arises, it is dealt with by the person (e.g., teacher or principal) who has authority to make an appropriate decision. If the decision is contested, it may be appealed to an educator with greater authority. But because decisions typically are based on explicit rules, there is little room for an individual to seek preferential treatment by working his or her way up the "chain of command." Those with greater authority (e.g., members of the board of education or superintendent) tend to make the rules and pass these down the chain of command to educators with less authority. Because everyone knows what's expected, the system works smoothly and efficiently. (We hope some readers find this familiar!)

The contrast between these two high schools reveals a great deal about how bureaucracy is organized and how it works. Its typical features include separation of functions, specialization of roles, employment based on credentials, hierarchically organized offices, explicit rules, and opportunity for advancement based on seniority (see, e.g., Presthus, 1962; Weber, 1924/1968). Table 2.1 shows how these features often play out in schools.

Although the bureaucratic features of schools are evident, schools are not "perfect" bureaucracies. Compared to other organizations, the hierarchy in school districts is relatively flat. And the structure in many small districts is so simple and the community so close-knit that explicit rules and communication based on "chain of command" seem unnecessary and out of place. Generally speaking, in fact, the larger the district, the more bureaucratic it will be (see, e.g., Astley, 1985; Raadshelders, 1997).

Table 2.1
Bureaucracy in Schools

Feature	School Examples
Separation of functions by job	The principal has one job, the teacher another, the guidance counselor another, and the bus driver another.
Specialization within jobs by role	Teaching assignments are specialized by level (e.g., early childhood, middle childhood, adolescent) and by field (e.g., math, English, social studies).
Employment based on credentials	Teachers are licensed for particular roles; districts hire appropriately credentialed (i.e., "highly qualified") teachers.
Hierarchically organized offices	Teachers report to principals, who in turn report to superintendents. In large school districts the hierarchy tends to be steeper than it is in smaller districts and much more complicated.
Explicit rules	Details about personnel are provided in districts' master agreements; codes of conduct and specified punishments for infractions are provided in student handbooks.
Opportunity for advancement	Seniority represents an important basis for salary increments; with additional preparation, teachers can become administrators.

Human Resources.   Although bureaucratic theory provides an excellent example of the focus on organizational structure, it was only one approach to scientific management. Other approaches devoted somewhat less attention to organizational structure and somewhat more attention to the structuring and supervision of work. These other "classical" approaches, far more than theories of bureaucracy, began to give scientific management a bad name.

Douglas McGregor (1960) offered what is perhaps the most persuasive argument against classical management. In the book, *The Human Side of Enterprise*, he contrasted classical management (which he also called "theory X") with a proposed alternative, "theory Y." According to McGregor (p. 33), underlying assumptions about human nature distinguish these two theoretical approaches. Such assumptions guide the practices that managers use in order to motivate employees to perform work. Whereas McGregor did not doubt the connection between motivation and work, he disagreed with the theory of motivation held by classical theorists. McGregor identified the foundational assumptions of theory X, explaining how these led to management practices that turned out to be counterproductive. He contrasted these assumptions with others that he claimed were more accurate and, therefore, more likely to support desired organizational outcomes. Table 2.2 presents the assumptions of these two theoretical approaches

According to McGregor, the approach to management supported by theory Y involves the establishment of conditions that link the individual goals of workers to the needs of the organization. He calls this linkage "integration." The logic of theory Y is this: (a) When employees are pursuing their own goals, they are motivated to perform work, (b) integration involves aligning the goals of employees with the goals of the organization, therefore (c) when individual and organizational goals are integrated, employees will be motivated to perform the work of the organization. For McGregor the individual goals of most consequence are those resulting in personal satisfaction and "self-actualization" (see Maslow, 1962). These types of goals are achieved when work is structured in ways that enable employees to direct their creative energies toward solving organizational problems.

Not all organizational problem solving, however, calls forth commitment from employees, as studies about "site-based management" in schools demonstrate. The rationale for this approach was to increase teachers' commitment to schoolwide policies and practices by asking them to participate in school deci-

Table 2.2
Assumptions of Classical (Theory X) and Human Resources (Theory Y) Theories

Assumptions of Theory X	Assumptions of Theory Y
Most people dislike work and seek to avoid it.	Most people derive satisfaction from work.
Most people must be coerced into doing work.	Most people motivate themselves to perform work when they are committed to its goals.
Most people prefer to take direction from others.	Accomplishment of worthy goals results in satisfaction.
Most people avoid taking responsibility.	Most people accept and even seek responsibility.
Most people seek security above all else.	Most people exhibit creativity in performing work and ingenuity in solving problems.
Most people lack ambition.	Most work underutilizes the intellectual capacities of workers.

sion making. Many teachers, however, resented this initiative, believing that their goals were attained through the work they performed in their classrooms, not through their participation on school management teams (e.g., Kemper & Teddlie, 2000). Empirical studies showing the limited success of this initiative suggest that, in many cases, site-based management does not result in meaningful integration of teachers' personal goals with those of the school (e.g., Leithwood & Menzies, 1998; Shen, 2001). Efforts to give teachers significant roles in decision making about classroom practices appear to be a lot more effective in fostering the type of integration of goals that McGregor advocated (Fullan & Watson, 2000).

Institutional Theory. Proponents of bureaucracy and human resource theorists differ with regard to many fundamental assumptions, but they have one important assumption in common. Both groups of theorists see organizations and the people who comprise them as "rational" actors. In other words, they believe that (a) organizations set up formal structures for linking means and ends and (b) employees make use of these formal structures in order to accomplish the work of the organization. For bureaucratic theorists, the formal structures relate to the chain of command, the specialized division of labor, and the explicit rules that govern technical and social processes. For human resource theorists, such structures relate to the system of motivation that managers use to elicit and channel the commitment of employees. They share the belief that when formal structures are arranged correctly, productivity will automatically result.

Most people's experience with organizations, however, suggests that the reasoning is flawed. In the real world, and at almost every turn, it's apparent how remarkably "irrational" most organizations seem to be. Schools, businesses, and government agencies seem always to be doing things that get in the way of optimal productivity. This apparent truth frustrates and confuses many people, including many educators. Sidebar 2-3 provides some illustrations of schooling

Sidebar 2-3

Practices that Undermine the Link between Means and Ends

Educational Aim	Undermining Practice	Preferable Practice
Students will attend school.	Suspending students for absenteeism.	Making school attendance desirable.

Students will take responsibility for their actions.	Deploying arbitrary punishments (e.g., writing sentences, detention).	Deploying consequences that teach responsibility (e.g., social restitution).
Students will achieve to their greatest potential.	Tracking students based on a measure of their ability.	Using differentiated instruction with mixed ability groups.
Students will achieve to their greatest potential.	Enforcing age-grade placement.	Allowing talented students to skip grades or otherwise accelerate their progress.
Students will achieve to their greatest potential.	Filling up the school day with irrelevant activities (e.g., movies, assemblies, etc.).	Focusing on instruction in academic subjects.
Students will use higher-order thinking skills to solve problems.	Using lecture and recitation methods of instruction.	Using inquiry and discovery methods of instruction.

practices that seem to undermine the link between educational means (i.e., teaching) and educational ends (i.e., learning).

Thus, with the painful recognition that schools and other organizations seem to behave in ways that interfere with productivity come two important questions: Why and how? Institutional theory offers answers to both.[1]

In answer to the question "why?" many institutional theorists maintain that whatever its espoused mission, the fundamental purpose of an organization is survival; and survival requirements cause organizations to develop implicit "rules" that sometimes seem counter to their espoused interests. For example, an organization that is under threat may engage in a process that some theorists call *rationalization*: It will avoid making substantive changes by devoting a great deal of energy to superficial changes with the intent to convince the public that change is indeed taking place (e.g., Meyer & Scott, 1983). Illustrating such dynamics are interpretations of why, despite ongoing reform initiatives, schools

---

[1]A large number of different ideas have been attributed to "institutional" and "neo-institutional" theory (Scott, 1995). The discussion in this chapter seeks to identify common themes in this large and complex literature and to provide illustrations of some of the dynamics revealed by theorists working in this tradition.

have failed to change in meaningful ways (e.g., Cuban, 1990; Sarason, 1971). Like other organizations, schools want to look good, especially in situations where things aren't going all that well. (Many of us have worked for organizations in which things "aren't going all that well.")

Threats to survival also elicit other "irrational" behaviors. For instance, rather than changing their strategies, organizations may actually intensify their use of ineffective strategies. Faced with attendance problems that reflect badly on a school, administrators often increase the punishments associated with absenteeism, thereby exacerbating the school's attendance problems. Or organizations may attempt to expand the scope of their work (a practice known as *mission creep*) when they experience pressure from the external environment. Schools that have trouble teaching core subjects adequately decide to add electives; schools where teachers are resisting one innovation choose to adopt a second innovation.

Institutional theorists have additional answers to the question "How do organizations respond to threats to their survival?" Another response is called *isomorphism*. This is a process of homogenization that comes into play because threats to organizations cause them to want to "blend in." According to DiMaggio and Powell (1983), there are different sources of isomorphism. Direct external regulation often results in what these authors call "coercive isomorphism" because it specifies the programs and practices that organizations must deploy. The educational standards movement, for instance, has pressured many schools to engage in curriculum alignment—a process that tends to increase the similarity of curricula across schools.

Mimetic isomorphism occurs when one organization mimics the practices of another, even if those practices are inappropriate for the "borrowing" organization. School-related examples of such mimicking abound, as the history of educational fads reveals. For example, the graded school was an urban innovation designed to help educators deal with the large numbers of children of immigrants who needed to be educated. But rural schools quickly adopted the innovation, even if they didn't have enough students to justify classrooms at every grade level. Rather than rejecting the "innovation" as unsuitable to their circumstances, educators adopted it and then consolidated small rural schools in order to make them more like large urban ones (Kliebard, 2002; Reynolds, 2001).

Responses such as isomorphism, mission creep, and rationalization reveal that organizations develop and sustain (i.e., institutionalize) tacit rules that often deflect their explicit goals and formal procedures. These practices respond to the political environment in which organizations operate, representing reactions to the pressures that organizations face. Unlike theories focusing on structure (e.g., the theory of bureaucracy) and those focusing on human relations, institutional theories rest on the assumption that organizations are "open systems" that respond to and influence the larger political, social, economic, and cultural environment (e.g., Handel, 2003).

Thus far, our consideration of institutional theory has provided examples of organizations' seemingly irrational responses to external pressures, but internal pressures also divert the formal structures of organizations and their means-ends relationships. One well-known discussion of such dynamics is presented in David Mechanic's (1962) article, "Sources of Power of Lower Participants in Complex Organizations."

Mechanic used examples from mental hospitals, universities, and prisons to show how participants who are positioned toward the bottom ranks of organizational hierarchies nevertheless exert control over those positioned at higher ranks. He described several strategies that lower participants use to acquire and retain power. Some lower participants, for example, have expertise they can choose to share or withhold in order to control higher participants. School secretaries, for example, have a wealth of knowledge about school rules and procedures (Rimer, 1984). Depending on their appraisal of new teachers (or principals), for instance, they can reveal useful information, remain silent, or provide misinformation. School secretaries also have access to resources (e.g., supplies, keys, account codes), and they often serve as gatekeepers, deciding on their own which staff members will gain an audience with the principal and which will not. These sources of power provide lower participants with leverage, enabling them to negotiate with those further up in the hierarchy for privileges and perquisites. Even students—arguably the lowest participants in school organizations—use such techniques to bargain for concessions. For example, Sedlak, Wheeler, Pullin, and Cusick (1986) showed how urban students struck this type of bargain with their teachers: They "agreed" to exhibit compliance in exchange for course work that did not require much engagement and effort.

Theories of Change.   With their focus on the internal and external politics that influence how organizations operate, institutional theorists opened the door to theories of organizational culture. Institutionalization represents the mechanism through which the features of organizational cultures (e.g., their norms and rituals) are sustained (Zucker, 1977); and organizational cultures play a critical role in mediating means–ends relationships (the things an organization does to achieve its ends). When organizational cultures are healthy, their norms encourage the performance of meaningful work, and workers experience the satisfaction associated with a job well done. Very often, however, because of the complex dynamics that affect them, organizations develop cultures that are not as healthy as they might be, and in extreme cases, they develop "toxic" cultures (Peterson, 2002). Such organizational cultures are characterized by inertia, low morale, hostility among staff members, and sharply impaired productivity (Peterson, 2002, p. 11). Unfortunately, in schools that serve children with the most pronounced needs, toxic cultures often develop and persist for years (e.g., Deal & Peterson, 1999; Muijs, Harris, Chapman, Stoll, & Russ, 2004).

Low-performing schools, in fact, cry out for cultural change.[2] Change, however, is never easy (e.g., Marris, 1975). For one thing, participants in a culture, no matter how toxic, become comfortable in that culture (e.g., Deal & Peterson, 1999; Schein, 1992). For another, cultural features are mutually reinforcing, so that real change often requires a major overhaul of the whole system. Moreover, if change is to result in positive outcomes, it must incorporate features that make sense to participants and that work to increase their productivity (Fullan, 2001; Rogers, 1995).

In a general sense, cultural change involves what Lewin (1951) described as a process with three steps. First, norms and practices from the existing culture need to be "unfrozen." Then new norms and practices need to be introduced and incorporated through "cognitive restructuring" (i.e., so that participants develop new ways of looking at the world and a new set of beliefs and commitments). Finally, the new culture becomes institutionalized or "refrozen." Fullan (2001) discussed similar stages, terming them "initiation," "implementation," and "institutionalization."

Describing the steps in this way makes them seem simpler than they actually are, and several theorists have provided detailed elaboration showing what is needed at each stage. Table 2.3 shows how the steps Lewin described are further specified in two models of social change, one formulated by Everett Rogers (1995) and another by Gene Hall and Shirley Hord (2001).

In addition to describing the stages of the reform process, theories of change also focus on participants' levels of engagement with a reform. According to Hall and Hord (2001), two continua show where participants stand. One continuum describes their stages of concern about an innovation, and another, their levels of use. These theorists suggest that participants cycle through all of the stages as they implement a reform. Rogers (1995) presented a somewhat less dynamic continuum, suggesting that members of an organization tend to pick up on an innovation at different rates (see pp. 263–265).

---

[2]Educators and policymakers typically refer to such change as "reform," "continuous improvement," or "capacity building."

Table 2.3
Models of the Change Process

Lewin	Rogers	Hall and Hord
Unfreezing	Knowledge	Awareness
	Persuasion	Orientation (informational)
	Decision	
Cognitive Restructuring	Implementation	Preparation (personal)
		Mechanics (managerial)
Refreezing	Confirmation	Routine
		Refinement
		Integration
		Renewal

Theorists also describe the characteristics and functions of change agents. Hall and Hord (2001), for example, believe that leaders charged with overseeing an innovation exhibit three facilitator styles (i.e., "innovator," "manager," or "responder"). Evidence suggests, moreover, that innovators and managers are more effective in initiating reform than are responders (Hall & Hord, 2001). For this reason (and also because the change process is long and complex), these theorists contend that a team approach to the leadership of change may work best.

Fullan (2001) talked in somewhat different terms about the role of change agents, explaining that they confront a fundamental dilemma: (a) Inertia characterizes most organizations, (b) leaders must exert considerable influence in order to overcome inertia, but (c) change efforts instituted by leaders typically do not have sufficient "buy-in" from organizational participants. Recommending a blend of "top-down" and "bottom-up" activity in the implementation of change, Fullan provided a practical (although only partial) resolution of the dilemma:

> You can get away with top-down or assertive leadership ... under two conditions: first, in situations where it turns out you have a good idea; and second, when assertive initiation is combined with empowerment and choices as the process unfolds. (p. 67)

In other words, Fullan (2001) argued that, no matter what action starts a change process, it must be followed up with efforts to bring a majority of participants "on board." Change agents, according to most change theorists, need to direct attention both to the attitudes and to the competence level of participants.

Illustrative Theories of Leadership

As with positivist theories of organization, there are hundreds of positivist theories of leadership, representing a few major traditions. Here we discuss three theories, each exemplifying a different tradition. The discussion of *charismatic leadership* illustrates important tenets of the various trait theories. Behavioral and contingency theories are so closely connected that we use one simple example, *situational leadership,* to demonstrate their fundamental claims. And we use Bass and Avolio's (1994) characterization of *transformational leadership* to illustrate the theoretical approach inspired by the work of James McGregor Burns (1978).

Charismatic Leadership: A Trait Theory. Trait theories of leadership focus on the personal characteristics of leaders that distinguish them from followers. Whereas some such traits concern the body of the leader (e.g., leaders tend to be taller and more robust than followers—seriously), others are more abstract, even ineffable. For example, *charisma,* which comes from the Greek word for "divinely inspired gift" (Yukl, 2006, p. 249), is hard to describe precisely. Nevertheless, followers recognize charisma when they see it, and they attribute exceptional (even miraculous) powers to individuals who possess this trait (Weber, 1947).

Although some explanations of charisma focus on psychodynamics or on processes of "group-think," many popular theories identify the personal characteristics of individuals who are perceived to be charismatic (e.g., Conger & Kanungo, 1998). Such individuals are seen as visionary risk-takers who propose unconventional methods to achieve their goals (Yukl, 2006). Followers also tend to attribute charisma to leaders who appear confident, persuasive, trustworthy, self-sacrificing, and enthusiastic.

Because charisma relates to the emotional appeal of the leader, it may have little to do with the effectiveness or moral value of the "vision" that the leader promotes. For example, a principal who has charisma might convince school staff to adopt a new program even if research shows that the program has a mediocre "track record." The charisma of the principal, however, is likely to inspire teachers to devote extra energy to the new program and, as a result of their efforts, the school will improve its performance. Charismatic leaders need to accomplish such feats in order to retain their mystique and its accompanying power. According to some writers, organizations seek charismatic leaders when they face crises (e.g., House, Spangler, & Woycke, 1991). Others suggest that the effectiveness of charismatic leaders tends to be transitory (Yukl, 2006).

Situational Leadership: A Simple Contingency Theory.   Leadership theorists could not take trait theories very far (Bass, 1990). In this view, leaders are
born, not made: Traits are something a leader already has; they aren't developed.
But war—World War II—and an expanding postwar population and economy
called for lots of leaders—perhaps more than might be expected to be born into
the role (Bass, 1990).

A more useful theory, then, was one that helped organizations, especially the
military and large corporations, nurture leadership talent rather than waiting
for it to arrive on their doorsteps. In the late 1940s, two teams of researchers,
one at Ohio State University and one at the University of Michigan, began similar studies of leadership behavior. According to these researchers, understanding leadership behavior and its effects would enable organizations to select and
train employees who would become effective leaders.

The fundamental insight arising from this work on leadership behavior concerned the existence of two distinct dimensions of leadership: the task dimension and the relationship dimension.[3] Leaders could be high on one dimension
and low on the other, high on both, or low on both. The Ohio State researchers
developed a questionnaire (the Leadership Behavior Description Questionnaire or LBDQ) to measure individuals' performance on the two dimensions;
and research using the questionnaire examined the relationship between leader
behaviors (i.e., task and relationship) and organizational outcomes (e.g., employee satisfaction, turnover, productivity, and so on). This research was less
conclusive than had been hoped. Sometimes high task behavior was positively
associated with organizational outcomes, sometimes high relationship behavior
was positively associated, and sometimes the combination of high task and high
relationship was positively associated (see, e.g., Yukl, 2006). Rarely, however,
was the combination of low task and low relationship behavior associated with
positive outcomes (e.g., Blake & Mouton, 1961).

The inconclusiveness of this research led some theorists to speculate that the
effectiveness of leadership behavior might be contingent on relevant features of
the situations they confront (e.g., Hersey & Blanchard, 1982). Situations relating to the character of the work, the abilities of the workers, and the nature of
the workplace all might play a role in moderating the relationship between leaders' behavior and organizational outcomes. A school-related example—presented in Table 2.4—illustrates these dynamics.

Clearly the list of relevant situational moderators could be enormous, making contingency theories so complex that their practical value would be seri-

---

[3]The Ohio State team called these "initiating structure" (task) and "consideration" (relationship),
but we prefer the simpler terms.

Table 2.4
Situational Moderator Variables in Schools

Principal's Behavior	Moderator Variable	Possible Consequence
The principal is strongly relationship-oriented.	The school hires a teacher who has difficulty controlling classroom behavior.	The teacher might interpret the principal's friendliness as a sign that the classroom management problem isn't a serious issue.
The principal is strongly task-oriented.	The school faces the threat of closure.	Teachers might see the focus on task as evidence that the principal is callous.
The principal is strongly relationship-oriented.	A grant proposal is due to a funding agency on very short notice.	The principal may be unable to get staff to focus quickly enough on the task of writing the grant proposal.
The principal is moderately task-oriented and moderately relationship-oriented.	The school has decided to adopt a math curriculum that is quite different from its previous curriculum.	The principal may be viewed as effective because change processes require both structuring and concern for teachers' emotional well-being.

ously compromised. Several such theories, in fact, do exist (e.g., Fiedler & Chemers, 1984; Vroom & Jago, 1988). Examining a simple contingency model, however, reveals the way this theoretical approach works without overburdening the reader with unnecessary details.

Hersey and Blanchard's (1982) situational leadership theory incorporates two dimensions of behavior (i.e., task and relationship) from the Ohio State model. According to these theorists, leaders not only *can* control the extent to which they use these behaviors, they *should*. The theory suggests that leaders' manipulation of task and relationship behavior should respond to a situational moderator variable known as "worker maturity," which relates both to the employee's ability to perform a task as well as to his or her self-confidence. Employees might have low maturity for a task if they lack necessary skills; but even if they have the requisite skills, their maturity levels will remain low if they lack confidence.

Situational leadership theory recommends four leader behaviors that are responsive to the maturity of employees. The behaviors combine different levels of focus on tasks and relationships (Hersey & Blanchard, 1982).

- For the least mature workers, high focus on task combined with low focus on relationships constitutes *telling.* A principal, for example, might want to tell new teachers how to fill out attendance sheets.

- Somewhat more mature workers respond better to *selling*, with its high focus on both relationships and tasks. As teachers get past the challenges of their first months on the job, the principal may want to continue to provide explicit instructions. At the same time, however, he or she will also want to encourage teachers' engagement with the work of the school.

- Once workers are knowledgeable and committed, high relationship and low task behavior on the part of the leader—what Hersey and Blanchard call *participating*—elicits ongoing commitment. The principal might treat seasoned teachers as colleagues by inviting them to become members of a school-based leadership team.

- *Delegating* is reserved for the most mature workers, those that require neither the structuring nor the collegueship of the leader. In a school, for example, highly capable teachers might simply be left in peace to perform their jobs.

Although Hersey and Blanchard did not explicitly tie situational leadership theory to educational administration, it is certainly possible to do so. In fact, one noted writer on instructional supervision, Carl Glickman (1981), elaborated on an approach (what he called "developmental supervision") that draws heavily on Hersey and Blanchard's contingency theory.

Transformational Leadership.   Up through the 1970s, most of the leadership literature that had an influence on educational administration came from work in industrial psychology and organizational sociology. Leadership, however, was also an important concern of political scientists. Arguably, in fact, the earliest "leadership theories" came from philosophers like Plato and Machiavelli who thought about how states ought to be governed.

Ancient and early modern political philosophers focused mostly on the ways leaders—through the force of their character or the ingenuity of their actions—realized their political aims. Leaders on this view were sovereigns whose aims coincided with the aims of the state. As a result, followers—and efforts to influence or engage followers—were not central in most early theories of leadership. With the inception of democratic theory, during the Enlightenment of the late 17th and 18th centuries, however, the idea of the consent of the governed became very important to political theory. The role of citizen-followers consequently assumed a more prominent role. Nevertheless, as James McGregor Burns (1978) argued, leadership often devolved to manipulative influence over followers (citizens) on behalf of those with power.

For Burns, leadership has the potential to call followers to moral purposes that exceed their own wants and needs, thereby expanding followers' horizons and increasing the good they accomplish in the world. Leadership along these lines *transforms* followers and the world in which they take action. Burns contrasted it with a lesser form of leadership based on *transactions* between leaders and followers: Followers do what leaders ask of them in order to assure that their needs will be met and their desires realized. According to Burns (1978, p. 258)

> This theory … conceives of leader and follower as exchanging gratifications in a political marketplace. They are bargainers seeking to maximize their political and psychic profits. In this marketplace the bargaining is restricted in scope because the process works only in easily identifiable, calculable, tangible, measurable properties.

Even though Burns focused attention on the large-scale political, intellectual, and social advances that transformational leadership makes possible, others soon realized that transformational leadership might be useful in all organizations. The essays in Bass and Avolio's (1994) collection, for example, examined transformational leadership in large corporations and small work teams. In fact, not too long after the publication of Burns' book, educators began discussing the applicability of this approach to K–12 schools and universities (e.g., Leithwood, 1992).

Contributing the insight that transformational leadership is an extension of transactional leadership rather than its opposite, Bass and Avolio (1994) provided practical guidance to managers and administrators looking to transform their organizations. These authors described four practices that characterized this approach to leadership: (a) idealized influence, (b) inspirational motivation, (c) intellectual stimulation, and (d) individualized consideration. In Sidebar 2-4 we provide brief definitions of these practices as well as school examples of each.

Sidebar 2-4

Transformational Leadership Practices in Schools

Idealized Influence: The leader inspires trust and proves trustworthy. He or she is a moral exemplar, a role model whom followers seek to emulate. In her book, *In Schools We Trust*, Deborah Meier (2002) described her work in creating a school community in which students trust adult staff enough to learn from them. Meier described the actions she first needed to take in order for staff, students, and parents to see her as trustworthy.

Inspirational Motivation: The leader contributes a vision that compels followers to become involved in shaping the future. The movie *Stand and Deliver* tells the story of Jaime Escalante, an inspirational teacher in East Los Angeles who, over the course of several years, convinced increasing numbers of low-income Hispanic students that they could learn calculus and pass the Advanced Placement exam in that subject.

Intellectual Stimulation: The leader encourages creative thinking among followers, often by asking provocative questions, reframing dilemmas that confront the organization, or soliciting innovative solutions to problems. A high school principal in a small Ohio town challenged her teachers to find a way to increase student engagement. One teacher designed an elective course in which students identified and found solutions to local problems. Over the years, increasing numbers of students have taken an interest in the course, and the students have solved problems relating to traffic flow through town, water pollution, and school funding.

Individualized Consideration: The leader cultivates the talents of each individual in the organization by getting to know each personally and helping him or her set and achieve worthy professional goals. A principal in one of Ohio's "Schools of Promise" met one-on-one with every student in his 7–12 school to discuss ways to improve performance on state proficiency tests.

THE LEGACY IN SCHOOLS OF TRADITIONAL THEORIES

As suggested earlier in this chapter, positivist theories dominate the way we think about schools. These theories provide important insights, but they also introduce blinders that keep us from thinking about other possibilities. In the discussion that follows, we explore briefly the legacy of positivist theories in today's schools. Our aim is to show the value of the practices supported by these theories as well as some of their drawbacks.

Schools as Factories

By the late 1800s, the 19th-century dream of providing a ubiquitous system of common schooling for all children had become a nightmare, especially in cities (Rice, 1893). Increasing numbers of immigrants teemed into the slums and ethnic neighborhoods of U.S. cities, particularly those on the East coast, and schools struggled to make space to accommodate their rapidly expanding enrollments. Because they were founded, at least in their urban version, to prepare masses of children from immigrant neighborhoods for "responsible adulthood," the common schools were becoming a large-scale enterprise.

Moreover, educators felt pressure to use the schools to inculcate the virtue of compliance (Tyack, 1974). From the perspective of social reformers of the day, immigrants (and their children) represented a serious threat to social stability. In their view, if the children of immigrants were left unschooled, they would eventually become a lawless mob of unemployed ruffians (Katz, 1968; Tyack, 1974). And in this "primitive" state, such youth and young adults would be unprepared to meet the demands either of citizenship or of participation in the growing economy.

In fact, harnessed to the economic needs of mass production, the system of common schooling rapidly evolved into a system of *mass* schooling (Tyack, 1974). What resulted were large, overcrowded "factory schools" where the requirement to impose (or just maintain) crowd control overshadowed the requirement to promote even basic literacy. Furthermore, these schools confronted pressure from business leaders to minimize costs per student, based on the positivist theory of scientific management (Taylor, 1911; see also Callahan, 1962). Educators developed various practices—reminiscent of those used in factories— in order to improve schools' efficiency. Among these were age-grade placement, strict time schedules marked by the ringing of bells, attendance rosters, seating charts, and report cards (Parkerson & Parkerson, 1998; Paterson, 1989).

These features of schooling persist in most schools today, and they still contribute to schools' efficiency. After all, without predictable and well-enforced routines, it's difficult to imagine that the typical staffing ratio (i.e., something like 1:30) would be sufficient to allow teachers to control the behavior of students, let alone teach them anything at all. Efficiency measures clearly have played a key role in sustaining the system of universal schooling in the United States.

But there have been costs. For example, faced with an impersonal system of schooling, many students become disengaged (e.g., Fanning, 1995). In fact, large schools tend to be quite bureaucratic, alienating staff and parents as well as students (e.g., Haberman, 2003). Even among students who remain attentive, learning does not proceed in lock-step fashion. Arguably, the routines that maintain school efficiency (e.g., the bell schedule, age-grade placement) work counter to efforts to cultivate students' independent thinking and self-directed learning (e.g., Gatto, 1990; Gibbons, 2002).

Didactic Pedagogy

Despite official lip-service for constructivist pedagogy, instruction in U.S. schools continues to draw heavily on lecture, recitation, drill, and practice (e.g., Battista, 1999). Grounded in behaviorist theories of learning, these practices *do* enable students to acquire basic skills and factual information. They are, however, less effective in helping students learn to think critically and creatively, solve relevant problems, and make sense of important ideas (Howley, Howley, & Pendarvis, 1995).

Furthermore, didactic approaches to pedagogy—what Freire (1970) referred to as the "banking model" of education—encourage students to take a passive role in their own education. This banking model prizes compliance over independence, inculcation over thoughtfulness, and silence over critique. Ultimately, according to Freire and others, this approach sustains prevailing relations of power by keeping those with the least power from using self-directed education on behalf of their own liberation.

Accountability

Current accountability policies and the practices they support draw on two positivist traditions: the psychometric tradition and the scientific management tradition. Earlier we explained how theories of scientific management influenced educators' quest for school efficiency (Callahan, 1962). At the same time, these theories also encouraged educators and policy makers to become more concerned about school effectiveness.

Arguably, public interest in the effectiveness of educational institutions actually preceded theories of scientific management. In 18th and 19th centuries, for example, examiners visited local schools to evaluate students' performance (Callahan, 1962; Mazzeo, 2001; Riley 1977). Even early accountability schemes, like those of today, linked the performance of students with the effectiveness of teachers and schools. Efforts to hold schools accountable, however, became far more extensive and far more systematic beginning in the 1970s (Marcoulides & Heck, 1994; Mazzeo, 2001).

The development of standardized tests in the early 1900s, multiple choice item formats in the 1920s, and machine scoring in the mid-1950s provided the technical means for widespread measurement of school performance (Clarke, Madaus, Horn, & Ramos, 2000). Although early uses of such tests focused more on guidance functions (e.g., determining students' eligibility for programs or their learning needs), standardized tests also enabled comparison of schools

(Clarke et al., 2000; Mazzeo, 2001). Such comparisons were first made via the national norms that were published by test-development companies. Later, states began to make use of criterion-referenced tests, focusing on cut scores and pass rates as the basis for comparing schools.

Throughout most of the 20th century and into the 21st, strong advocacy has promoted psychometric testing in schools, but there has also been much resistance. Supporters argue that testing has contributed to school improvement by making school performance visible to parents and community leaders (e.g., Ravitch, 1995). Opponents claim that accountability testing narrows the curriculum, places unwarranted stress on students, unfairly discriminates by race and social class, and undercuts local control over education (e.g., McNeil, 2000; Ohanian, 1999).

WHAT HAPPENS TO THE LANGUAGE OF POSSIBILITY UNDER POSITIVISM: CASE STUDY

Jurassic Middle School seems to be in free fall. Student performance has been declining for the past 5 years, teacher turnover is at an all-time high, and parents are exercising their option under NCLB to move their children to other schools in the city. At this point, long-time principal Nate Henderson isn't sure what's really been happening or what to do.

In actual fact, Henderson seems to have been doing all the right things for the past several years. He's involved teachers in school governance; he's helped teachers develop individualized professional development plans; he's used staff opinion leaders to help convince colleagues of the need for reform.

All of these initiatives, of course, rest on traditional theories about schooling, leadership, and organizational dynamics. Human resource theory justifies the involvement of teachers in school decision making; transformational leadership theory supports the use of individualized professional development plans; corralling early adopters to help change the opinions of colleagues comes from change theory.

Why might it be that Nate, a seasoned and previously effective principal, is having so much trouble now? Is he using the theories in the wrong way? Or are the theories wrong?

As we see throughout the rest of the book, other theories besides traditional positivist theories offer insights unsupported by positivist theories. Perhaps dynamic systems theory could help Nate identify an unproductive feedback loop. Communitarian theory might suggest to him that the breakdown is not in the school itself but in the way the school interacts with the community. Thinking about the racial and ethnic dynamics within the school community might re-

veal deeply entrenched patterns of domination. Or it might be that gender relations among teachers are creating a school culture that functions to restrain or
even disable positive initiatives.

The schooling enterprise and the world in which it operates are, indeed, complex. As a result, powerful tools are needed by those who think about schooling
and the good it might do. Although traditional theories of organization and leadership provide some insights, their assumptions keep us from seeing important
possibilities. A "language of possibility" is opened up through theories that go beyond educational means and ends to explore how education—construed broadly
as personal and social liberation—might constitute an end in itself.

CHAPTER SUMMARY

This chapter reviews the assumptions of traditional positivist theories and functionalist research that are usually seen as the legitimate guide to how to be a
principal (in fact, to the practice of school administration overall). Exploring
the connection between a positivist view of the world and research based on
that view, the discussion considers the hopes and possible illusions of social engineers.

Turning then to specific positivist theories of organization, the chapter provides exemplars characterizing significant theoretical traditions. Among theories of organization, bureaucratic theory illustrates the focus on organizational
structure. Human resources theory, institutional theory, and theories of change
exemplify descriptions about and prescriptions for social relations, political
dynamics, and culture in organizations.

Traditional leadership theories are explained next. To exemplify trait theories, the discussion considers charismatic leadership. Linking behavioral and
contingency theories, the narrative explores theorists' expansion of two-di-
mensional behavioral theories to incorporate important situational moderator
variables, such as worker maturity. Representing more recent theories of transformational leadership, the chapter considers how Bass and Avolio operational-
ized the practices distinguishing transactional from transformational leaders.

The chapter concludes with a brief look at the legacy of traditional theories
in contemporary schools. It considers constellations of practices grounded in
scientific management, behaviorism, and psychometrics, examining the value
and limitations of each. Perhaps most significantly for people who are starting to
think critically about school administration, the discussion reveals the influence of scientific management on the structure and operation of schools as well
as on efforts to hold schools accountable for particular outcomes.

3

Why We Need to Think Differently About Schools

CASE STUDY, PART 1: NOW WHAT'S WRONG?

Ellen Farber is principal of Penn Hills High School in a populated suburban district in the Northeast. She's led Penn Hills now for 6 years and is the first woman to hold the position. Penn Hills enrolls 1,703 students and has a subsidized meals rate of 4.7%. The community is reasonably affluent: Nearly all the kids go to college, with a lot of competition and anxiety over hoped-for admission to the great universities of the nation. It's been a stimulating ride up until now. Ellen works with three assistant principals to manage the complexities of the enterprise; one essentially for discipline and related matters, one for postsecondary articulation, and one for teacher support.

For the 10 years prior to becoming principal, Ellen taught mathematics at the high school. She adored math, and she liked teaching it. Ellen also coached a very successful girls' volleyball team. She was highly respected by team members and their parents, and she was an enormously popular teacher. Now, as principal, she knows the school and the community like the back of her hand.

Toward the end of her years as a teacher, Ellen's problem seemed to be that she wanted—she didn't know exactly—something more than what she'd achieved. Teaching wasn't giving her the challenges and pleasures it once had. Out of what seemed like boredom, she began, once again, taking classes—this time in school administration. Her fellow teachers thought she was nuts for a variety of reasons.

She'd wanted to understand more about Penn Hills High School as a system, and about the wider system of schooling in the United States. And during her master's program in educational administration, she discovered that she liked thinking this way; the whole entity, Penn Hills High School, was a fabulous and messy enterprise, with the challenge being to help more individual kids and more teachers make the most of their talents.

This view of the school, and of schooling, was not something, she observed, that most of her teacher colleagues wanted to share. To her, they seemed to be stuck in the perspective of the classroom; they often said, "We'd be fine if the district and the state would just *leave us alone to teach*." They didn't get the idea that the school wasn't *just* a school, that it was also part of a major social institution—an institution with a unique and wonderful and strange mission. Nor did they understand how little this institution and Penn Hills in particular was able to confront crazy threats to its well-being and success. These threats, it seemed to Ellen, were part of what made the institution *strange*. Her teacher colleagues tended to take it all upon themselves: the failures, the challenges, and the successes. And taking on this burden seemed to confuse and frustrate so many of them. Many got burned; and too many got *burned out*.

Ellen wasn't going there; she wanted to keep contributing. And that meant she needed to keep growing. That's why she became a principal—a successful one, it had seemed, until recently, when she found herself asking more and more often, "What's wrong with this picture?" Interestingly, these doubts have come at a time when Ellen is the top contender and presumed heir-apparent to the superintendency of the Penn Hills School District. (to be continued…)

THEORY AND PERSPICACITY

Theory is not, as chapter 1 explains, a remote, abstract, or bloodless view of the world. Quite the contrary: We all hold theories and we defend some of them with considerable passion. Theories, however, are—or should be—subject to revision as we get new information or have experiences that force new insights upon us. It's this quality, after all, that distinguishes a *theory* from a *belief*. Theories are supposed to be tentative; beliefs are often timeless, with belief in God the typical example.

A theory, in this view, is a work in progress. It makes sense to reexamine a theory from time to time, to revise it or even abandon it as our reexamination indicates. Good theorizing requires continuous thinking and updating.

Arguably, it's the special role of the leader of an organization to take charge of theorizing—helping members of the organization examine and explain the situations they confront and helping them revise their explanations in light of new information and accumulating experience. A school leader, then, would become a school's or district's leading theoretician. Of course, this view of the school leader's role doesn't mean that every principal and superintendent necessarily will become the leading theoretician.

But it is almost always a good thing when the people who hold leadership positions actually do assume intellectual leadership. Certainly, when an administrator is *not* the equal of others in the organization, he or she loses considerable leadership potential—and loses actual as well as potential power and authority. A poor leader is, after all, one whose ideas are dismissed, and an administrator without ideas is not even in the running.

Should the potential leader's ideas come principally from those represented in chapter 2, from the body of traditional theory on leadership and organizations that has been used to prepare school leaders for several generations? It seems a dubious idea!

Scientific management, for instance, could have been taught to the grandparents of people now preparing to become principals. And yet, that theory is a key part of contemporary accountability arrangements. Is the application of scientific management still appropriate? How do we know? How can we judge? If so, does scientific management of schools represent good leadership?

Chapter 3 presents some of the evidence and develops some of the arguments to address these questions, such as "Is scientific management still appropriate?" as well as other related questions. It's important to note, however, that this chapter and, in fact, the whole book intentionally refuses to take an all-or-nothing perspective. It neither views the old theories as all bad, nor claims that any of the new ones are all good. How could it? Schooling is not an all-or-nothing proposition, and the same is true of ideas about schooling.

What's worrisome to some of us, however, is that too many people in schools, perhaps administrators especially, seem to be looking not only for ready-made solutions to eliminate particular problems, but also for a single, enduringly valid way of viewing the world of schooling. In school administration, for a long time, this "true way" has been offered as the path of progress. Among the signposts thought to stake out the path are the theories presented in the previous chapter. For many observers, though, the path and the signposts are no longer adequate in themselves. And for some observers, the old ways of viewing schools seem on balance to be more damaging than they are helpful (e.g., Bruner, 1996; Theobald, 1997; Wenger, 1998; Wheatley, 1994).

The goal of this book is not to help readers find the one best path to certain success, but to help aspiring principals become more *perspicacious*[1] about how they think about their jobs and how they provide leadership to schools. We can, each of us, decide what we find "best," but that choice is sure to be of limited value if the thinking behind it is restricted. This book, therefore, encourages broad thinking, inventive theorizing—in short, contemplation of views of schooling and of the context for schooling that go well beyond the mainstream. This chapter opens up this exploration with a distinctly nonmainstream consideration of the contemporary context in which schooling takes place.

TAKING AND MISTAKING THE CONTEMPORARY CONTEXT OF SCHOOLS

There was a time, two generations ago perhaps, when schools were being perfected, seriously perfected, across the nation. Americans were working hard after 1945 to move forward after a long depression and a horrific global war. It was a moment of intense optimism. People widely believed that life in general was getting better and better, and it seemed almost natural to conclude that the anticipated improvement would certainly make schools better (see, e.g., Lasch, 1991).

Writing in 1959, for instance, the former Harvard President James Conant, chemistry professor emeritus, and president of the American Association for the Advancement of Science, advised the nation that no American high school enrolling fewer than 400 students in Grades 9–12 could hope to provide an adequate curriculum (Conant, 1959). Conant wrote with considerable prestige, of course, and between 1959 and 2005, the size of the average high school increased from about 300 to over 800 (Snyder, Plisko, & Sonnenberg, 2004) as small high schools everywhere were closed. About the same time, new ideas about teaching and learning math, science, and foreign languages—the new math of the early 1960s, for instance—were unrolled. The proportion of youth attending high school rose after falling during the war and increasingly more high school students were graduating and going on to college.

In spite of such changes, by all accounts, our public schools have not become perfect. Some doubt whether they are very good or even good enough. Many people appear to believe that they leave much to be desired. In fact, whether or

---

[1]*Perspicacious* is a great word for leaders, implying "unusual power to see through and understand what is puzzling or hidden" (Mish, 1984, p. 1091, under "shrewd").

not curricula are more adequate today in our larger schools than was formerly the case in our smaller ones is an open question. A distressing number of sober observers are claiming that high schools—in part because of their large size—have become dysfunctional institutions (e.g., Marsh & Codding, 1999; Raywid, 1999). This claim, by the way, does *not* mean that every high school is dysfunctional. Rather it suggests, for instance, that society as a whole might be better served by some other kind of arrangement than by high schooling. What happened along the road to perfection? What caused an institution once thought to be perfectable to become so troubled and perhaps even to have become dysfunctional?

The reasons may have something to do with demographic shifts, social disintegration, and the various school wars. The views presented in this chapter, however, may seem surprising in that they don't blame the changes on these conditions, as is so often the case. The argument is not that we need to think differently about schools because these things have made our work so much harder. The argument is more like this: These changes alter the terms we accept, the bargains we make, and the way we ought to think about negotiating the terms and bargains. What does this mean?

Demographic shifts, social disintegration, and the school wars aren't going away anytime soon, so it's not a question of solving a problem or overcoming a barrier. It's not a question of silver bullets, of just adopting "best practice." And rather than solving problems, school leaders would need to deal wisely with rather durable dilemmas (e.g., Cuban, 2001a). These may seem like subtle points, but they aren't. They concern how administrators imagine schooling and how they lead and manage actual schools.

Disturbing Populations

One development, often pointed to in explaining why teaching and leading schools has supposedly become more difficult, is the shift in "demographics," particularly the racial, ethnic, and cultural structure of the U.S. population. Certainly a "shift" has taken place, and the transformation continues. But there is more to be said.

In 1940 and 1950, about 10% of the U.S. population was "minority"—almost entirely Black (Gibson & Jung, 2002). Hispanics, according to the U.S. Census, comprised 1% or 2% of the population. At the time, of course, numerous people still regarded Italians, Jews, and members of other White ethnic groups as, well, not quite kosher—definitely inferior to Anglo-Saxon Whites, which didn't include the Irish.

Not only was the minority population of that time composed predominantly of a single group (i.e., African Americans). Black people were nearly invisible to White people. African Americans attended segregated schools (that's not much different from today), but, as most readers know, they were also legally barred in many states from attending schools with Whites. The prevalent images of Blacks we now see in the media, and have come to expect to see, would have surprised and probably disturbed most Whites from 1900–1960, for whom the invisibility of this population was an expectation. The cultural norm of the mainstream, reinforced by law, was to ignore and discount the needs and dreams of this 10% of citizens (Woodson, 1933/1996). The fact that it was easy to do, however, didn't make it right. Nor does the size of the proportion, small or large, ever make it right. This moral argument, in fact, is a cornerstone of democracy: Protection of the minority and its voice is a principle of democratic governance and is inscribed in Constitutional law.

The story of "the demographic shift" begins with that reality, and not with what is after all an inevitable change in the national and linguistic make-up of a land founded to help realize the dreams of ordinary humans far and wide. In this light, it has to be understood as strange that to nearly all White Americans in 1945, the coming postwar epoch did not seem to harbor much of a place for the Black Americans already in their midst. How could it, of course, if they were invisible and if that invisibility was understood as proper? Blacks returning from the war just happened to see matters quite differently. And many other Blacks, educated by several generations of perspicacious African American educators, also saw through the White complacency.

The moral argument is augmented by 40 or 50 years of population growth, such that by 1990, about 25% of the nation was Black or Hispanic. In 2005, Hispanics alone accounted for about 14% of the total U.S. population or 41.3 million people—proportionately more than the entire minority population in 1950, and far larger in absolute numbers (Bernstein, 2005).

By the start of the new millennium, a number of populous states had already become what the Census Bureau called "majority-minority" states—that is, states in which racial and ethnic "minorities"—dark-skinned people, to make matters simple and blunt—now comprised more than half the population. According to a 2005 Census press release,

> Texas has now joined Hawaii, New Mexico and California as a majority-minority state, along with the District of Columbia, the U.S. Census Bureau reported today. Five states—Maryland, Mississippi, Georgia, New York and Arizona—are next in line with minority populations of about 40 percent. The minority population includes all people except non-Hispanic single-race whites. (Bernstein, 2005, August 11, p. 1)

Dark-skinned people outnumber white-skinned people in the nation's most populous states: California, Texas, and New York. Such facts are still disturbing to some, perhaps many, White people. The implications for culture, economics, politics, and schooling are momentous. It's a far cry from being invisible.

One thing this change in "demographics" does *not* mean, however, is that schools have to figure out how to cope better with deficient students! The word *demographics* appears in scare-quotes in this section to highlight a continuing misconstruction, namely the belief that people whose skins aren't white are somehow mentally deficient.

Of course there *are* demographic changes (no scare-quotes), but that's merely what happens with the passage of time; if time passes, the character of a population changes. Why is it then that the expression "demographic shifts" often serves as a code word for "difficult-to-educate students?"

One answer to the question reflects insights that come from institutional theory. Put most sharply, we might conclude that minorities are viewed as a "challenge" for the mainstream school system because the K–12 educational system doesn't engage the relevant cultural, economic, and political issues—a refusal that is based on the legacy of invisibility. Instead, the system—the *institution*—insulates itself from these "irritants." It remains, according to some observers, largely a 1950s or 1960s institution, stuck on whiteness, on naïve and unrealistic views of improvement, and on the continuing belief that dark-skinned people are invisible (e.g., Brown & Land, 2005; Shapiro & Purpel, 1998). The institution sees itself as being challenged merely because it remains so stolidly unresponsive. With this view, at any rate, it earns the reputation of being dysfunctional.

Readers need not accept this view, but many Blacks, Hispanics, and American Indians do accept it. Unlike in decades past, Blacks and Hispanics today are culturally, economically, and politically visible—even without the sorts of institutional change that might otherwise affirm and make productive use of this reality. Today, they are not only visible, but influential.

Responsibility for addressing the argued short-sightedness of schooling lies, however, in significant measure with White educators. Many "minority" observers conclude that the association between the whiteness of the profession and its argued nonresponsiveness is anything but coincidental. Rather, its whiteness explains its nonresponsiveness.

A different argument can also be made; namely, that what "these people" require is to learn the ways of the mainstream middle class. This argument is precisely the one made by Ruby Payne in her immensely popular publications and workshops (e.g., Payne, 1998; see Sidebar 3-1 for some implications behind this popular position).

Sidebar 3-1

There *is* a lot to be said on behalf of the role of schooling in cultivating a strong middle class, and Ruby Payne's workshops are perhaps very popular for that reason. The middle class has been regarded historically as a balancing force in American society. Its demise, in this view, is a bad sign for America's future.

Some observers, however, identify two related misconceptions hidden within an approach that otherwise seems generous and helpful to many educators: (a) a deficit theory of poverty and (b) an uncritical theory of the middle class. These alleged shortcomings relate to what the poor might lose and what they are supposed to gain. What does it mean to help a poor child or dark-skinned child enter the White middle class?

What the Poor Might Lose. Payne *does not* claim that the bad habits she says characterize the poor cause poverty. What she does say, however, is that those who shed their home culture—its bad habits and lack of planning—have a better chance of escaping poverty. Even if one agrees with the proposition that poverty is structured by bad habits and bad planning, say the critics of Payne, one needs to acknowledge that, when poor students shed their home culture, they also lose something. It's perhaps notable that, according to Payne, "In generational poverty, education is often feared because it is equated with loss" (as quoted in Shaughnessy, 2005, August 30, ¶ 5, 8). The loss being spoken of here is the loss of family. Of course, as anyone with a family knows, and anyone who has been divorced, it's a lot to lose. The promise had better be worth the sacrifice.

What the Poor are Supposed to Gain. In recent decades, the percentage of unionized workers has declined, and the proportional size of the middle class is shrinking, according to a variety of objective measures. Its historical existence has been brief so far, and its staying power seems uncertain. Beyond this, of course, the epithet "middle class" also signifies complacency, self-righteousness, and mediocrity. Is the middle class such a terrific destination? There are reasons to doubt. Is a good job preferable to wretched poverty? It certainly is. A good job isn't synonymous with "middle-class."

What's the Truth? The truth is that most poverty, as Payne claimed, is about survival. Struggling for survival sharpens and sometimes, perhaps often, also narrows one's vision. The poor's struggle for survival is grim, for reasons having as much, or more, to do with racism and classism as with bad habits and poor planning. Surely good habits and planning are helpful; but what's believed to be good and what's being planned must be considered by the poor themselves, and not merely assumed by educators certain of what's best. Perspicacity is applicable here.

SCHOOLING AS A DISTURBED MICROCOSM OF SOCIETY: OR VICE VERSA?

Public schooling in the United States has been under concerted attack for quite some time. The character of the attack has changed in recent decades, however. In the middle of the last century, that is, in the late 1950s, criticism centered on reform of curriculum and instruction. The launching of Sputnik, the first "artificial" satellite by the Russians in 1957, was thought to reveal the need to retool U.S. schools in ways that would enable them to produce more engineers and scientists and thereby to safeguard national security. Today, however, criticism from across the political spectrum is more and more directed at public schooling as an entire institution (e.g., Arons, 1997; Chubb & Moe, 1990; Mathews, 1996) and less and less at its specific shortcomings. Nevertheless, public schooling certainly retains some defenders, prominent among whom are professional educators.

But the visible criticism overshadows the visible support. There are clear threats that governments will take bold steps if adequate improvement isn't forthcoming soon (e.g., Hanushek & Raymond, 2002). Already the "monopoly" of public schooling is being disrupted by home schooling, charter schools, public support of private schools, vouchers and other mechanisms, and various experiments with electronic schooling. Some observers predict that the accountability movement and the standards movement, which are related to one another, will serve to widen this breach (e.g., Bracey, 2002; Dorn, 1998; Walberg & Bast, 1998).

In the more distant past—during the era of high modernism from about 1920 to about 1980—the idea of doing away with the state's "monopoly" on schooling was barely thinkable. Only radicals, mostly libertarians, voiced such ideas (e.g., Everhart, 1982; Illich, 1971) and they weren't taken very seriously the mainstream. Free, publicly funded schools for everyone, right through high school, was an amazing accomplishment, the result of at least 100 years of struggle. The monopoly was a mark of success, not of failure.

Today, however, the radical ideas once dismissed by the mainstream have powerful supporters in the American right (see Walberg & Bast, 1998, for a thoughtful account of this perspective). What's responsible for the change?

One view—a common one—is that recent disappointments with schooling simply reflect changes in society as a whole. The nature of these changes, however, goes well beyond the "demographic shifts" previously identified. In fact, the changes may be so momentous that they shake the ground under the institution of schooling, including public schooling as we have known it.

But the traditional theories typically called on in the preparation of administrators take little account of this shaky ground. Principals who limit their vision to traditional theories, moreover, already find themselves unprepared to handle many of the challenges that confront them. Alternative theoretical perspectives attend more directly to these social changes, and the remaining chapters of this book examine these perspectives in an effort to help new and aspiring school leaders think about schooling in the contemporary, postmodern context.

The changes that seem to be causing the ground to shake are readily revealed in simple national statistics, viewed over time. The following statistics are examples, in round numbers, and all are drawn from authoritative sources (the following are given from longer to shorter time-span):

1. Since 1900, the *divorce rate* has quadrupled (source: Department of Health and Human Services).
2. After 1950, *drug usage* increased five-fold —10 drugs used by at least 6% of those born after that date as compared to two drugs previously (source: Department of Health and Human Services).
3. Since 1950, *youth suicide rates* have doubled (source: American Association for Suicidology).
4. Since the late 1960s, the *ratio of the minimum wage to the poverty level* has been cut almost in half and now stands at about 50% or 60%, with exact ratios varying by size of family (source: Congressional Research Service).
5. Between 1970 and 1990, the rate of *35–44 year-olds living alone* tripled (source: Bureau of the Census).
6. Since 1980, the *rich have gotten a lot richer*: The richest fifth of American wage earners claimed a larger share in 2000—20 % larger since 1980—of all income, whereas all other fifths lost income share (source: Bureau of the Census).
7. Since about 1990, a minimum of 75% of American students in the fourth grade have watched *at least an hour of TV per day*, with as many as 20% watching 6 *hours* or more each day (source: National Center for Education Statistics).

Such statistics are indicators of disintegrating social bonds—in communities, among members of families, between individuals, and within individuals themselves.

The circumstances indicated by the statistics make it arguably more difficult to conduct schooling as it has been designed so far. That's because such circumstances directly influence the behavior of all of us—most of us are touched personally by at least one of the foregoing statistics—but all of these circumstances also indirectly influence all of us collectively. It's not only that children and youth bring such baggage to school, but that teachers and administrators do as well.

Again, as with "demographic shifts," the issue is not that there is some problem outside the control of educators that educators are nevertheless expected to solve, but a difficult circumstance that really does involve all of us, professionals and lay people alike. It means we need to think about schools differently—not "how to fix the problem," but how to manage thoughtful experiences for students within an environment shaped by such developments.

Sure, maybe better schooling will alter the course of such developments—but maybe not. Whatever happens, we can be absolutely sure that the need will remain for thoughtful people who can argue issues, who have intellectual interests and other capacities, and who see beyond their own needs and desires to those of neighbors and fellow citizens. Cultivating such people sounds like a good mission for schools, whatever the circumstances—at least to many educators on both the political left and the political right (e.g., Bruner, 1996; Gatto, 2002; Ravitch, 2000). It seems reasonable to the authors of this book, too, but we also think that many other aims are arguable and worthy. So one response to the disintegration is to think more broadly about schooling.

Often, however, school administrators interpret within-school reflections of the wider social disintegration as (a) a failure of parents and (b) a failure of school discipline. Principals who see matters this way typically but not always do two things. First, they give up on parents because they blame them. Second, they tighten school discipline: "If they're not getting it at home, we'll give it to them here."

For instance, principals and superintendents impose strict "zero tolerance" policies. When it comes to weapons there's good reason for such policies, although the media have reported seemingly ridiculous incidents of students being suspended or expelled for dubious infractions of them (e.g., Sughrue, 2003). What's happening in these cases? Are the school leaders stupid? Have they gone nuts? Probably not.

First, schools had to adopt zero-tolerance policies if they wanted to remain eligible for federal funds (Fiscus, 2000). Schools and districts, having already incorporated these funds into their cash flow, seldom declined to take the funds even as "small" prescriptions of this sort have been added—new strings attached to federal funding. Playing the zero-tolerance policy game wasn't optional. It was mandatory. Hardly anyone refused, although refusal always has remained an option.

Second, the zero tolerance framework reinforces a custodial tendency that is already too strong in most schools (e.g., Haberman, 2000). Custodial functions are those that replace education with confinement and the discipline needed to ensure confinement, ideally with maximum order and safety. Strongly custodial environments are harsh and miseducative, at least in the judgment of centuries of perspicacious observers (e.g., Dickens, 1854/1907; Gatto, 2002; Montessori, 1946; Rousseau, 1762/1911).

Under zero-tolerance thinking, a rather wide range of misbehaviors can be treated as if the infractions were as serious as bringing a gun to school. In these situations, students develop a variety of devious and clever forms of resistance. They can systematically provoke harsh responses with toy weapons, phone calls, and rumors. From an administrative and organizational standpoint, strict disciplinary routines too often become ends in themselves. Worst of all, they can be a lot harder to get rid of than they were to impose (e.g., Perryman, 2005). This is surely the case when the federal government is mandating the programs and holding 7% of school funding hostage (7% is about the average federal share of a school's funding).

Breaking Down the Commitment to the Common School

If the school can be viewed not just as a microcosm of social disintegration but as a contributor to such disintegration, then it's easier to argue that public schooling has lost its legitimacy. In other words, if the public can be kept ignorant about social disintegration (its extent, its structure, its causes), then public schools can be easily blamed for incompetence, for disorganization, and even for failing to adequately protect the safety of the nation's children. One solution is to remove schooling from public control, handing more of it over to varied private operators—privatization.

Work along these lines is not new. The National Commission on Excellence in Education, established by the administration of Ronald Reagan, made this stunning pronouncement about the schools in 1983:

> If an unfriendly foreign power had attempted to impose on America the mediocre educational performance that exists today, we might well have viewed it as an act

of war. As it stands, we have allowed this to happen to ourselves. We have even squandered the gains in student achievement made in the wake of the Sputnik challenge. Moreover, we have dismantled essential support systems that helped make those gains possible. We have, in effect, been committing an act of unthinking, unilateral educational disarmament. (National Commission on Excellence, 1983, p. 50)

In this way, the Commission took the unique position that schooling was *not* in fact a microcosm of society, but that society was a microcosm of *schooling*; if the nation was at risk, it was the schools' fault!

The argument may seem odd at the present historical moment, but in the early 1980s, the Japanese economy was booming and the U.S. economy stagnant; Japanese schools and industry outshone their American counterparts (Japanese schooling is still held up as a model for American educators, see, e.g., Stigler, Gonzales, Kawanka, Knoll, & Serrano 1999). The argument found a wide audience, despite its unique reading of what causes what (Ravitch, 2003).

Nation at Risk seemed to suggest that if the public schools are capable of such an act of betrayal, perhaps nonpublic options would be worth thinking about. Not surprisingly, private and parochial schools are listed in its discussion of "the tools at hand" (National Commission on Excellence, 1983, p. 16). The Commission, in effect, said that because public schools had threatened the national security, private schools would help restore it. The logic has made sense to many people since that time (e.g., Chubb & Moe, 1990), although there are many who take exception to it (e.g., Masini & Edirisooriya, 2000; Ravitch, 2003). Others (e.g., Berliner & Biddle, 1995) have suggested that the Commission helped shape a fall from grace for American public schools, and more particularly for the American ideal of the common school—an institution to which the children of all citizens go in order to become citizens themselves (e.g., Cremin, 1980).

It's a substantial historical change. Earlier, private schools had been a small, and contested, part of schooling in America. In fact, it took a Supreme Court ruling to establish the constitutional right of parents to send children to private schools (*Pierce v. Society of Sisters*, 1925).

As the legitimacy of public schooling was increasingly challenged after 1983, James Coleman and Thomas Hoffer published a book in the late 1980s that presented substantial evidence of the inferiority of public as compared to private schooling (Coleman & Hoffer, 1987). It was about this time that other research studies began to use "sector" comparisons in their analyses, which, in effect, legitimized a new view of the structure of the U.S. educational system. Henceforth, it was composed of two parts, a "public sector" and a "private sector."

The research by Coleman and Hoffer provoked vigorous reaction from the defenders of public schooling—denials, reanalysis of the data, and so forth—but the slight superiority of schools in the private sector seemed, on balance, genuine. After all, at each grade level, private schools were on average a lot smaller than public schools. Private schools seldom, if ever, existed in the huge and embattled district organizations with tens or even hundreds of thousands of students that are so common in the public sector. Their teachers and administrators were less burdened with paperwork. The private schools were able to make bargains with parents enrolling their children (e.g., abide by the rules or go elsewhere; we offer this sort of instruction, but not that; take it or leave it). Their administrators seldom had to cope with the demands of teacher unions.

In short, the range of such structural differences in organization *ought* to have imparted considerable structural advantages to the private sector. There's new evidence that supports Berliner and Biddle's argument. Chris and Sarah Lubinski (2006) reported rigorous new analysis that show public students outperforming their counterparts at every income level. Previous studies did not compare students within quartiles of socioeconomic status, but only reported overall averages. That gave a false picture, according to the Lubienskis. The averages are distorted in part because of "Simpson's Paradox," a well-known statistical illusion. In essence, the averages misstated reality.

What's really at issue, as a series of books point out, is whether or not America's schools will be *privatized*. This is where the voucher issue comes in: Should the nation's public funds enable the private sector to school more students, because the public sector is allegedly doing such a terrible job?

David Berliner and Bruce Biddle, however, in *The Manufactured Crisis*, make the case that the public sector is actually doing better than ever (Berliner & Biddle, 1995). The performance isn't excellent—but neither is the performance of private schools on average. Moreover, if the private sector develops further in response to changed funding patterns, there's no guarantee that what emerges won't look more and more like the public sector does now (larger, more bureaucratic, and less responsive).

So why manufacture a crisis? Subsequent chapters take up this issue from different perspectives. For the moment, readers should understand that many analysts (e.g., Bracey, 2002; Giroux, 2000; Levin, 2001; Molnar, 1996) have argued that since the days of *Nation at Risk*, corporate interests have been invited by politicians to take a more and more active part in the reform of public schooling. These analysts have argued that cities that offer contracts to private firms to run their public schools do so as a result of 20 years of corporate effort to create the political climate needed to give them the chance. The idea of privatization, after all, is contrary to long-standing national commitments, as *Pierce v. Society of*

Sisters (1925) demonstrates. One recent study has suggested that privatization works a lot better, however, when preceded by lengthy and open public discussion that defines the scope and terms of the effort (Maranto, 2005). Quick deals that put a private firm in charge of the public good, especially in large cities, are not only undemocratic, they are less effective than a slower arrangement that results from public debate, according to this study.

What's at stake with the privatization of schooling, according to some analysts, is the idea of the citizen's role in a democracy (e.g., Bauman, 1998; Saltman, 2000; Sassen, 1996). Public schooling is supposed to create informed and thoughtful citizens capable of ruling themselves collectively with a measure of wisdom. It's always fallen short, as it inevitably would. But the corporate version of schooling harbors lesser goals—the teaching of skills and attitudes, and the formation of good workers and eager consumers instead of wise citizens. There's a lot more to be said about this, but it is a real, a serious, and an ongoing struggle in which school administrators play a tremendously important role. Do we want workers/consumers mostly or free and thoughtful citizens mostly? Will we have good workers if we have free and thoughtful citizens? Will we have free and thoughtful citizens if we have good workers and consumers? Administrators need to answer such questions for themselves. They can't do so with traditional theories of administration alone.

Urban Schooling.   America's cities, especially its largest cities (e.g., Atlanta, Boston, Chicago, Houston, Los Angeles, Miami, New York, Philadelphia, and Washington) operate huge districts and have created extremely large schools that now enroll many impoverished "minority" students. These students arguably have the greatest educational needs, and the school systems that are supposed to engage these students do so under the worst possible conditions (e.g., Lankford, Loeb, & Wyckoff, 2002). Indeed, many observers find that such systems are ungovernable, chaotic, corrupt, and dysfunctional (e.g., Ayers, 1994; but see Cuban, 2001b, for a different, and thoughtful, view). Teachers, principals, students, and parents—claim the critics—all get a pretty bad deal. Instead of remarkable changes to humanize the system, to provide appropriate levels of resources and (more importantly) to develop appropriate ways of applying the resources, these stressed schools and districts face a variety of sanctions enacted by state and national accountability systems. What's one result in such desperate circumstances?—the privatization of such systems (see Maranto, 2005, for two contrasting examples).

Rural Schooling.   Rural schools don't present the same face of disaster that urban schools seem to do, but high poverty levels and the disappearance of farming as an occupation have indeed had disastrous effects on the social structures that underlie rural schooling. Rural areas have higher poverty rates than urban areas, and the farm population now makes up less than 7% of the *rural* population (Jollife, 2002; Kalbacher & DeAre, 1988). A lot has been lost in rural communities, and the nation is mostly ignorant and silent about this mostly White and only partly visible minority.

More than half of the school-funding lawsuits that have been heard in the past 30 years, however, were brought by coalitions of rural districts. The disappearance of a school in a community means long bus rides for kids, reduced parental involvement, and fewer opportunities for student engagement; and it has long-term implications for the community's quality of life (Lyson, 2002; Howley, Howley, & Shamblen, 2001). The rural disaster is expressed by the permanent out-migration of young people (destroying the community's future in one way) and school closures and district consolidation (destroying the community's future in yet another way).

As public schools are withdrawn from rural communities (hospitals are being similarly affected, by the way), a sort of privatization occurs: The state is reducing the level of public service and expecting private alternatives to fill the gap. Although private vendors are unlikely to establish rural bricks-and-mortar private schools at the same rate they do in urban areas, virtual schools are more than a possibility; they are already functioning to serve disaffected rural families (e.g., Jaycox, 2004).

Suburban Schooling.   For the first time in the nation's history, according to results of the 2000 census, more than half the population of about 280 million lived in the suburbs—up from 7% in 1910. In fact, the largest growth in metropolitan areas was not in central cities during the 20th century, but in the suburbs (Hobbs & Stoops, 2002). Surely, in the suburbs things are fine for schooling!

Unfortunately, the sorts of social disintegration evident in the statistics cited earlier are common in suburbia too. Yes, the suburbs are on average more affluent than other areas. But more than in any other locale, they are the product of social and physical mobility. If rural places confront the destruction of communities, and urban zones confront the evil legacies of slavery and industrialization, then the suburbs often confront their own brand of instability and isolation (e.g., Hawkins, Campanaro, Pitts, & Steiner, 2002; Merten, 1996; Miller, 1990; Reardon & Yun, 2001). Also, the greater affluence of suburbs may point to the triumph of consumerism over citizenship—the very sort of educational shift that critics of corporatism deplore. Suburban schools, one might argue, are already, in a sense, paragons of privatization. When David Mathews (1996) charged that "public sector" schools lack a public, the corporate mentality of many suburban schools is part of what he's worrying about.

UNDERSTANDING AND MISUNDERSTANDING
OUTSIDE PRESSURES: THREE FLASHPOINTS

Educators sometimes come to the conclusion that, because educational aims and sometimes educational methods are contested publicly, sometimes with considerable acrimony, schools have fallen victim to outside pressures. This conclusion leads some educators to despair of ever gaining sufficient control; for others, it provides a rationale for trying to shield schools from external forces and thereby to out-maneuver society.

It's important to realize, however, that few schools—more likely none—can out-maneuver the society in which they are embedded. Society creates as well as destroys schools (for example, by closing them), and it also sustains or undermines their work (for example, by requiring things that are unlikely to succeed). This embeddedness, in other words, accounts for what educators take to be "outside" pressures. In fact, however, the outside is inescapably inside the school from the start.

Nevertheless, for much of the 20th century, school administrators actually worked hard to widen the distance separating schools and communities. Arguing for the "professionalization" of education, school administrators tried to narrow the scope of the domain over which citizens had control (Callahan, 1962; Lutz & Merz, 1992). School district consolidation also removed citizens from oversight of local schools, and the number of school boards, in fact, declined more than 90% during the 20th century.

What has been steadily replacing local oversight is the oversight of state legislatures and the federal government. The outside is coming back into schooling, but it's a very different sort of outside—and no wonder, therefore, that it's conceived as pressure. The use of force is deployed at high, and powerful, levels. The accountability movement is hardly a grassroots citizens' movement (Arons, 1997), but originates with government and business, working with allied professionals.

Related political struggles have sharpened the intensity of the contest unrolling in and around the institution of schooling and also in many local schools. The flashpoints—including not only accountability but also safety and responsiveness—are interpreted as unwanted "outside" pressures that make running a school, and teaching in one, so much more difficult than seems necessary to many educators: "If they would just leave us alone!" It isn't going to happen.

The old sense of professional security, based on separation of school and community, started to crumble after 1960. The civil rights and antiwar movements intruded sharply at that time into the schoolyards, classrooms, and administrators' offices, and into the institution of schooling as a whole. With good, although in retrospect wrong-headed, reason at the time, those intrusions were regarded as a temporary unpleasantness. With good, but wrong-headed reason, many educators believed things would change (e.g., civil rights would be affirmed and the war would end and the world would get back to normal—as it had in 1945).

But because the old version of "normal" really encompassed so much that was inequitable and unjust, the idyll of the "good old days" was not idyllic at all. Getting back to normal meant getting back to the circumstances that had provoked unrest in the first place. Normal, it turned out, continued to be a sore spot. Desegregation, for example, was successful for a time, but its effects soon eroded. Schools have, in fact, been resegregated, and now more than 70% of African American students attend predominately minority schools; Whites and Blacks are more likely to attend school together in the South, but schools there are now more segregated than they were in 1970 (Orfield, 2001; Orfield & Yun, 1999); the struggle with race hatred and xenophobia continues in shocking ways. The war in Vietnam ended, but its issues persisted—not only the role that the armed and economic might of the United States played throughout the world, but also the eternal interplay of war and economics throughout the regions of the world. Globalization brings all of these issues—race hatred, conflicts in distant lands, the effects of war and genocide—dramatically together. And improved transport, communication, and ways of doing business bring these accumulated influences much, much closer to home.

Would we expect the schoolhouse to be a continuous refuge from these volatile matters? It seems terribly naïve to think it might.

It's rather simple to explain what was happening here. The difficulties in the real world impinged on educators' roles in schools and on their conceptions of what schooling is and might be. The traditional theories of educational administration, and their substantial accomplishments, it can be argued, were outstripped by developments in the wider world. In fact, the development of what we're calling "traditional" theories corresponded with the period in which school administration on-the-ground, as well as in theory, separated itself from local communities and from citizen control (e.g., Christy & McNeal, 1999; Lee, 2002; Strang, 1987; Timar & Tyack, 1999; Tyack & Hansot, 1982). Schooling didn't just separate itself from the real world, it *isolated* itself, and it did so quite intentionally.

One serious complaint against the traditional theories is that they construct a version of reality—of the way schools work—that is increasingly less accurate. Instead of taking a perspicacious view of the evolving institution and of the nature of professional practice, the traditional theories operate from the belief that separation of school and community is both possible and wise (for aspects of the argument see, e.g., Arons, 1997; Fontaine, 1998; Theobald, 1997; Timar & Tyack, 1999).

The protected domain may be disappearing inside real schools, but the aging theories unfortunately continue to regard outside pressures as manageable threats. Thus, in the view of the critics of those theories, successful administration is seen to hinge, in part, on successful management of outside pressures. The theoretical terms laid down by these theories make it difficult to engage, or even see, the things that need to be dealt with. At least, that's the thesis of this book.

In order to provide examples of this point, the discussion here is going to examine three flashpoints of outside pressure (safety, accoutability, and responsiveness) that illustrate the decentering of traditional practice that is occurring in the real world. The real world includes schoolhouse, state house, the neighborhood, and the dinner table. We start with (1) outside pressures for safety, then move to (2) accountability, and conclude with (3) responsiveness.

Three Flashpoints

1. Imagine that you are the principal of Adams-Franklin Elementary School, one of three K–8 elementary schools in a district neighboring another district where, at the high school, there was a shooting last week. An assistant principal was wounded; fortunately no one was killed and students were never directly threatened. The story, inexplicably, didn't make the national news. School violence, moreover, has never before been an issue in this mostly rural area. But it is now.

2. Imagine yourself as superintendent of Rosa Parks Alternative School, a regional alternative school that serves secondary kids, Grades 7–12, in trouble in three small suburban districts near a big city in the Midwest. The arrangement under which the school operates actually calls you a "superintendent," but you're really a principal with three bosses. This gives you some autonomy, at the cost of comparative isolation. Your three bosses like the arrangement, however, because it means you're solely responsible for the accountability performance of the 73 kids in your school. Lucky you.

3. Finally, imagine that you've just been transferred to PS 43B Middle School in this year's shuffle of principals in a large city district in the East. This is your second year as a principal, and you thought you'd been doing a decent job at PS 11. You don't know why you're being transferred, but you do know your predecessor was an unusual character with previous experience as a community organizer. During her 2 years at the school, she'd worked to get local "community development" groups into the school and

had been unusually successful. The community reportedly loved her, and there's a lot of anger over her departure. Your car was egged the first day.

Questions.   What do you do in these situations? What will you be *told* to do? How will you respond to such directions? What will laypeople ask or demand? What will your staff expect? How will you respond? How will the system respond to that? How will you respond to the system's response to you, and to the system's response to the demands? Does this sound like chaos? No, it's real administrative life in schools.

Alternatives.   How a school leader handles such dilemmas depends on how he or she thinks about them. And the discussion in the next section compares two alternatives.

STORIES OLD AND NEW

What an incumbent administrator is most likely to do in any of these quite real situations is not actually so difficult to predict. Their responses are predictable, because most administrators accept the "old story" about schooling.

The old story is based on the understandings previously described (i.e., that the inside of the school or district is distinct from the outside forces surrounding it and from which it needs to be protected). These understandings lead principals, through a family of likely responses, to affirm the status quo as described in the old story. Change may be the stated goal, but the likely result is that the status quo will persist. For example, a dramatic and sustainable rise in test scores will be unlikely for administrators following the old story. Whereas silver bullets are sought in these situations, band-aids are the usual application. In the scenarios above, the predictable responses would be (a) a zero-tolerance discipline policy for the elementary school, (b) a series of maneuvers to exclude kids from testing at the alternative school, and (c) a period of community unrest as new principal succeeds new principal.

Predictions for the new story are more difficult, because it is still being created. The major point, however, is that the new story challenges the old story for good reasons, and it takes a wider view of the issues. Applications other than band-aids are possible when administrators give up the search for silver bullets—and for job security and professional exclusivity. Chapter 12 provides examples of extended real-world dilemmas and alternatives based on the new story.

The Old Story of School Administration

In the old story, each of the preceding flashpoints presents a threat to the "real work" of the school, particularly its processes of curriculum and instruction, known as "the technical core." The old story, suggested by the discussion of how the separation of school and community came about, regards outside pressures as temporary intrusions. The goal in dealing with the intrusions is first to protect the staff from the ill-effects, and, second, to return the system to the previous equilibrium. All of this is done in the name of permitting professional educators to "do their jobs" (e.g., Thompson, 1967). Those who are teachers may well feel that this is a perfectly proper and sensible role for administrators, a role they'd like to fulfill once they become school leaders. Working with the old story in mind, some school districts can in fact hire many people whose purpose is to buffer the organization from outside pressures. The role of principal, especially in very large schools, is sometimes refashioned to serve this purpose.

Districts act this way precisely because the supposedly temporary threats represented as outside pressures have proven to be unexpectedly persistent. In large districts, staff members hired to play the "buffering" role can comprise a substantial layer of the bureaucracy. In fact, they can provide a truly tough layer of insulation, enabling the district to be somewhat successful in resisting outside pressures. This longstanding and successful buffering may be one reason large urban districts are so difficult to change.

This way of looking at the issue depends on the vantage of the old story. The traditional response is endemic to the claims that the old story makes about the institution of schooling, namely (a) that it is most appropriately the province of professionals, (b) that its purpose is to maximize benefits to individuals rather than to communities, and (c) that the content of what is taught is primarily relevant to students' subsequent jobs and employability.

Sidebar 3-2

What Is Schooling For?

If schooling were not primarily concerned with giving deserving individuals more employment, career, or job choices, then what might concern it? Perhaps readers don't agree that this is what schooling now mostly does, but both critics of this way and its supporters seem to agree that this is what schools are mostly up to at present.

But what about alternative purposes for public schools? The options are as wide as geography, as long as history, and as deep as human aspiration. The list that follows hardly scratches the surface:

- To create good citizens.
- To sustain the community.
- To cultivate thoughtful human beings.

- To develop people who will become caring adults.
- To help children learn important knowledge with understanding.
- To form obedient members of the faith.
- To train children and youth to serve the national interest.
- To prepare young people to serve in the military.
- To create proud members of the race.

Given such actual and possible variability, it's remarkable that school mission statements so prominently focus on the service to individual potential (e.g., "helping each child reach his or her potential"). It's a version of education that lacks definite character, as many observers have written. A standard vanilla sort of schooling may not actually provide suitable education in a democracy.

The way forward under the terms of the old story is for schools to "do their job," narrowly construed as development and implementation of the "technical core" of schooling (Hoy & Miskel, 2001). That technical core concerns, for teachers, the professional skill needed to plan, conduct, and assess teaching; and (for administrators) the professional skill to organize, manage, and change the same things. Under the terms of the old story, the paramount importance of these tasks appears self-evident. If readers find them so, that is to be expected. Such appearances are, this book maintains, deceptive. Now that the old story is clearly in view, what about responses to the three flashpoints?

A family of responses to the three flashpoints is possible under the terms of the old story. But all of them will turn on the key assumption of the old story that intrusions into the technical core of schooling—the content and process of teaching—by nonprofessionals are illegitimate. For instance, in this view, safety issues are an embarrassment for professional educators. What does that mean? It does not at all mean that incidents like the ones described as the flashpoints are trivial, but rather that when they happen, they are widely understood as a professional failure of the basic trust the public puts in schools— namely, that children will be kept safe at school. The expectation is certainly reasonable.

But because schools are the nearly exclusive preserve of professionals, the fault and the blame logically falls to professionals. Never mind that many children are not safe in their neighborhoods: That's not an excuse for educators. In bad situations (demoralized or dysfunctional schools,) the thought that neighborhoods are even less safe than schools can provoke a measure of frustration or cynicism in professional educators. They almost rightly wonder why they must uphold standards that students' own parents and neighborhoods can't be counted on to uphold. In the end, under these terms, it is very easy for professional educators to blame parents and children for the failures to which educators are held so publicly accountable. The "blame game" is, indeed, a very common feature of schooling in America, according to some observers (e.g., Saunders, 1995). It's also, arguably, a direct result of the theory that schools should be run by professionals. It's an old story.

Similar logic theoretically applies to issues of accountability and responsiveness, as in the other preceding flashpoints. The flashpoint described for responsiveness—a predecessor who worked with the community and got transferred because of her success—confronts the incoming new principal with some sharp challenges. In the case described, the incoming principal is literally a new principal—in the second year as principal. The principal can go along with the system (governed by the theory that schools are for professionals, for the advancement of individuals, and ultimately about jobs). This is the most likely response. After all, we believe that our jobs are at stake.

Possibly, however, even if our particular jobs are at stake, our careers are not at stake. Or possibly, our careers are at stake in quite a different way.

That is, if, in the third flashpoint, the principal makes the decision to undermine the work of the previous principal—which is easy to do if the community is not well organized—the principal may be choosing a professional development path grounded in the status quo, taking the familiar rather than the unfamiliar road. The choices are seldom reversible according to the poet: "Yet knowing how way leads on to way/ I doubted if I should ever come back" (Frost, 1921, p. 9). Making bad choices defines us, and bad choices can be formative. Perhaps they are too often formative.

Schooling *can* be thought of differently, however. It is, in fact, *already* being thought of differently by many people, including some who work in K–12 schools, some community development activists, and some university professors. The subsequent chapters deal with this thinking, but we want to introduce the overall shape of what we're calling the "new story of school administration." (The two "stories" constitute a shorthand expression for the different theoretical perspectives we have in view, not just in this book but in the world at large, where ideas about schooling come from, now and in the past, and possibly into the future.)

The New Story of School Administration

The new story is not, for instance, a way-out-there radical proposal. It has a long history because it is by no means utterly new, and in fact, the old and new stories have common ancestors. Ideas evolve, and so ideas about schooling evolve.

What this chapter is calling "the new story," is, in part, a reclaiming of ways of looking at the world that the "old story" abandoned when theorists imagined schooling in the early 20th century. But the new story also includes recent thinking about related issues, and this is the story told primarily in chapters 4 through 11 in this book.

Dynamic systems theory, for instance, which is considered in chapter 4, is a way of looking at the world, and at schooling, enabled by the capacity of computers to mimic the behavior of complex systems over time. The related ideas have implications for better understanding how schooling works and, more particularly, for how change transpires. Therefore, it's something that prospective administrators ought to consider if they imagine themselves as involved in *changes* at their schools. At the same time, however, what's now called "dynamic systems theory" is a work in progress. Its future is not clear, but it has a longer past than many people realize. Two points seem most relevant.

First, dynamic systems theory (to stick with this example) treats schools not as machines—what they are in the old story—but as organic entities, and more specifically, as organic entities that follow a logic of change and development that is well hidden. This hidden logic is impossible to learn, some argue, if one's vision and one's interpretations of what's going on are guided by the old story (Wheatley, 1994). Naturally occurring, organic behavior has proven complex and difficult to model until recently, and that's where computers have come in. They've made it possible to see this behavior, to develop models of it, to generate data from the models, and to analyze this behavior to see the patterns hidden in the apparent chaos. That's what's new. But the theory is much older.

And so, the second point is that such insights (in this case insights about the organic quality of organizations and of society) substantially predate the rise of (in this case) dynamic systems theory as an outgrowth of computer analysis. Van Bertallanfy (1968) is one of the originators of nondynamic "systems theory." His insights concerned the broad outlines of what a "system" might be. Interestingly, he was a biologist whose significant work appeared about the same time that a few scientists were just beginning to use computers to model weather and climate. But the theory that organizations are organic, evolving entities is much older than 1966.

Using this example to move beyond it, it's important to recognize that the origins of systems theory in biology suggest, quite rightly, that it is an ecological view of organizations. "Ecological" perspectives (putting things in systemic context) have roots that reach back through the early 20th-century philosophy (e.g., Edmund Husserl, 1859–1938) to 18th- and 19th-century views of society and culture (e.g., John Stuart Mill, 1806–1873; Adam Smith, 1723–1790). All of these theories looked at society as being composed of related systems, systems whose complexity and history were also motivated by a hidden logic that was different for each theorist. In fact, for at least 2,000 years, the traditional goal of science and philosophy has been an intellectual struggle to uncover these sorts of hidden truths. The various philosophers and sociologists arrived at quite different conclusions over the centuries, of course.

But all of their theories, unlike many traditional theories of schooling, and unlike the old story, generally, were synoptic—in other words, they aimed at "a view of the whole." The old story rests on dealing with the pieces of the whole separately. The new story seeks, instead, to restore a measure of wholeness—although it may be a complex, contested, and divided wholeness—to the way we think about and come to understand schooling.

The basic critique of the old story given by the new story is that the old story is so narrow that it mistakes the trees for the forest. This critique is a very old one in the history of theory, and theorists have actually thrown the question back and forth for millennia. The reason the critique is again relevant to thinking about schools seems clear: Schooling was set up, conducted, and studied (theorized about) based on understandings of the nature of reality that have become increasingly doubtful. So it's time again for a wider view. There may be a time later on for a settled consensus, but it may well be a quite different sort of consensus than the one that seems to have prevailed from 1910 to 1970 (e.g., Habermas, 1987; Lyotard, 1984; Senge, 1990; Williams, 1989).

The new story doesn't accept the separation of school and community or society; it's skeptical about "best practice"; it regards professionalization as a doubtful project; and it understands complexity, ambiguity, and variation as advantageous. Such differences are salient to the outlook of this book.

THE CHANGING WAYS AND MEANS
OF SCHOOL LEADERSHIP

The insight that we need to look at schools differently is a "theoretical" position in the sense that it relates to certain explanations of how schools work in the real world. We've seen that traditional theories conceived the relationship between schools and society in particular ways. Resulting from a lot of work done before 1950 or so, these theories changed the way schools looked. Interestingly, this work also made subsequent theorizing possible and enabled empirical research based on that theorizing.

But just as, in decades past, changes in reality enabled changes in the way administrators could think about schools (that is, changes in how they "theorized" schooling), differing expectations for school leadership are already emerging—with or without the sorts of theoretical lenses offered in the rest of this book. Readers are likely already familiar with some of these changes: (a) focus on leadership as opposed to management, (b) the emergence of shared governance, (c) notions about distributed leadership, and (d) persistent concerns with affirmative action and equity.

Leading Practices

Practice can lead theory, and often does. This situation is likely, in fact, in realms other than natural science, although, even there, interesting theoretical connections become evident as a result of the accomplishments and insights of engineers, crafts workers, and self-taught thinkers. But in social science, theory is often confronted with the need to describe, explain, and influence new social inventions (not preexisting natural phenomena). With school administration, the new organizational inventions often accommodate some changed circumstance in the social world as a matter of apparent common sense among the inventive practitioners. This is decidedly the case with the four practices just listed.

Leading and Managing.   In the "classical" version of the old story, administration was primarily management—planning, organizing, directing, staffing, coordinating, reporting, and budgeting, according to one famous formulation ("PODSCORB," see Gulick, 1937/1992). Administrators still do these things of course—leadership does not operate without management, although it's certainly possible to manage an organization without leading it.

During the heyday of the industrial society and in many organizations still, workers spoke disparagingly of "management." Wherever workers are unionized, for instance, the distinction is often drawn between the interests of management and those of workers. It's quite interesting that the stated opposition is seldom, if ever, characterized as being between leadership and workers. In the world of management, and in the world of labor–management struggle, leadership is understood to be contestable and contested. Strikes are, in one manner of speaking, a struggle for leadership. Moreover, unions and management each have their leaders.

Leadership, then, is an elusive concept as compared to management. It's a more difficult concept and a more difficult practice. It makes references to a phenomenon whose occurrence is comparatively rare. One can have bad management, but bad leadership is sometimes merely ill-fated good leadership, taking people to a place they (after arriving there) don't want to be. Even Napoleon

Bonaparte, the iconic leader of the early 19th century (a middle-class hero according to the historian Eric Hobsbawm, 1962), was a bad leader by this criterion. Leadership, then, is a very high standard for administrators, and yet, it is considered much more important today than "mere" management. Each of the theories considered subsequently in this book has various things to say about the dicey business of leading, but the fact remains that everyone is talking about leadership—and everyone is finding it remarkably difficult to do something about it. Why is it so difficult? (Each of these sections will end with an unanswered question.)

Shared Governance. Governance deals with the highest levels of administration—organizational or political aims and the policies needed to realize them. Moreover, with governance, there needs to be a discrete and significant entity involved—a nation, a large organization, a school district, or a school. In fact, in education, some of the most familiar arrangements of "shared governance" occur at the level of the local school. Many education reforms have adopted school councils on which "outsiders" serve, and that, in addition to focusing on aims and policies, sometimes exert a certain amount of control over traditional management functions, including staffing and budgeting (e.g., Kannapel, Aagaard, Coe, & Reeves, 2000).

In the post-World War II version of the old story, principals rarely found themselves relinquishing their positional authority to outsiders in this way. This sort of "sharing" has not come easily to principals, and, in many cases, principals orienting themselves to the old story have undermined the work of local councils. Moreover, when teachers are expected to serve on the councils in addition to teaching a full day, shared governance often seems an unreasonable expectation. Obviously, sharing stretches the limits of the old story. How can new principals deal productively with the related struggles?

Distributed Leadership. The earliest—one might even say primordial—theory of leadership was the "great man" theory. It's primordial in lots of ways; first, it's the main theory informing official histories of ancient regimes, with these sorts of histories being written to this day. The theory is also applied to contemporary great businessmen, for example, Steve Wozniak and Bill Gates of microcomputer fame. Second, it's primordial in the sense of being a male fantasy, having been named while leadership was nearly the exclusive province of tall White males. Third, and more critically, it's primordial in the sense of primitiveness: leadership as the rare heroism of a single man. The great man theory, of course, is not a very subtle theory, and it's not anywhere near sufficient to guide widespread educational reform.

After 1945, however, this and other "primitive" theories, such as the trait theories of leadership, gave way to more contextualized and complex views of leadership as involving a dimension of group life different from management. These more complex and more contextualized theories began to push theorizing about leadership to a strange turn: distributed leadership. Curiously, though, the more complex and contextualized views of organizations, especially business organizations, and also more sophisticated views of power, made the idea of distributed leadership seem much less strange.

Indeed, to return to workers and managers, it would seem clear that a successful business organization, in the context of unionization, would require leadership from a number of quarters—union members and management, and not only formal, but also informal, leadership. Theories of distributed leadership take such insights and attempt to apply them, or at least realize them, in planned ways.

These plans can easily come to grief against the expectations of the old story of school administration. If the school is the preserve of specialists, the community's informal leaders can easily blindside the principal (even a principal who is practicing distributed leadership inside the school), on the supposition that only professionals are capable of taking leadership roles. How can principals avoid such grief?

Persistent Concerns.   The great man theory makes many people—especially women and also some men—quite uncomfortable. The idea that men, as opposed to women, are better suited to be managers or leaders isn't just offensive to many people, there's plenty of evidence that it's wrong-headed. The simplest evidence consists of the historical record. There have been heroic women for as long as people have existed. The human condition is a tough existence, and one encountered equally by men and women, and arguably not more successfully by one sex than the other.

Strangely, though, the ranks of school administrators are still primarily the preserve of tall (maybe not so great) White men (see chaps. 6 and 8 for the details). And the often unionized workers in this field are predominately women. Students, moreover, are arriving in greater numbers with skins that are dark (see chap. 6 for the details).

What's perhaps strangest of all is the persistence of the "old demographics" of leadership. Given the change in the student and teacher populations (more dark-skinned people and the prevalence of women teachers in the U.S.), one might have predicted that we'd see something closer to a 50-50 division of leadership roles by gender and a more substantial representation of African Americans and Latinos in leadership positions. This observation isn't a silly illusion of "political correctness," it's a simple puzzle. What's going on?

One approach to such developments (leadership, shared governance, distributed leadership, equity concerns) is a standards-based approach to the principalship and superintendency. The Interstate School Leaders Licensure Consortium (ISLLC), a project of the Council of Chief State School Officers, takes that approach, as does the National Council for the Accreditation of Teacher Education (see Sidebar 3-3).

Sidebar 3-3

ISLLC Standards for School Administrators

A school administrator is an educational leader who promotes the success of all students by:

1. Facilitating the development, articulation, implementation, and stewardship of a vision of learning that is shared and supported by the school community.

2. Advocating, nurturing, and sustaining a school culture and instructional program conducive to student learning and staff professional growth.

3. Ensuring management of the organization, operations, and resources for a safe, efficient, and effective learning environment.

4. Collaborating with families and community members, responding to diverse community interests and needs, and mobilizing community resources.

5. Acting with integrity, fairness, and in an ethical manner.

6. Understanding, responding to, and influencing the larger political, social, economic, legal, and cultural context. (Interstate School Leaders Licensure Consortium, 1996, pp. 10, 12, 14, 16, 18, 20)

NCATE/ELLC Standards for School Administrators

This standard addresses:

1. The need to prepare educational leaders who value and are committed to educating all students to become successful adults.

2. The need for educational leaders to position teaching and learning at the focal point of schools.

3. The need to enhance student learning through effective, efficient, and equitable utilization of resources.

---

4. The fact that cooperation among schools, the district, and the larger community is essential to the success of educational leaders and students.

5. The educational leader's role as the "first citizen" of the school/district community.

6. The need for educational leaders to understand and be able to operate within the larger context of the community and beyond, which affects opportunities for all students.

7. The importance of structured, sustained, standards-based experiences in authentic settings. (National Policy Board for Educational Administration, 2002, pp. 3, 6, 8, 11, 13, 15, 18)

The idea is the same as it is for students, but in this case the standards are an official specification of what every *administrator* should know and be able to do. Readers of this book who are enrolled in administrator preparation programs will likely be held to one or another of these sets of standards.

Each formulation describes briefly and succinctly a complex set of values, practices, dispositions, and skills. In fact, to do any of these things even moderately well requires a great deal of perspicacity: the capacity to see things that are hidden from many people. By its nature, perspicacity is not amenable to standardization. If it were, we would all be much wiser than it seems we are.

CASE STUDY PART 2: HOW THINKING DIFFERENTLY ABOUT SCHOOLS HELPED

Recall that Ellen is unsure where she's going as an educational administrator, a thought that disturbs her profoundly. Ellen knows that she is not essentially ambitious. She looks ambitious to most people—those who don't know her very well. There's tremendous pressure… well, not exactly *pressure*, but a heavy air of expectation related to her possible move to the superintendency. Ellen's just not sure that the move is right for her. She's disturbed by much of what she has come to see in the Penn Hills District.

She keeps asking herself what she should do. She's bothered, in particular, by all the wrangling over college admissions that seems to sweep up kids, parents, and teachers, and certainly the well-staffed counseling department at Penn Hills High. Shouldn't all kids go to college? Shouldn't they go to the best colleges they can get into? Isn't this frenzy a mark of the school's—of her—success?

She's completely unsure. There's nothing in her preparation as an administrator that seems to be providing any help. The question is not really about how to run the school, nor is it about how to motivate teachers and kids. That's disturbing Ellen too: They don't seem to require much motivation.

Although this job is certainly not easy, it seems like almost anything they do at Penn Hills High is regarded as a big success. The school has a slew of state awards for excellence in this or that. She finds herself no longer able to make a big deal out of any of these awards. The problem is not with the skills needed to make good things happen.

The problem, Ellen concludes, is that she is starting to think differently about schooling, and she needs help. She doesn't know much history or philosophy; she doesn't know much sociology; and she's barely heard of anthropology. So that's where she starts. The only thing is, she wishes she could talk to other folks about the things she's learning and the troublesome questions that keep popping into her mind. She doesn't know it, but she's beginning to think that what she needs professionally is another district—one with new challenges for her, possibly even as a teacher, at least for a while. She's discovering how much she has to learn.

CHAPTER SUMMARY

We need to think differently about schools because the traditional theories are based on an accord about schooling that no longer pertains. It no longer pertains because that accord, fashioned between about 1945 and 1960, wasn't an eternal state, but a very brief moment in history.

The accord centered, in many ways, on professionalizing the institution for providing formal instruction to citizens of an industrialized national republic. "Becoming professionals" is a phrase with a history that predates 1945, of course, and the phrase resonates strongly with educators because it implies equality with lawyers and doctors, who cannot be said to contribute more importantly to the well-being of society than teachers. Gallingly, educators have never enjoyed the prestige of lawyers and physicians or ministers—this latter group seldom mentioned in the longing for professional status. These three professions were the traditional preparations for promising, and wealthy, young men from colonial times forward. Teachers were never on this list, quite likely because their work came to being much later, in the late 19th and 20th centuries. In fact, it was an occupation for hard-working sons and daughters of members of the working class.

There was one result of professionalization, however, and that has to do with the "accord" just mentioned. Professionalization meant that the public was pushed out of schools. One way to interpret this development is to say that the century-long work of administrators was to push the public out of schooling.

Certainly the 90% reduction in the number of school districts eliminated the influence of hundreds of thousands of citizens. Perhaps, as claimed at the time, this change was an improvement in that it "removed politics" from local schools. On the other hand, most of those districts were quite small, so the "politics" in question were probably more about personal rivalries and contested motives than about the corruption of any political machine. Politics may have been an issue in the many local districts that were then operated within large cities, but the creation of huge urban districts seems not to have banished politics there, either.

The benefits are not the issue in this, or in other examples. Instead, what the field of administration accomplished was the separation of community from education in the name of schooling. That was the essence of the 1945–1960 accord: less community influence, the school as an insulated professionally operated institution. The tense role of managing the enterprise and maintaining the accord fell mostly to White male administrators.

What's arguably wrong with the accord? First, communities and families *are* primary educational institutions, so maintaining a formal institution separate from communities and families puts the formal institution at a remarkable disadvantage. Second, educators come to view themselves as superior to parents, commonly blaming parents for the institutional difficulties manifested in classrooms and schools. Third, professional control means the institution cannot even listen, not widely, to the voices of concern in the public; instead, these voices reach educators' ears sometimes as distortions and more usually as the manipulations of power brokers—among whom one might number some highly esteemed national professional organizations. Fourth, and most practically, the accord isn't holding. Reasons are numerous, including changes in society, struggle over institutional expectations for schooling, and changes within the profession—including marginal and incremental changes in the outlook of practicing administrators.

The discussion in this chapter argues, therefore, that administrators need perspicacity more than a set of theory-based skills in order to thrive, or at least to actively struggle, as they lead schools today. A new accord may emerge in the future, possibly around the role of community, or the role of globalization, or the role of culture, or of social justice. Even if that happens, though, the relevant concepts will remain relevant for a long time to come.

4

Dynamic Systems Theory

Schools are complicated and changeable places, yet most traditional administrative theory rests on the assumption that, even in such changeable places, leaders can take actions that will foster predictable outcomes. The outcome most often sought these days by principals and superintendents is school improvement.

Those new to the field of professional education may arrive on the scene thinking, "It's about time schools did *something* to improve." But old-timers will recognize that calls for and programs on behalf of school improvement go back a long way. Educational historians—even those whose work predates all of the reform initiatives in recent memory (e.g., Callahan, 1962; Tyack, 1974)—tell the story of ongoing efforts to improve schools through a variety of primarily top-down (i.e., management driven) reforms. Despite the almost 100 years of improvement talk, schools, according to some historians, remain largely unchanged (see, e.g., Cuban, 1993). According to others, schools have improved markedly since the mid-20th century and ought to be left alone to continue making progress (see, e.g., Berliner & Biddle, 1995).

Whatever the interpretation, calls for school improvement are increasingly strident. School leaders are caught between trying to defend what schools already do and trying to promote changes that respond to outside pressures. No wonder the principal's office is a tough spot!

The theories considered in this chapter can, in a broad sense, help. In particular, they provide compelling explanations of what's going on, by describing schools and districts as complex, even chaotic, systems. In addition, they offer alternative frameworks for responding to the quintessential leadership dilemma: "How can I get the results I want?"

Theories that construe organizations as dynamic systems build on, but in some ways counter, the open systems theories discussed briefly in chapter 2. They derive most directly, however, from two sources: (a) insights about the natural world that come from what Margaret Wheatley (1994) called "the new science" and (b) insights about complex industrial and electronic systems that come from a field of engineering known as systems dynamics. Curiously, though, the insights derived from these sources seem to explain things about complex social systems, such as our complex system of schooling, much more cogently than earlier theories have been able to do (Forrester, 1975). Even though these explanations embody important insights, they appear to be much less precise than earlier theories of cause and effect. For this reason, we might prefer to think of a dynamic theory of educational systems as a metaphor rather than as a definitive and complete model of how such systems always work. (See Sidebar 4.1.)

This chapter explores three critical insights supported by dynamic systems theory and applies these insights to our ways of thinking about systems of schooling:

- Social systems—including systems of schooling—are unpredictable, and unpredictable systems are difficult to control.
- Systems of schooling are complex; understanding them requires us to take into account direct and indirect influences, short-term and long-term influences, and linear and noninear influences. Accounting for all of these influences can be very difficult, so our almost-always-imperfect interpretations of what's happening in a system of schooling are quite often misleading.
- Systems are self-organizing, developing regularities of function that correspond to the dynamics of underlying structures. The tendency for systems to organize their activity according to specified patterns does give us leverage for shaping systems in desired directions. As school leaders, we are not helpless observers of totally random activity in the system of schooling. Rather we can play important roles in supporting and elaborating those underlying structures that advance school aims, thereby contributing to upward spirals of performance. At the same time, we can work to diminish the influence of counterproductive structures that contribute to schools' stagnation and failure.

Sidebar 4.1: Dynamic Systems Theory as Metaphor

You are watching the clouds, and suddenly observe that they are not just moving across the sky, but constantly changing their shapes in the process— taking other shapes, merging, and even disappearing. It seems a strange, slow dance. You watch a previously unappreciated complexity, although it was there all along, changeably suspended above you.

Perhaps as a teacher, you've had a similar experience observing a classroom of students at work, or standing playground duty over swirling groups of children. Perhaps you've even thought of your school, your district, or the whole educational system in this way; and perhaps you can imagine the forces of politics, economics, and culture at work in this way. It's a startling thought, but not an idle one either, according to the perspectives of dynamic systems theory.

Clouds don't simply move from point A to point B, of course. Winds often rotate, so that even the positions of points A and B—toward which the clouds might be considered to be moving—are not fixed with respect to on-ground positions.

Can we get a precise fix on where our students are moving? From the perspective of dynamic systems theory, it seems doubtful. Much of the discussion on school reform, however, seems to say that we *ought* to get a fix on where they are going! It seems to say that there is a specified set of outcomes for all students and that the things we do in schools can and ought predictably to lead to those outcomes. Perhaps we ought to be looking at the issues of schooling in ways quite different from those we traditionally use, different from the way most of us have been told to look at them, for instance, by school reformers and top-down administrators.

If you are a fan of "The Weather Station" or of web-based weather images, you'll certainly appreciate the metaphor of changing cloud patterns. But time-lapse photography has also made the transformations of the sky accessible, and scientists have long used it to study changes in features of the natural world over time. In time-lapse representations, the sky becomes an ocean, which it is, in a way, because clouds are in fact a vast body of water. Strangely, then, the flow of the sky and of the ocean must have something in common.

Stranger still to say, both the clouds and the ocean have something in common with the flow of rivers; not just the flow within the riverbanks, but also with the way in which rivers and river systems in a watershed cut through the landscape over time, joining each other, continuously making new courses. One could see this process easily if time-lapse photography could be used over the course of millions of years. And, if one observes this continual branching and joining of river systems, even in the present, one is likely to note the resemblance of a river system to a tree or plant, both in its roots and in its branches. And this branching and joining in both watersheds and in plants, and even in animals (for instance, the branching that occurs in the unfolding of an embryo), takes place as a time-dependent process.

Very soon, thinking such thoughts, you might begin to suspect that this sort of patterning is all around us in the natural world, which it is. You may begin to suspect, with "dynamic systems theorists," that perhaps these patterns characterize the *social world* as well as the *natural world*. And, just perhaps, you might suspect that this sort of patterning characterizes schools, school districts, and state and national systems of schooling as well.

Interestingly, dynamic systems theory builds on an earlier version of systems theory, which also drew parallels between systems in the natural world and systems in the social world. The major difference between the two approaches is that, in earlier versions of systems theory, an understanding of a system was purported to enable scientists or social scientists to control the events taking place within the system. The unique insight of dynamic systems theory is that events in complex systems are unpredictable and, therefore, not amenable to direct control.

THE LIMITATIONS OF CONTROL

From the Enlightenment onward, efforts to understand the world have been linked with efforts to control it. These efforts, however, have often been frustrated by unanticipated turns of events. Life in schools, in fact, gives us countless reminders of the tenuous connection between means and ends. We try for weeks to teach a student about common denominators, but nothing clicks. Then one day, the student understands and performs addition and subtraction of fractions with apparent ease. What happened? We can speculate, of course, that his parents or a friend gave him some help. Or perhaps he just "grew into" an understanding of common denominators. In subsequent weeks, we observe that the student's new level of competence seems to lead to a productive learning spurt. But then the student catches the flu and stays home for a few days with a babysitter. When he comes back to school, he doesn't even remember fractions let alone common denominators! Again we can speculate about what happened; but our speculations—even when they're right—don't really tell us what to do next.

The Shock of Unpredictability

As educators, we are quite often bemused by our inability to predict and control what happens in schools. For dynamic systems theorists, the unpredictability of events is a key point to remember in thinking about all organizations, including schools. Taking this point to heart means that many of our traditional assumptions—about children, families, learning, motivating, and leading—no longer apply. It also means that the traditional ways of doing research may be misdirected, and that findings from that research—the predictions that are supposed to guide what teachers and administrators *ought to do*—are not only *misguided* but in all probability *dead wrong*! The old approach to scientific research aimed at control; but without accurate prediction, attempting control can be a desperate, even repressive, act (Mintzberg, 1994; Wheatley, 1994).

The elusiveness of control can be especially troubling to school administrators who, after all, are supposed to exert important kinds of control in a variety of domains. Dynamic systems theory, however, can help administrators distinguish between domains in which some control is necessary and possible and domains in which control is inappropriate. Furthermore, it offers a practical alternative to control, namely the use of leverage points in the deployment of "strategies." This approach enables administrators to foster systemic learning, which points members of a school community toward avenues for making use of the system's opportunities while at the same time diminishing the impact of its defects.

Wishing for a greater level of influence than this, school leaders might wonder why we must tolerate so much uncertainty. According to dynamic systems theorists, uncertainty is tied to the complexity of systems. Imagine, for example, a day in the life of a complex system. On that day, we might take measurements that describe the state of the system. Our measurements, like all measurements in science, cannot be perfectly accurate. They contain "error." Right from the beginning, therefore, there is a difference between the real state of the system and our representation of it, based on the measurements we have taken. In the old science, these small differences made little, often no, difference at all (see Sidebar 4.2). But in dynamic systems, small initial differences ("inaccuracies") on day one—and this is a key principle of dynamic system— create *huge* differences a relatively short time later. Predicting the weather a week from now, for example, is a very dicey business. Atmospheric conditions exist as part of a complex system. So do schools. Just as meteorologists cannot be sure of making accurate predictions of the weather that will take place just a few days in the future, educators cannot be sure of making accurate predictions about school outcomes— student achievement, teacher performance, or the progress of educational reform. Unable even to predict what might affect these outcomes, school leaders cannot reliably choose courses of action that will necessarily produce them.

Sidebar 4.2: Regression Analysis as Prediction: What it Means to Ignore Error

Much of our "scientific" knowledge in the field of education is based on the faith that we can predict many things quite far into the future, not just weeks but years and even decades. Educational reform programs are based on this faith and on the scientific methods that purport to make predictions.

Let's say we have an innovative reading program, call it "Reading Dynamite." To show that "it works," we might want to evaluate reading comprehension scores of similar groups of children who differ only on the basis of whether or not they participated in the program. Let's also say that Reading Dynamite uses five key practices. If this is the case, we can measure how well each practice was implemented, not just whether or not a child went through the program. By using this method, we should be able to show the extent to which each of the five practices contributed to the higher reading comprehension of children who participated in the program.

But what if the groups of children, participants and nonparticipants, were different before the program was instituted? We must find a way to even out these initial differences, and we can do this by including the children's previous reading test scores, their reading grades, plus a variety of background information in an equation that shows the extent to which conditions (either background conditions or conditions associated with the reading program) contributed to their reading scores. In a conceptual sense, the equation would look something like this:

reading comprehension = the sum of all the program effects + the sum of all the other effects + *error*

This method of evaluating the effects of educational programs makes use of a very common statistical tool called "regression analysis." Often a regression equation such as the one just presented can combine enough relevant variables to account for a great deal of the variability in children's reading achievement. But there is always error.

Despite error, social scientists find the equation useful for more than just explaining what happened to the two groups of children—participants and nonparticipants in Reading Dynamite. The equation can also be used to predict the eventual reading scores of children who *haven't yet* participated in the program!

Using the equation in this way constitutes a leap of faith. That leap is based partly on social scientists' willingness to discount the relevance of error and partly on their willingness to see the dynamics that will contribute to reading comprehension in future groups of children as identical to the dynamics that produced reading comprehension in the previous groups of children. This view of dynamics, however, is curiously static. It suggests that schools, districts, and even children do not change in ways that might influence the effectiveness of the key practices of a particular reading program. Interestingly, our experiences as educators tell us to expect just the opposite. The stuffed animal "letter pals" that children of a generation ago found cute and cuddly now appear hokey to the more sophisticated, media-saturated youngsters of today. Or the call–response format that resonates with African American children, who associate it with practices in their churches and neighborhoods, seems overly rambunctious and inappropriate to the classroom of 6-year-old Mennonites. The old science relied heavily on "all things being equal," yet our intuitions about schools suggest that all things are rarely equal.

Losing Control

Organizations, communities, and schools are part of a social world that, it seems, behaves more like clouds, bodies of water, or plant and animal populations than like absolutely predictable machines or manufacturing processes. Short-term prediction might be possible for these "dynamic systems," but long-term prediction usually turns out to be a fool's errand.

In fact, the whole idea of administrative control might be seen as irrelevant from this perspective. Attempts to impose control, in light of the impossibility (not just the inaccuracy) of prediction, would probably be counterproductive. In a dynamic system, for example, planning would look very different from the various "improvement planning processes" now prescribed by almost every state department of education. Anyone who has served on a school or district "improvement" committee will have no trouble imagining how much professional time such planning processes involve. Committee members devote their time because they imagine that the plans they formulate will result in important educational improvements. Imagine, however, that all that time is wasted, that it is work based on a hopeless misconception.

Such a possibility is an insight offered by dynamic systems theory. In the field of administration, this theory provides a surprising way of looking at organizations, as surprising as its way of looking at patterns in the natural world. In fact, however, we'll see that these ideas have a good deal in common with some very old ideas largely ignored by the field of education.

Still, we have very little evidence about whether the concept actually applies to schooling, because research methods in education have not yet—not by any measure—caught up to the new theorizing. The viewpoints and insights, however, seem credible to a large number of observers (e.g., Senge, 1990; Sungaila, 1990; Wheatley, 1994) and, from our perspective, they help educators make sense of some very puzzling features about schools as organizations and schooling as an institution.

THINKING COMPLEXLY ABOUT WHAT WORKS AND WHY

The vague feeling that "nothing seems to work" is an everyday challenge for many, probably most, educators at all levels. This observation applies widely in our experience—in reading groups within a single classroom, in classrooms within a school, in schools within districts, in school districts within states, in state departments of education, and in the U.S. Department of Education. We know the feeling is common because we, as a team, have worked in all these settings—and in other nations as well.

Maybe this commonality is actually a blessing in disguise. Perhaps by acknowledging that all things are never equal and that, therefore, what is supposed to work often doesn't, we will be able to examine issues more productively. Some teachers and administrators manage to do just that, it seems. Some find meaning and energy in the midst of seeming chaos. How do they do it? Without necessarily putting a name to it, these educators may be drawing on the insights offered by dynamic systems theory.

Some of us, of course, have been skeptical about claims that this or that educational product "works," even when the claims are attached to pretty convincing evidence. We skeptics may tend to think that what works varies by setting—by types of students, types of communities, and by intended purposes—so that, indeed, nothing can be expected to work universally. Something that works with one student might flop with another, and something that works to improve test scores might also have the effect of undermining parent involvement. We don't usually study these possibilities in education. The traditional view in education is that even acknowledging these possibilities would make our jobs far too complex to manage.

Nevertheless, imagine the all-too-familiar plight of Belinda Hammond, who was until recently the principal of a consolidated elementary school in a rural district. Ever since she started work on her master's degree, Belinda had been attuned to the research about instructional effectiveness. Careful reading of that research led her to select a nationally validated instructional strategy as a way to improve the academic performance of the children in her school. Impressed with the program's theoretical foundation and with the reported evidence of its results, she decided the program was worth a try in her school. She even spoke with other principals throughout the region who had used the program and found it effective. And she followed the guidelines of the program carefully, taking all of the steps supposedly necessary for success: She cultivated staff buy-in, she provided extensive and intensive professional development, and she garnered community support. Three years after implementation, students' academic performance was about the same, teachers' morale was lower than ever, and citizens were questioning the board about expenditures for the materials and workshops associated with continued use of the program. When the superintendent offered Belinda the opportunity to take over the principalship at the high school, she jumped at the chance.

As was the case with the nationally validated program that Belinda selected, much evaluation of educational programs, products, and practices has been carried out expressly to show whether or not something works *universally*. Evidence of gains is offered, but the gains are usually slight. The underlying logic that links such findings (of small but "statistically significant" gains) to prescriptions for school or classroom practice usually goes like this: If a program shows slight overall benefits aggregated across evaluation sites, it will be judged to work, and if it works, it is presented as working everywhere.

Developers or publishers make this claim, even though in some places where the program was piloted, it was not associated with any gains, and in others it was actually associated with losses. Sadly, when, later on, the program does not work as well as it should in *many* places, the program's failure is assumed to lie with the teacher or with the school and *not* with the program or the research that "validated" the program!

Embracing Complexity

Let's admit it. The organizational world is a complex place, and it just doesn't look like we can make straightforward claims like "A causes better Z," for instance, "block scheduling causes better student learning."

A causes Z is hardly the only possible causal link between, say, block scheduling and student learning. For instance, isn't it more likely that A (block scheduling) and other influences (let's say 24 of them, C through Y) interact with each other in complex ways to facilitate, but maybe not exactly cause, improvement in student learning, Z? There may be causal links here, but they are certainly neither straightforward nor direct.

This idea might be tough to grasp, so let's examine it further. Very rarely in schools is one change made while holding all other conditions constant. In fact, schools tend to adopt constellations of changes. Perhaps a district might institute a high-school reform program that incorporates block scheduling, a new student advisement system, and a new discipline policy. At the same time, other changes that might have some influence on the school are also taking place. The superintendent may have made changes in the structure of district administration, there may be an upturn in the local economy, and a new youth program may have just been established by a neighborhood church. Could we really tell which of these changes (or which combination of them) is most likely to result in improved performance on the high-school graduation exam? Even if we could predict the unique influence of each of these changes, could we ever understand the optimal sequence of their implementation? For example, perhaps the odds of getting higher test scores are improved if the implementation of block scheduling is preceded by changes in the structure of district administration. Maybe, however, this sequence for maximizing the odds is totally unique: Perhaps it wouldn't apply to any other school system on earth!

Each scenario might, in this complex way, be a productive path for a particular district to follow, but not for *all* districts, and probably not for any other district. Given the complexity of the influences, moreover, it is hard to imagine that this path to improvement could actually be predicted by anyone at the outset. Furthermore, if improvement actually does take place, educators are likely to have a difficult time identifying the influences with the greatest effect. Their tendency, however, would be to simplify the causal path, viewing as the most promising influences the ones that seem most immediate (see, e.g., Mintzberg, 1994). In this case, the teachers and administrators would be more likely to attribute the improvement in test scores to block scheduling and the more stringent discipline policy than they would be to attribute it to changes in the local economy. In the face of complex circumstances, human beings are prone to make sense of matters by simplifying them. Doing so saves us all a great deal of time and reduces our consternation, but it may also lead us to make wildly inaccurate inferences about cause and effect (Mintzberg, 1994).

The vision of causality in dynamic systems theory, then, is dramatically different from the one that we get by reading most social science studies (including educational research) or by reading most of the practical works intended to guide school administrators. From the vantage of dynamic systems theory, there is good reason to be skeptical of the claims made by those who advocate data-based improvement and educational "best practice."

Dynamic Linearity and Nonlinearity

Dynamic systems theory takes account of two sets of processes that complicate cause and effect relationships. The first of these processes, known as feedback, alters the straight-line association between cause and effect, enhancing or dampening the original association. Because the process of feedback interacts with a cause–effect relationship in an active way, it is sometimes referred to as "dynamic" linearity.

Feedback occurs when an initial effect produced by a particular cause itself becomes a contributor to future effects. Let's look at this situation as it applies to an all-too-common systemic effect in schools—an epidemic of head lice. Starting with just two head lice with the propensity and ability to reproduce themselves (i.e., the cause), we find in short order that the result is the production of, let's say, 100 head lice. Now the effect of the reproduction of the first two lice has led to an addition to the system of 100 head lice, all equipped with the propensity and ability to reproduce themselves. Anyone who has experienced a head-lice epidemic in a school will recall what happens next—an exponential growth of head lice. Exponential change (either as an upward or downward "spiral") results from positive feedback to a system.

Policymakers and school administrators would, of course, like to see exponential increases in some domains (student achievement, for example), and they would like to see exponential decreases in other domains (discipline problems, for example). Unfortunately, however, few schools reap the benefits of feedback that contribute to a desired upward or downward spiral. Instead, schools sometimes experience the frustrations and even tragedies associated with undesirable upward and downward spirals. For example, the ripple effects of one episode of school violence—media attention and public outrage—often contribute to an increased incidence of school violence (i.e., an undesirable upward spiral). And certain consequences of low student achievement in a school—for instance, the all-too-frequent decision of the best teachers in that school to transfer to other schools—have the effect of reducing achievement even further (i.e., an undesirable downward spiral).

Given the tendency for positive feedback to result in unwanted consequences, schools are perhaps lucky that they are not subject to the effects of positive feedback all that often. They are, however, much more likely to experience the influences of various sorts of negative feedback. With negative feedback, an effect of a system functions to limit the influence of an initial cause. Systems governed by negative feedback are self-limiting: They embed correctives that restrain growth, and, therefore, they tend to promote equilibrium rather than change.

The typical experience of site-based councils illustrates these dynamics. When they are initiated, site-based councils give teachers (and sometimes parents) increased control over school governance. As teachers assume greater control over school-wide matters, however, they realize that they are expending increasing amounts of time and energy on school governance. This realization disturbs them because it makes them wonder if they are neglecting their most important work, namely the design and delivery of classroom instruction (see, e.g., Conway & Calzi, 1996). As a result of their worries, teachers cut back their commitment to the site-based council, often returning to their original (lower) level of involvement with school-wide matters.

Contingency is another process that complicates cause and effect relationships, producing what are often called "*nonlinear*" associations. These associations exist, but they change their character in response to changes in circumstance. Take, for example, the simple process used by some teachers to restore quiet to a noisy classroom—the process of flicking the light switch on and off. This trick works extremely well in many classrooms of primary-level students, but it works less well once these same children reach middle school. It may have almost no effect when the children are in high school. Undergraduates, in our experience, however, respond to this same practice almost as readily as kindergarteners.

Not only are cause and effect linkages problematic (because of the inevitability of error, the complexity of ordinary influences, the presence of feedback, and the existence of various contingencies), but all sorts of extraordinary influences are likely to contribute in unspecified ways to organizational outcomes. A sudden catastrophe or disaster, for example, will impose a new set of contingencies on a previously stable relationship, disrupting a smoothly increasing or decreasing influence.

Although we can all think of plenty of unfortunate (even tragic) examples of catastrophes that have profound effects on schools, we may not always appreciate the fact that catastrophes can be an expression of productive change. Let's return to the subject of Sidebar 4.2, the innovative "Reading Dynamite" program.

Most of us realize that buy-in is essential to the success of an improvement effort. So, if a clueless superintendent says, "We're all going to start using Reading Dynamite on Monday morning," as sure as Tuesday follows Monday, we'll soon be saying "We *tried* Reading Dynamite and it doesn't work!"

But let's say the district has five elementary schools, and in one of them, Reading Dynamite actually *takes off*, despite the ineptitude of the superintendent. The teachers there understand the five key practices of the program, and, in fact, have been working toward them on their own—they just didn't know it. When Reading Dynamite got shoved their way, most of them said, "Hey, this is us!" The backlash in the other four elementary schools, however, is furious, and it precipitates heated debates about reading instruction that eventually involve the board and lead to a buy-out of the superintendent's contract.

Catastrophe!

The next year, the new superintendent enlists some of the teachers in the Reading Dynamite school—teachers who know enough to steer clear of direct references to the Reading Dynamite program—to help her facilitate district-wide conversations about teaching and learning. Whether Reading Dynamite becomes the program of choice in all of the elementary schools is not at all important to the new superintendent, but she is committed to professional dialogue. In this illustration, the Reading Dynamite program served, complexly, as a platform for a disaster and then for a recovery that actually had positive systemic implications.

Dynamism

The "dynamic" quality here is easy to grasp in broad outline. The passage of time joins the mutual influence of one thing to another and animates the complexity of events in the system. Moreover, complexity expresses itself in changes (whether smooth or catastrophic) that suggest to theorists that *systems spontaneously adapt to their surroundings*. In fact, it almost seems that systems (organisms, ecological niches, organizations, or societies) and their surroundings adapt *to each other*. This concept is called "coevolution."

Consider what happened in the Red Rock School District, a poor rural district in a southern state. Because of its low per-pupil funding, Red Rock could not pay its teachers as well as surrounding districts could. But Red Rock had an advantage that other districts did not. Because of its dramatic scenery, it was home to a large number of urban transplants—many of them retired professionals. Some of these individuals were concerned about the local infrastructure and were willing to contribute energy to improving the schools. The district decided to recruit a few of these individuals, particularly those with backgrounds in math and science, to provide instruction to high-school students.

As soon as the transplanted teachers began working in the schools, however, they encountered practices that were unfamiliar to them. From their perspective, the high school placed far too much emphasis on athletics and far too little emphasis on academics. When the newcomers voiced their concerns, the local teachers began to resent them and took actions designed to undermine the entire initiative. Their most serious action involved a written complaint to the State Department of Education that the new "teachers" were practicing without appropriate teaching licenses.

Recognizing that their jobs were in jeopardy, the newcomers became less vocal about their discontent with the school culture. Rather than criticizing the culture, they began to observe it; and, in doing so, came to notice that the focus on athletics actually encouraged reluctant students to become more engaged with school in general, including academics. Once they saw some positive effects of the athletic program, the newcomers actually started to support it. At the same time, the local teachers began to recognize the benefit of having a cadre of newcomers at the school. Their workloads became more manageable, professional conversations became more varied, and the students actually seemed a little bit more attentive to academic requirements. In response to these changes in the school culture, the morale of local teachers began to improve, and their classroom performance reflected a new level of energy. In effect, the newcomers had adapted to the system, and the system had adapted to the newcomers, with the eventual effect of altering the system, in this case, for the better.

Coevolution of this sort is a dynamic process that occurs frequently in schools, which are, like many other systems, subject to continual pressures for change. The coevolution of systems, moreover, is often complex—making them seem sometimes to lose energy, sometimes to stabilize, and sometimes to create new energy. For this reason, social systems such as schools might reasonably be viewed as "complex adaptive systems." Open to a myriad of internal and external influences as well as to the effects of positive and negative feedback, such systems operate beyond the direct control of the human beings who comprise and participate in them. For this reason, complex adaptive systems are some-times characterized as "self-organizing" (see, e.g., Wheatley, 1994).

SYSTEMS AND THEIR STRUCTURES

The concept of a "system" is easy to grasp. In fact, we are so used to thinking of social organizations as systems that we frequently use the term "school system" as a synonym for "school district." If thinking of schools as systems is old news, what makes dynamic systems theory so different? Here we briefly review fea-tures of dynamic systems (complex adaptive systems) that are important to our understanding of school as organizations:

- Dynamic systems are unpredictable.
- Causal chains are difficult to interpret accurately in dynamic systems.
- Complex, contingent, and nonlinear associations are more typical than direct linear associations.
- Dynamic processes happen over time, but the speed of change can be extremely variable.
- Because dynamic systems are adaptive, the human beings who comprise and participate in them cannot control them.
- The human beings who comprise and participate in dynamic systems can learn to understand and make productive use of the possibilities such systems offer.

One variation of dynamic systems theory is known as "chaos theory." Chaos is indeed an interesting phenomenon, but it's more properly considered a spe-cial case of *complexity* (Kellert, 1993). Sidebar 4.3 gives a quick glimpse at chaos theory for those who are curious.

Sidebar 4.3: Chaos Theory

Chaos theory develops images of the behavior of a nonlinear dynamic sys-tem (e.g., the stock market) by using a few variables to describe it, collect-ing data over many observations (in the case of the stock market, say, every day for 3 years) and plotting the "movement" of the system over that time period. The images produced in this way reveal that chaos is both *orderly* and (unpredictably) *deterministic*.

Chaotic natural systems, by the way, consist of all sorts of phenomena: weather, population growth and decline, turbulence in flows of fluids and gases, and so forth. Note that complex adaptive systems need not exhibit

chaotic behavior; it's just that they quite often do. Fluid can flow without turbulence; population growth can be regular and predictable. But "disasters"
or "catastrophes" or simply the small change that spawns feedback cycles that
amplify it can push a system to behave chaotically (i.e., turbulently).

More detail is provided in James Gleick's very readable 1987 book *Chaos:
Making a New Science*. No one to our knowledge has yet applied this way
of studying actual data to schools or school districts. A study of this sort,
however, probably will appear soon—perhaps by the time this book is
published. So far, the applications of chaos theory to social organizations
like schools are mostly metaphorical.

There's one more thing to understand about systems theory—dynamic or not.
What counts as a system is not set in stone. What's a system and what's not is more
about *relationships* than about precise operational definitions (Wheatley, 1994). To
identify a system of interest, look at the relationships that define it.

For instance, a system might be a single person in a school district—the
superintendent perhaps—or the set of people with whom the superintendent interacts. More often, though, we call social interactions systems when
they entail a series of complex relationships over an extended period of time.
A classroom, for example, is a system that incorporates at the very least the
relationships among the teacher, the students, and the parents of the students. We might exemplify a more inclusive system as the schools in a district, the communities that comprise the district, and the economic
circumstances of the district. In each case, though, we define the system by
its relationships. Defining a system, then, is not at all arbitrary. It's an idea
about things that "hang together" rather than things that "hang separately."
Hanging together indicates relationships.

Underlying Structures

In a dynamic system, the things that hang together consistently form identifi-
able structures. Although alterations in the conditions affecting a system also
affect these structures, the structures often persist undisturbed. Part of the reason why such structures tend to persist is that the participants in an organization consciously and unconsciously reinforce them by believing in and basing
actions on their supposed inevitability. Senge (1990), for example, discusses the
way "mental models" of what's going on in an organization actually serve to reinforce existing structures—for good and ill.

Schools, in fact, offer some of the best examples of how mental models work.
And they also demonstrate the benefits that result from making dramatic

changes in certain mental models. Perhaps the quintessential mental model operating in schools involves teachers' expectations of student performance—the so-called "Pygmalion effect" (Cooper & Good, 1983; Rosenthal & Jacobson, 1992). Here's how it works. Teachers develop expectations about the performance capabilities of the various children in their classrooms. These expectations can result from teachers' knowledge of students' past performance, or they can reflect prejudicial stereotypes (e.g., "students from impoverished homes start off with a learning deficit"). Whatever ways they are acquired, these mental models of how students are likely to perform (i.e., the teachers' expectations for students' performance) influence a host of teaching practices such as the selection of "appropriate" instructional materials, the pace of instruction, and the methods of instructional delivery.

For the children whose teachers hold low performance expectations, the resulting feedback cycle can be devastating. When teachers hold low expectations for students, they often design slow-paced instruction using simplified materials accompanied by repetitive practice exercises. These methods are the least likely, however, to stimulate children—any children—to become engaged in learning. As a result, children who are required to participate in these "learning activities," that is, the students purported to have low ability, quickly lose interest. They exhibit their boredom in different but characteristically unproductive ways: as laziness, insolence, and disruptiveness. No wonder their academic performance turns out to be poor. Unfortunately, however, their poor performance reinforces teachers' original expectations, thereby producing the self-fulfilling prophecy that characterizes the Pygmalion effect. The situation usually is worse than this, however, because the classroom is part of a larger system.

But let's first draw attention to what happens in the classroom where the bored but low-performing students engage in disruptive behavior, possibly in order to get attention or possibly just to relieve the tedium. Through repeated patterns of misbehavior and punishment, many of these students become classroom discipline problems. Once they achieve this status, word about their behavior reaches beyond the confines of the classroom. Their teachers talk to other teachers; the principal is asked to support or enforce disciplinary measures; the counselor and the school psychologist become involved. Soon, parents begin to hear their children talk disparagingly about the troublemakers. In fact, in some communities, almost everyone will eventually come to know these students by reputation. When, as adolescents, these children get tangled up with the juvenile justice system, no one will be surprised.

Whereas teachers' low expectations do not always result in eventual jail time for students, this downward spiral happens much more often than it ought to

(Kozol, 1991).[1] Moreover, many less devastating, but nonetheless destructive, consequences follow from practices—tracking, for example—based on educators' predictions about how well certain students are likely to perform (Oakes, 1985). Indeed, school structures based on performance expectations are so pervasive that they are among the most difficult to change (Lipman, 1998).

Changing these structures can be accomplished, however, and the effects can be dramatic (see, e.g., Meier, 1995). In fact, many educators credit impressive "turn-arounds" to shifts in the expectations teachers hold for certain (typically underprivileged) groups of children (see, e.g., Cantor, Kester, & Miller, 1997). Such turn-arounds are what most school leaders claim to want, so attuning themselves to the undesirable effects of persistent school structures and the mental models that sustain them seems to be a key part of the principal's and superintendent's jobs. Actually managing these structures on behalf of children constitutes the heart of school leadership; and even in complex and unpredictable systems, such strategic leadership seems to offer a great deal of promise.

Strategies and Leverage

Dynamic systems theorists argue that when leaders find the important leverage points in a system, they are able to identify strategies capable of altering persistent but undesirable organizational structures (Senge, 1990; Wheat, 2000). Indeed, taking action at key leverage points is the only way that leaders can counter the unwanted feedback cycles that threaten organizational effectiveness. Moreover, as Senge and other dynamic systems theorists warn, leverage points are not necessarily found in the obvious places.

Wheat (2000), for example, provided a compelling discussion of the way that Virginia's school accountability policy actually undermined efforts to improve student achievement in low-performing schools. By defining schools' effectiveness only in terms of a high pass rate on the State's accountability tests, the policy continually punished low-performing schools, even when they were demonstrating marked improvement. Wheat's analysis suggests that a policy focusing on improvement in achievement offers leverage for nurturing success in low-performing schools, whereas a policy focusing on absolute standards of achievement contributes to a continued cycle of poor performance in such schools.

Strategic leadership depends on the administrator's ability to identify important leverage points, to decide what actions to take, and to convince others of the benefits of taking those actions. Each of these steps requires the school

---

[1]Of course, in a dynamic system, many forces are at play all at once. We would never conclude, therefore, that teachers' expectations alone would have such dire consequences.

leader to act with conviction in the face of uncertain outcomes. Moreover, un-certainty increases considerably if there is turmoil in the environment sur-rounding the school or district (Mintzberg, 1994).

Two Challenges

Dynamic systems theory seems like an appealing way to understand school sys-tems. It offers a concise and reasonable explanation of some of the most puzzling dilemmas that educators face. And it seems to offer the promise of opening up opportunities for strategic as opposed to managerial or reactive leadership. There are two challenges, however, associated with bringing insights from dy-namic systems theory to bear on what happens in schools and districts.

The first challenge concerns the temptation to take dynamic systems theo-ries too literally, believing that science *conclusively proves* that this is how organi-zations *must* work. Science has not proven any such thing (see, e.g., Hunter & Benson, 1997). But even if the corroborating research never materializes, the framework will probably endure as a helpful metaphor, in the spirit of Lao Tzu. (See Sidebar 4.4.) It's a very different approach from the old com-mand-and-control outlook of the traditional and still dominant "administra-tive science."

The second challenge is the opposite, but probably less tempting, one. So lit-tle social science research has been done with the research techniques of dy-namic systems theory that teachers and principals with a keen scientific turn of mind may be apt to dismiss out of hand the analogy from natural to social sys-tems. The big idea, however, is not that this is *science* per se, the once-and-for-all truth. What's useful is the straight-on consideration of complexity and unpre-dictability in organizational life, a complexity that is inherently obvious, but that traditional theories mostly ignore.

Even if we cannot consider the insights of dynamic systems theory as valid in a strictly scientific sense, we can appreciate and use them to help us interpret the organizational life of schools and districts. In fact, similar types of interpre-tations were being offered long before there was a field of school administration. Notably, modern (as opposed to ancient) philosophers and historians did have a complex view of societies, nations, cities, and the political and social arrange-ment of life. In many ways, the modern era is traceable to the Italian Renais-sance, where the "old science" of 1600–1900 had its origins. Niccoló Machiavelli was there, with a watchful eye on politics. His famous treatise, *The Prince* (1515/1999), reads like a contemporary political science text.

Machiavelli definitely understood the complexity of political life. He was also interested in the changeable nature of political organization and the ways in which political change related to the governance of states and the conditions surrounding that governance. Focusing on relationships (e.g., between the Prince and his subjects, between competing princes), Machiavelli explained how states co-evolve through the interplay of internal (within state) and external (between states) dynamics.

Unfortunately, nearly all traditional educational researchers—like the scientists who consistently failed to examine chaos in the natural world—neglected the previous understandings of complexity evident in thinkers like Machiavelli (and legions of other thinkers from the 17th through the 20th century). They neglected them, in fact, in order to narrow their focus on regularity, predictability, and control (Kellert, 1993).

Sidebar 4.4: Historical Antecedents of Dynamic Systems Theory

Dynamic systems theory, as applied to social science, rests on perceptions of experience that are really quite ancient, going back to very early accounts of the world. Heraclitus (1969), a philosopher born before both Christ and before Socrates (about 500 B.C.), remarked famously, "You cannot step twice into the same rivers; for fresh waters are ever flowing in upon you." Heraclitus believed that swirling change was the hallmark of nature and society.

About the same time, on the other side of the world, the Chinese philosopher-poet, Lao Tzu, elaborated a philosophy for negotiating personal and social change with grace and wisdom. The way to do this, according to Lao Tzu (1997), was to fit oneself into the flow of life. The indirect approach was always better than the direct approach according to Lao Tzu (Stan Rosenthal's translation):

Act without contriving;
work naturally, and taste the tasteless;
magnify the small; increase the few,
and reward bitterness with care.
Seek the simple in the complex,
and achieve greatness in small things.

It is the way of nature
that even difficult things are done with ease,
and great acts made up of smaller deeds.
The sage achieves greatness by small deeds multiplied.

Promises easily made are most easily broken,
and acting with insufficient care
causes subsequent trouble.
The sage confronts problems as they arise,
so that they do not trouble him.

> Remarkably, this passage mentions complexity and even seems to recommend using leverage as a practice of leadership: "The sage achieves greatness by small deeds multiplied."

WHAT DOES ALL THIS HAVE TO DO WITH SCHOOLS?

The life of a teacher and the life of a principal are rapid-paced; every day hundreds, more likely *thousands*, of interactions take place. Just the pace of the action in a school leaves most of us exhausted at the end of a day. Keeping track of all that was done, everything that we are in the middle of, and everything that remains to be done is extraordinarily demanding, difficult work. People who have never taught or led a school don't realize this; often, when they have spent a day teaching, however, they develop such an appreciation. Talk about a dynamic system!

And "change" is certainly a watchword in schooling. International, national, state, and district-level reform efforts are working continuously on systems of schooling. The social context of schooling (the "surroundings" of the educational system) have undergone dramatic change as well, worldwide, in the past half-century. As time passes, the planned and unplanned changes, many of them contradicting one another, produce actual changes in systems of schooling that only partially resemble any of the original plans. In order for school improvement efforts so often to misfire or flop, all the parts of the system and its surroundings, it seems, must be influencing one another in ways that we can only dimly perceive.

Applications in School Life

Although there may be other ways that dynamic systems theory can help school administrators think about the issues they confront, three applications seem particularly germane. These relate to (a) planning and strategy making, (b) mental models about what works, and (c) leadership and the self-organization of systems.

Planning and Strategy Making.   If organizational life is unpredictable, what use is it to plan? Good question. Recently, two of the authors were conducting a study of principals' planning. We developed a draft of our questionnaire and sent it to a small group of principals in order to get feedback. The principals absolutely hated the following question: "Are you a rational planner or an improvisational planner?"

Most of them wrote comments like this on the draft questionnaire: "This question is dumb. It doesn't make sense. A *plan* is always carefully considered. Planning is the opposite of improvisation." We eliminated the question because—whether there "really was" such a thing or not—it looked like improvisation was *not* the story about planning that principals had been hearing.

Despite the apparent self-contradiction in the phrase "improvisational planning," however, dynamic systems theorists argue that this approach constitutes the *only* kind of planning capable of producing effective strategies. According to Mintzberg (1994), strategy making requires deep understanding of the structures of a system and the ways those structures interact with significant features of the environment. Through intuition (Mintzberg's word for "improvisational planning"), leaders ascertain the points of leverage that provide access to productive avenues for change.

As the case study later in this chapter shows, a strategy achieves its effect by altering the prevailing logic of a dysfunctional system. Identifying such a strategy is difficult, of course, because the leader, like everyone else in the system, accepts the system's logic. In the school described in the case study, teachers are acting in ways that might be called "untrustworthy," and according to the prevailing logic of the system, the appropriate response to untrustworthy behavior is the withdrawal of trust. That approach, however, leads to a downward spiral in which teachers take less and less responsibility while the principal (and perhaps the parents as well) treat them with greater and greater wariness.

To alter the logic of the system, as we'll see, the principal in the case study, Mary Fletcher, needs to *increase* the trust she invests in the teachers, while at the same time providing appropriate support. In effect, Mary needs to take actions that seem wrong-headed under the prevailing logic of the system. Why should the principal trust teachers who seem to be untrustworthy? Isn't that the very worst thing to do? And why should she give support to teachers who appear to be unworthy of it?

The strategy Mary chooses seems like the exact opposite of what the logic of the system tells her to do. And that fact alone might clue her into the strategy's potential to effect meaningful change.

Mental Models About What Works. "Mental models" represent commonly held understandings that define the "logic of a system," such as the one in which Mary and her teachers operate. Such models incorporate rulelike generalizations about what will and will not work in a particular system. Although mental models do develop in response to the experiences shared among members of a system, they do not *necessarily* represent "the truth."

Of course, many—perhaps even most—mental models actually do provide accurate guidance. Furthermore, in schools, as in all systems, routine functioning depends on the reliability of our mental models. At the same time, some mental models simply codify arbitrary conventions. For example, many schools make an issue when boys wear hats, but pay no attention when girls do. Although this mental model regarding acceptable dress may not contribute to serious dysfunction in the school, it may introduce unnecessary—even counterproductive—"noise." Some mental models, however, cause more serious problems by contributing to undesirable feedback loops. Our earlier discussion of teacher expectations illustrates such dynamics.

Productive change in organizations often depends on convincing participants to revise their mental models about how things work (Senge, 1990). Leaders may first need to ask members of the organization to "suspend their disbelief" in order to get them to substitute new models for the old ones. Sometimes it's helpful to pilot test a new model, but pilot testing provides time for resisters to mobilize support. Senge (1990) suggested computer simulations as another approach, but this option does not seem particularly workable for schools. He also recommended candid dialog as a way for teams of employees to surface unproductive assumptions and formulate more productive alternatives. Reports from educators involved in establishing new schools or reforming existing ones demonstrate how important such dialog can be (e.g., Meier, 1995). According to Senge, a "learning organization" is one in which work teams engage in dialog that enables them to uncover organizational "learning disabilities" and replace them with more functional mental models.

Leadership and the Self-Organization of Systems.   Leadership looks constantly to the future, identifying implicit strategies and purposefully designing innovative ones that position the organization to take advantage of emerging opportunities (Mintzberg, 1994). Organizational effectiveness, in fact, depends on an organization's ability to exploit such opportunities.

This perspective is hardly unique to dynamic systems theorists; in fact, it is shared rather widely among contemporary organizational theorists. But dynamic systems theorists put a somewhat different spin on leadership because they understand that systems are self-organizing. As a result, they view leaders primarily as capacity builders and catalysts.

Because schools are so often under attack, we educators may have a hard time imagining what it would mean for a school to "exploit opportunities." For many of us, "respond to mandates" sounds more like it. Nevertheless, schools *are* presented with opportunities all the time, particularly if we view opportunities as occasions to do things better or in more interesting ways. In fact, every time a school gets its state report card, it is offered an opportunity. Teachers and principals, however, often view such occasions as threats. That's because they believe they are being asked to do more with the same or fewer resources.

And here's where capacity building comes in. Imagine what it would be like if a school were able to increase its resources in preparation for each significant occasion to do things better. For example, anticipating that community demographics were likely to change, the school might increase bilingualism among its teachers. Or recognizing that children's lives were becoming more and more complex, the school might help teachers acquire counseling skills. A school that was able to prepare for change in this way would be well positioned to turn challenges into opportunities. Teachers, for example, would have the opportunity to use (and increase) their skill with a second language or their ability to provide counseling services. And as some teachers began to expand their roles to encompass these new skills, other teachers would follow suit. Perhaps, in fact, as parents and community members began to see the school taking the lead on an important new initiative, they would become involved as well. These events (what dynamic systems theorists might call "self-organizing processes") would signal a sea change—an adaptation enabling the school to perform as well or better than it did before and to do so under new and possibly more difficult conditions.

Of course, getting the teachers to recognize the future need (e.g., for bilingualism or for counseling services) would not be easy because, like everyone else, they rely on mental models that have been created from their past experiences. And, in dynamic systems, past experiences serve as a limited (and often misleading) basis for thinking about the future. As a consequence, someone—most likely the principal—must develop and communicate a compelling vision of what the future holds. Moreover, a vision that is sufficiently compelling to stimulate teachers to devote extra energy to a major new initiative must ring true, accurately depicting the present while at the same time presenting an image of a worthy and more desirable future. Such a vision—and if Senge (1990) is right, only such a vision— catalyzes strategic change.

CASE STUDY: TRUSTING TEACHERS

Background

Mary Fletcher was in her second year as principal of Sugar Creek Middle School, located in a rural community in western Oklahoma. A former Oklahoma City teacher, Mary had received her master's in school leadership just before accepting the Sugar Creek job. Mary had lived in a rural community as a child and was pleased to be back in a rural locale.

During her principal preparation program, Mary had learned about the relationship between instructional leadership and school improvement. And she understood how important it was for principals to play a major role in supervising teachers. She also thought of herself as a master teacher, having spent 13 years refining her own instructional and classroom management skills. To Mary, teacher professionalism not only meant that teachers behaved respectfully in their interactions with students, parents, and colleagues, it also meant that they spent time after school hours making sure they had up-to-date professional knowledge. Professional development programs had often provided her with opportunities to stay current, and she subscribed to and read many articles from two professional journals, one that focused on trends in middle-level education and one that focused on math education, the field in which she was licensed to teach.

The School Situation

Mary's first year at Sugar Creek had taught her that most of the teachers there weren't as professional as she thought teachers ought to be. Drawing support from the master contract negotiated by the union, the teachers tended to "work to the rule," arriving at the specified work time and leaving as soon as the school day was over. Rarely did they take work home with them. And when Mary asked them to participate in after-school curriculum meetings, they insisted on receiving overload pay.

Mary realized that cultivating the professionalism of her teachers was a project that would take time. But she also came to the conclusion that the behavior of certain teachers was likely to frustrate her work to improve professionalism more broadly. Two teachers in particular took excessive liberties. Close relatives of long-time board members, these teachers tended to come to work late, miss required meetings during school hours, and pressured newer teachers to cover duties (e.g., monitoring the lunchroom) for them. These teachers also tended to make life harder than it needed to be for the children with disabilities in their classrooms. And, on occasion, each of these teachers had reportedly engaged in questionable teaching practices. One, for example, periodically let her students watch videos all day on Fridays if they exhibited good behavior during the other four days of the week. The other routinely read students' grades aloud to the class when she handed back students' work, and ridiculed those students, typically the LD children, who had earned the lowest grades.

Late in October, a contingent of parents contacted Mary about the way one of the two "problem" teachers was treating their children. This situation gave Mary an opportunity to talk with the teacher about her attitudes and classroom practices. The meeting, however, did not go well. The teacher immediately accused Mary of siding with parents rather than with teachers. And then she told Mary to watch out because she was tempted to talk to her brother-in-law, currently the president of the board of education, about nonrenewal of Mary's contract. She explained that she was tired of being harped on by Mary to attend extra meetings and to give special breaks to the students with disabilities.

Given these circumstances, Mary had to make some decisions about what to do next. First, though, she decided to reflect on the situation, using her knowledge of dynamic systems theory.

How Dynamic Systems Theory Helped

Based on what she had read about dynamic systems theory, Mary knew to look for the mechanisms within the school community that tended to be counterproductive. She noticed, for example, that some teachers and parents seemed to be creating a downward spiral of mistrust. And, unfortunately, the negative feelings resulting from the mistrust felt by these members of the school community were becoming contagious. Feeling that they weren't trusted, teachers became defensive; then acting on the basis of defensiveness, they ultimately became less trustworthy.

These insights led Mary to speculate that trust might be the lever she'd need to apply in order to reverse the downward spiral. But what specific approaches might she use in order to build trust? Thinking back to Senge's "five disciplines," Mary considered how (a) personal mastery, (b) mental models, (c) team learning, and (d) a shared vision might help her build trust widely within the school community.

Mary decided that, before trust could be established widely, each participant would need to learn to trust him- or herself. So she would start with Senge's notion of personal mastery and build from there. And teachers would be the first group with whom she'd work: Parents would without doubt need to see evidence of the trustworthiness of school personnel before they'd agree to participate.

With teachers, then, Mary decided to get things started by showing them that she trusted their professional judgment, while at the same time expecting them to increase the fund of knowledge on which that judgment was based. To show her trust, she asked clusters of teachers to join together in problem-solving teams to address issues of concern, such as the behavior of particular students or difficulty in communicating with parents from particular social groups. And she gave each team a budget to use at its discretion to pay for books, consultants, or training workshops that would assist them in arriving at workable solutions to the most difficult problems they identified.

She knew, however, that without some way to offer critique, the teams would be likely to fall back on persistent mental models. They might, for example, explain the achievement difficulties of some children in terms of those children's family backgrounds rather than looking for evidence of conditions in classrooms that might be impeding children's progress. So she decided to meet monthly with each team to help them analyze the thinking that was taking place in their problem-solving sessions. And, at the meetings, the teams would use an agreed-upon rubric for analyzing their own problem solving. Mary was well aware that a process, not a person, would need to be responsible for surfacing criticism. She also knew that, with repeated practice with this approach, teams would begin to learn about more than just the problems occurring in classrooms. Their problem-solving activities would enable them to learn about how things work in the system—the school community—as a whole.

Once these activities were well underway, Mary knew it would be time to codify the teams' learning in a vision statement that could be shared widely. And she suspected that a tentative vision statement coming from the work of the teams of teachers would serve as a good point of departure for broadening discussion about the school's future with parents and community members.

CHAPTER SUMMARY

Viewing dynamic systems theory as a useful, if metaphorical, way to understand the circumstances that confront school leaders, this chapter examines a set of interrelated insights. The foundation stones on which these insights rest include the ideas of complexity, unpredictability, dynamism, feedback, self-organization, structure, leverage, and strategy.

These ideas connect to form a new way of understanding organizations (including schools) that approximates the real world better than do simplified models of cause and effect. Because the world of schools is complex, multiple influences—some known and some unknown—are always at work. In fact, there are so many different and interdependent influences that educators are rarely able to understand the whole picture, even the whole picture of one school or classroom. Given this degree of complexity, prediction becomes extremely dicey. Not only does the error implicit in measuring influences and outcomes compromise the accuracy of prediction, influences themselves can be dynamic, contingent, nonlinear, or cataclysmic. Direct efforts to *control* outcomes seem like so much wasted energy given the dynamism of social systems.

Does an understanding of the dynamism of school systems therefore mean that principals and superintendents ought to pack up and go home? That might be a reasonable option if there were no way to get a handle on what's going on in school systems. But, as dynamic systems theory shows, complex processes lead to self-organization of systems, producing persistent patterns and structures that leaders can use to leverage change. By learning how feedback moderates or intensifies outcomes in their particular school systems, principals and superintendents cultivate a base of experience from which to identify significant leverage points. Doing so is extremely important, because leverage points represent the places in the system where productive strategies are most likely to take hold. From the perspective of dynamic systems theory, the quintessential acts of leadership involve designing or discovering productive strategies, promoting mental models that enable participants to make sense of and embrace the strategies, and persuading participants to take the action steps necessary to put those strategies in motion.

Clearly this view of leadership connects to a commitment, first on the part of the leader and then on the part of participants, to engage in deep and ongoing learning about the nature of their work and the systems that enable or constrain it. In fact, action rooted in dynamic systems theory depends so heavily on learning that some writers use the term "learning organization" to refer to schools or corporations governed by its principles.

At the same time, dynamic systems theory provides a context for understanding the limits to human learning by reminding us that—even if patterns do exist in chaos—we are not always able to see or make use of them. Recognizing that the world of schools is often chaotic and sometimes toxic, we reiterate the line from Lao Tzu: "Reward bitterness with care." Dynamic systems theory does not always attend explicitly to this idea. Nevertheless, we can hardly imagine a better strategy for school leaders to embrace as they work to foster meaningful organizational learning in systems historically stymied by overreliance on command and control.

5

Communitarianism

Communitarianism is useful to school leaders because of its concern for the schooling that forms citizens who are disposed and prepared to care for the common good. Moreover, it acknowledges that care for the common good represents difficult work in particular communities. Unlike many discussions of schooling, this chapter considers the pertinence to school leadership of the real-world communities in which schools are embedded, or from which they are too often alienated. It also critically considers "community" as a metaphor that can describe the social relationships of school life.

Because communitarianism is a practical theory, it helps educators deepen their understanding of the connection between schools and communities. Such insights are not accessible elsewhere, either in traditional theories or in the alternative theories presented in other chapters in this book. Indeed, although most educators have been convinced that "parental involvement" improves students' achievement, the field of education itself doesn't value community connections very strongly, according to a number of perceptive observers (e.g., Arons, 1997; Bickel & Dufrene, 2001; DeYoung & Theobald, 1991).

In fact, communitarian thought can help teachers and principals think more deeply about the *purpose* of schooling than they are apt to do without it. Communitarian thinking fills a gap left by the many leadership theories that focus on the organization but completely ignore questions about the nature of a good society and the link between a good school and a good society. There is a link, or there should be a link, according to these thinkers—and many practicing educators would probably be inclined to agree. As a collective enterprise, such higher purpose is always in play when it comes to schooling. Communitarianism is more education-specific in its bones than some of the other educationally relevant theories represented in this book. Like the other theories considered in this book, however, communitarianism is decidedly a work-in-progress.

Sidebar 5-1 summarizes Henry Tam's account of the roots of communitarianism (Tam, 1998). The theory has its roots deep in the history of philosophy, as it must, because it deals with momentous issues concerning knowledge, power, and social organization.

Sidebar 5-1: The Roots of Communitarianism (from Tam, 1998, pp. 18–23)		
Illustrative Thinker	Time	Justification of Contribution
Aristotle	384-322 BC	for asserting the value of common knowledge (in contrast to Plato's elite knowledge)
Francis Bacon	1561-1626	for promoting cooperative inquiry (i.e., 'empirical science')
Robert Owen	1771-1858	for inventing community-based social transformation (i.e., 'communitarians')
John Stuart Mill	1806-1873	for promoting participatory democracy (i.e., as the route to 'the common good')
Emile Durkheim	1857-1917	for articulating the role of social norms in sustaining communities (i.e., morality as the good)

What is Communitarianism?

The contemporary world, according to communitarians (e.g., Theobald, 1997), is dominated by institutions and cultural habits that dissolve the glue holding society together: community. (Sidebar 5-5, which appears later in this chapter, provides a variety of formal definitions of community.)

Some communitarians, like Henry Tam and Amitai Etzioni, envision "community" as encompassing very large nations like Britain and the United States. Others, coming from a rural perspective, like Paul Theobald and Wendell Berry, ground their version of communitarianism in local places. Some, like Tam and Etzioni, espoused universal standards for "the good" (love, wisdom, justice fulfillment in Tam's version) whereas others, like Michael Walzer, argue for a process of local construction of such ideals as "the good" (see Walzer, 1988, for this argument). In all versions, however, notions of the common (versus private) good predominate. Cooperation, rather than competition, is the dominant organizing principle. Struggle, debate, and conflict nonetheless receive prominent billing in communitarian theory as requirements of common effort.

The opposing theory to communitarianism is commonly identified by communitarian writers as *neo-liberalism*, the internationally held philosophical and economic perspective that, among other things, theorizes and justifies late capitalism as it operates around the world. "Neo-liberalism" should not be confused with the way Americans use the word "liberal" to mean a mild left-leaning ideology associated with the U.S. Democratic Party. Neo-liberal ideals are those held most frequently by conservatives, but they are also held strongly by most members of the Democratic Party in the United States.

Communitarians tend to be critical of globalization, of big business, and also of big government. Most communitarians are *not* opponents of capitalism, however, but of its excesses, which they most often attribute to the philosophical commitments of neo-liberalism. They oppose all forms of authoritarian rule, whether from the left (e.g., Communism) or the right (e.g., fascism). They support participatory democracy—by which they mean active participation in debate and policy formation rather than just voting. Among the world's varied political platforms, communitarians might be most likely to endorse those typically espoused by the Green Party, for instance, nonviolence, sustainability and limited growth, appropriate technology, decentralization, and community-based economics.

The variety of positions to which communitarian thinkers and activists are led in viewing the world this way understandably puts them at odds with the tenor of the times. Communitarians are critical of institutions (e.g., the penal system, the banking system, the military) that have developed under the sway of neo-liberal commitments, and their concern prominently includes the educational system (Tam, 1998; Theobald, 1997).

For communitarians, humans need to be educated—raised up—to *debate* the common good and decide the relevant issues with others in their lives, in their communities, and so they regard public schools as logical institutions for preparing people to live this way. Thinking is a centerpiece of schooling among communitarians, not just skill development or generic problem solving. Schools, communitarians argue, should cultivate the disposition to read, write, and analyze information as part of engagement with the important work of building robust communities. The ideal of the common good, however, receives varied treatment among communitarians, and we turn next to a discussion of their conception.

MASS SOCIETY AND THE CONSTRUCTION OF THE COMMON GOOD

What difference does the common good make to how schools work, and, especially, to how schools *should* work? This question is a critical concern among communitarians. Understanding their answer requires a bit of background in sociology, history, and philosophy, but it won't be particularly difficult to grasp. The discussion turns on *mass society* as developed during the 20th century. Schooling is an important part of this history because *mass education* is the form of education that serves mass society. Most of what contemporary Americans think about education is determined by this history.

The Rise of Mass Society

When thinking about these historic changes, however, it is important to remember that education is not just schooling; it is the upbringing of children. And childrearing has (of course!) always been practiced. Before the development of mass education, especially in the 20th century, education was the province of families, communities, religious organizations, and guilds. Schools were much less important than any of these other institutions. Indeed, schooling of any sort was a comparatively rare experience before 1800. Most people—that is, ordinary people as compared to aristocrats and the very wealthy middle class—had no experience of it whatever.

The difference in how people regarded schools before 1800 and after 1945 can be summed up like this: Before 1800, schools contributed to education; after 1945 or so, we came to regard education as synonymous with school. Those preparing to lead schools enter the field of "educational administration," not "school administration," and in most states, one cannot become a principal without going to school to study educational administration. These circumstances are not abstract considerations, but real-world matters that govern the daily behavior and mind-set of people who work in schools. Communities still have an extremely important educational function, a dominant one according to some observers, but educators sometimes fail to recognize the fact, and school reformers have historically ignored it, according to David Cohen (1988). In Cohen's telling, the widespread failure of school reform efforts is due to almost total ignorance of the importance of community conceptions of education.

Historical Context of Mass Society.   According to educational historian Michael Katz (1987), the educational system as we know it was not invented until the last half of the 19th century. Two historical facts go a long way to showing how different the world was before the emergence of mass education, and mass society, in the 20th century.

First, the world had been controlled largely by hereditary elites—aristocrats whose economic and political force typically came from royal grants of land and related privileges. This was certainly the case throughout Europe and in the colonies held by European powers (including the North American colonies).

Second, the realm in which people were born and died was much more local than it is now. In fact, the idea of "society" itself barely existed before 1750, and society was conducted mostly on a scale determined by walking distance. A famous history of the industrial revolution begins like this: "The world of 1789 was overwhelmingly rural, and nobody can understand it who has not absorbed this fundamental fact" (Hobsbawm, 1962, p. 1). Society arguably remained small scale, in fact, until very recently—perhaps until as late as 1920 or even 1945 (as in those reruns of the *Andy Griffith Show*, which first aired, in fact, in 1960 with some nostalgia for the lost world of 1945).

Historians have identified two organizing principles governing the changes begun about 1750: the *nation state* as a political practice and the unfolding of the *industrial revolution*. The changes are ongoing today: They continue in the political realm with globalization (see chap. 11) and in the industrial (or technological) realm with the digital revolution. The nation state has an historical beginning and likely an historical end, and the industrial revolution has already been overshadowed by the digital revolution.

There is good reason to wonder what the future will look like. Schools will change, and principals will make some of the choices involved. Some will be quite concerned, in this possibly dangerous context, about community as the glue that holds society together.

Political Context of Mass Society.   Although the contemporary nation state is associated with ideal characteristics relating to a unified culture and language (Hobsbawm, 1992), two key points need to concern us: (a) the geographic size of the sovereign nation state and (b) the conception of rights on which the politics of the nation state, under the sway of neo-liberal thought, is most often founded. We deal with each separately in the next two paragraphs.

The geographic size of nation states has a special significance under the conditions of mass society. Markets for goods, services, and information that were once distinctly local no longer exist. Mass society is served, and an identity is engineered for it through images and stories marketed nationally and globally. These latter connections—cultural and ideological ones—bear on how schools should be run and on what the purpose of schooling should be. Communitarians note that the communications infrastructure (particularly video and audio markets and delivery systems) constitutes a powerful educative force—arguably more influential than schooling—that is firmly in the grip of private, rather than common, direction. The idea of local community is significant to some communitarians because its smaller scale offers opportunities for common action not accessible through national politics.

Neo-liberal rights are founded not on the golden rule (treat others as you would like to be treated) but on the antithesis of the golden rule: Leave others alone as you would like to be left alone. This is what neo-liberal political regimes mean by "freedom." It is not a *positive* system to govern relationships among citizens, but a *negative* one (instead of the right to something, it is the right to do anything that does not harm others). Communitarians object that such a system lacks the commitment needed to support the substantive development of the common good. Many communitarian theorists put it this way: Neo-liberal political thought revolves around the idea of what is right or fair, whereas communitarian thought deals with the idea of what is good or virtuous.

Economic Context of Mass Society.   Trade was locally based before railroads provided quick transportation starting in the mid-1800s. Most goods and services were produced and consumed in the same place, with production and distribution centered on small family farms and businesses. It's particularly dangerous, however, to believe that things were necessarily better in the past (see Sidebar 5-2).

Sidebar 5-2: Communitarianism Is not a Nostalgic Project

The comparative poverty of the past suggests something important about communitarianism. The past was not an ideal world, and communitarian-sim does not aim to model the future on an idealized misconception of the past. Not only was poverty common in the past, but racism, sexism, and class prejudice operated with arguably greater viciousness. Although it sometimes seems that the past must have been a better place than the present, the past is commonly romanticized to the point of falsehood. According to some observers (Williams, 1973), people who accept the falsehoods are easy prey for authoritarian political agendas. Fabled "golden ages" make poor models for strengthening the common good in the contemporary world and into the future. Community, from this vantage, is not

> something to be retrieved or recaptured, but something to be developed
> now, and into the future in interaction with contemporary issues. Com-
> munitarianism can be seen as a theory with a future orientation, one that is
> dissatisfied with both present and past.

Contrast the economics of previous historical societies with ours, for a quick impression of the economic changes. Manufacture has become wildly produc-tive, but, according to communitarian theorists, this productivity is tied to a frenzied and unhealthy consumerism. Additionally, many goods and services—perhaps most of the goods and increasingly many of the services—are produced outside the localities in which consumption occurs. The production of goods and services takes place very often in nationally centralized locations, and dis-tribution is also highly centralized and nationally organized (Walmart and Amazon.com are current strong examples of this tendency).

The Common Good in Mass Society.   According to communitarians, the contemporary market system embeds a stunted view of the common good (Katz, 1997; Orr, 1995; Tam, 1998). Shopping and television are the main lei-sure-time activities. Most other purposes (including concepts of learning, work, family, and community) are deformed and even neglected by comparison, and mass society provides few openings to debate what forms those other purposes should take. Everyone remains separate despite engaging in the quite similar pursuit of amusement. The educator Neil Postman summed up this sort of world in an apt book entitled *Amusing Ourselves to Death* (Postman, 1985).

Communitarians conclude that a lack of public concern for fellow citizens is a major casualty of a life based on private consumption. They charge that equal-ity and solidarity are not features of the neo-liberal version of the good life in the mass society. Indeed, the proposition that these qualities might be part of the good life probably sounds strange these days to most American ears. These val-ues are nonetheless the basis for constituting community, and they are neces-sary to sustain it, in the view of communitarians.

Responses to Mass Society and Its Discontents

Mass society is beset by a particular set of problems, and because the cultural products of American mass society are purveyed worldwide, its contents and discontents, its good and its ill, beset humanity throughout the world. The dis-contents may be especially intense in the United States, the headquarters of neo-liberal thought and practice, according to many communitarians (Tam, 1998). Can this be right?

In fact, in comparison to Western European nations and the developed Asian nations of Japan, Korea, and Singapore, our nation is surprisingly deficient on such basic indicators of well-being as infant mortality, primary school attendance, income equality, and even life expectancy (Bellamy, 2004). Sidebar 5-3 illustrates some of the facts.

Sidebar 5-3: The State of the Social Contract in the United States: An International Illustration

Country	infant mortality rate*	life expectancy	primary attendance rate	income of poorest 40% [†]	income of richest 20%[‡]
Canada	5	79	99%	20%	39%
Finland	4	78	100%	25%	35%
France	4	79	100%	20%	40%
Japan	3	81	100%	25%	36%
Spain	4	79	100%	20%	40%
United States	7	77	95%	16%	46%

*per 1,000 live births
[†]proportion of national income going to poorest 40% of population
[‡]proportion of national income going to richest 20% of population

Notice that, in this table, the United States has the highest infant mortality rate, lowest life expectancy, lowest primary school attendance rate, and (last two columns) the most unequal distribution of income. These statistics are representative of a range of such measures: This information was drawn from a much longer table in a recent UNICEF report (Bellamy, 2004). The data are available for some 200 countries in an Excel spreadsheet from the United Nations: http://www.unicef.org/files/Table1_english.xls.

The discontents in mass society go well beyond these simple indicators, of course. Many are familiar to sociologists from decades of study in the developed world and are of concern to scholars and activists across the political spectrum:

- Economic inequality (growing poverty, shrinking middle class);
- Apathy (political disengagement, cynicism);
- Isolation (narcissism, greed, disintegration of family and community);
- Crime and violence (desperation, addiction, danger to self and others);
- Anomie (meaningless, prevalent clinical depression); and
- Thoughtlessness (rudeness, bigotry, rage).

Such discontents are certainly part of the enduring human condition, but most sociologists observe that they are dramatically sharpened in mass society.

The discontents of mass society help to explain the many controversies that bedevil contemporary schooling. The various "school wars" that swirl around how to teach math and reading properly, proposals for school privatization and competition, high-stakes testing, and school funding litigation—all these can be read as symptoms of the discontents of mass society.

Responses deal with the discontents in two principal modes, both relevant to schooling: standardization and differentiation. In mass society, they are two sides of one coin, according to many sociologists (e.g., Lasch, 1991) and communitarians (e.g., Tam, 1998).

Standardization.   Standardization is a traditional response to the problems of organizing mass society, and so educators have actually used it for a long time. As we mentioned in chapter 2, standardization was a goal, and later a tool, of scientific management, a movement to improve the organization of firms and factories in the early 20th century. Scientific management was quickly imported to schools from business (Callahan, 1962). Standardized testing, and school and district consolidation became, well, *standard practice* early in the century. Bringing the real world into line with such standards, of course, required decades of struggle. Indeed, these two efforts—standardized testing and school consolidation—continue with great force in the present.

There is a deeper meaning to "standardization," though. The purpose of standardization is to reduce variation, which can be regarded as fault or error rather than as welcome diversity. Now, errors or mistakes in industrial production are one thing, but they can be taken much more seriously, as moral failings, when human behavior is at stake, as it is with schooling (see Cohen, 1988, on Christian purpose in education). That is, in the field of education, standardization harbors a moral purpose because the upbringing of children so often has to do with the imposition of moral values. Mass society thus—through mass education—introduces the opportunity to impose a standardized morality.

A famous text about the history of educational administration is titled "managers of virtue": School leaders in the 19th and early 20th century were understood—and still are—as probable but uncertain upholders of a sort of moral standardization (Tyack & Hansot, 1982). Superintendents and other educators working in mass education were then expected—as they still are in many communities—to convey a certain moral tone that is subjected to very little doubt or reflection. According to thinkers like Cohen, most citizens are by no means convinced of the position that virtue requires reflection, judgment, doubt, and debate. Many prefer a managed virtue with norms of behavior inculcated rather than examined and questioned. Communitarians, who value the role of thinking, inquiry, and imagination in education, generally have trouble with this approach to the development of character.

In support of the view that ethical issues and morality are inherently debatable, it must be said that convincing examples of the role of introspection and moral insight come from the great stories of literature: from Shakespeare, to Jane Austen and Henry James, and to the American Nobel-prize-winning novelist Toni Morrison. In great stories, virtue is very much a dialogue internal to individuals and between individuals and their families, communities, and societies.

Differentiation. Standardization, although effective in organizing industry, is not a mode of life that sits particularly well with, or has been easily sold to, Americans. The sale is difficult because of the place of freedom in the American imagination; and Patrick Henry set the pattern for subsequent generations—"Give me liberty, or give me death." He didn't say: "Make me like everyone else, or shoot me."

Perhaps because of the American devotion to freedom, the 20th century marketplace promoted differentiation with exactly the same vigor as it promoted standardization. This looks like a paradox, perhaps, but it isn't.

The two concepts are not necessarily opposites, or at least their evident opposition has served to strengthen both tendencies. This is because mass society knits the two together to support and deepen prevailing habits of production and consumption. Production is standardized, creating efficiencies and great productive capacity. Great productive capacity, however, enables an impressive differentiation of product lines, resulting in American consumer choices that are fabled worldwide.

Indeed, contemporary society offers so many choices to consumers that some people experience substantial difficulty in actually making a choice. Which mustard, food processor, DVD player, car, house, spouse, neighborhood, lifestyle, or set of beliefs is best? Even those things we don't normally think of as commodities (spouse, neighborhood, lifestyle, beliefs) can be "commodified." Personal relationships (spouse), community relationships (neighborhood), and ways of being in the world (lifestyle) are subject both to market-based standard-ization *and* to differentiation, each process reinforcing the other. Thus, making the choices, Americans also differentiate themselves—but in the context of standardization and marketing.

Take the family as a case in point. In the 1950s, following decades of depres-sion and war, new media—like television—marketed a differentiated, but also a temporarily standardized, version of the family that is well-remembered by adults who are now in their 50s and 60s. Men were to be corporate breadwin-ners, children were to be winning but unchallenging, and women were to be homemakers almost exclusively—keepers of the "haven in a heartless world," which is the title of a famous book by social historian Christopher Lasch (1977). Lasch wrote that this market-driven version of the family offered a constricted and weakened "haven," compared to previous versions. Weak-ened from within by its constriction to a nuclear core, it was also weakened from without by the sharp dislocations operating in and for mass society. In particular, in Lasch's view, the erosion of community in the mobile postwar world was a major blow to the family.

Differentiation, however, also exists in varieties less useful for propping up the status quo of mass society. This sort of differentiation can center on commonly ex-isting differences such as gender, sexual orientation, skin color, or occupation, as the following discussion explains. Let's stay with gender and the family. The fam-ily of today is not what it was supposed to be in the 1950s and 1960s, nor what it once was in the premodern world. Most women in mass society now position themselves far differently than did their predecessors. What happened?

One answer is that discontented members of mass society (largely women) have elaborated alternative forms of sex-based differentiation. Not only Simone de Beauvoir (*The Second Sex*) and Betty Friedan (*The Feminine Mystique*) but millions of women before and after them articulated new roles that pushed back against the expectations, especially after 1945. (See chap. 8 on gender, sexual-ity, and school leadership.) Several generations of women pried open the way to graduate schools, and into the ranks of physicians, lawyers, and engi-neers—all-male preserves of power and knowledge through the 1950s and 1960s. They insisted that childbirth was optional, and some women even in-sisted that men were optional as partners.

Differentiation of this sort constitutes a prominent irritant within mass soci-ety, and one that is not necessarily regarded as in-step with the smooth func-tioning of neo-liberal institutions. Most communitarians, by contrast, not only welcome, but insist on, vigorous debate and inquiry into such matters (e.g., Tam, 1998).

Social Change Grounded in Humanism

Communitarians tend to ground their beliefs about change in humanism, rather than in science or technology. Educators, of course, actually believe in changing the minds, and even the destinies, of individual students. Learning is by definition change, and teaching is an institutionalized attempt to guide that change. This dedication to change can go further, in fact, than the classroom.

Looking beyond the classroom, a visionary teacher might imagine that certain sorts of teaching and curriculum will contribute to making the world a better place. Many have done so, and a substantial minority of educators has always worked to establish that sort of schooling (see chap. 9 on critical theory). Communitarians, however, take up such change as their most important work, whatever profession they follow. But they repudiate violent revolution and, more importantly, they are committed to dialogue—to talking and writing (that is, to educational tools)—as the means of bringing about change.

Change, according to communitarians with a local focus, must be grounded in human needs and outlooks—on the common good variously construed by varied communities. They believe that to base change either on the presumed requirements of national economic development—or on the alleged "laws of history" (as with the followers of Karl Marx)—is to invite greed and brutality to rule. Humans must, according to the communitarians, *debate* good and evil. These debates, and the courses of action decided in them, are a responsibility of everyone according to communitarians, as the only feasible path to a good society. In their view, the good cannot be imposed on humans.

Social Institutions and the Quest for Sustainability

Momentous social changes, as many observers now realize, have momentous implications: Global change not only has a trajectory, it could have an ultimate and unfortunate destination. Communitarians worry about this possibility, which seems likely to them.

They are concerned about the sustainability of the sort of economic development practiced under the auspices of neo-liberal ideology. Unlimited growth is the foundation of neo-liberal economic development, but communitarians doubt that unrestricted growth is sustainable, particularly unrestricted exploitation of the world's natural resources. Before 1800, the world's resources seemed vast and the idea that humans might so befoul the planet as to make it uninhabitable would have seemed an absurd and evil fantasy.

Communitarians accept the notion that unrestrained economic development not only threatens the social world, but also the natural world. Population growth occurs exponentially, but the world's resources are finite: Communitarians see the logic in doubts about the sustainability of the neo-liberal perspective on economic and social development. For some of these writers, however, a schooling improved along communitarian lines would inevitably help citizens question the neo-liberal presumptions about limitless growth, and thereby contribute to a sustainable economic life and, ultimately, a sustainable planet—not to mention sustainable communities.

SCHOOLS AND COMMUNITIES

Many educators, at least in our experience, argue that caring for the local community is outside the sphere of professional concern. For these colleagues, "being a professional" means that decisions about schooling should be separated from concerns for community.

Communitarians, however, regard such thinking as a misconception for two reasons. First, they find that schools really do have connections to community, no matter how much schools, as currently operated, work to frustrate the connections. Second, they believe that if schools are not helping to foster community, they are likely to be subverting it—that is, when schools profess a disinterest in community, they are, in fact, harming it.

These beliefs apply, moreover, to both the real-time communities that surround schools and to a *concept of community* that might help strengthen the relationship between schools and communities. Communitarians, in short, find that community is one of the major purposes of education, and hence, the exclusion of community is worse than unprofessional. It's educational malpractice in the eyes of communitarians.

Education and the Common Good

The common good is a rough equivalent for the concept of community. The phrase, "the common good," begs a great many questions, but such an observation, communitarians might respond, is part of the point. People need a schooling that, as part of its higher purpose, helps them pose such questions, investigate possible answers, and decide matters wisely. Under communitarian principles, exactly what constitutes the common good in any particular place, or across numerous particular places, is an urgent matter for public consideration.

Compare this perspective on educational purpose with neo-liberal conceptions. One can look almost anywhere for such statements. Take a state, Kentucky for instance, that has a well-articulated set of goals for students.

Kentucky operates perhaps the most systematically reformed school system in the nation—because the entire Kentucky system, not just its financing of schools, was declared unconstitutional by the state supreme court in 1990. A great deal of thought and struggle have gone into its reform agenda as a result.

Nonetheless, when this chapter was written, all roads leading into the state proclaimed: *"Welcome to Kentucky: Where Education Pays!"* The signs show a graduate, in mortarboard, grasping a diploma. The state thus advertises the role it expects schooling to play on behalf of individuals' private gain.

Other readings are possible, of course. One might argue that well-educated people pay higher taxes, for instance, or that such advertising demonstrates a high level of support for schooling. Either way, the emphasis in all readings is that schooling's highest good is to turn knowledge into money. We have already seen that this position strikes communitarians as unworthy of a democracy.

The expression "put your money where your mouth is" applies also to Kentucky's six "learning goals" for all students, one of which states, "Students shall develop their abilities to become responsible members of a family, work group, or community, including demonstrating effectiveness in community service" (Kentucky Department of Education, 2004, ¶10). Perhaps surprisingly, this goal is specifically *exempted* from the state's academic assessment program (Education, 2004). The failure to honor this goal cascades downward into the 62 "academic expectations" tied to the six goals—only one of which mentions community, and it is not about contributing *to* the community, but taking *from* it (i.e., demonstrating the skill of finding information and resources in the community).

The point of this example is *not* that Kentucky falls uniquely short as compared to other states—far from it. The state is justly identified as a model of reform. Rather, the point is that even in a prominent reform effort driven by very serious concerns for equity, the aims of schooling reflect neo-liberal commitments. Communitarian commitments are predictably invisible—even in an effort like Kentucky's. As a result of such evidence, communitarians suggest that the institution of schooling in the United States actively avoids the sort of work needed to develop the idea of community with a citizenry that is *active* in building democracy.

Among communitarians, the theory and the practice of community is not an optional, or a minor, aim. For them, it is the organizing central aim of schooling, requiring an education that helps develop everyone's capacity to think; to critique plans; and to carry out civil discourse about complex, debatable issues. Inevitably, one might note, these sorts of capacities require students to use written language fluently and to think competently using mathematics. Communitarian discussions of educational purpose tend, in short, to articulate a "larger" view of schooling than the neo-liberal discussions—as the Kentucky case illustrates.

School Governance and the Tradition of Democratic Localism

Communitarians agree that a profound relationship exists between schooling and democracy; many, like Theobald (1997), believe that local schools help sustain the American tradition of democratic localism. This tradition is reflected in the fact that among industrialized nations, the United States retains a decentralized educational structure. Our schools are not administered by a National Ministry of Education and the national constitution does not establish education as a right, as do the constitutions of many other nations. Individual states are free to structure and govern education within the bounds of other provisions of the U.S. Constitution and relevant laws.

Centralization, Decentralization, and Local School Governance. As the nation grew, so did the number of states, and decentralized schooling became an entrenched American institution. At the same time, however, the industrial age created large, increasingly centralized business organizations—railroads, huge mining companies, steel factories, automobile factories, giant utility companies, and so on. Communitarians observe that the business developments entail commitments and understandings that exert dominant political and economic influence everywhere. As a result, schools have been under continuous pressure to adopt business practices (Callahan, 1962), and that has included continuous pressure from State Education Agencies (SEAs) to centralize schooling within states.

Systematizing the schools for an entire state, of course, had to be imposed from the outside by entities with sufficient authority, and that meant state legislatures, and their creation, the SEAs. Local Education Agencies (LEAs) continue to exercise authority at the local level, and they have traditionally exercised considerable, but steadily weakening, authority. Today SEAs, under the color of state authority and laws, regulate the operation of LEAs to such a degree that, in many states, the options confronting local school boards are prescribed in considerable detail, and such options are being increasingly restricted.

The principle historical evidence is the severe decline in the number of public school districts (LEAs) operating historically. Table 5.1 shows the change in number of districts and schools by decade and school level since 1929, together with enrollment changes at each level.

The raw data in Table 5.1 reveal some trends—significant factoids—of which most citizens remain unaware:

Table 5.1
U.S. Schools and Districts by Decade, 1929–1999

Year	Districts	Elementary Schools	High Schools	K–8 Enrollment	9–12 Enrollment
1929	127,000[a]	238,300	23,900	21,279,000	4,399,000
1939	117,108	221,660	25,467	18,832,000	6,601,000
1949	83,718	128,225	24,542	19,387,000	5,725,000
1959	40,520	91,583	25,784	26,911,000	8,271,000
1969	17,995[b]	65,800[b]	25,352[b]	32,513,000	13,037,000
1979	15,929	61,069[c]	24,362[c]	28,034,000	13,616,000
1989	15,367	60,699	23,461	29,152,000	11,390,000
1999	14,928	68,173	26,407	33,488,000	13,369,000

Note. From Table 3 and Table 87 by T. D. Snyder and C. M. Hoffman, 2002, *Digest of Education Statistics 2002*, p. 12 and p. 87 respectively.
[a]From "Sizing up schooling: A West Virginia Analysis and Critique," by C. Howley, 1996b, p. 6. Copyright © 1996 by C. Howley.
[b]1970
[c]1980

• The United States now maintains 90% *fewer* districts than it did in 1929, whereas the student population *increased* by 90%;
• The number of high schools remains constant across the century, but enrollments have tripled; and
• The United States now maintains 70% fewer elementary schools, but elementary enrollments have increased 60%.

Some observers, communitarians among them, suspect that the "systematization" of U.S. schooling will end with the overthrow of local governance altogether, and with the federal authority firmly in charge of directing action at the local level (e.g., Arons, 1997).

School Governance and the Health of Local Democracy. As noted previously, communitarians judge the health of democratic life by the vigor of political debate and the quality of the debate. The debate is not a spectator sport to communitarians, who judge its vigor by the quality of talk about the common good among ordinary people, not by the soundbites or televised "debates" of candidates for high office.

In their view, decent public schools are needed so that ordinary people have the capacity, the will, and the habit of talking about the common good, a deep subject, whose engagement is supported by reading, analysis, and conversation. In fact, for communitarians, this sort of conversation *is* politics—not the machinations of political parties. Politics, in the larger sense of the word favored by communitarians, is the route through which the common good is enacted, but when left to the small cadre of politicians in Washington, DC, or even to an elite handful of local politicians, communitarians conclude that the common good is endangered. The need for ordinary people to take the common good seriously is one reason that public schools, in the view of some communitarians (e.g., Theobald, 1997), need to be local. Only local schools, in this view, can help children and youth interact with the significant ideas in literature, history, and mathematics in the context of the varied issues important to where they live.

There is, according to the communitarian perspective, another and perhaps more compelling reason for locally grounded schools. They claim that schools ought to be part of a network of familiar and well-established organizations that together have the potential to help a local people interact, cohere, and develop common purpose. Synergy among local institutions—their potential to enlarge the good each might do separately—creates a productive "infrastructure" that supports the common good. Banks; stores; churches, temples, or mosques; hospitals; restaurants and cafes; and other institutions with distinctly local allegiances have the potential, together, to contribute to a promising future in local places. There is evidence that good community connections improve school safety (e.g., Bickel & Dufrene, 2001), and such findings provide support for the views of communitarians. The fact that communities with an adequate institutional infrastructure possess such potential, of course, hardly means that it is always, or even commonly, fully realized. As with most such insights, the matter is a question of improved odds.

Bases of the School–Community Disconnect

Too often in recent decades, according to communitarians, local institutions—notably including schools and school districts—have been distanced from the communities they might otherwise serve. Why do communitarians think this has happened?

First, they might explain that schooling focused on individuals tends to slight community. In Alan DeYoung's (1995) *Life and Death of a Rural American High School*, the superintendent who closes the school says it is not the school system's business to concern itself with helping the community.

Second, for nearly 100 years, the field of educational administration has trained leaders to keep communities at a distance. Relationships with the community are mostly handled as "public relations" in order to minimize the damage potential of the community. In short, the profession is more apt to view the community as a liability than as an asset, with administration leading this view.

Third, the distancing has also taken place through a substantial reduction in the influence of citizens, largely through district consolidation. A 90% reduction in the number of school districts has meant a 90% reduction in the strength of citizen influence (see Table 5.1). At one time, citizens had a very strong influence on the day-to-day operations of hundreds of thousands of schools. Even the size of school boards is smaller than it once was. Today, moreover, school boards receive formal training that teaches them how to fulfill their role as defined by state regulations. So the influence of citizens is much weaker, and school boards listen much more attentively to the voice of administration (as lodged in state education agencies).

Fourth, the professionalization of teaching, following the factory model, makes the participation of nonprofessionals in instruction very difficult. This is a curious turn of events, actually, because nearly every human, including most children, really is a teacher in some aspect of daily life (Cohen, 1988).

Many communitarians conclude that "stay away" is a message given by schools, and by the institution of schooling in general, to communities. The insistence on "highly qualified" teachers, however, is stronger than ever (see Sidebar 5-4).

Sidebar 5-4: Highly Qualified Teachers, Professionalization, and Community (One View)

It's hard to argue with the need for qualified teachers for all students in all schools all the time. It's a need that is dramatically unmet because the poorest schools in the poorest communities often struggle just to get enough warm bodies to stand at the front of the classroom and take roll. The need is obvious and strong, but where are the needed teachers going to come from? Many well-intentioned observers argue that opening the schools to anyone with a liberal arts degree will supply the needed teachers. The available research, however, suggests that such experiments have supplied "warm bodies" ill-prepared to tackle the tough jobs they are given.

Perhaps communities and better connections to teaching talent in communities would help. "Full qualification" is a strategy that intensifies professionalization, but, absent sharply increased purchasing power for impoverished rural and urban school districts, narrowing the talent pool through increased professionalization seems a strange way to improve the overall equity and excellence of the teaching force.

Community Size and the Relationship Between School and Community

Although communitarians might read the general message from school to community as stay away, the strength of such a message would naturally vary from place to place, in particular by community size. Communication is usually easier in smaller groups, whereas communication in a large bureaucracy is notoriously difficult—and these findings are well known to researchers (Gooding & Wagner, 1985; McCroskey & Richmond, 1978; Morgan & Alwin, 1980).

The idea of community size, moreover, raises the issue of what the word "community" indicates. If communication is easier in smaller groups, are smaller communities more likely to engage a common good? Some readers may have been waiting for a definition. Sidebar 5-5 gives a number of them, including a definition recently proposed for "communitarianism."

This issue is related to the earlier distinction between communitarians whose concerns were national and those whose concerns were primarily local. The question of what constitutes a "real" community is related to that distinction. Is a small hamlet one community? A town? A small city? Can a large city, like Los Angeles, be one community? A nation? The world? The typical approach among educators, of course, is to consider the human beings residing in the attendance zone of every school, or within every school district, as "the community," no mater how many hamlets, neighborhoods, towns, villages, or cities it might contain—or whether it can be said to contain any community at all.

Sidebar 5-5: Definitions of Community

Life in association with others; society, the social state.
  (*Oxford English Dictionary*, 1971, p. 582; definition 4)

A body of men living in the same locality.
  (*Oxford English Dictionary*, 1971, p. 582, definition 7a)

A body of nations acknowledging unity of purpose or common interests. (Esp. in the titles of international organizations, as European Defence Community, European Economic Community.)
  (*Oxford English Dictionary*, 1971 p. 582, definition 7e)

Community is best defined as a network of social relations marked by mutuality and emotional bonds.
  (Thomas Bender, *Community and Social Change in America*, 1978, p. 77)

A real community need not consist of people who are perpetually to-gether; but it must consist of people, who precisely because they are com-rades, have mutual access to one another and are ready for one another.
  (Martin Buber, *Paths in Utopia*, 1949, p. 145)

An organic commonwealth will never build itself up out of individuals but only out of small and ever smaller communities: A nation is a community to the degree that it is a community of communities.
  (Martin Buber, *Paths in Utopia*, 1949, p. 136)

A community is a group of people who are socially interdependent, who participate together in discussion and decision making, and who share certain practices that both define the community and are nurtured by it.
  (Robert Bellah and colleagues, *Habits of the Heart*, p. 333)

A community is a relatively self-sufficient population, residing in a limited geographic area, bound together by feelings of unity and interdepen-dency.
  (Bryon Munson, *Changing Community Dimensions*, 1968, p. 1)

The OED defines "communitarianism" as follows (origin given as 1984, United States):

A theory or ideology which rejects as divisive both the market-led theo-ries of political conservatives and the liberal concern for individual rights, advocating instead a recognition of common moral values, col-lective responsibility, and the social importance of the family unit.
  (in-process entry in 2005; see http://dictionary.oed.com)

There are some ideas common to all the definitions of community included in Sidebar 5-5. They are (a) a shared place, (b) shared history and future, and (c) a probability of mutual action. Clearly, at every level of human existence, from schoolyard to planet, such matters can be said to pertain and to shape common purpose. But with each increment of size, such interests become more abstract, until the probability of mutual action becomes slim indeed. The diffi-cult history of national and international common purpose may suggest this fact to readers.

When considering a school and its relationship to community, however, local definitions therefore seem appropriate—more useful and more meaning-ful—than those focusing on state, nation, or world. Some researchers also be-lieve that developing community is more likely in smaller than in larger schools (e.g., Husen, 1985; Sergiovanni, 1994).

Renewal of School–Community Connections

What do communitarians advise for reconnecting schools and communities? From their perspective, principals should embrace a more subtle conception of community than the typical one—everyone in the school's attendance zone is not sufficient, in their view. Communities are places where we live our lives and realize a common destiny: They are not merely potential allies in the struggle to help children grow, but the real beneficiaries of the results of successful schooling. This circumstance can be accepted as true, on communitarian principles, even for the most challenged of communities.

Another task for educators, from this perspective, is to reconceive the professional stance as serving community rather than as serving individual students. In a sense, the school and its leaders exercise stewardship on behalf of the school's community (or communities). Educators usually believe that the focus of their professional attention is the student, on the student's learning, and on "individual needs." This chapter describes how communitarians view that belief—that is, as a distortion of neo-liberal thinking. Elaborating the alternative—stewardship of community—would therefore be challenging work. Although some portion of such work has already been started (e.g., Hutchison, 2004; Sobel, 2004), comparatively little community-centered professional development exists for educators and none that we know of for educational leaders. School leaders will mostly have to do the necessary professional development for themselves—by reading the relevant works, making long-distance contacts with other interested educators (see those cited in this chapter), and taking appropriate action.

Ironically, appropriate models for action are more fully elaborated than the pathways to internalizations (thoughts, reflections, analyses, value structures—the theoretical perspectives that this book seeks to introduce) that can help educators grasp a communitarian outlook. The reason is perhaps cultural: The United States is a practical nation, and introspection is a relatively weak tendency in our culture (but there are plenty of counterexamples among American novelists, philosophers, musicians, and artists).

Relevant practical work has actually been carried out (for instance) under several banners for a very, very long time—and a great many resources are available to the curious would-be school principal:

- Vocational agricultural education (from 1900 onward),
- Outdoor education (from at least the 1920s onward),
- Community education (from the 1930s onward),
- Environmental education (from the 1960s onward),

- Cultural journalism (from the 1970s), and
- Place-based education (from the 1980s).

Each of these movements persists to this day, and information about all of them is readily available on the Web and in libraries. Of all these forms, however, only place-based education—because it does focus on the particularities of place—synthesizes the big picture of community in much the same way that this chapter does (for a thoughtful consideration of the link between critical theory and place-based education, see Gruenewald, 2003; for a readable overview of place-based education, see Smith, 2002).

Because the disconnection with communities (of whatever sort) is so prevalent in U.S. schooling, principals face stiff and interesting challenges when they try to refocus educational purposes on community. In such a situation, the best strategic advice may be to work steadily in a low-key manner to make the border between school and community more porous.

The opportunities to do this work are, in fact, numerous: using community people to teach (especially in informal roles), finding places where students can be taught outside the school, involving more students in service-learning activities, revising curriculum to develop a community theme across the curriculum, altering pedagogy so that demonstrations and apprenticeships displace lecture and seat work, holding events that draw community members to the school (these should *not* be ones that directly help the school, but should instead be those that easily show the school helping the community), getting teachers to visit families in their homes on a regular basis. So many things are possible, but, in our experience at any rate, comparatively few schools do these things. That circumstance, communitarians would say, shows how right they are about the disconnection between schools and communities.

Community as a Metaphor for School

Most communitarians argue that schools can hardly contribute to the well-being of real-time local communities if they fail in their own operation to embrace communitarian principles (e.g., Tam, 1998). They argue, in fact, that the metaphor describing the structure of mass schooling ("organization") is ill-suited to the work of education, and that the concept "community" is a more appropriate way of thinking about the social entities we call "schools" (Sergiovanni, 1993, 1994). According to this line of thought, which is advanced by some communitarians but not all, schools that are run on an authoritarian, individualist, and custodial basis will never have the resources or the courage to engage the real-time communities from which they draw their students. They would have no basis even for talking about community, let alone practicing it.

In this sense, then, an additional place in which to start rebuilding connections to communities is *within* the school. The previous section outlines the substantial work already done that could be useful to principals interested in cultivating connections with real-time communities. This section focuses on the parallel work that might be done within the school.

One point to remember here, however, is that some of the work needed to connect schools with communities takes place within the school and some outside. Moreover, the community inside the school is a metaphorical community, as Sergiovanni (1994) recognized, and it is important to remember this fact. School communities—especially in consideration of compulsory attendance laws—lack the organic quality, the durability of members, and the presence of families and, in fact, of varied other embedded institutions (churches, businesses, civic organizations, local government), that comprise what this chapter calls "real-time communities." Nonetheless, schooling can be conducted to focus on a common good rather than on benefits to individuals, even exclusively within the school.

Educators, of course, are more comfortable working within the walls of the school and within the organizational boundaries of the school system, and this makes the temptation to focus solely on within-school community very strong. Teaching and leading within schools is already very difficult work, after all. Communitarians would argue, however, that making connections to real-time communities will make that already difficult work more successful in the long run by building better local regard for educators, more commitment from students, and stronger community ownership of the school (e.g., Howley, Pendarvis, & Woodrum, 2004; Sergiovanni, 1993; Sobel, 2004; Tam, 1998).

Finally, educators who embrace the idea of schools as communities must understand that they are embracing a progressive view that can be an uncomfortable fit with many traditional real-time communities. This situation is by no means a reason to reject a communitarian approach to leadership in such places, however. Rather, such an observation constitutes a reason to take care. A school with an aggressive vision of itself as different from the real-time community from which it draws its students is likely to widen the prevailing school–community gap—whatever the perspective from which the principal operates. Many traditional communities would welcome a communitarian approach that takes up stewardship of the community as an important contribution of the school; indeed, many local school board members in traditional communities already operate from such a vantage.

Shared Vision

What is needed in schools on which to found community? Many writers agree that *shared vision* is a starting point, or a passage along the way. From the communitarian vantage, however, this shared vision is not an abstraction that might take any form. A shared neo-liberal vision (common in many fine suburban high schools) would be considered inadequate by communitarians. They want, rather, to see a *shared vision of the common good.*

Most communitarians insist that the common good be sufficiently generous to include everyone in the group (in this case, the school). A common good that ignores the needs of the least privileged members of the community is a particularly impoverished misconception, as is one that privileges the needs of the most privileged members. Again, too many schools—especially those fashioned on the metaphor of the factory—operate systematically to the advantage of the already advantaged (see Lankford, Loeb, & Wyckoff, 2002, for a recent example of this tendency).

An active leader operating on communitarian principles would help a community articulate a worthy vision of its own good. Subtle and difficult, the work has to rest on long experience of grappling with this issue already. It's not something that can be taught in a lesson, but an adept mentor could show a receptive apprentice a great deal about the struggle. The alternative to such good fortune, again, is reading. Sergiovanni's (1993) *Building Community in Schools* is a decent place to start.

Keep in mind, however, that the point of this work is not merely to supply, within the walls of the school, the community absent from, or deteriorating in the real world. That's a project unlikely to succeed. If community disappears outside the school, it is unlikely to thrive within it. Schooling can hardly be a special treatment for children suffering from deteriorated real-time communities. Rather, from a communitarian perspective, the point is to reconnect schools and communities in order to help realize, locally, a more vibrant connection *between* the real-time community and the school to benefit the common good. Whether any of this can be achieved widely is surely anyone's guess. Some reports, however, suggest that schools located in all sorts of communities are succeeding to some degree (e.g., Hutchison, 2004; Sobel, 2004).

Learning Community

The shared vision most commonly articulated in writings of within-school communitarians, not surprisingly, is the "learning community." In most existing schools, however, a community of learners would be a goal far more than a reality because of the enduring influence of the factory model of schooling: large size, bureaucratic organization, separation from community, primary emphasis on benefits to the individual ("education pays"), and accommodation to the needs of business and industry (e.g., Apple, 2000; Arons, 1997; Sher, 1995; Theobald, 1997). Creation of a community of learners under the factory model, as Sergiovanni and others have noted, is unlikely, and a far too common course of events is the insertion of a "small learning communities" initiative into a large factory-model school. The first casualty is likely to be the idea of community (Raynor, 2005).

As typically imagined, however, in learning communities, those who receive instruction, those who give it, and those who lead schools share a common fate determined by one another's success and failure. But what is the purpose of a learning community? Academic success only? Like shared vision, focus on the academic success of a learning community is not really enough to constitute a school as a community. The phrase again reminds us that "learning community" is usually a simulated community created in the school by educators, most often as another way to meet accountability requirements. Communitarians typically want to go further than this.

Among communitarians, Tam (1998, especially pp. 57–84) stressed the way in which schools might model, in intellectually relevant ways, the salient features of democratic communities. Tam was particularly concerned that students learn to explain and defend (with logic and evidence) ideas and positions, particularly in the spirit of collaborative inquiry. Visions like Tam's are notable for defining a strong common good, and not merely for meeting existing accountability goals. Improved equity is an urgent goal, communitarians would agree, but—they would also observe—neo-liberal schooling can accommodate it, as artifacts of the neo-liberal agenda suggest, for instance 2001's "No Child Left Behind."

One can press a bit deeper, however. Martin Buber's characterization of community in Sidebar 5-5 notably mentions comrades whose fates are bound together by a common enterprise and who are accessible to one another. In a learning community in particular, one might infer that the comrades should be intellectually accessible to one another. When teachers are intellectually accessible to students, and model such behavior themselves, however, they are teaching adventurously. Surely, one might think, in learning communities, adventurous teaching would be more evident than elsewhere.

Adventurous teaching, however, is enormously difficult because its central ideas contradict most human beings' understanding of what counts as knowledge and what counts as learning (Cohen, 1988). According to Cohen, adventurous teaching, in the spirit of intellectual accessibility, treats knowledge as contingent rather than definitive, and learning as actively productive rather than passively receptive. But this is not what most people think, nor how most teachers act, according to Cohen. Hence, learning communities may represent an aspiration for a quality of shared effort that rarely exists in schools and is completely uncharacteristic of the world at large.

On this logic, requiring that engagement with real-time community await the development of a learning community within the school could be a misguided strategy. It could drive school and community further apart. Principals most interested in building community in schools and those most interested in helping to sustain communities ought, perhaps, to consider that the two seemingly separate realms are mutually dependent: Neglect of one may undermine efforts in the other.

Talk and Civility

Schooling is practically all talk, even when demonstrations and apprenticeships are involved, and so the quality of the talk that occurs is extremely important to what is done (or what fails to be done). Ideas about adventurous teaching, moreover, are very much concerned with the quality of talk in schools. The kind of talk used in the classroom, especially from a communitarian vantage, determines what and how students learn. Bad talk is likely to constitute bad education, miseducation, and ignorance—just as bad talk makes for bad politics and bad laws.

This idea is not an abstract possibility, either. Rexford Brown in *Schools of Thought* (1991) wrote of "talkinbout" as the language of the typical mediocre classroom (see Sidebar 5-6). Talkinbout dances around the subjects of instruction without ever demonstrating, engaging, or using real knowledge—or inviting students to do so. It's a phony language that enthrones classroom subjects as dead things suitable for fearful worship, rather than as lively matters that require students and teachers to inquire about and actively address real problems, including real intellectual problems.

Sidebar 5-6

Talkinbout (from Rexford Brown's *Schools of Thought*):

Brown describes *talkinbout*:

> In most schools, the language of the classroom is primarily a language about the process of teaching something; it is not itself a language of learning. "Talkinbout" is … an adult reconstruction after the fact of an

experience that the student is not allowed to have firsthand. It is a rumor about learning. (p. 234)

And gives examples:

Ms. Burden asks, "What do you notice about Houdini and Boudini?" The students make some guesses, and finally one says, "The words sound alike," and she says, "Yes, they rhyme." She says, "Someone who does a trick is a ..." and the students all chime in at once: "Magician." When she gives directions, she says, "Do you have any questions?" The class replies in unison, "No, ma'am." (p. 17)

Ms. Bledsoe says, "This is to help us improve our written and oral what?" The class isn't sure, and so she says, "Speech, our written and oral speech" ... "What does a predicate adjective do?" she asks. (pp. 38–39)

A great deal has been written about the quality of classroom discourse in recent years, but classroom practice is difficult to change. Particular sorts of change are, however, needed if schools want to develop learning communities in which adventurous teaching and the sort of talk that sustains it are the norm. This type of change, moreover, requires extended effort. In particular, as Cohen (1988) noted, developing the kind of talk needed requires considerable forbearance on the part of students, teachers, and community members: a forbearance known as civility.

This sort of forbearance is not common in American society. The United States is known the world over as a brash and blunt society. Our public debates exhibit little civility; they are often vulgar, offensive, and even narrowminded, and it's no surprise that the public thereby comes to regard talk as a form of battle (as in "talk" radio), even a form of hate-speech. In schooling, moreover, talkinbout and other custodial practices make it hard for most of us to imagine how inquiry, discussion, and debate can be managed in the classroom—of all places—with civility. The word "civility" even seems quaint—outdated and weak. It seems to indicate a diffidence, or deference, characteristic of the interaction of lower orders with hereditary elites. That's passive civility, and it has too much in common with *servility* to appeal to Americans.

Civility has another meaning, however: active and respectful engagement with others (Walzer, 1995). "Forbearance" indicates the tolerance needed for such engagement in the name of working together, especially working together on difficult issues where differing views are likely, and where the differences need to be fully articulated and thoughtfully explored. By contrast, the factory-model of schooling seems absolutely to require force, muscle, and stringent discipline—the familiar range of authoritarian practices needed just to keep order.

This section of the chapter proceeds in three steps to the heart of teaching and learning in schools. Leadership is clearly needed to articulate shared vision, to build a "community of learners," to address connections with real-time community, and to cultivate the kind of talk capable of sustaining adventurous teaching. The discussion shows, at each step, the forms that hostility takes in factory-model schooling toward the proposals of communitarians. As David Cohen and others have noted, such resistance is to be expected. Dealing with that resistance is the work of leadership, especially a leadership grounded on the communitarian outlook.

Community of Leaders

The common good must be fashioned, by definition, by many people together, as they make inquiries and debate options. This is why communitarian principles reject authoritarianism (e.g., Tam, 1998), the polar opposite of distributed (or participatory) leadership. An authoritarian leadership cannot authentically cultivate the common good, even if under some circumstances it believes it knows what the common good is. (Nazism and Soviet-style communism are perhaps among the examples of such elite misconceptions of the common good.)

In schools that operate on communitarian principles, the need for distributed leadership seems evident, but how does leadership function in a communitarian framework? Initiating new work defines leadership in all contexts, but sustaining the work requires partners, and a communitarian leader, more than other sorts of leaders, needs allies and fellow travelers. It's not a solo act. There are two reasons.

First, as the discussions in this chapter indicate, the common good, from a communitarian perspective, requires the widest possible participation. Beginning this work in a school must start someplace, with someone; the principal, as positional leader in a school, is a logical center for the alliance, but the success of the effort depends on the creation of a "community of leaders" within the school. Charisma could be helpful to a principal, but it isn't sufficient and probably isn't even necessary. What is necessary to cultivate the common good, in an environment somewhat hostile to it, is an alliance of several like-minded people with the courage to initiate and sustain the difficult work: people who are open to each other, especially intellectually and emotional open (see, e.g., Meier, 1995).

Second, building and sustaining community in schools, and simultaneously connecting it to real-time local communities and sustaining it there as well, cannot even be begun alone. Keeping it going, in fact, means extending the leadership circle rather steadily, inside and outside the school—and helping to make the line between school and community increasingly more porous. In the end, ideally, this process increases the sense of agency—the capacity of people involved with the school to initiate work on behalf of the community (the common good), and the overall capacity of both school and community. Sergiovanni concluded his chapter on becoming a "community of leaders" with a brief characterization of the principal's role in such circumstances:

> What do principals do in schools that are becoming communities of leaders? Many things. They preach and teach, they encourage, they help, and sometimes they even yell and tell. But mostly they serve. (Sergiovanni, 1993, p. 189)

VIRTUAL COMMUNITIES, VIRTUAL COMMONS

The varied ways in which the word community has been used indicate the nature of the human struggle with the concept of the common good—the so-called "commons." One of the contemporary classics on communitarianism and schooling, Paul Theobald's (1997) *Teaching the Commons*, uses that concept—the commons—in the title. The term refers in particular to the practices and commitments that a group of people hold in common, but it also refers to the property that communities once actually held for the common use of all members—communal property.

Communal property sounds like a pretty radical idea these days, but it was once a very ordinary, daily practice (a commonplace, actually) for rural and urban people in Europe, and in the European colonies in North America. A residue of these practices exists in the name of Boston's central park, the Boston Commons. Common land was available to all members for grazing, wood gathering, and other harvests of naturally growing products. In some European places up through the early 20th century, town councils apportioned commonly held village lands for the use of farmers, every few years adjusting the allocations to take account of changed circumstances (Scott, 1998).

The idea of the commons as community property points back to a recurring theme in this chapter: the relevance of locality—of physical place—to the idea of community. In some of the definitions in the *Oxford English Dictionary*, all that is required for community, in fact, is local residence (much like the usual professional understanding of "everyone out there").

Metaphorical human communities, however, need not be restricted to any particular place (a stretch of land or a school, for instance). Humans can create virtual communities. The application of the metaphor of "community" in this way is very appealing, moreover, if one agrees with communitarians that the cohesive pull of communities has been damaged by the intrusion of neo-liberal commitments, practices, and institutions into everyday life. What can take the place of real-time community? One seemingly hopeful alternative is the rise of virtual communities. Why not, for instance, establish a virtual community of learners working together in a virtual school?

Communities of Place and Virtual Communities

Humans—unlike plants and animals—can make the leap from real to virtual communities because they have thoughts and languages with which to capture, construct, and convey knowledge. They can attach their affections to commonalities of thought, language, and understanding—to varied forms of culture disconnected from immediate, or even actual, location.

In fact, school communitarians like Sergiovanni, who focus almost exclusively on building community within schools, are, to a large extent, already engaging in this sort of move away from actual, real-time communities. Why? Arguably, any community created exclusively within a school is a virtual community. A number of things suggest the virtual character of in-school community—for instance, the few adults responsible for so many children, the characteristically total lack of other institutions in school, and the fact that the school community exists physically for only a fraction of the 24-hour day (the school being empty for most of the day).

The human need for community arguably remains strong, despite the contemporary assaults from a variety of quarters, so individuals are on the lookout for the opportunities that do exist to establish common bonds. Individuals today find considerable fellowship in virtual communities. Friends and lovers establish new relationships with inspiring frequency online; and groups of like-minded individuals discuss issues and take action because communication is so much easier, especially shared communication in groups. In fact, professional educators are especially good at establishing such communities and in finding fellowship in them. In particular, telecommunications has enabled many educators and educational organizations to sustain long-term contact with colleagues across district, state, and national boundaries.

This typical practice points up another aspect of virtual communities: They can flourish at the expense of communities of place, by absorbing energies that might otherwise play out locally, face to face. There's an irony here for educators. They can sometimes, maybe often, more easily find online community than real-time community.

Communitarian-minded principals, however, would arguably need to recall that the communities most likely to sustain democratic practices are not virtual ones, nor are they only the ones within the school, but the real-time ones of which the school is—or might be, or ought to be—a part. Like other leaders, however, principals working from a communitarian outlook may well begin their work alone, and taking part in a supportive virtual community of communitarian thinkers and activists would, for them, be a logical source of counsel, encouragement, and resources for the ongoing local struggle.

The Promises and Disappointments of Virtual Worlds. Beyond the notion of virtual communities as stop-gap associations to make up for the lack of real-time communities, the promise of a largely virtual reality seems to loom—an entire simulated world enabled with powerful electronic simulations. This is the realm of science fiction (e.g., StarTrek's "holodeck"), but it also connects with the ideas of some postmodern thinkers (e.g., Baudrillard, 1983; Lyotard, 1984). Rather than a utopian future (as in StarTrek), however, these postmodern thinkers see trouble in such worlds.

On the upside, virtual worlds could seemingly be designed to overcome the frustrations and shortcomings of the real-time world. Assistive devices for persons with disabilities, for instance, suggest a potential for good. On the downside, and according to many postmodern thinkers, the likely development and marketing of virtual worlds is dystopian, not utopian improvement of the efficiency and control of the existing global economic and political system (see, e.g., Burbules & Callister, 2000). Communitarians would also predict that the business of creating and marketing virtual worlds would be conducted with scant regard for authentic community—whether real-time or virtual.

The Global and the Local. Virtual worlds can be made sufficiently appealing that they will sell widely. The video game market quite clearly establishes this point. The market for such virtual realities—and arguably for all to come—is global. This means that the products created for it will exhibit almost no regard for local cultures.

Some communitarians argue that the scale of social organization is becoming so vast that the fabric of people's lives around the world is increasingly threadbare, with life (in an era of comparative security and abundance, at least in North America) apparently an unsatisfying experience for many people worldwide, including those in the developed world. Families and local communities are arguably the institutions that make life most meaningful, but in so many places around the world, the terms under which families and communities now operate destroy the meaningfulness historically associated with them, according to communitarians (see, e.g., Bellah, Madsen, Sullivan, & Tipton, 1985).

Increasing rapid geographic mobility, for instance, means that families have been scattered, and many towns and villages have become suburbs—indistinguishable residential zones where the residents seldom interact, and where no goods or services are produced, but only consumed. Moreover, the production of goods and services has been removed from communities and families and lodged in firms that grow larger and larger, selling their products over the entire globe. (For additional perspectives on the relevance of globalization to schooling, see chap. 11).

Sometimes the press of a one-world system is attributed to the United Nations as an authoritarian plot sponsored by international heathens. Most communitarians, by contrast, would find that globalization stems from the spread of business and commerce across national borders under the leadership of transnational corporations operating on, and further developing, neo-liberal principles (see, e.g., Burbules & Callister, 2000). They believe that the firms organize politics and international law, creating a world system, smoothing their global reach (for the argument from a globalization theorist, see Sassen, 1996).

Localities almost everywhere represent the past in such a scheme. Connecting deeply to localities, from the communitarian vantage, cannot ultimately be a central project of organizations guided by neo-liberal interests. Perhaps surprisingly, however, connecting to local communities is not a priority for some communitarians. The introductory discussion noted differences between communitarians whose focus was local, for instance Michael Walzer and Paul Theobald, and those for whom the nation (or even all humans) was the focus, for instance Amitai Etzioni and Henry Tam. The global communitarians articulate universal values that they believe can and should be embraced by all humans.

Readers should think about what makes sense to them, given these distinctions. Perhaps it is already obvious, but the authors of this chapter—without actually being communitarians themselves—tend to side with localists. Let us list some of the reasons:

1. Families and communities are necessarily local phenomena.

2. Experience suggests that durable communities are possible only when the members of them live together in the same place, and this view implies that places exist on a very small scale, that of villages, small towns, and neighborhoods—not of counties, cities, states, or nations.

3. A "sense of place" defines the humane experience of life on earth, and without such a sense, inhumanity arguably multiplies.

4. Negotiating right and wrong is a matter of local practice—situated practice, practice in particular places; claims of universal educational truths seem appealing, but ancient and recent history shows them as not very helpful abstractions—or fantasies.

5. Justice actually occurs only through local experience—in local action, but also in local inquiry, discussion, debate—and struggle. Humans have no choice but to learn to deal with another about difficult matters locally.

The local and the global will continue, inevitably it seems, to exist, perhaps in increasing tension, but each giving to and taking from the other. The perspective taken by any communitarian-minded educator may perhaps hinge on experience as much, or more than, on reading. Experience, however, comes in two forms for educators; professional and personal.

Very often, so far as schooling practices go, however, the two forms of experience are not talking to one another. A traditional mark of professionalism is objectivity: The education profession is bureaucratic in this way, partly to ensure impartiality. Personal involvement is commonly considered unprofessional. This is one reason teachers are advised not to teach their own children: They are said to be "too involved." This outlook, moreover, extends to educators' personal experience of places and communities, as the discussion has previously suggested. Communities, from the traditional professional outlook, are none of our business.

Interest in communitarian practices motivates some teachers and principals to question this norm. In many places in the United States, teachers are themselves local people, rather than transplants or transients. For such educators, a localist form of communitarianism can make a great deal of sense, but only if they can overcome the alienation from community that is a typical part of a teacher's training. For educators already personally disconnected from a particular place or from the idea of place, making this sort of sense can be more difficult, but it is still possible: One makes a home where one is.

Stewardship: Sustaining Intellect and Community

This chapter concludes with a brief look at a concept referenced tangentially earlier in the chapter: *stewardship*. The concept is a familiar one with a long history, but it has enjoyed comparatively little play in American schooling for a variety of reasons.

One theory for this oversight is that stewardship belongs to a different ethical code from the one so enthusiastically embraced by contemporary American culture. According to a leading urban communitarian, politics and commerce are founded on two distinct moral codes (Jacobs, 1994)—the guardian code (politics) and the trader code (commerce). The trader code perhaps prevails in neo-liberal practice, with ideas about business administration dominating writings about how to run schools. Ideas about market development, privatization, and innovation—all reflections of the trader code of morality—shape leadership in many schools. As a result, the guardian perspective may receive less emphasis in American schooling. Certainly, more and more traderlike practices have appeared in schooling in the past 20 years.

The point of the guardian perspective is conservation of the body politic, and in the case of the theory considered in this chapter, the body politic may be the nation or the world (for universalist communitarians) or the local town, city, neighborhood, or country place (for localist communitarians). Clearly, as we have seen, a schooling based on either version of communitarianism would cherish educational aims, and ways of doing school business, that differed from the allegedly dominant neo-liberal ones.

Now, Jacobs's analysis is more subtle than this short characterization of some of her ideas suggests, but this idea of differing moral perspectives does help explain why the communitarian notion that schools *should* play a role in sustaining communities is very much at odds with the conventional wisdom about what schools should do (preparing individual students to serve business and industry) and how they should be run (as business and industry is run). Communitarians seem to recommend—in the name of sustaining communities—the reintroduction of a guardian perspective into interpretations of what schools should do and how they should be run.

What sort of leadership might be appropriate? Communitarians—some grounded in the tradition of religious leadership—recommend "servant leadership" or "stewardship" (Greenleaf, 1977; Sergiovanni, 2000). Stewardship is leadership that focuses on conservation of the good that exists internally (to the locality or the nation—to the relevant "body politic") rather than on rapid adaptation to the demands of external forces. Inevitably, good school management does require such adaptations—but under the regimen of more stewardly leadership; it's a question of striking the right balance between conservation and adaptation.

We might predict that this sort of school leadership would be practiced more often in traditional, stable communities than in other places. We personally know school districts that are very traditional, in which a de facto concept of servant leadership and care for the local community is practiced. Because U.S. culture in general tends to be anti-intellectual, however, stewardship (e.g., of the school or of the community) does not always entail "stewardship of the intellect" (see, e.g., Howley et al., 1995). Nevertheless, absent a care for intellect— for a community's intellectual power—stewardship loses its potential to be generative. In some rural districts, for example, academic learning (which certainly might add to a community's intellectual power) is positioned as a tool that individuals use in order to escape from the local community (Howley et al.,

2004). Academic learning could, of course, be positioned differently—as a tool
for sustaining and building community. The arguments of some communitarians imply that, unless school stewardship nurtures intellect, it ultimately will
undermine community (see, e.g., Sher, 1995; Theobald & Curtiss, 2000).

CASE STUDY

Background

Jack Bobineau is serving his third year as principal at Jackson High School,
which enrolls about 1,400 students in Grades 9–12. The school is doing a barely
adequate job on the state accountability tests, but it isn't meeting the "Adequate Yearly Progress" goals under NCLB. The test-score gap between disadvantaged and nondisadvantaged students is proving to be persistent, as is the
gap between its small African American population and other students.

The School Situation

Jackson High School is a consolidated school, now the only high school in the
Lee-Kingston-Billville Unified District—known locally as "LKB." The school
serves a rather diverse student population, but is predominately White: About
40% of the students come from the affluent and growing town of Lee, which, in
the 14 years since the consolidated school was built, has become something of a
bedroom community. Most of those of students are in the college-prep track,
and they do exceedingly well academically, for the most part.

The rest of the students are a more motley crew. Most of the African American students, about 15 % of the student body, come exclusively from little
Kingston, which has a history as a center of African American population going
back to the years before the Civil War. Historically, Kingston was also a farming
community, but that history is long over. Its population, unlike Lee's, is slowly
dwindling. Only a few of the Kingston kids are in the college-prep track.
Billville is a working-class enclave due to the two light-industry plants located
there. About a third of these kids are in the college-prep track. Billville is
ethnically diverse.

LKB maintains three middle schools—one in each community—and Jack is
good friends with the principal at Kingston. Kingston Middle School actually
serves not only Kingston, but also the western section of the Billville area. What
concerns Jack is that the African American kids at Kingston Middle School do a
lot better there than they do at the high school. In fact, none of the middle

schools has any problem with its AYP goals. Jack's convinced that the Billville and Kingston kids—especially the Kingston kids—somehow "get lost" at Jackson High.

The Problem

All three middle schools are housed in the old high schools, which were consolidated to make Jackson High. The problem is that they are regarded as antiques, especially by board members from Lee, who are vexed that the district's children are housed in buildings with asbestos problems, heating and wiring problems, and unattractive locations in the middle of the towns. A building program is being discussed, and the issue seems to be which school to close—or where to locate a single middle school to serve the entire district.

How Communitarian Theory Helped

Ordinarily, the high school principal wouldn't worry much about what happens at other levels in the system. Not Jack. First, he understands very well that he and his school *are* part of a system. Second, he knows from his reading about communitarianism and from his experience (he grew up on the Kingston side of Billville township) that the system includes the three very different communities that feed his school. Third, he knows that something is right in the middle schools and something is wrong at the high school. Fourth, he's aware of the research that suggests smaller schools serve mixed-SES communities better than do large ones. If he had his way, he'd make the high school smaller and leave the all middle schools where they are. This is not at all an idle thought for Jack, because he has a shot at the superintendency in coming years. Chief in his mind here, though, is helping to do what's right for the system, and, with Jack, the foundation of that system is the communities. At the same time, he sees a link between what is right for the communities and what is right for their kids.

The Solution

The current superintendent, who recognizes Jack's leadership skills and community standing, makes Jack the vice-chair of the school-study committee. This gives Jack a "bully pulpit" from which to talk about the interface between kids' needs (as documented by test scores, a bit of evidence that compels some attention these days) and the attachment of Billville and Kingston to their schools.

At this moment, no one knows what the outcome will be. One thing is sure, though: Jack's position in the community and in the district ensures that his perspective will get a hearing, even from the two board members from Lee township. When it comes to a vote, Jack is pretty sure that the system will avoid what he regards as a catastrophe—the creation of a huge middle school that looks and functions like the high school.

Down the road, Jack is beginning to wrestle with how to make his school more personable for students, and more firmly connected to its three communities. There are lots of options, none of them ideal, but all of them a lot better than the status quo. He realizes, on one hand, that he may well make connections, in the coming school-study work, that will prove useful in the future, maybe even strategically useful. On the other hand, there's some chance that he may be looking for work elsewhere—but that seems unlikely.

CHAPTER SUMMARY

According to communitarians, communities are not just sources of potential support and aid for the work of the school, but constitute the reason for them. This chapter considers that perspective and what it indicates. At the core is the idea that schooling should not only reflect, but strongly implement, a vision of the common good. The idea of community, in short, represents one view of the common good.

The chapter describes essentially two communitarian positions—the universalist and the localist. Universalists regard community as capable of expression over substantial territory—a nation and even the entire world. Localists, by contrast, regard the common good as a project of local action and local negotiation.

The communitarian perspective is peculiarly useful for school leaders because it suggests why, lacking the glue of a common good (community), schools can become increasingly dysfunctional. Typical American schools are patterned, according to communitarian theorists, on a schooling that tries to advantage individuals in their future economic struggles. This sort of aim, moreover, tends to play out in schools that nearly all communitarian educators find to be too large—certainly too large to sustain community.

A major challenge for educators contemplating communitarian ideas is the traditional professional attitude toward community. School administration, in particular, has tended to view community as the enemy of responsible professionalism; the community as meddlesome busy-bodies (or worse). The 90% reduction in numbers of school board members since about 1900 is substantial evidence of this position. Moreover, in contemporary practice, and with this history as influential background, educators most often speak of cultivating community exclusively within school walls, in a metaphorical fashion. Unfortunately, the durable factory model tends to subvert even well-intentioned efforts of this sort (Raynor, 2005). For many communitarian theorists, by contrast, the community exists in real time and is situated in a particular place. Honoring place and the relationships it sustains, community members struggle equally to make ends meet and to make sense of life. That "making sense" of life, communitarians believe, is substantially strengthened by joint effort among strong democratic institutions, which should include the school.

6

Cultural Bases
of Leadership

Jerry D. Johnson

In this chapter, we describe the views of a wide range of writers, whom we call "culturalists," because their work focuses principally on educationally relevant ideas about culture.[1] What do we mean by "culture"? Sidebar 6-1 offers some insights from an anthropologist, Clyde Kluckhohn, and two leading culturalists, Raymond Williams and Clifford Geertz.

By the way, we use "culturalists" instead of "multicultural educators" because we're talking here about the idea of culture, and the interaction of leadership with culture, and not so much about multicultural education. Whatever they think about multicultural education, nearly everyone agrees that culture is relevant to schooling. That's because, in many ways, culture *is* education. Multicultural educators, of course, also observe that teachers and administrators are not typically *ready* or *able* to think and talk about cultural issues in productive ways (Chavéz Chavéz & O'Donnell, 1998; Howard, 1999; Jackson & Solis, 1995), especially about cultures other than their own. We agree. That's why this chapter is here.

In the U.S. context, though, educators in most schools remain aware of the cultural struggles of *people with darker skins*. (This chapter uses that down-to-earth phrase in preference to the inapt "minorities" or "people of color" in order

---

[1] This chapter considers the issues of culture, race, and ethnicity in national context, whereas chapter 7 includes treatment of these issues in the international context from the perspectives of the field of comparative education. Educationally speaking, *culture* is the overarching concept, and the chapter uses the three terms in common-sense ways, without engaging the academic disputes that swirl around them (see, e.g., Martin, 1997; and the evidence of such disputes in Sidebar 6-1).

to emphasize the fearfulness behind race hatred.) Readers will get the point, however, whatever the finesse.

The ideas engaged in this chapter apply to everyone, but they perhaps have the sharpest implications for those whom schooling actively disadvantages.

THE SCOPE OF THE CHALLENGE

Working well with people raised with different cultural outlooks and values from one's own—whatever the cultures—requires a broader understanding of the range of human cultural variation than most educators, seasoned and aspiring administrators alike, have so far been prepared to embrace. The United States continues to become increasingly varied culturally, and that has implications for how to lead schools. Considering the implications is just common sense for anyone who wants to be a principal. The main advantage, however, may be a better appreciation of the role of culture in education.

Sidebar 6-1: What Does Culture Mean?

Clyde Kluckhohn was an influential North American anthropologist (1905–1960). His *Mirror for Man* (1949, pp. 17–24) includes the following senses for "culture":

- The total way of life of a people. (p. 17)

- A way of thinking, feeling, and believing. (p. 23)

- A theory on the part of the anthropologist about the way in which a group of people in fact behave. (p. 23)

- A set of standardized orientations to recurrent problems. (p. 24)

A persistent issue in considerations of culture, however, is the difference between elite "high" cultures (fine art, classical music, poetry) and the supposedly "low" cultures of everyday life. Anthropologists like Kluckhohn focus on everyday culture, and generally ignore high culture. One of the great culturalists, Raymond Williams, insisted that the two were related as sources of deep personal meaning and were apparent in every human being:

> A culture has two aspects: the known meanings and directions, which its members are trained to; [and] the new observations and meanings, which are offered and tested....Some writers reserve the word for one or other of these senses; I insist on both, and on the significance of their conjunction. The questions I ask about our culture are questions about deep personal meanings. Culture is ordinary, in

---

every society and in every mind. (Williams, "Culture is Ordinary,"
1958/2001, p. 11)

Clifford Geertz, like Williams, was a great culturalist, and in the following
passage, Geertz wrote about how to study culture. Like Williams he took
meaningfulness as the root of culture:

> Believing, with Max Weber, that man is an animal suspended in
> webs of significance he himself has spun, I take culture to be those
> webs, and the analysis of it to be therefore not an experimental sci-
> ence in search of law but an interpretative one in search of meaning.
> (Geertz, *The Interpretation of Cultures*, 1973, p. 5)

Culturalists, in fact, argue that culture is the greatest institution of education: It encompasses language learning and use, ways of knowing about
things, and it harbors the potential and power that individuals access and
use. On this basis, it would be difficult to deny the relevance of thinking
about culture for school principals.

It's probable that most readers of this book will be White, non-Hispanics. It's
even more likely, however, that most people enrolled today in principal preparation programs will one day assume leadership positions in schools that actually
enroll students from cultural backgrounds that differ from their own. What
does this mean for our work?

It means, according to the culturalists, that schools of education should develop a school leader population that better represents the communities
schools serve (Darling-Hammond, 1997; Futrell, 1999; King, 1993; Siegal,
1999). Some states have undertaken broad-based and aggressive initiatives,
and a few—including South Carolina and Illinois—have met with considerable
success (see, e.g., Serafin, 1998; Thompson, 1992). Is this sort of thing sufficient
to meet the challenge?

No, say the culturalists. There's a life out there in the real world, and it influences how kids deal with school, how whole communities interact with schools,
and how differing cultures deal with the institution of schooling itself. All
school leaders, of whatever cultural background, need to work toward an understanding of the ways that race, culture, and ethnicity shape the everyday experience of ordinary people—their "life-worlds" (see chap. 5, and Sergiovanni,
2000). The effectiveness of a school leader, the culturalists would claim, depends in significant ways on the willingness to develop understanding of the relevant life-worlds—the everyday experience of belonging to a culture.
Objectively, of course, even those who remain skeptical about the ideas of the
culturalists or about the value of multicultural education need to pay attention

to race, culture, and ethnicity, because equality among ethnic groups is now a prominent goal in the nation and all the states (e.g., NCLB).

The Tough Work of Engaging "Other" Cultures

Engaging unfamiliar cultures is tough work because, as the views in Sidebar 6-1 suggest, cultures are strongly bound to personal identity, and encountering (and even contemplating) cultural differences is, for that reason, always personally unsettling. This is no mere academic observation, either.

As North American society grows ever more culturally varied, the terms "majority" and "minority" will reverse their meanings (changes that are well underway, incidentally). The identities of millions of individuals are involved in such changes—including those of nearly all educators who are beginning or in the middle of their careers. The culturalists argue that we have no alternative to engaging in this tough work, and we can get the best results by doing it thoughtfully, rather than in fear and haste.

Of course, one reaction is to retreat into denial and isolation: "How dare 'they' (the minority) overwhelm 'us' (the majority)?" Such retreats lead through sentimentality and nostalgia to hate acts, according to some observers (e.g., West, 1999). Looked at in a nearsighted way, this cultural work can be unpleasant, especially for White people, many of whom are unused to it. It requires us (them) to be discomfited, decentered, doubtful of things taken for granted, and open to other ways of encountering life and making sense of it. It asks us (them) to deal with some very uncomfortable or seemingly unbelievable features of the real world such as race hatred, de facto segregation, white privilege, justifiable outrage, elective separatism (e.g., "Black separatism"). Not only are these issues unpleasant, but, for many White people, including some educators, the issues remain just so much liberal clap-trap; knee-jerk reactions arising from a foolish misunderstanding of the dog-eat-dog quality of the real world.

The culturalists, however, find that all of these issues—race, culture, and ethnicity—are very much a part of the dog-eat-dog "real world" and so deserve attention on those terms at the very least. However, more than cultural *understanding* is required of educators, whose work, after all is to help others learn. Educators, in the view of the culturalists, have to use cultural knowledge to help others learn, and principals have to lead schools in this direction. We don't see much of this sort of thing represented in contemporary educational standards, however.

The Demography of School Administration

Contemporary American society presents schools with a challenging paradox:

1. The United States is a multiracial, multiethnic, multicultural society, and our K–12 student populations are even more diverse[2] than the society as whole, *but*
2. The staffing of schools and enrollments in preparation programs are dramatically less diverse than in either schools or society at large.

To begin this chapter's engagement with the influence of race, culture, and ethnicity on schooling and school leadership, then, let's consider these two issues; (a) the cultural misalignments that result from the poor representation of minorities in school leadership, and (b) the pressures on some school leaders to make accommodations to the "White mainstream."

Cultural Misalignment

Students in today's K–12 schools make up an exceptionally diverse population, but minority and majority proportions are moving in opposite directions—the minority is growing as a percentage of total population, whereas the majority is shrinking. See Sidebar 6-2 for some of the illustrative statistics.

As the minority becomes the majority of students, however, their teachers and especially their school leaders are likely to remain largely White. Just five percent (around 150,000) of America's three million K–12 educators are from racial minority groups—*a drop from 12% in the 1960s* (American Association of Colleges for Teacher Education, as cited in Futrell, 1999). And a mere 5% (401) of 8,029 superintendents from a 1998 survey were members of minority groups (Siegal, 1999). In fact, of the nation's 85,000 schools, *more than 40% do not have a single person of color* on their faculty (National Center for Educational Statistics, as cited in Darling-Hammond, 1997).

Sidebar 6-2

Trends That Tell of Things to Come

- Approximately 52 million students attended K–12 schools in the United States in 1999.

- Of that 52 million, approximately 35 % were from families classified as linguistic- or racial-minority.

- By 2008, the total number of school-age students is expected to top 55 million.

---

[2]The diversity of the population is increasing more sharply among the young, in part because of immigration and in part because of differences in birthrates among "majority" and "minority" cultures.

> • By 2008, nearly half—49%—of that 55 million will belong to linguis-
> tic- or racial-minority families.
>
> (Source: *National Commission on Teaching & America's Future*, as cited in
> Futrell, 1999.)

Clearly, the demographic makeup of the K–12 profession does not reflect the
pluralism of the students they serve or the communities in which they operate.
We might call this a case of *cultural misalignment*. So what? What makes this lop-
sidedness of the profession significant in the eyes of the culturalists?

The significance, they might claim, lies in the strong impact of the hidden
curriculum inevitably imposed on children in school (see chap. 9). The argument goes something like this:

1. Schools are the primary institutional entity in most children's lives,
and schooling goes a long way toward shaping the ways in which children
come to view power and authority.

2. Most children therefore spend their formative years in a place where
power and authority are exercised and controlled mainly by White males of
European ancestry and where darker-skinned people (if there are any)
most often fill subsidiary roles as secretaries, or cafeteria and custodial
workers.

3. Repeated exposure to this pattern is a cultural lesson of schooling:
*Children learn that White men are the bosses for whom others (perhaps people who
look like them) work.*

The culturalists suggest that this lesson is miseducation, and that, to the
contrary, people from all cultures can be and *are* leaders, and so they should
be principals. A logical alternative to the conclusion of the culturalists, of
course, is simply to accept the lesson of the hidden curriculum as valid, to believe that there *is* something inherent in White males that makes them the
best leaders, and something about White people that makes them better humans than other humans. Those who take this alternative, however, need to
know that such views are practically a dictionary definition for "racism" (see
Sidebar 6-3).

Lack of demographic symmetry is not the basic problem, then, although
news stories about "quota systems" and "affirmative action" make it look that
way to many people. The disparity is a symptom of racism: personal racism and
institutional racism. The flip side of racial discrimination (prejudice and oppression directed against dark-skinned people) is White supremacy.

Sidebar 6-3

Racism and Race Hatred: Two Definitions and a Culturalist Reflection

Racism (Gove, 1976, p. 1870):

> The assumption that psychocultural traits and capacities are determined by biological race and that races differ decisively from one another, which is usually coupled with a belief in the inherent superiority of a particular race and its right to domination over others. (*Webster's Third New International Dictionary*)

Racism (Tasmanian DE, 2005, ¶ 3):

> The assumption of superiority of one group over another, based on real or perceived racial characteristics and/or culture. Examples of demonstrated behaviours: demeaning and excluding individuals and/or groups; prejudices and fears based on real or assumed stereotypes and ignorance.

Raymond Williams (*Keywords*, 1983, p. 250) writes tellingly about race hatred. He observed that race hatred is founded on a confusion of meanings for "race" and that this confusion (a) enables cruelty and bigotry and (b) disables our linguistic capacity to be fair:

> Physical, cultural, and socio-economic differences are... so confused that different kinds of variation are made to stand for or imply each other. The prejudice and cruelty that then often follow...are not only evil in themselves, they have also profoundly complicated, and in certain areas placed under threat, the necessary language of the (non-prejudicial) recognition of human diversity and its actual communities.

Recent work on the human genome suggests that the variations in physical appearance by which humans have traditionally identified themselves as so very different are genetically superficial. Such differences as skin color are not, in biological fact, associated with systematic differences in capacity or talent, let alone a constellation of systematic differences capable of establishing "race superiority." Out of fear and ignorance of each other, a fear that attaches itself to *how we look*, humans very often respond with bigotry and cruelty.

Now, Williams's analysis suggests a startling role for educators, because the fear, bigotry, and cruelty that are the hallmarks of race hatred, in his view, deepen our collective ignorance of each other. Surely deepening ignorance is the enemy of education. The culturalists, therefore, see a profoundly educative purpose in antiracist education.

Comparatively few writers suggest that African American, Mexican-American, or American Indian students can learn well *only* when they are taught by people with similar backgrounds, although a reasonable argument can indeed be made. Instead, most culturalists argue, the relevant cultural issues need to be taken into account, and addressed in the everyday practices of schools—in all schools, but especially in those with student populations that come from differing cultures. One team observed that

> when the dominant ideological discourse tolerates diversity as a cultural value while the effective cultural practices, in society and in the school, promote the exclusion of ethnic and cultural groups, the effect for the minority child is one of great confusion with negative consequences for his or her development. (Lima & Lima, 1998, p. 335)

These writers are talking about double messages, and the passage implies that when it comes to valuing culture, schools need to "walk the talk" because double messages are as harmful in school as they are in family life.

Imagine that a basically authoritarian school leader reluctantly agrees to allow his school to hold a culture fair, but he continues to act in autocratic ways among students and faculty, and he continues to act like the community and parents are the enemy. In this case, one message—the far weaker one—says "We value you and your culture." The other—the stronger and louder one—says, "Shut up; stand back; keep your hands in the air" (see, for example, Sherwin & Schmidt, 2003, on the connection between school and prison for African Americans). According to many writers, double messages of this sort are given to poor people, especially poor people with darker skins, all too often in our schools and in our society (e.g., Purpel, 1999; Sergiovanni, 2000; Spring, 1994; Theobald, 1997).

So, although there may be definite benefits for any child of being educated by teachers with backgrounds similar to their own (King, 1993), it is not, according to many culturalists, a *necessary* condition of learning. Others also note that in monocultural locales, understanding the cultural diversity of the world may be an even stronger need, and one with its own challenges.

One more point, to illustrate the extent of this problem, and to extend the application from *schooling* to *school administration*: The passage just quoted (Lima & Lima, 1998) is taken from a discussion of the schooling experiences of *immigrant children in France*. It's been argued that the struggle of these children to adapt to a new culture is a lot like the struggle of minority teachers in joining the ranks of school administrators. Here's the argument:

1. Leadership traits are influenced by cultural background (e.g., Washington, 2005).

2. School leadership has long been an exclusive domain of White males.[3]

3. For this reason, the "culture of school leadership" is that of White males.

4. Leaders with darker skins enter organizational cultures that present them with challenges the organizational culture doesn't usually recognize.

Much like the immigrant children in the cited study, aspiring school leaders must make difficult decisions in the face of differences between their own culture and the dominant culture into which they have stepped.

Pressures to Make Accommodation to the White Mainstream

Minority school leaders, operating from primary cultural experiences different from those of the dominant culture, offer distinctive perspectives that could benefit schools and districts. All too often, however, the educative potential inherent in their cultural experience is lost, or its impact diluted, by the pressures on minority school leaders to assimilate to a "culture of leadership" informed by the primary cultural experiences of a White mainstream. We turn, now, to a consideration of this situation.

Although they are poorly represented in the profession, American K–12 schools and districts *do* employ *some* minority administrators at present. According to the National Center for Educational Statistics (2002), in 1999–2000, there were a little over 12,500 minority principals in the nearly 120,000 public and private schools in the United States.[4] As previously suggested, moreover, most of these principals—from a culturalist perspective—operate within an organizational leadership culture that owes its assumptions to White privilege.

The extent to which these minority administrators retain the diverse perspectives they bring to the table can be approached through the culturalist lens of assimilation. Bill Hing (1997) drew on Gordon's (1964) theoretical work in describing the processes involved in the assimilation of an immigrant group into a dominant culture. Gordon's theory consists of two parts: (a) acculturation, or *behavioral* assimilation; and (b) structural, or *social*, assimilation. In behavioral assimilation, members of the immigrant group exchange their original ways of

---

[3]That is, White non-Hispanic males; see chapter 8 for an examination of feminist theories as an alternative grounding for leadership.

[4]The representation of minorities in the principalship is increasing in public schools, but it has remained about the same in private ones according to NCES (2002).

acting (cultural patterns) for the patterns of the dominant culture. Structural or social assimilation, on the other hand, is the actual large-scale acceptance of the immigrant group into the receiving society.

Behavioral Assimilation. It's no coincidence that acculturation comes first in the paradigm. To be accepted by the receiving society, immigrants have to reject (or at the very least, hide or obscure) certain aspects of their own culture in favor of those of the dominant culture in the host society. This is often an individual act, and it is inherently lonely. For an immigrant, acculturation means denying or disposing of much of what comprises individual identity, a loss that can sharply disrupt individual development (e.g., Lima & Lima, 1998). The loss is akin to an earthquake, and the resulting split or shakeout can be so great that it compromises both social and intellectual development.

Are the dangers less for, say, an individual African American or American Indian joining the ranks of school administrators than they are for immigrant children? After all, such people are already adult Americans, not really immigrants. They've been fully socialized to American society, right? Not quite, argue the culturalists. Ethnic groups—principally those with darker skins—can easily remain outside the dominant cultural mainstream, consistently experiencing constricted employment options, more prevalent poverty, and bad schooling—from generation to generation

This is where institutional racism comes into play with special force. The history of exclusionary practices is sedimented, layer by layer, in U.S. institutions, the culturalists would argue. Institutionally, to White people, these practices appear "normal." (Evidence of race-based disparity in views of reality is apparent in nearly all polls that contrast the view of African Americans and Whites on race issues; in general, the two races see remarkably different and very durable versions of reality.) In the case of aspiring administrators from varied non-White cultures, these "normal" (White) practices constitute sharp challenges to be met with either few organizational resources or none. This situation is arguably the result of a long history, and it seems that only a long struggle will change institutional practices. Without this sort of change, argue the culturalists, schools and districts lose perspectives that would otherwise contribute to their organizational vigor (cf. National Commission, 1987).

Structural Assimilation. Structural assimilation would seem to occur with a reasonable degree of acculturation—perhaps very little; "the salad bowl" metaphor of North American culture as opposed to "the melting pot." For members of the cultures that most concern some of the thinkers in this chapter (African Americans, Mexican-Americans, and Indian cultures, for instance), structural assimilation has been slow. This means that administrators entering the ranks of the profession from these cultures are faced with a continuum from cultural capitulation at one end to cultural separatism at the other. (Don't forget that demographic reality suggests the need of the profession to welcome these aspiring administrators.)

Capitulation—giving up one's culture and the perceptions and perspectives grounded in that culture—is the seemingly easier choice. Culturalists suggest, however, that capitulation damages both the school leader and the school itself.

Of course, in contrast to a culturalist perspective, education leaders can think it a proper goal for schooling to reproduce existing society exactly, with all its inequities and injustices. Many people think this way, and it should not surprise anyone. It's simply another mark of the enormity of the task proposed by the culturalists.

CULTURAL, TRANSFORMATIONAL, AND OPPOSITIONAL LEADERSHIP

The perspective described in this chapter may imply that U.S. society requires a fundamental transformation. From the culturalist vantage, such a transformation is fundamentally cultural. It's well to remember that stewardship of culture is a traditional role for schooling—conserving it, conveying it, cultivating it, and developing it further. This is the rich cultural purpose of education to which Raymond Williams alluded in Sidebar 6-3 (see also Williams, 1961).

Writing at the close of the 20th century, the education critic David Purpel (1999) offered this observation on where America stood as a nation:

> In the United States…culture that emphasizes competition, conquest, and domination at the expense of compassion, caring community, and dignity…a growing…fear and loathing of the other. A dismal record indeed for a talented and enterprising people and a shameful state of affairs for a powerful and wealthy nation…founded on the principles of liberty and justice for all. (pp. 187–188)

At this juncture, an important question to think about from the culturalist perspective is: *Does schooling contribute to these problems? Can it contribute to resolving the problems?*

Educators have asked these questions since the establishment of public schooling, but they are especially important questions for prospective educational *leaders*. Culturalists argue that such questions are more educationally important than questions like *Which reading program works best for preparing fourth graders for a proficiency exam?* or *Which attendance software package offers the greatest versatility for administrators?*

Questions of this sort will inevitably seem more educationally relevant to most teachers. That's because the way of talking about professional matters with which most teachers and aspiring administrators are familiar is the one focused almost exclusively on psychological perspectives and explanations, on the study of things like learning theories, human development, instructional methodologies, or curriculum planning (Shapiro & Purpel, 1998). It's a huge leap to consider the questions deemed important by the culturalists. The perspectives of culturalists, however, give one reason for extending administrative practice beyond the usual structures of technical rationality (see chaps. 2 and 3): Education is culture, they claim, and according to them, schooling can and should become more educative by better engaging cultural meanings (both "high" and "low" cultural meanings).

School leaders who choose this way of looking at things find that they have to confront the norms of professional school administration. The confrontation, however, leads from the profession to entrenched parts of American life, and ultimately to the underlying power structure. If this sounds like dangerous work, it's important to remember that leadership is dangerous work—no danger means no leadership. Of course, each sort of leadership perspective is associated with differing interpretations of the dangers and to differing sorts of action. When we choose our leadership perspectives, then, we choose our dangers—and our likely battles.

Exactly this sort of work, however, is what transformational school leaders undertake as their defining purpose. It's not for everyone, but it is particularly germane to leadership from a culturalist vantage, as the next sections demonstrate.

We turn next, then, to practical implications: (a) cultural identity as a grounding for leadership, (b) oppositional leadership in the face of power politics, and (c) leadership as moral outrage. These issues can be grasped as a three-step sequence from orientation to contextualization to application. For example, imagine the organizational leader, grounded in a strong sense of cultural identity, attempting to enact transformation in a highly politicized environment, and responding to barriers to transformation with moral outrage. This progression characterizes many recipients of the Nobel Peace Prize, incidentally, so it's easy to see that they apply to transformational leadership.

Cultural Identity as a Grounding for Leadership

By definition, new visions of the possible have always been enacted by transformational leaders. Ghandi, King, Mandela, and others brought about sharply different social arrangements than had previously been thought likely. Significantly for our discussion, the transformations brought about by their leadership have cultural as well as social implications. The idea that cultural identity is a foundation for leadership, at least as conceived in this chapter, turns as well on the leader's sense of social justice, and thus shares some of the insights of "moral leadership."

Leaders who work to transform an organization, according to many observers, operate from a well-defined core set of beliefs held by their organization and about the legitimate uses of organizational power (e.g., Sergiovanni, 2000). They operate from passionate commitments. It's important to recognize, however, that their commitments stem partly from an intellectual grasp of matters; ethics, after all, is a subject that demands considerable thought, particularly when the ethical issue is how best to enable social justice. The transformational leader is an agent of a larger purpose—and that kind of commitment can only evolve from deep within the individual, brought into being by reflection on personal and professional experience.

Moreover, the culturalists would note, the imagined transformation is inherently cultural (Abalos, 1996; Connell, 1993). This means, first, that such leaders believe that schooling is an extension of American society, and of the dominant ideologies operating in that society (see chap. 13). Second, the leaders also understand that changing the purposes and practices of schooling means challenging the dominant ideology. School leaders can't do this without a thorough understanding of the organizational cultures of their schools and, at least as important, the cultures of the students in them. But in order to reach those understandings, leaders must first develop a clear sense of their own cultural identities and those of their students and faculty. Thus, cultural identity can and should embolden the individual to develop the kind of ideological center and passionate commitment essential for dramatically changing organizations for the better.

Certainly, this claim seems relevant for school leaders grounded in the cultural experiences of historically dominated groups (e.g., Mexican Americans, African Americans, American Indians, Alaska Natives, Hawaiians Natives, Appalachians, the Irish in Massachusetts circa 1860). But cultural identity is something we all have—although many White people have difficulty identifying the cultural features of "whiteness." Whiteness, for the most part, entails unexamined assumptions relating to privilege, and these assumptions can be read as the mirror image of the lessons taught to African American children in the hidden curriculum. But White people—like Indians and African Americans—also have particular cultural backgrounds and ancestries that tie them to the previous worlds in which their families lived—in many cases, in poverty, bondage, or tragedy.

White leaders who are open to the culturalist perspective—that is, those who appreciate the educationally generative qualities of cultural engagement from an antiracist perspective (again, see Sidebar 6-3 for the educational connection)—can also claim the work of cultural leadership. This perspective cannot be reserved for one culture, although leaders from oppressed cultures may well find it instinctively compelling.

One awakens, perhaps, to the mission of cultural leadership. This awakening has two parts—an awakening to one's cultural identity as well as an awakening to the dynamics of cultural domination and the strongly felt need for transformation. Such an awakening can overtake anyone who looks long and hard at the relationship between culture and power in consideration of one's place in it. Passion for the mission, at least for school leaders, comes from assessing the implications for one's own life as it connects to the lives of students in the context of their families and communities. School leaders only rarely make these connections (as many of the theories considered in this book claim). With understanding one is freed to ask: What can I do? What dare I do? How can I do it with best effect? How will I manage the setbacks? What will success mean?

"Transformation" ought to be a frightening word. The recommendation that principals and superintendents become "transformational leaders" is given all too lightly, often, it seems, by those who have themselves transformed nothing. Transformational leadership is real leadership in the classical sense of history: thinking very big and being at the edge of monumental changes. Often, things go badly for transformational leaders, and so innate courage, imagination, and an appreciation of contingencies are essential. One's eyes need to be open wide.

Sidebar 6-4 tells the story of one principal who accomplished much as a cultural leader in her school. Although the story in Sidebar 6-4 concerns an African American principal in South Carolina, it shouldn't be too difficult for readers to transfer the scenario to other circumstances, including their own. In every local community and every local culture, similar arrangements are in play. Land-use controversy is a durable part of the human landscape, for instance, and for that reason, issues of justice are always at stake when land-use controversy erupts. By the way, the story of the principal in Sidebar 6-4 isn't over. She has a reputation and a following, and even without her old job, she retains stature and influence. In fact, according to Quigley (2005), community members organized and received approval to establish a public charter school. Guess who they want to lead it?

Sidebar 6-4

School Leadership in the Sea Islands: A Story of Cultural Leadership

During her 19 years as principal at the St. Helena Elementary School (14 as principal), Laverne Davis built strong links with the community, adopted a math program designed with the rights of African Americans in mind (the Algebra Project), saw kids' math scores go from the worst to the best in the Beaufort County School District, and helped establish a boys choir that traveled to Africa to give performances. The school, in 2002–2003, enrolled 638 students, 92% African American, and 82% of students qualified to receive *free* (not just reduced-price) meals.

Laverne Davis was dismissed in 2004 by the leadership of the large county district of which the school is a part. No reason was reported to the press at the time of the dismissal (Strueber, 2004). But a year later, school district officials were quoted as saying that the dismissal was the result of "repeated violations of district policies" (Quigley, 2005, ¶ 4). According to the newspaper story, the position has remained vacant for a full year (Quigley, 2005). What's going on?

One view is cultural. The people of St. Helena's Island, South Carolina, are part of the Gullah-Geechee culture. The fate of the culture is an issue of immense local importance. The Gullah are African Americans with a unique history (see final paragraph). Ninety percent of St. Helena's population is reportedly Gullah, whereas nearby Hilton Head Island (vacation resort of the affluent, including former President Clinton) has about 5% Gullah population (Betton, 2004).

What about Davis's dismissal? One journalist (Betton, 2004) has offered an interpretation of events related to cultural leadership at the school. According to community members with whom the journalist spoke, the St. Helena school, under Davis's leadership, made the community dangerous to the plans that commercial developers and local vested interests have for St. Helena's island. The children's pride in their culture, one interviewee reportedly claimed, "could ultimately instill a resistance in their children against selling off their birthright—and the prized land that underscores it" (Betton, 2004, ¶ 5). The battles over property, moreover, are complicated because the Gullahs reportedly practice a tradition of communally held property. (Communal land-holding is unstable when land is treated as a private commodity; see Scott, 1998, for one account.)

Oppositional Leadership in the Context of Power Politics

"Power pervades the social world as thoroughly as gravity pervades the physical world," wrote Patrick Moore (1999). Power, in this analogy to physics, exists as a differential. That is, if the balance of power is equal, then neither side in a power play actually "has" power over the other (Shuy, 1987, as cited in Moore, 1999). The transformational leader's role in changing the organization's culture and ideological foundation in the face of an existing power structure suggests that the goal is not "getting" power, but altering the balance of power. In this view of power, no defeat, and no victory can ever be permanent. The culturalists agree with this perspective because they understand culture as an inevitable struggle between stability and change (e.g., Bruner, 1996).

It is worth noting, however, that power is a negative force only when it aims at unworthy or evil ends. Indeed, effective educators (like the principal in Sidebar 6-4) are effective precisely because they exercise power for worthy ends. T. H. White's version of the King Arthur character (*The Once and Future King*, 1958) is a leader whose personal transformation takes him to this understanding of power. Operating in a world of "might makes right," Arthur comes to the realization that power can just as readily be turned to positive purposes ("might for right").

This observation is particularly important for leaders who want to transform a school from a culturalist standpoint. By their nature, they are underdogs. Their natural work is to challenge an existing power structure, using their side of the power equation to accomplish a worthy mission. How? We now look at an approach to engagement—"moral outrage"—that is centered on both ideological commitment and emotional honesty.

Leadership as Moral Outrage

The leader's approach to conflict deserves attention. Sergiovanni (2000) and others (e.g., Purpel, 1999) have argued for *moral outrage*.

One of the major themes in cultural leadership in American schools, as illustrated all along, is intolerance for racism—opposition to bigotry and cruelty. Such opposition, though, is not an end in itself; antiracist efforts are necessary to remove barriers to learning and to facilitate engagement with cultural issues, both low and high, that constitute the substance of education from the culturalist perspective.

Moreover, in this scheme, injustice can never be overlooked in favor of "accentuating the positive." Evil must be confronted. Given the commitments of this perspective, then, it's no wonder that a moral outlook on leadership prevails. The defining quality of "moral outrage," of course, is a passionate honesty, something Purpel (1999) saw as uncommon among school leaders:

> Rather than rage at the injustice of needless suffering, the culture and the profession instead persists in avoiding its responsibilities through a thorough-going process of denial that includes blindness, self-absorption, and victim-blaming. (p. 4)

One reason the approach advised by Purpel (and also by Sergiovanni) may seem shocking and impractical to principals is that for 100 years, the profession has trained school leaders in technical rationality (see chaps. 1 and 2). This training demands that one hide one's commitments so as to approach leadership dispassionately.

Purpel insists, however, that rationality alone is insufficient for effective leadership (Purpel, 1999). School leaders must also, he claimed, be as passionate as their opposition, must be open about and make use of their passion, and must be willing to meet the opposition with an outrage grounded (in this case) in their cultural commitments.

SCHOOL-BASED LEADERSHIP MODELS

The concluding section of this chapter explores some of the ways that school-level leadership might respond to local cultures, particularly along antiracist lines. In general, school-based leadership seems to require a degree of autonomy, especially as part of the way a principal operates. Cultural leadership, in particular, requires it.

Great variety remains, of course, with respect to autonomy embedded in the way schools in a jurisdiction operate. In some states (e.g., some midwest and Great Plains states) more autonomy prevails at local levels (school and district) than it does in others (e.g., where district consolidation has resulted in dominant power favoring the SEA). But in any school organization, there is always work for a principal, the culturalists would argue, to foster schooling that engages cultural issues as a primary aim of schooling.

The discussion that follows examines school-based leadership from three vantages: (a) separatist impulses (intentional separation from the White, middle-class mainstream); (b) multicultural and antiracist curricula (fostering a culture of pluralism and respect within the school); and (c) identity politics and culture wars (school-level cultural leadership that is politically engaged). The third section is specifically framed to concentrate on the culturalist leadership understandings of the principal.

Separatist Impulses

Prospective school leaders interested in culturalist perspectives should realize that administrator organizations have worked toward district consolidation and the other forms of centralization for at least a century (e.g., Callahan, 1962; Peshkin, 1982; Strang, 1987). Centralizing tendencies—which, in addition to consolidation also manifest themselves in administrative regulations, requirements for curriculum and instruction, and accountability provisions—are seen by some as limiting the local cultural engagement of schools. Apparently just one state—Alaska—has even acknowledged standards related to cultural responsiveness (Alaska Native Knowledge Network, 1998), and these standards were created and apparently promoted by a Native coalition, not by the SEA. Centralizing tendencies have also been shown, not surprisingly, to constrain the scope of principals' leadership (e.g., Wiseman, 2003).

These two conditions—diminished cultural engagement and constrained local autonomy arguably associated with centralization—suggest that cultural leadership will often find itself opposing the fact and process of centralization. Thus, in extreme forms, the push for autonomy can result in separatist ideas and actions on the part of the leader, the school, and the local community: For instance, as African American schools run by African Americans and enrolling exclusively African American children, or as American Indian schools run on the same basis. There are, of course, substantial historical examples of such arrangements (see, e.g., Spring, 1994).

Hing (1997) provided a two-part taxonomy of separatism that can assist us in approaching this idea. The first, sociological separatism, is the version with which most Americans are acquainted. This occurs when people with similar cultures live together in one area or neighborhood. The other form is ideological or political separatism. This form of separatism is based on active rejection of the dominant culture, largely as a result of repeatedly frustrated aspirations. Ideological separatism, according to Hing, can result in physical separatism, but it can also exist as a state of mind; the perspective is not relevant only to African American, Hispanic, or Indian leaders. White principals who find themselves at odds with the cultural outlook prevailing in their district, or among a subgroup of teachers in their school, may find a separatist approach useful. Readers should realize that, whether in the wide world or within the culture of a single school, separatism is seen by some observers as undermining "the commons" (see chap. 5). One's assessment may depend on reading separatism, on the one hand as a tactic, or, on the other as a strategy. This chapter presents separatism as being more a tactical response than a strategic initiative.

Separatist impulses, especially political separatism, are a sharp challenge to those who actively promote a "multicultural" society in which individuals with adequate understanding and openness readily embrace cultural differences, valuing and expecting contributions from all corners of society. Hing himself gave qualified approval to the idea of separatism, and his analysis is consistent with the nature of transformational leadership as an oppositional project for leaders willing to undertake it.

Obviously, separatist impulses can lead to internal conflict that undermines the unity of an organization, and it's certain that conflict can disrupt the smooth process of schooling. Put another way, however, conflict can disrupt the objectionable business-as-usual process of schooling, a real benefit, according to the culturalists, if tendencies like institutional racism are understood as guiding the process of schooling (see Ayers, 1994).

Conflict can, moreover, sometimes constitute real education. The culturalists would advise that principals need to recognize this possibility and *sometimes*, wisely and forthrightly, to embrace it. Nicolò Machiavelli, the misunderstood 15th-century philosopher of political action, taught this very lesson. Battles need to be chosen, and carefully, he counseled.

Multicultural and Antiracist Curricula

The philosopher Terry Eagleton (1991) contended that members of marginalized groups must be actively taught the ideology that condemns them to their fate. Schooling, in this view, is one of the institutions that fulfills this task, and its teachings are delivered not only through the hidden curriculum, but through the overt curriculum as well. This is an unsettling thought because the overt curriculum, by contrast with the hidden, is widely understood as the major role of the teacher. Can teaching the overt curriculum well have serious harmful side-effects?

Good teachers struggle mightily to "get the material across" to students. The thought that the hard-won success of good teaching might be the undoing of some students (for instance, those with darker skins) will likely offend good teachers. How on earth can this disaster happen? Can this really be true?

According to culturalists, of course it can. See Sidebar 6-5 to see how the mathematics curriculum has been understood as racist.

Sidebar 6-5

Is Algebra I a Racist Plot?

Algebra I is the familiar course in elementary algebra taught almost universally in American high schools. This is their first chance to grasp the distinction between *mathematics* and *arithmetic*. Unfortunately, and for a variety of reasons, students too often retain little of what they are taught in the course. Many even become frightened of mathematics, without, tragically, understanding what it is (see Smith, 2002, for this argument).

Nonetheless, students *are* repeatedly told, and they *do* learn well, that completing these courses is required if they want to get into college. "College-prep" students receive this message relentlessly.

Guess what? The gateway to college really is Algebra I (Moses & Cobb, 2001). Students who don't complete it don't move on to the rest of the high-school math sequence, and find getting into college more difficult. Those who do complete Algebra I follow the path straight to college (more or less). This circumstance has caused Algebra I to be known as the "gatekeeper" course to college.

Guess what else? African Americans complete Algebra I a whole lot less than do White students (Moses & Cobb, 2001). They also attend college—of course—at a lower rate. Is the relationship causal? Unlikely, but the association is strong: African Americans don't accumulate the college-prep credits, which hurts, and their relative exclusion from the course teaches the lesson that mathematics isn't for African Americans.

Mathematician and civil rights activist Robert Moses founded the Algebra Project to disrupt this situation. See Sidebar 6-4 for the story of a courageous African American principal whose school joined the Algebra Project.

Now, none of this makes algebra a racist plot. Algebra is a delightful way of thinking (a claim that will surprise readers who have learned to hate math), and a delightful way of thinking *cannot* be a racist plot. What *can* be read as a racist plot, however, is the way curriculum and curriculum leadership far too often function in the way described. Sadly, in this account, curriculum and teaching can also subvert the learning of mathematics (see Stigler & Hiebert, 1999, for international comparisons with math teaching in the United States).

It's also easy to imagine that schools *might*, at least hypothetically, teach quite different lessons from those characterized in Sidebar 6-5. Teachers would ordinarily need appropriate help and guidance, of course. In fact, in the case of mathematics, the work of the National Council of Teachers of Mathematics is arguably relevant. For the Council, equity is the first of its *Principles and Standards for School Mathematics* (NCTM, 2000). The Council also supports dissemination of many versions of math curriculum it judges to be in step with its thinking. Only a minority of districts have adopted these curricula, and that track record is a partial indicator of how much effort it takes to make (arguably) appropriate changes.

The principal, however, is a logical arbiter or spokesperson for the appropriateness of any change. Changes designed and imposed by a national authority, for instance the NCTM, will often go badly in local places (Scott, 1998). After all, as leaders we ought to consider closely the ways that *what we teach* (curriculum) and *how we teach it* (viewed broadly, as not only instruction but how the school operates in general) define *who we are as a school*. Recommendations for change require local judgment, adaptation, and knowledge. One motive for this book is the insight that "best practice" is not the same everywhere, nor is it the same for every thoughtful educator.

Extending the culturalist argument a bit further, it's possible to compare the inequitable distribution of material goods in society to the inequitable distribution of curricular goods in schooling. The White professional upper middle class enjoys considerable net worth, and considerable well-being, whereas much of North American society enjoys considerable net debt and stress. Raymond Williams (1961) offered pertinent commentary on this idea, as follows:

> The cultural choices involved in the selection of content [will be seen to] have an organic relationship to the social choices involved in the practical organization [of society]. If we are to discuss education adequately, we must examine, in historical terms, this organic relation, for to be conscious of a choice made is to be conscious of further and alternative choices available. (p. 125)

Put simply, choices about what goes into curriculum follow the usual social distinction between the haves and the have-nots. This is why, as we saw at the start of this chapter, Williams insisted on the importance of both "high" and "low" culture—and about the meaning making that is the center of culture generally.

If the leader imagines a society in which everyone has a place in defining and sharing the common good, then creating a legitimate place for those groups in the school curriculum is a logical place to start. Robert Moses and colleagues are doing this for mathematics with the Algebra Project.

But another route is explicitly antiracist curriculum. Excellent materials (and instruction) of this sort might help to undermine the obstacles to learning created by some common ideas and images, and to pose new ones that more closely represent the complexity of the nation and of society. At least, this is what many multicultural educators claim, with arguable reason. Like establishing a degree of school-level autonomy or adopting a separatist outlook, however, the implementation of anti-racist and multicultural curricula is not productively viewed as an end in itself. An improved organizational culture, exhibiting the mutual respect of members for one another, and for one another's culturally based ways of acting and knowing is one end. A world of that sort is another end said to be worthy for education (e.g., Rorty, 1999).

Identity Politics and the Culture Wars

A further culturalist model for school-based leadership takes the principal beyond separatism and curriculum development to an appreciation of "the culture wars" in a national context (see Arons, 1997). Readers might ask "Why is what happens at the national level with 'culture wars' relevant to being principal of a local school?" One answer is NCLB. The Act has shaped the behavior of teachers and administrators in all public schools, especially those serving impoverished and minority communities. National battles clearly, and even directly, affect what happens to local schools. This influence, however, is not a new development. NCLB had decades of precedents, most recently (in the past 15 years or so): the National Education Goals (Executive Office, 1990), Goals 2000 (Goals 2000, 1993)United States Department of Education, 1993), and, of course, the various national standards and accountability movements.

Some readers may not think of these developments as battles, but it is good to remember that all reforms provoke resistance. Resistance always slows down the reform process. Moreover, resistance is often reasonable; according to Scott (1998) resistance is, in fact, usually a good idea. What actually happens when reforms are deployed, moreover, is always some sort of compromise between the official agenda and the agenda of local resisters (Scott, 1998). So, the national reform battlefield is strikingly relevant to the everyday life of principals of local schools. In the era of NCLB, of course, this assertion will now seem obvious to many educators.

Because the culturalists view culture as the foundation of education—not merely high culture, but most critically the ordinary, anthropological everyday variety of culture (see Sidebar 6-1)—they object to a one-size-fits-all curriculum fashioned for the undistinguished masses (e.g., Bruner, 1996). In the view of such thinkers, this sort of schooling is both miseducative (because it severs connections with relevant cultures) and undemocratic (both because it removes local voices from curriculum debate and because it excludes stories about injustice from the curriculum).

Stephen Arons, a law professor, defends the right of varied local cultures to determine the kind of schooling appropriate to their children. For Arons, using standing U.S. Supreme Court rulings to make the case, the national efforts are *unconstitutional* attempts to impose "official knowledge" on students in public schools (Arons, 1997). Instead of national standards and requirements imposed by national or state government or by professional fiat, Arons would have localities make their own determinations for good and ill (for a relevant example, see Rural School and Community Trust, 2000). Arons believes that the diversity of such a system—in line with an older American tradition—contributes to a vital society and a vital democracy.

Where do the culture wars come in? They come in over who gets to define official knowledge at national and state levels. Major battles, for instance, were waged over "history standards." Those proposed by historians drew complaints from education officials who had served in the Reagan and Bush I administrations. From the perspective of these former policymakers, school history was necessarily different from the practice of history by historians; school history should help create a single national identity, with stories of the founders, of American leadership in free trade, and of military valor. School history was to have a patriotic function, not an intellectual one (Nash & Dunn, 1995).

Every disciplinary field has seen the struggles, moreover—not just history and literature (e.g., Goodson, 1994), but also mathematics and science. In the case of mathematics, the standards articulated by the National Council of Teachers of Mathematics (NCTM, 2000) have come under concerted attack from some university mathematicians (e.g., Ross, 2001) who generally favor a larger role for memorization, formulaic approaches to problem solving, and extended practice sets than does the Council. Both sides to the debate make reasonable points, and both sides harbor extremists. The vexing business with the culture wars, however, is that sloppy polemic and outright propaganda tend to displace thoughtfulness, because the stakes (what counts as school knowledge) are so large.

Also at stake, from a more narrow culturalist perspective, is the answer to the question, "Whose culture is this?" The extremes of each side in the culture wars answer, "Mine!" The result of such warring is a polarization of national perspectives that makes conversation more difficult at best, and at worst, multiplies intolerance and hatred. The culture wars may represent a full-scale societal conflict about the meaning of life, and a great deal has been made of them in both the media and in the academy. The "wars" have arguably contributed to the political polarization of the nation evident since the 2000 presidential election.

Do the objections raised by the culturalists mean that schools should throw out the current curriculum, creating a new one that reverses the roles of who dominates and who is pushed to the margins? Should schools banish Shakespeare and Hemingway from the literature anthologies and replace them with Alice Walker and Maya Anjelou? This sort of reversal is apparently what many of the opponents of multicultural curricula fear, but bell hooks, prominent among culturalist thinkers concerned with curricular change at universities (where the culture wars are said to have originated), calls this fear "the gravest misperception of cultural diversity" (hooks, 1994, p. 32). Raymond Williams and bell hooks seem to take the broader rather than the narrower culturalist perspective. From their more broadly culturalist perspective, the question is perhaps not so much "Whose culture is this?" as "What does culture, and the phenomenon of culture, have to teach us?" The answers are very different. In this case: "Nearly everything!"

CASE STUDY

Background

Michael Raleigh became principal of East Malvern High School in July, 6 weeks after finishing his master's degree in school administration and 5 weeks before the start of the new school year. EMHS was located in an area of central Virginia that had retained some rural farming areas, but was largely a collection of suburbs providing a bedroom community for commuters to Richmond.

Michael had lived in the area for 5 years. He was originally from the coalfields area of southwestern Virginia, and his own upbringing was considerably different from his wife's. He'd been raised in poverty, and had "escaped" through a combination of doing acceptably well in school and exceptionally well on the football field, where he was a quarterback. A serious knee injury in his sophomore year, along with a previously unrecognized, and undeveloped, aptitude for math led Michael to finish his undergraduate years doing acceptably well as a football player and exceptionally well in the classroom. Following graduation, Michael was hired to teach math at Malvern Central High School. Michael recognized, even if he never openly discussed it with anyone, that *success* and *fitting in* went hand-in-hand for him—that is, being successful at college, in his teaching career, and now in his administrative career, meant not being like his family and the people he grew up with at home but, rather, being like the people he met at college and, now, the people with whom he worked in Malvern County.

The School Situation

Having been hired as principal in the summer, Michael inherited a school that was largely ready to go for the coming school year. The master schedule had been developed prior to the end of school, students had preregistered, teachers had been assigned the courses they would be teaching, and a few new teachers had been hired to replace retiring teachers. Thus, for Michael, the weeks before school was to start were not taken up by getting the school year ready, but by learning what was already in place and preparing to manage it. He learned it, and managed it, all the while making notes about what he would do differently when he had the opportunity to lead efforts for planning the next school year.

In early spring, as part of reviewing the plans for the coming year, Michael asked department chairs to meet with him to go over scheduling and budget matters. In his initial review of the math department back in the summer, Michael had noticed that the eight teachers in the department each had very few daily preparations, with all of the general courses taught by one of four teachers who, as a group, taught the courses through elementary algebra, with three others teaching geometry and Algebra II exclusively and the remaining two teachers responsible for the "higher-level" college-prep courses: trigonometry, precalculus, regular calculus, and AP calculus. A de facto tracking system at the middle school meant that students entering ninth grade would enroll in either an "advanced" course (geometry or Algebra II) or a "basic" course (e.g., prealgebra or algebra). These two teachers had an extra planning period, supposedly because of the difficult nature of their subject matter.

One of the things Michael was planning to discuss with the department chair, Susan Martin, was a practice they had employed at Malvern Central where every teacher taught at least one introductory course of integrated math, prealgebra, or Algebra I, and the other courses were rotated around a bit (within the bounds of qualifications) to keep everyone "fresh." The practice had been in place when he arrived at Central, so he didn't know a lot about the decisions involved in putting it in place. He knew that it meant that every kid (including kids who were tracked into a lower level at the middle school) had access to a wide variety of teachers, and that the best teachers taught both advanced courses and the "building block" courses that prepared kids for success at higher levels. He had been told that the change was controversial, but that was about it. He had found it to be a good system, that it improved his own teaching, and it gave students access to a wider variety of teaching styles and instructional strategies.

The Problem

Michael met with Susan Martin, the math department chair, on the first Monday in April. He set out to share with Susan his ideas about making changes to the teaching schedules in the math department, offered his rationale for it, and told her about his own experiences working in such a system and what it offered for him and for the students. Based on the scant knowledge he had of the experiences at Central, he was prepared for some controversy. Susan herself taught four sections of Algebra II, along with a regular planning period and a department chair planning period.

To his surprise, Susan was positive about his suggestion. She told him that she had long felt that the present system was demoralizing to the teachers who were "stuck" with only introductory courses, and that it also meant that only a handful of students ever got to experience the two really exceptional teachers who only taught precalculus and calculus. Her excitement quickly dissipated, though, when she began to tell Michael what kind of resistance he would face, which, she suggested, would not entirely come from the teachers. In fact, the teachers had tried to initiate a change of this sort a few years back and were put off by the principal. The real resistance, Susan told him, would come from parents by way of the division office. Parents in the community had come to associate high levels of academic success not only with taking higher-level math, but with taking Mr. Stevens or Ms. Skeens for higher level math. These were the teachers who taught "their" kids. If students received schedules indicating that they would have Ms. Kinner or Ms. Parks for AP Calculus, she predicted, parents would complain to board members, board members would complain to the superintendent, and the superintendent would send the assistant superintendent for instruction and assessment to persuade or, if necessary, direct Michael to change his mind. That their children would not necessarily have Mr. Stevens or Mr. Skeens because those instructors were teaching Algebra I for part of the day would satisfy neither the parents nor the assistant superintendent. Given some of the dynamics between parents, board members, central office staff, and school staff he had observed, Michael was not surprised by her prediction

Michael met with the entire math department and, with Susan, presented his plan. The department members were supportive for the most part, as Susan had predicted (the one teacher she had predicted would be displeased simply stayed quiet). Michael proceeded with his plans, and developed a schedule for the following school year that had every teacher teaching at least one Algebra I section, and with adventurous and young, but extremely well-qualified teachers assigned to precalculus for the first time. The call from the assistant superintendent came before he had even distributed the actual schedule to the staff. She met with him the same afternoon she'd called, and advised him, strongly, not to proceed as planned.

How the Culturalist Perspective Helped

Reflecting on what he had learned in his administrator preparation program, Michael recognized that nothing in what he had studied—school finance, school law, personnel administration, and the like—had prepared him for this. But he remembered reading about the cultural roots of schooling and learning.

This was the politics of power and influence, in which a working-class culture was pitted against a professional-class culture, with the school board and central office working hand-in-glove for the latter set of parents. Michael knew that giving more students access to the best math instructors in the building was right and good, and that developing the skills and broadening the experiences of younger teachers was an important part of his own job. He was also beginning to realize that the parents of the "AP calculus kids" could influence the way the school operated in ways that most other parents couldn't (in fact, wouldn't even *attempt*). There were no "AP calculus kids" at Michael's alma mater of Mansfield County High School, but he had traveled to other high schools to play football and he had seen what their schools and athletic facilities looked like compared to his own. Michael had experienced inequity firsthand. As he considered the situation he faced in light of his own experiences, he began to realize that he was, in fact, working to enact practices as the instructional leader of East Malvern that would promote equity, with his experience of working-class culture as the foundation of his commitment.

The Solution

This realization seemed to provide Michael with a sense of direction and purpose that he had been looking for. As the instructional leader of the school, Michael knew he had the legal authority to proceed with his planned schedule. He also knew that asserting that legal authority would not resolve the controversy, that it might not be resolved, or that it might be resolved by his dismissal or transfer. He was prepared for any of these outcomes.

Michael knew he needed to be proactive in responding to the questions and concerns of his superiors in the school district and to the parents, students, and community members he served. He began with his superiors by scheduling a meeting with the superintendent and assistant superintendent. At the meeting, he fully elaborated the instructional equity rationale for his planned changes, and spoke from the heart about what he saw as the moral and ethical bases for it. He stressed that the changes were made—and that additional changes would be forthcoming—in the interests of better meeting the needs of all students. Neither the superintendent nor the assistant superintendent questioned the validity of what Michael had presented; each, however, did attempt to caution him about making enemies so early in his administrative career. Michael explained that this was something more important than his immediate career trajectory, that he intended to be as honest with parents as he had been with them about what he stood for and what he intended. In any case, he explained that he was prepared to face opposition and consequences.

CHAPTER SUMMARY

This chapter examines some of the ways that schooling and school leadership in the United States is grounded in culture, including race and ethnicity, and it examines some of the ways that interested educators can use the culturalist vantage to lead schools. We consider the challenge of increasingly diverse K–12 school populations being served by relatively homogenous leadership populations, as well as the complexities of responding productively. Members of distinctive cultural groups—especially if they are dark-skinned people—who do become school leaders, however, confront pressures to change their cultural identities and conform to the schooling practices of a White mainstream. For leaders who resist assimilation, an in-tact cultural identity can provide a solid grounding for leadership, especially transformational leadership.

Transformational leaders, by definition, encounter opposition. The chapter suggests that for the transformational leader who operates from a grounding in cultural identity, such opposition is often broad-based and rooted in the power politics of the organization. With that in mind, the chapter examines the culturalist claim that leadership grounded in an individual's cultural identity is desirable and should be cultivated.

There are several ways that individuals might approach oppositional leadership in the face of a dominant ideology and organizational culture. One approach is leadership as outrage, wherein the leader responds to barriers to organizational purposes and abuses of power with a "passionate intensity." Another response is separatism and the chapter considers Hing's (1997) qualified support for separatist thought; school-level autonomy is a possible first step in enacting substantive change on such a basis. Third, antiracist and multicultural curricula can be deployed to assert varied culturalist conceptions—either on behalf of a specific local population or on behalf of the interplay of high and low culture.

The chapter closes with a discussion positioning these issues within the center of a much broader societal struggle, as examples of the ways that identity politics play out in the nation's culture wars. The chapter maintains that leadership perspective grounded in an understanding of the importance of culture is important and useful to school administrators in leading schools and school districts. From the vantage of the key thinkers in this chapter, culture is education, and a schooling that aims to truly educate must take cultural forms seriously, as the centerpiece of schooling, and not as an external threat to school leadership.

7

Schools and Administration in Comparative Context

James H. Williams

Anthropologists have been equated metaphorically with fish that are learning to see the water in which they swim (Spindler, 1982). To the fish, the water usually is invisible. Similarly, the features of a culture are usually invisible, particularly to those who live in that culture. Anthropologists and others who study culture set out explicitly to make its features visible. They believe that doing so promotes understanding of one's own culture and appreciation of the cultures of others. In the practical realm, moreover, cultural understanding provides a basis for evaluating the features of a particular culture in order to decide which ought to be preserved and which ought to be changed.

One way to make cultural features visible is to make comparisons between cultures. For example, whenever we travel or work in a country other than the United States, we experience cultural differences firsthand. Within this country even, when we move to a new and unfamiliar area or start work in a new organization, we begin to see differences between our everyday ways of doing things and those of other groups of people. These experiences prompt us to reevaluate the assumptions and ways of operating that we typically take for granted. Looking at familiar things comparatively is an important way to gain insight into our own practices and theories, especially those we have come to take for granted.

This chapter presents several comparative perspectives that help us examine schools, revealing important—but often taken-for-granted—characteristics of their cultures and the cultures in which they are embedded. Analyses from a comparative perspective involve systematic efforts to look outside or beyond one's experience and conventional ways of seeing and doing things, to others' experiences and to new ways of understanding and behaving. Analyses based on a comparative perspective yield insights that enable educators not only to make sense of what they see in their own schools but also to think about alternatives. A comparative, particularly an international, perspective is well suited to surfacing the basic underlying assumptions and systematic patterns of thinking that make up a worldview—whether that of a country, an organization, or even a person. This perspective is useful for all leaders interested in seeing common problems in new ways.

Of course, comparison can take place at many levels: One can look at other classrooms, other schools, districts, states, or regions. This chapter, however, focuses specifically on the comparison between schools in the United States and those in other countries. And it also adopts a "cultural" approach because different countries typically have different cultures. International comparisons that focus on culture are valuable for several reasons.

First, school systems are organized by governments, and there are substantial and instructive differences in the ways school systems are governed across countries. These differences affect both what administrators can do and what schools can achieve. The U.S. system of heavy reliance on local funding of schools, for example, both permits a high degree of community control and results in substantial differences in the resources available to schools in different areas. This feature of the U.S. system to some degree determines what school administrators in different parts of our country can do.

Second, citizens of a country share many ways of seeing things, ways that differ across countries. There are cultural commonalities, as well as a body of shared experiences, characteristic of each country. Americans tend to see things in particularly American ways—we ask American questions, are preoccupied with American concerns. American policy analysts who look at Japan, for example, are likely sensitized by American experiences of racism. As a result, perhaps, they tend to focus on discrimination faced by Burakumin, Koreans, or guest workers rather than, for example, on the low percentages of Japanese children in poverty as compared with the very high percentage of American children, of whatever ethnicity, in poverty.

Schools provide civic education, more or less explicitly. Schooled citizens thus share an experience of being taught who, what, and how "we" are, as well as who, what, and how "they" are. International comparison helps bring these shared perceptions to light. The intent is not to minimize important differences and comparisons within the United States, but to highlight aspects of the U.S. system that are easily taken for granted by its members.

Comparison is especially useful to those who are looking for new ways to see and act. It is not so much that comparison identifies what should be done, "what works," in the quick-fix language of those seeking silver bullets, but that it helps us see and understand what we cannot easily see—what we do, without thinking, and how we conventionally think. A comparative lens is, perhaps, especially important to Americans. In a large country such as the United States, with both diversity and a great deal of shared culture, an educator might not encounter anyone who questions the core assumptions underlying the system. There are at least nine reasons why we might want to adopt a comparative perspective (see Sidebar 7-1).

Sidebar 7-1: Reasons to Think Comparatively

A little bit of brainstorming revealed nine different types of comparative questions an educator might ask (Williams, 2003a). Each type of question provides a different reason for thinking comparatively.

1. How are we doing academically in comparison to other countries? Are our kids learning as much as kids in other countries? Are our schools doing as good a job?

2. How are we doing, in terms of other measures? For example, how big are achievement gaps between rich and poor in the United States and in other countries? How many scientists and engineers are we producing per population unit, as compared with other countries? How well does the United States meet its labor market needs?

3. What do other education systems do? For instance, do all systems have comprehensive high schools? How similar are unit expenditures in different education systems? How many years of teacher training do other school systems require?

4. How do other education systems manage common problems? For example, how do other systems organize early childhood care? How do other systems pay for public schooling? How do other systems manage trade-offs between access to higher education and costs of higher education?

5. What's possible? Is it possible, for instance, to educate all children at affordable cost? Can education help historically disadvantaged groups get ahead?

---

6. What works—when, where, and how? Under what conditions does school choice increase inequalities with a system? What cultural features promote and inhibit parental involvement?

7. What are other cultures and places like? For instance, what are the dimensions along which cultures vary? How do other cultures see things? What do their frames of reference look like? How are their ways of seeing things different than ours?

8. What is our role in the world? What does the United States do in the world? How do people in other countries see us? Why do they see us in those ways?

9. How do we see things? For example, what are our own frames of reference like? What alternatives are there to the ways we usually see things?

INTERNATIONAL COMPARISONS: HOW ARE WE DOING?

One reason for examining education from a comparative perspective is to see how our students score relative to students from other countries. This aim is probably what prompts the international comparisons of academic performance that are reported in the popular press. Generally, news reports list average scores on international assessments of achievement across a range of countries from Europe, East Asia, and elsewhere. Often, the U.S. scores seem rather weak, at least in light of our economic and military preeminence. Typical is the following excerpt from a report on the Third International Mathematics and Science Study (TIMSS, now Trends in International Mathematics and Science Study):

> U.S. twelfth graders performed below the national average and among the lowest of the 21 TIMSS countries on the assessment of mathematics general knowledge... U.S. twelfth graders also performed below the international average and among the lowest of the 21 TIMSS countries on the assessment of science general knowledge. (U.S. Department of Education, 1998, p. 13)

Reports that draw on international comparisons, moreover, often lament the mediocrity of U.S. education and propose reform. Indeed, current reform movements can be traced to the *A Nation at Risk* report which states, in high drama:

> If an unfriendly power had attempted to impose on America the mediocre educational performance that exists today, we might well have viewed it as an act of war.

As it stands, we have allowed this to happen to ourselves. We have even squandered the gains in achievement made in the wake of the Sputnik challenge. Moreover, we have dismantled essential support systems which helped make those gains possible. We have, in effect, been committing an act of unthinking, unilateral educational disarmament. (National Commission on Excellence in Education, 1983, p. 5)

Since that time, international comparisons, especially those based on TIMSS, have sparked considerable discussion among educational researchers. Some scholars have questioned the value of rankings as a way to compare the quality of school systems, given problems with sampling, differences in eligible populations, and other factors such as poverty that are known to affect learning but that are unrelated to school quality. Rotberg (1998, p. 1030) noted, for example, that only 5 of the 21 countries participating in TIMSS' general math and science tests and only 6 of the 16 participating in the advanced math and physics tests met the study's own sampling guidelines. Children excluded from the study tend, of course, to score lower than those included; so the smaller the percentage taking the test, the higher the average score.[1] It is difficult to interpret results of a study in which average scores do not include high percentages of students (e.g., exclusion rates of 18% for Austria, 22% for Cyprus, 30% for Italy, 16% for the Netherlands, and 43% for the Russian Federation on the General Knowledge Assessment in mathematics and science; U.S. Department of Education, 1998, Tables A1.1, A1.2, and A1.3).

Moreover, what is one to make of average scores on advanced physics and mathematics tests when the proportions of students enrolling in advanced physics and mathematics classes vary widely across countries? The percentage of the age cohort represented in the advanced mathematics test, for example, varied widely: from 2% in the Russian Federation to 75% in Slovenia (Rotberg, 1998, p. 1030). Critiques focused on sampling issues raise serious questions about the meaning of average scores on international assessments. Certainly, such critiques suggest that comparisons based on these assessments should not be accepted at face value. But should they be disregarded altogether?

Yes, but...

Some critiques of international comparisons have a "Yes but ..." quality, which begs the question of whether or not U.S. education should be improved. These critiques seem to come from defenders of the status quo. Such defenders say, for

---

[1] This same phenomenon can be observed in comparisons of average state SAT scores: The smaller the proportion of seniors taking the test, the higher the score. Indeed, the best single predictor of a state's average SAT score is the percentage of seniors taking the test (Powell & Steelman, 1996).

example, that, although U.S. average math scores are low, the United States has a higher percentage of children in poverty than do other countries. Yes, say these defenders, the United States ranked among the lowest of the countries tested, but most American students were enrolled in comprehensive high schools as compared with students in countries such as France, Sweden, and Switzerland, where everyone is tracked into academic or vocational schools. Yes, Japanese students do well on international comparisons, but who would want a child to attend a high school as rigid and punitive as those in Japan (Fallows, 1987). Yes, students from Asian countries score well on multiple-choice tests requiring memorization of facts, but do they learn how to think critically or to develop original ideas? One senses a certain amount of defensiveness in these responses to international comparisons.

Despite the defensiveness of some commentators and the methodological cautions of others, we can nevertheless learn from international comparisons of academic performance and practices. Indeed, a growing body of classroom research suggests that there may be important lessons in observations of curriculum and instruction in other countries (Ma, 1999; Schmidt, et al., 2001; Stevenson, Chen, & Lee, 1993; Stigler, Gonzales, Kawanka, Knoll, & Serrano, 1999). In terms of mathematics instruction, for example, analysis of video observations of a sample of U.S., German, and Japanese classrooms showed that U.S. classes "require less high-level thought than classes in Germany and Japan.... [U.S. mathematics teachers'] "typical goal is to teach students how to do something, while Japanese teachers' goal is to help them understand mathematical concepts" (Stigler et al., 1999, p. viii). While Japanese classes share many of the "features called for by U.S. mathematics reforms, U.S. classes are less likely to exhibit these features. Although most U.S. math teachers report familiarity with reform recommendations, relatively few apply the key points in their classrooms" (p. viii). Offering a similar analysis, Schmidt and colleagues argue in a series of research pieces that the U.S. school system lacks a challenging, coherent, and common mathematics curriculum (see, e.g., Schmidt, et al, 2001; Schmidt, Houang, & Cogan, 2002). Such findings call for further investigation, reflection, and perhaps corrective action.

Interestingly, the discourse on international achievement comparisons may speak a great deal more to the preoccupations and politics of those discussing the issue than to conditions in the countries being referenced. Use of a single score as "scientific proof," for example, gives advocates a great deal of room to project their own theories and agendas onto the evidence. And the public's faith in the precision and validity of numerical test scores lends legitimacy to the use of international comparisons in support of almost any credible story one wants to tell.

Nevertheless, like any single measure, test scores reveal little depth about the phenomenon, school system, or person being evaluated, and they tell us nothing about context. For example, we learn little about where a school system has come from or how to get it to where we want it to be. Still, scores provide a public and easily understood indicator of relative standing, and are thus useful in advocacy. We are all susceptible to the question, "How'd you do?"

Other Interesting Comparisons

It doesn't take a lot of thought to come up with a number of other interesting indicators to compare across nations. For example, given their values, the authors are drawn to international comparisons of equity. Moreover, data to make such comparisons are readily available. Recently, the Programme in International Student Assessment (PISA) has provided data that were used to calculate country-by-country correlations between socioeconomic status (measured by parental occupation, education, and income) and student test scores (Williams, 2003b; Willms, 1999). These statistics provide a gauge of educational equity. Although in *all* countries, student performance is correlated to some degree with socioeconomic status, the strength of the relationship varies quite substantially across countries. In some countries such as Japan, Korea, and Finland, family background characteristics are much less predictive of student achievement than in other countries, such as Germany, Austria, and, to a lesser extent, the United States. These findings, of course, say nothing about why family characteristics play a greater or lesser role in student achievement. But the variability of the correlations suggests that some countries *have* found policy interventions that reduce the influence of poverty on student achievement. Such a finding calls for further research, at both system and local levels, to discover more about the policies that seem to improve educational equity.

Other indicators also can be instructive. Rotberg, for example, provided an interesting set of measures that represent "alternatives" to test score comparisons:

- Productivity in science and engineering, as measured by breakthroughs in basic research, technological advances, and product development.
- The availability of qualified scientists and engineers to meet workforce requirements.
- Retention and graduation rates in science and mathematics education.
- Access to higher education in science and engineering for low-income students, students from racial and ethnic minority groups, and students with disabilities.

• Availability of science and mathematics education for students who do not attend college. (Rotberg, 1998, p. 1031)

Such indicators can tell us more than academic test scores alone, but they still paint only a superficial picture. In short, the "How're we doing?" approach to comparison can raise "red flags," but it cannot offer much guidance on how to think about, make sense of, or improve an education system. If the purpose of comparison is to learn, knowing how we're doing doesn't tell us much. Maybe that's one reason international comparisons are so infrequently used in educational administration and policy analysis (Plank, 2003). A recent report by the National Science Foundation came to a similar conclusion:

> The U.S. approach to education is not systematically informed by experiences with education in the rest of the world. Since the 1980s, many calls for domestic education reform have been justified by citing large gaps between the academic performance of U.S. students and their peers in other countries. Nonetheless, the U.S. public has been offered little evidence to explain these results and knows little about the limitations of the studies that produced them. Nor have U.S. policymakers and researchers used the limited information they do have about differences in education systems in various countries to systematically explore these results. This is surprising given both the ways that results of international comparative studies are so often used to justify domestic education reform and, even more, the ways that other sectors of U.S. society—such as business, science, and popular culture—have reached out to become more knowledgeable about practices in other countries. (Chabbott & Emerson, 2003, pp. 1–2)

LEVELS OF CULTURE

It may be helpful at this point to describe an education system in terms of levels of culture, as presented in Figure 7.1. This schematic and the accompanying discussion of it draw on—but with considerable latitude—Schein's (1992) ideas about organizational culture. Schein proposed a three-level model. The top level consists of "artifacts," or visible organizational structures and processes. The second, deeper level consists of "espoused values," that is, the strategies, goals, and philosophies that members of the organization say they endorse. The third and deepest level consists of "basic underlying assumptions," the unconscious, taken for granted beliefs, thoughts, perceptions, and feelings, which function as the ultimate source of action and values.

For our purposes, it may be useful to think of the top level—the artifacts—in terms of *outputs and outcomes* of a system: average international assessment scores, for example, or other skills, knowledge, behaviors, and attitudes that students acquire. Underlying and producing outcomes at the second level are

(Visible)
    Level 1:   Outputs & Outcomes

                                    /\

Level 2: Organizational Practices & Institutional Arrangements

                                  /\

(Less Visible)

    Level 3:   Frame of Reference
                          (basic underlying assumptions;
        taken-for-granted beliefs, theories, & explanations;
                core beliefs; cultural patterns;
                political and social context)

Fig. 7.1.   Levels of education system culture.

the *organizational practices and institutional arrangements* associated with a particular education system. These organizational practices include a variety of things—school calendar, authority patterns among teachers and students, the curriculum, examinations, and so on. The third and deepest level is the *frame of reference*, corresponding closely to Schein's "basic underlying assumptions"— the taken for granted beliefs and theories that an education system draws on to make sense of what it sees and to plan its activities. The frame of reference is created by system participants, who continually revise it and pass it on to the next generation of system participants, who also revise (and even recreate) it.

Whereas the top two levels in the model are relatively visible and can be "observed" empirically, Level 3 cannot be seen directly. Rather, it must be inferred from careful observation and analysis, as well as from theory. Because variations at levels one and two are visible, moreover, people readily acknowledge them. For example, most people accept the fact that learning outcomes and instructional practices vary. People have much more difficulty believing that there are different but equally valid ways of seeing things. Nevertheless, one cannot understand what someone from a different culture means without grasping, to a certain extent, his or her frame of reference. Lacking awareness of how someone else sees something, one can only interpret events in light of one's own frame of reference, which is likely to lead to incorrect conclusions.

Whereas Schein's focus was on variation across organizations, our emphasis is on important variations across countries. And comparison may be carried out at any of the three levels. For example, "how are we doing?" is usually a Level-1 comparison. An important point to remember is that even when we make a Level-1 comparison, we make sense of it in light of Levels 2 and 3. A deeper purpose of comparison, as we have suggested, is to increase awareness of our own theories, explanations, core beliefs, and cultural patterns by examining those of others, which are much easier to see than our own. Increasing awareness of our own and others' frames of reference can be profoundly uncomfortable, but it increases our options for understanding problems, determining what to do, and evaluating how well we are able to understand and communicate with others.

How Do Other Systems Do Things?

Thinking in terms of the second level of culture (i.e., organizational practices and institutional arrangements), one can look across systems by asking questions such as: What are others doing? How do things work in other systems? How do other systems work?

One obvious use of this type of Level-2 comparison is to generate ideas that can be adopted by a system seeking to improve. Ideas, large and small, can be borrowed from other countries. At the local level, for example, individual teachers or entire school faculties may adopt ideas—innovations or novel practices—that they observe in their travels abroad. Representatives of state or national systems also read about and observe practices used elsewhere. Several years ago, for instance, one of the authors met with a delegation of ministry officials from Egypt, who were interested in the instructional technologies used in American schools. Their intent was to "import" to Egypt some of the technologies that they saw in use in U.S. classrooms.

Of course, not all efforts to import ideas turn out to have their intended effect. During the late 1980s and early 1990s, a number of practices were identified from other education systems and proposed as remedies for deficiencies in the U.S. system. These included increases in the length of the school day and of the school year, increases in the volume and expectations for homework, the requirement that students wear school uniforms, and so on. Transplanted into different social ecologies, such practices assumed different functions and meanings, generally not gaining wide support or spreading throughout the system.

Whereas the rationale for promoting adoption of an international policy or practice varies by country or state, ultimately the success of the transplanted policy or practice depends on the level of local support it receives. In fact, at the national level, relatively few practices are adopted wholesale, just as true reform is relatively rare. Exceptions are times of national crisis such as the Sputnik threat or the fears in the 1980s that the United States might lose its economic edge. Japan underwent a major reform following World War II (e.g., Anderson, 1962), Russia and Eastern Europe in the early 1990s (e.g., Batioukova & Shaposhnikova, 1997), and Britain in the late 1980s (e.g., Elliott & MacLennan, 1994). At such moments, education systems are more likely to borrow ideas and practices from other systems (e.g., Steiner-Khamsi, 2004).

Because of the way context influences reform, international comparisons tend to be more useful when they are viewed broadly as the basis for reflection, rather than narrowly as prescriptions for particular policies or practices. Level-2 comparison, for example, is sometimes instructive by showing that alternative arrangements are possible. In contrast to the United States, for example, most industrialized nations have established far-reaching policies for early childhood education. Neuman and Bennett (2001), for instance, examined early childhood education and care policies in eight European countries. In advocating for development in the United States of a comprehensive early childhood care and education policy, they identified the elements of successful programs, the issues facing all systems, and implications for adoption of such a policy in the United States.

Sometimes, other countries' educational policies and practices can stimulate debate at home. Liping Ma's study of mathematics instruction in elementary schools in China and the United States, for example, provoked considerable discussion among mathematics educators about the nature and depth of teacher knowledge of mathematics and the ability of teachers in different settings to foster deep conceptual understanding in children (see Ma, 1999).

Comparison can also spur the development of new concepts, even catch phrases that convey a certain truth. TIMSS, for example, elaborated the distinctions among "intended," "implemented," and "acquired." curricula. And early reports from TIMSS characterized the teaching of mathematics and science in the United States with the expression "a mile wide and an inch deep," a phrase that appears to resonate among many U.S. educators.

Finally, it's enlightening to see how different countries see things. Foster and Nicholls (2003), for instance, compared the portrayal of World War II in English, American, Swedish, and Japanese textbooks. Not surprisingly, the different countries emphasized different aspects of the war. No facts were found that contradicted others, but the portrayal of the roles of different countries varied considerably. Moreover, the ways lessons were presented also varied. Japanese textbooks tended to present material in an authoritative factual manner, with no reference to interpretation or multiple views of the same event. U.S. textbooks were the most entertaining, visually engaging and reader oriented. Still, there was little sense of the interpretive nature of history. English textbooks, by contrast, were organized in terms of evidence and possible conclusions drawn from that evidence from the perspectives of different groups. Students were invited to review the evidence, develop their own interpretations, and defend them against classmates' contrary interpretations. Sidebar 7-2 provides another example of how countries differ in the educational approaches they adopt.

Sidebar 7-2: Seeking Equality in Different School Systems

As part of a larger comparative study of teachers in England and France, Osborn, Broadfoot, Planel, and Pollard (1997) examined the effect of history and culture on the beliefs and practices of teachers. Both countries face the challenge of dealing with impoverished children, and both countries enact policies to help counteract the disadvantages that impoverished children face. Moreover, teachers in both countries consider the education of impoverished children to be a major problem. But the approaches of the two countries differ.

In France, with its centralized, constitutionally organized, and secular educational tradition, it is "considered morally unacceptable to treat children differently" (p. 377). Schools are expected to provide all children—even those whose abilities differ—with access to the same curriculum, regardless of where they live, who they are, or what their economic circumstances might be. The system seeks equality by avoiding differentiation.

The English system, by contrast, evolved in a more piecemeal fashion, with a much stronger role for voluntary associations and religious groups. As a result, perhaps, the English system emphasizes a more diversified, individualistic approach. The development of individual potential is an important theme at all levels of the system: The English primary system in particular has enshrined the notion of differentiated teaching according to the perceived needs of children. In this view, greater equality within education cannot be achieved without understanding that children start school from rather different points and therefore require different teaching approaches. (p. 377)

NATURAL EXPERIMENTS: INVESTIGATIONS
INTO "WHAT WORKS"

International comparisons also enable educators to learn from the "natural experiments" being carried out in different education systems around the world. Natural experiments are systematic changes in policy or practice whose effects can be studied scientifically (e.g., Nagel, 1964).

Over the past two decades, for example, Chile has adopted what has been described as the world's most comprehensive choice and voucher system (e.g., Delannoy, 2000; Gauri, 1998; Parry, 1997). Observers can learn from what has happened there, and some studies have already been conducted. One of these looked at merit pay. Chilean teachers are awarded merit pay by school rather than by individual—a practice that tends to reinforce the cohesiveness of the school community as well as rewarding high performance. In recognition of the different resources available to schools in communities of varying wealth, high-performing schools are selected from within similar strata—those from wealthy communities, or those from low-income communities, for example. In this way, schools compete with others that face similar circumstances. Teachers are said to find the merit pay system fair and to view it as an impetus to work hard (McMeekin, 2004).

Other natural experiments show the negative effects of tracking on low-ability and low-income children. Studies of this type have been conducted in several countries. Sweden, for example, introduced comprehensive high schools in the 1960s in an effort to reduce the inequality and elitism of its previous tracking system, whereby students were assigned to more and less academic schools at an early age. Studies at the time compared the achievement of students in southern Stockholm, where comprehensive schools were introduced immediately, to that of students in northern Stockholm, where tracked schools were maintained for a longer time. Results showed that low-ability students fared much better in the comprehensive schools than in the tracked schools, whereas high-ability students performed equally well in both types of schools (Husen, as cited in Brint, 1998). Similar results were reported for children in Britain (Kerckhoff, 1986), Scotland (Gamoran, 1996; McPherson & Willms, 1986), and the United States (Ayalon & Gamoran, 2000). Interestingly, however, in Israel tracking did not seem to lead to inequality of outcomes (Ayalon & Gamoran, 2000).

Because they focus on policies and practices, natural experiments represent level-2 analyses. Some international studies of this type are somewhat superficial, however, examining discrete practices out of context. These studies address the question, "What do other systems do?" Other analyses examine policies and practices in light of national context and promote deeper understanding of the processes by which learning takes place in different countries and the policies that work in particular contexts to improve learning outcomes. These studies address the more complex question: "How do things work in other systems?" For most educational issues, "What works?" is more usefully rephrased as "What works when, where, and how?"

WHAT'S POSSIBLE?

One other use of level-2 comparison is to show what's possible. Countries, like people, get stuck in habitual ways of doing things, ways that limit their vision of the possibilities. Counterexamples, however, can help "unfreeze" habitual practice. Within and outside education, examples abound of social accomplishments thought to be impossible until someone achieved them. Who would have thought at the end of World War II, for instance, that a nonviolent people's movement would end British rule in India? Who would have thought in 1986 that South Africa would manage a peaceful transition to a multicultural society with African American majority rule? Who in 1980 foresaw the fall of the Soviet Union? Who would have thought that Korea, with a per capita GNP in 1960 equal to that of Ghana, would grow into the one of the world's leading economies?

Ideas travel far. Universal public education, democratic self-governance, and freedom of speech, largely American ideas, once considered impossible in many places, are now within realistic reach of most nations in the world. Mandela was influenced by King who emulated Gandhi who read Thoreau. Universal literacy, once thought to be too costly for much of the world, has been achieved, at low cost, in Kerala, one of the poorest places on earth. Costa Rica has eliminated its army, and is alone among the nations of Central America in its lack of conflict.

Unfortunately, human beings are capable of bad as well good. Comparison allows us to see the evil that humans are capable of, and there are many examples. In the past century alone, genocide has been attempted in Germany, Rwanda, Serbia, and the Sudan. The human tendency is to see such things as aberrations, events that could never take place "here." The record suggests, however, that the most advanced and enlightened human societies are as capable of great evil as other societies.

To sum up, the most insightful Level-2 comparisons look beyond current and received practice to understand how the things others are doing work for them. Deeper than just comparing the results of what different systems do, these Level-2 comparisons look at the practices and institutional arrangements that seem to produce different outcomes. Such comparisons recognize that national contexts differ and, as a result, they focus on practices in context. Level-2 comparisons can also show what others have achieved—what is possible, for better or worse. Knowledge of such possibilities helps us think about what we might want to do differently.

HOW DO OTHER PEOPLE THINK?

To recap, comparison, at its simplest, asks how we are doing compared to others. International test scores provide ready material for such comparisons, even if we don't learn much from looking at them. Somewhat more instructive are comparisons that look beneath test scores to see what others are doing. Teachers and principals find these comparisons most useful when they enable us to understand the interactions between different practices and different contexts.

The model of the culture of education systems presented in Figure 7.1 suggests that the outcomes of school systems result from their organizational practices and institutional arrangements. These practices and arrangements are created, maintained, and recreated by the theories, understandings, core beliefs, and cultural patterns of the people who make up the system. The invisible, yet potent features of a system represent the deepest level of culture, and they tend to be difficult to study. Some characteristics of these Level-3 features of culture are presented in Sidebar 7-3.

Sidebar 7-3: Characteristics of Culture at Level 3

The theories, understandings, core beliefs, and cultural patterns at Level 3—what are sometimes referred to as "cultural assumptions"—have the following characteristics:

- They generally pervade the thinking of group members, but not of non-members.
- They vary in important ways across countries (as well as across subcultural groups within a country).
- They are usually invisible to (or at least not noticed by) group members.
- They focus and limit how members see problems and solutions.
- They serve as the interpretive lens through which members understand themselves, their systems, and their options.
- Despite the fact that other groups have their own frames of reference, they serve as the lens through which members interpret the behavior and intentions of non-members.

- They tend to be seen by group members as the most (or only) legitimate or natural ways of thinking, understanding, believing, and behaving.
- They are defensively maintained, and sometimes fiercely so.

Despite the difficulty of bringing cultural assumptions to the surface, Level-3 comparison seeks to understand some of the ways these theories, understandings, core beliefs, and cultural patterns vary systematically. In the case of this chapter, variation across countries is of interest. Sidebar 7-4 illustrates this type of comparison, suggesting the types of assumptions that tend to undergird cultural practices.

Sidebar 7-4: Epistemological Ethnocentrism

Comparative studies of human development in different societies have started to challenge some of the basic assumptions of developmental psychology. Until recently, most of the research on human development was carried out in middle-class European or European-American communities. Theories were generated based on the frames of reference of these cultural communities and then generalized to people in all communities worldwide (Rogoff, 2003).

Nevertheless, different yet clearly adaptive practices of other cultural communities challenge the "epistemological ethnocentrism" of many theories of human development. For example, in many U.S. families, children under age 10 are not seen as capable of watching themselves or caring for younger siblings. In a number of other cultures, however, children as young as 5 assume increasing levels of responsibility for the care of younger children. Rogoff quoted Hewlitt: "By three or four years of age children can cook themselves a meal on the fire, and by ten years of age Aka [Central Africa] children know enough subsistence skills to live in the forest alone if need be" (1991, p 34).

North American childrearing deemphasizes hierarchies between older and younger children, encourages verbal reasoning, seeks to provide even young children with choices, and construes physical punishment as abusive (Edwards, 1994 as cited in Rogoff, 2003).These values are not universal, however, even within the United States. Some cultures value hierarchy, whereas others downplay verbal reasoning in favor of other behavioral modes. Not every culture views choice as equally important, and relatively few see the development of a child's individuality through presenting him or her with choices as an important aim of childrearing.

When they make Level-3 comparisons, researchers inevitably encounter problems of difference and the ways that individuals, cultures, and education systems deal with difference. In focusing on cross-national differences, therefore, researchers need to be careful not to downplay the within-country differences among individuals and subcultural groups. In addition, they need to portray group characteristics as tendencies, not absolutes, and as influences on behavior, not as determinants of it. Individual members of a group may or may not act or see things according to the cultural assumptions of the group in general. In this regard, it is important to remember that individuals, although often influenced by shared group beliefs, also play an active role in helping to shape those beliefs quietly by affirmation or more dramatically through resistance and transformative change. Moreover, individuals almost always see themselves as members of multiple groups. Rarely does a single group label adequately capture an individual's complex identity.

Understanding Patterns of Difference: Illustrative Theories

Among the many theorists of culture, Geert Hofstede has carried out some of the most thorough investigations of cultural differences in industrialized countries (see, for example, Hofstede, 1986, 1997). Administering over 100,000 questionnaires to employees of a multinational business corporation operating in over 50 countries, Hofstede initially derived four dimensions along which national cultures varied:

- *Individualism* relates to a culture's tendency to equate individual accomplishment with identity. Members of individualist cultures are concerned primarily with their own interests and those of their immediate families, as compared to members of collectivist societies, who typically extend concern to several tight "in groups" (e.g., extended family, clan, or organization) from which detachment is difficult. In-groups protect their members but expect continuing loyalty.
- *Power distance* is the degree to which less powerful members of a society accept inequality as normal. High power distance cultures are more hierarchical. Managers in high power distance cultures are less likely to use consultative management strategies, and subordinates are less likely to challenge or even question their supervisors.
- *Uncertainty avoidance* is the extent to which members of a culture become nervous in situations seen as unpredictable, unclear, or unstructured. Individuals in high-uncertainty-avoidance cultures "try to maintain strict codes of behavior and a belief in absolute truths" (Hofstede, 1986, p. 308).

Participants in low-uncertainty avoidance cultures are much more willing to tolerate ambiguity.

• *Masculinity* refers to the degree to which a culture strives for "maximal distinction between what men are expected to do and what women are expected to do. [Masculine cultures] expect men to be assertive, ambitious, and competitive, to strive for material success and to respect whatever is big, strong, and fast" (Hofstede, 1986, p. 308). In a "masculine" culture, external success and competition are prized over personal relationships, nurturing, and security, which are seen as "feminine" and therefore inferior.

A fifth dimension, *long-term orientation*, has been identified more recently (Hofstede & Bond, 1988). Long-term orientation refers largely to the values of Confucian societies: thrift, persistence, respect for hierarchy in relationships, and responsiveness to shame. Short-term orientation involves greater concern for immediate security and stability; protection of one's reputation; and the reciprocal exchange of greetings, gifts, and favors.

These dimensions of culture play out in interesting, oddly familiar ways (Hofstede, 1986). For example, in schools in a *collectivist* culture, individual students tend to speak up only when called on personally by the teacher, whereas in an *individualistic* culture such as the United States, individual students speak up whenever the teacher issues a general invitation to speak (and presumably when the student has something to say). What would a teacher from an individualistic culture be likely to think about students from a collectivist one?

In *low-power distance* cultures, such as the United States, teachers tend to be treated as the equals of parents or even of students. In *high-power distance* cultures, by contrast, teachers are accorded high levels of respect by virtue of their role. Imagine what would happen if a student from a low-power distance culture were studying overseas in a high-power distance culture. How might that student greet his or her teachers if he saw them in the street? How might those teachers react in response to such a greeting?

In a *strong uncertainty-avoidance* culture, disagreement of any kind with a teacher represents rudeness and disrespect, whereas in a *weak uncertainty-avoidance* culture, such as the United States, intellectual disagreements are more often viewed as stimulating—providing evidence of critical thinking on the part of students. Weak uncertainty-avoidance cultures tend to leave situations open ended, while high uncertainty-avoidance cultures prefer more structure.

In a *feminine* culture, relationships are given more value relative to achievement and success than they are in a masculine culture, such as in the United States, where performance is paramount. Imagine the difficulties of a student from a masculine culture in a feminine classroom, or the difficulties that would confront a culturally unaware teacher from a feminine culture in the first few weeks teaching in a masculine school.

Although there has been some criticism of Hofstede's theories (e.g., McSweeney, 2002), they do provide a useful starting point for understanding the ways that people from different countries see things. Some other concepts that are useful in comparing underlying cultural assumptions were developed by Edward Hall (1963, 1976, 1984). These contrast "high-" with "low- context" cultures and cultures that view time as "monochromic" with those that view it as "polychromic."

Hall's distinction between high- and low-context cultures relates to communication style. In *high-context cultures*, for example, much of the meaning of a message lies in the context surrounding the message itself, for example, in the relationship of the people speaking, or in the timing or location of the interchange. With high-context communication, relatively little of the intended meaning is communicated through the content of the message. By contrast, in a *low- context culture*, the focus is on the content of the message, which has meaning independent of context. According to Hall (1976), cultures can be classified as high context (e.g., China, Japan, and many countries in the Middle East) or low context (e.g., the United States, Scandinavia, and Germany).

This contrast in communication style becomes quite apparent in business negotiations between members of high- and low-context cultures. Members of high-context cultures begin negotiations by working to establish trust and good personal relations. Negotiations tend to be slow and somewhat ritualistic, and the eventual contracts that come out of such negotiations are often broad and rather light on detail. Negotiators in low-context cultures, by contrast, try to get down to business fast. They value expertise, efficiency, and detailed, highly specific contracts. Negotiators from low-context cultures often have a hard time figuring out why their high-context counterparts don't get to the point.

In schools, students from high-context cultures will typically seek cues from the context as to the meaning of events, often reading in meaning unintended by a teacher from a low-context culture. Students from low-context cultures, for their part, will likely miss many of the subtle signals sent out by a high-context teacher or classmates.

Hall's second concept relates to the understanding and management of time. A *monochronic* view of time construes it as linear, one track, compartmentalized, and goal oriented, whereas a *polychronic* view construes it as nonlinear, multiple track, open ended, and lacking clear boundaries. As with context, cultures can be classified as being primarily monochronic or primarily polychronic. Monochronic cultures focus on schedules. When the time is up, it's time to go home regardless of whether or not the task has been completed. Members of monochronic cultures also tend to focus on one topic at a time. People from polychronic cultures, by contrast, pay less attention to schedules and more to the completion of tasks or the conclusion of interchanges, and they tend to juggle multiple tasks rather than completing one at a time.

In educational settings, students from polychronic cultures may appear to a culturally naïve monochronic teacher as lacking discipline and the ability to attend to tasks. Because students from polychronic cultures usually value relationships over tasks, however, the savvy teacher will work to develop relationships first, and later to introduce specific assignments. Polychronic teachers, by contrast, are prone to view monochronic students as impolite, unfriendly, and hurried.

Other dimensions than the ones discussed here have been identified, of course, to characterize differences across cultures. The main point of examining some of these dimensions, however, is to illustrate the importance of cultural frames of reference to the interpretation of events and interchanges. Often when people interact with others from different cultures, miscommunication occurs. This is because members of a particular cultural group, raised among people "programmed" in similar ways, typically look through but do not see the cultural lenses they wear. They tend, instead, toward *ethnocentrism*, the belief that their own native culture and modes of behavior represent the norm and therefore are superior to other cultures and modes of behavior (Reagan, 1996, p. 4).

From an ethnocentric perspective, members of other cultural groups appear deficient.[2] Cultural "deficit theories," in fact, are implicit in a great deal of educational thought and practice. Nevertheless, discussion of cultural deficits is typically grounded on the false premise that the norms and values of one's own culture are an appropriate basis for understanding the intentions and behaviors of people from other cultures. Moreover, in a context in which cultural differences are associated with power differentials among social groups, dominant groups often define what is normal for everyone.

Dealing With Cultural Difference at the Individual Level

Even with awareness and a willingness to see and understand the perspectives of others, the fact of difference is hard to deal with constructively. Psychologically, people find it difficult to see how two seemingly contradictory perspectives can both be correct, especially when their own perspective is involved.

---

[2]Alternately, members of other cultures may be romanticized as "noble savages." Both deficit and romantic perspectives, however, define the "other" in terms of the meaning system of the observing culture, rather than in terms of the meaning system of the culture being observed.

The patterns are easiest to see in other cultures and most difficult to deal with in one's own.

Interested in such difficulties and in ways to overcome them, Milton Bennett (1986, 1993) developed a six-stage framework to explain the predictable reactions of individuals to cultural differences. In his model, individuals move from stage to stage as they develop intercultural sensitivity. The first three stages are ethnocentric, where the individual's culture is *experienced* as central to reality.

The first stage is *denial*, in which individuals experience their own culture as the only one possible. Other cultures are avoided, and individuals seek to maintain psychological or physical distance from those who are different.

Slightly more tolerance is exhibited at the second *defense* stage in which one's own culture is experienced as the only good one. Because other cultures are seen as inferior, people at this stage experience cultural differences as threats. They view the social world in polarized terms, seeing people as either "us" or "them."

A variant of defense is *reversal*, where individuals see another culture as superior and their own culture as inferior. Reversal is a stance sometimes taken by individuals who have a profound and positive experience of another culture, as the expression "go native" suggests. To some degree, reversal also captures the experience of "internalized oppression," whereby members of an oppressed group come to believe the negative stereotypes about their own group that the dominant group promulgates.

The third stage entails *minimization*. At this stage, individuals experience the features of their own culture as universal, while at the same time obscuring, trivializing, or romanticizing the differences represented by other cultures. People at the minimization stage emphasize the similarities of others to themselves. Nevertheless, minimization actually requires greater cultural sensitivity than denial or defense, because it acknowledges differences and moves beyond polarization and over-simplification.

Bennett explained that the next three stages incorporate an ethnorelativist perspective—one in which a person's own culture is experienced in the context of other cultures. Ethnorelativism does not require that a person endorse others' actions, but it does require him or her to try to *understand* those actions in their own cultural context.

Acceptance represents the least sophisticated of the ethnorelativist perspectives. From the vantage of acceptance, a person understands his or her own cultural worldview as one of many. Individuals at this stage may not agree with others' frames of reference, but they recognize and accept the existence of those other frames. Because they can see things from other cultural perspectives, individuals at the acceptance stage are able to "frame shift." And, although individuals at this stage may have disagreements with others, such disagreements do not result primarily from the unconscious projection of their own cultural values onto others.

Adaptation is the next stage. At this stage, a person experiences another culture in ways quite similar to those of native members of the culture. Individuals who have adapted to another culture are able to see through the lens of that culture, and they can make use of communication strategies that are appropriate to either their own or the other culture. In fact, such individuals are truly bicultural because they are able to "code shift," that is, to act differently depending on the culture in which they are operating.

Integration is the final stage. At this stage, individuals experience themselves as full members of two or more cultures. Individuals at the integration stage, however, may actually find themselves in a position of "cultural marginality," whereby they sometimes operate in a realm that is beyond the boundaries of any one culture. Sometimes cultural marginality can have negative consequences, rendering an individual incapable of feeling like he or she belongs anywhere. A more constructive version of integration occurs when an individual is not only able to take part in two or more cultures, but also feels that he or she belongs to both.

Interestingly, in speaking about organizational culture, Schein (1992) urged leaders to become "marginal" in their own organizations so as to be able to recognize the organizations' maladaptive assumptions and envision new solutions. Schein's insight that organizations represent cultures on a small scale is particularly useful to school leaders. Denial, defense, and minimization, for example, are responses commonly seen in schools when staff members' underlying assumptions are challenged. Some innovations in recent history—such as full inclusion of children with disabilities—threaten many teachers in ways that trigger "ethnocentric" responses.

Nevertheless, ethnorelativism is certainly not an easy or popular stance. To people at the defense stage, for example, respectful understanding of the cultural values of others seems to disrespect their own cultural values. Also, ethnorelativism is sometimes confused with moral relativism—the belief that because morals are a social construct, no one can really distinguish "right" from "wrong." Ethnorelativism, however, does not mean that people must give up their values and commitments, but it does require moral reasoning that evaluates behavior in light of the actor's, rather than the observer's, cultural understandings. As Bennett explained,

> … ethnorelativism does not imply an ethical agreement with all difference nor a disavowal of stating (and acting upon) a preference for one worldview over another. The position does imply, however, that ethical choices will be made on

grounds other than the ethnocentric projection of one's own worldview or in the name of absolute principles. (1993, p. 15)

Dealing With Cultural Difference at the System Level

Not only is it important for individuals to deal with difference, it is also important for school systems and even nations to do so. Although these matters were discussed in detail in chapter 6, here it is useful to explore a typology of *systemic* perspectives that in some ways parallel the stages of individual acceptance of difference that Bennett developed.

In their typology of systemic responses to difference, Smith and Vaux (2003, p. 27) described the following perspectives:

- *Assimilationist*: single institutions organized around the values of the dominant group, with minority interests less well represented;
- *Separatist*: different institutions serving different, relatively homogenous populations; and
- *Integrationist [or pluralist]*: common institutions with internal diversity.

The history of the United States provides examples of all three responses. In the 19th and early 20th centuries, the expectation was that people who immigrated to the United States would become "Americanized," giving up their native languages and customs for those of their new homeland. The result of such assimilation, however, was the loss of the richness that cultural variability offers. The post-Civil War treatment of African Americans in the United States illustrates the separatist perspective. African Americans retained their own traditions and ways of life, but they did so in segregated churches, schools, and voluntary organizations. Illustrations from U.S. history of true integration are rare, but there are some examples of partial integration. For instance, although people with different religions worship in separate institutions, they are often integrated into other social institutions in the United States (e.g., schools, workplaces, government).

Contemporary schools' responses to children from different backgrounds tend to run the gamut between assimilationist and integrationist. School leaders can gauge their schools' perspectives by examining the practices that are used to address students' differences. For example, schools with large numbers of students whose native language is something other than English—let's say, it's Spanish—might take an assimilationist perspective by requiring that instruction be conducted in English only, or they might take a separatist perspective by providing bilingual instruction to Spanish-speaking students, or they might take an integrationist or pluralist perspective by providing bilingual instruction to all students, native English speakers and native Spanish speakers alike.

Among those who take a pluralist perspective, there is also some variability in the response to difference. Smith and Vaux (2003, p. 27), for example, distinguish among conservative, liberal, and critical pluralists.

- *Conservative pluralists* tend to emphasize similarities across groups and do not encourage public expression of cultural identity. They treat schools as neutral public spaces, believing that religious and cultural symbols are appropriate primarily in the private spheres outside of schools.
- *Liberal pluralists* tend to emphasize the cultural uniqueness of different groups, treating schools as an appropriate space for the display of symbols and the enactment of practices that define cultural identity. They do not, however, encourage discussion of the power relations among different cultural groups.
- *Critical pluralists* acknowledge power relations among social and cultural groups, recognizing differences in status and privileges. They believe that the proper role of public institutions is to understand and address the deeper causes of injustice.

In general, public schools in the United States, even those with an integrationist perspective, tend to adopt conservative or liberal versions of pluralism. Educators who advocate critical pedagogy (see chap. 9), however, believe that schools ought to confront injustice by giving students opportunities to examine power differentials across groups.

LEARNING ABOUT THE REST OF THE WORLD IS BROADLY EDUCATIONAL

Despite (and perhaps even because of) the difficulties of dealing with difference, it is useful, as well as broadly educational, to learn about the world beyond our own schools and districts. The United States is large and distant from much of the rest of the world, and it has often been able to isolate itself from daily encounters with other countries. In fact, as a people, we know relatively little about other countries. For one thing, we don't hear much about them. Indeed, citizens of other countries hear a great deal more about us than we do about them. And because we lack information, we sometimes find it hard to show empathy.

Few American citizens, moreover, spend much time in contexts where American values and ways of doing things are not the norm. Many of us do not speak another language. We're not, as a people, very good at understanding how different countries are different—either from us or from each other. And we often don't see the direct effects of our institutions in other countries. As a result, it is often difficult for us to understand why people in other countries act the way they do toward us—why people in some countries may even "hate us" and seek to inflict harm on our citizens.

In the broadest sense, however, the task of understanding ourselves in relation to the rest of the world is one of the most important curricular challenges that educators face. Not only will on-going "globalization" bring us into contact with people from many different parts of the world, but the political tensions resulting from our post-industrial economy are likely to pose serious challenges to international peace and understanding (see chap. 11). In an era in which U.S. educators are increasingly asked to focus narrowly on academic content, it may be wise to remember that creating and teaching understanding is, indeed, the larger work of schools.

CASE STUDY: UNDERSTANDING THE "NEW KIDS"

Background

Bob Michaels is the principal of Emory Middle School. It's his third year there and his second as school principal. Bob is from the Emory area, having grown up in a town about an hour away where his mother still lives. Bob got his M.Ed. at State College, and is working, slowly, on a doctorate. The degree has a number of requirements, including (and mysteriously to Bob) an international-comparative education class where, among other things, the students are asked to look at intercultural communication. Bob hasn't had a lot of experience with people from different countries and doesn't see much need for the class, but he is intrigued by a member of the project group to which he was assigned—a high school teacher from Paraguay, who married an American and taught in Los Angeles for a couple of years.

The School Situation

Emory is a small town with a traditional economic base of small-scale farming and light industry. Recently, a number of new businesses and industries have moved into the area, attracted by lower costs of living and of labor. The new businesses have attracted a group of immigrants seeking work. Town has traditionally enjoyed good race relations between Whites and a small number of African Americans whose families have lived in the town since the late 1890s, although the sudden influx of a large number of immigrants has strained ethnic relations.

Although the school year seems to be off to a good start, a fight breaks out among 20 or so students at a football game, and Bob decides he has to act. But what should he do? What can he do? To buy time while he figures out how to respond, Bob talks with local religious and community leaders.

The Problem

First, Bob convenes a meeting of teachers, parents, and community leaders from all groups. When he asks what's going on, parents of the new immigrants tell him that their kids feel excluded, patronized, not respected. Bob points out the efforts he has made to build the school's bilingual program. The parents respond by saying that the kids don't like the classes or the teachers. Students feel like the White kids get all the attention, and the "new kids" are shunted off to special classes, so regular teachers don't have to deal with them.

After two more incidents in the school cafeteria, Bob decides to organize a series of "dialogues" among different groups of students, both "old" and "new" kids, and among teachers. The dialogues seem to make everything worse at first.

"Old" kids and teachers complain about "new kids." "They just don't fit in," some students say. "It's our country," others complain. "The 'new kids' need to become American," "They need to learn English," according to others. Others wonder, "Why can't we all just get along?" Teachers also complain about the "new kids'" "lack of respect" and apparent unwillingness to take part in class. One teacher comments, "They don't even make eye contact when I talk to them."

The new kids, for their part, are quiet at first, but then raise a number of complaints of their own. "It seems like the teachers have us figured out as soon as they look at us." "They don't even know our names. We all look alike to them." "The 'old kids' don't ever talk to us. It's like we're not there." "They make fun of us and the way we talk."

The polarization gets worse. One more fight breaks out, and Bob holds an emergency meeting. An unusually large number of parents attend, many of them quite angry. A number of them are angry at Bob! Some parents call for more discipline and order. Others call for an end to the bilingual programs. Just as the meeting is about to end in a tense stalemate, the former mayor, a retired teacher himself, rises to speak. He begins with his own family history, the flight from persecution, the difficult early years as new immigrants. With his old-fashioned rhetoric of "the American dream," he calms the angry parents. He proposes that the community take on the challenge of learning to live with its newfound diversity. The parents agree, at least, to see what Bob comes up with.

How Cross-Cultural Communication Theory Helped

Bob turns to his books. He reads up on cross-cultural communication, some of which he finds useful, and some not. He talks to his Paraguayan friend who recommends a book about classroom interactions among students and teachers from different ethnic groups. Bob recognizes some of the patterns talked about in the book from his own experience as a teacher and principal.

As he explores these issues, Bob begins to get interested in the development of intercultural sensitivity. He starts to see how he and others look at things through the lens of their own culture, and how easily people see differences as bad. He recognizes his own tendencies to deny, defend, or minimize other cultural experiences as well as the tendency in his school to label the immigrant kids "deficient." Bob begins to empathize with the fearful "defensive" reaction of old-time residents as well as the anger of newcomers. Bob recognizes his own tendencies toward minimization. At the same time, he begins to see how minimization is almost as ineffective as polarization in dealing with the real differences across groups.

As he thinks about the situation, Bob becomes able to name the conflicts going on and to identify resources and strategies that might help his school. He talks with his Paraguayan classmate about his experiences, and reads a novel about the experience of a new immigrant in Texas schools. He enrolls in a workshop on intercultural conflict resolution and talks his Paraguayan colleague into helping him try it out.

The Solution

With assistance from an intercultural facilitator, Bob and his colleague from Paraguay set up a series of workshops with teachers. Over the next 6 months, teachers meet one Saturday morning a month to discuss the effects of culture in the classroom. Teachers are exposed to a variety of exercises that help them experience culture—feel and think about differences in more complex ways. Teachers at the denial stage are led to see differences. Those at the defense stage are encouraged to see their similarities with people from other cultural groups. Teachers who tend to minimize are helped to recognize and accept that people raised in different cultural communities see and experience the same things differently. The few teachers who are ready are prompted to learn and practice the codes of the other culture.

The experience of being different is personalized and supplemented with readings about cultural differences in teaching and learning styles. In teams of two, teachers interview parents of the new kids, with students serving as translators. Gradually, teachers become aware of their own cultural values and how these differ from those of the new kids and their families. Once the connections are made between differences in cultural beliefs and teaching and learning styles, the teachers are able to brainstorm about ways they might vary their teaching to better accommodate the learning styles of the new kids. Encouraged to bring examples of cross-cultural encounters to the seminars, teachers are led in a series of role plays and simulated encounters with new kids and their parents. Debriefing of these role-playing exercises helps teachers develop better ways to interact with the new students and their parents. Teachers work to apply what they have learned in lessons on conflict resolution focused on ethnic relations. In the meantime, a few new kids have joined the basketball team, and tensions ease.

The intercultural victory is likely not complete, and there is still some resistance. More than a few teachers wonder why they, not the new kids, "have to change." However, as a result of the family interviews, a few teachers who had originally asked "why we can't all get along" begin to see some of the barriers faced by the new immigrants. Most teachers still believe that the new kids need help to overcome the linguistic and cultural limitations of their background. A number, however, begin to enjoy some aspects of the newcomers' culture—food, a colorful religious festival, the dancing. Most parents—long-term residents of the Emory community—feel that the school should try to assimilate the newcomers as quickly as possible into the mainstream, but negative cultural stereotypes have become "politically incorrect." A few teachers overemphasize the differences between the cultures, prompting one new kid to complain, "We're not all like that, you know."

Still, most teachers and community members have passed from intolerance to tolerance, some to acceptance, and a few to respect. A few more "extreme" members of the community have begun to identify with the newcomers, wearing traditional newcomer clothes and peppering their speech with newcomer words. (Those members have always been considered a bit odd.) Some teachers begin to question their previously unquestioned acceptance of "familiar," "normal," and "dominant" attitudes and practices. Interestingly, some of the teenagers have started to "accessorize" with bits of newcomer culture. Few teachers question the basic assumptions under which they teach, but most have broadened their understanding of difference and, as a result, their classroom practice.

One teacher lands a scholarship to study overseas during the summer. As a result, an exchange student is invited to the school, and a number of pen pals are established. Although the changes are still relatively superficial and operate primarily at an individual level, they have made the school a much richer and more welcoming environment for all students.

CHAPTER SUMMARY

As this chapter points out, the most difficult culture to see is our own. The process of comparing cultures internationally, however, promotes our awareness of the general features of culture and how they function. Not only does such comparison enable us to evaluate our educational outcomes and practices in consideration of outcomes and practices in other countries, it gives us a way to see our own assumptions, taken-for-granted beliefs, and theories.

As Americans, we tend to want to do stuff, to get on with things. Don't bother us with theory, history, or philosophy! But our thinking doesn't come out of thin air. Our ideas, however much they may seem to reflect the reality in front of us, are a reflection of our history, our context, our experience, and the theories we've inherited and constructed:

This chapter argues for a comparative view of education, providing some theoretical tools for comparing the cultures and policy contexts that influence education systems around the world. As the chapter shows, comparison enables us to locate our own education system—its superficial and deeper characteristics—in relation to other systems. It also provides a view of what other systems have achieved and thereby offers a vision of what is possible. Comparison, moreover, gives us the opportunity to learn from other systems. And it permits us to see others more accurately, through increased awareness—of our own patterns of belief and behavior, of the *fact* of difference, and of others' cultural patterns. Most of all, by highlighting differences, comparison gives us the opportunity to make our habitual ways of acting and thinking visible, thereby allowing us to understand ourselves better, critique what we think and do, and revise or refine our policies and practices.

8

Gender, Sexuality, and School Leadership

Jerry D. Johnson

A highly revealing fact about the nature of public schooling may be this: Most teachers are women—almost 75% in 2000—but at the same time, only about 40% of principals are women (National Center for Education Statistics, 2004). And even fewer women occupy district superintendencies, an estimated 13%, according to Glass, Bjork, and Brunner (2000). Exactly what does this unequal representation mean?

According to some writers, it may mean that schools themselves, and the institution of schooling as a whole, have been structured to promote men to positions of formal power and authority. Indeed, according to some theorists, the very construct of "leadership" carries with it a bias toward males (e.g., Blackmore, 1993; Schmitt, 1994). If these theorists are correct—and the available evidence suggests that they very well might be—the schooling process itself probably communicates lessons about power relations in our society. And it communicates these lessons, not only to the adults employed by schools, but also, and arguably with even more profound consequences, to the children they serve.

This chapter considers the work of a wide range of scholars and theorists who have examined the male bias in school leadership, called into question its legitimacy and outcomes, and posited alternative approaches. These theorists and scholars do not represent the mainstream in the administrative sciences; they are, indeed, its critics. Moreover, their critique comes from a wider perspective on power relations in Western society. This perspective sees a world in which various functions—parent, worker, administrator, nurse, farmer, President—are handed down to successive generations already "gendered," already possessing a script. This script, which schooling helps to communicate, tells us what's permissible, or usual, or "normal" for boys and girls, men and women.

In exploring the work of gender theorists, this chapter helps both men and women understand the notion of "gendered roles" and the complexities of gender equity. One of the most important points suggested by the discussion that follows is that, ironically, socially constructed "female" characteristics may make women particularly well suited to lead schools and districts. Because these characteristics are constructs rather than biological features of the sex, men, too, can cultivate them; moreover, and perhaps more critically, both sexes can help to build organizations that cultivate them.

Importantly, moving beyond traditional male-biased thinking about school leadership is not simply a matter of replacing a singularly male perspective with one jointly shared by men and women. It is about moving beyond simplistic definitions of "man" and "woman" to acknowledge complexities in individuals' identities, and to consider the implications for leadership of varied identities and their perspectives. Thus, if we are to really move beyond simplistic definitions of male and female, we need to bring sexuality into the equation—and that's a real leap for many in education and school leadership. It's a leap that the authors feel needs to be made.

Sexuality and Education

Arguments against everything from sex education curricula to the formation of student organizations to combat homophobia take the position that *sex and sexuality have no place in schools*. As an example, the following statements were made by the president of the Massachusetts Family Institute: "Why should one impose what they do in their private lives onto students? Shouldn't we be spending our money on making sure they know American History rather than on exploring sexuality?" (Pappano, 2003, pp. 8–9).

These kinds of rhetorical questions are common in the discourse surrounding issues of sexuality and gender relations in schools. The first, in fact, points to an even broader question: whether or not learning itself is value free—the result of a direct and unadulterated transfer of information from teacher to student. In a value-free conceptualization of learning, personal characteristics of the student and of the teacher are irrelevant. Critics of this conceptualization see it as unworkable if students are to deal with more than simple "facts" and develop capabilities other than simple "skills." They argue, moreover, that value-free learning may never be possible, in other words, that learning even simple facts and skills implicates values.

In fact, the value-free view of learning, according to some, actually embeds a particular, if hidden, moral perspective. Interestingly, conservatives see the hidden perspective as too permissive (e.g., Doyle, 1997), whereas radicals see it as too wishy-washy (e.g., Cornell, 1991). Both sets of critics, however, agree that education is, by its very nature, value-laden; it's all about values. And it's also all about identity because—no matter how narrowly construed—education helps shape identity.

The second rhetorical question posed by Pappano really gets to the matter of the aims of schooling. Those who construe school's aims in a narrow way—as academic achievement, perhaps—see concern for other matters, such as sex education or gender equity, as an interruption.

But anyone who's worked in a school will know that gender dynamics and sexuality show up in schools every day simply because students do not (and cannot be made to) leave their identities at the schoolhouse door.[1] Moreover, the "hidden curriculum" conveys messages to students about sexuality and gender—and the connection between the two. As Epstein and Johnson (1998, p. 2) explained,

> As places of everyday-life activity as well as public or state institutions, schools are sites where sexual and other identities are developed, practiced, and actively produced. Pupils, but also teachers and to a lesser extent other participants (parents, usually mothers, and other carers for example), are 'schooled' there, as gendered and sexual beings. Sexual and other social identities, as possible ways of living, are produced in relation to the cultural repertoires and institutional conditions of schooling. School-based identity production is never final, nor can it encompass the whole of (even sexual) life—but it can have lasting, ramifying consequences in individual lives nonetheless.

With this view in mind, it seems clear that, if schools are to serve the interests of students and school personnel alike, understanding of and sensitivity to these issues is imperative. Ignoring or avoiding sexuality and gender dynamics won't make them go away, but ignoring these issues when they become evident in day-to-day experience can lead to physical, emotional, and intellectual damage to the individuals who learn and work together in a school. Two bodies of theoretical literature help educators think about these issues.

Feminist Theory

Feminist theory provides a useful starting point for examining the way education contributes to the social construction of gender roles, individuals'

---

[1] Here we are paraphrasing from the famous Supreme Court decision in the 1969 *Tinker v. Des Moines* case, which argued that "students do not leave their rights at the schoolhouse door."

gendered identities, and gender relations. And it's a complex body of theory. In fact, there is no single, easy-to-pinpoint, definition of feminism, so what it means to hold a feminist perspective differs considerably from theorist to theorist and from practitioner to practitioner (Bowen & Wyatt, 1993). In fact, much of feminist theory rejects the idea that we can characterize *anything* definitively. A better way to view feminist theory, then, is as a set of loosely related "feminisms," assumptions applicable to most (but not all) feminist theory.

One avenue for exploring these assumptions is to consider what the "project" of feminism is all about—what this body of theory hopes to accomplish. Bowen and Wyatt (1993) developed such an analysis, concluding that the following approaches seem to be shared across most "feminisms:"

1. Feminist theories focus explicitly on the experiences of women, moving their experiences from the margins to the center of attention.
2. They attempt to show how social relations and academic discourse have shaped our conceptions of gender and gender roles.
3. They explore the ways that society unfairly distributes valued resources (e.g., wealth, power, status, and access) on the basis of gender and other "differences."
4. They examine the ways language is used to reinforce a dominant view of social reality.
5. They recognize that society is complex and that, therefore, a variety of methodologies must be used in order to study it.
6. They question the conventional basis for valuing certain kinds of knowledge and excluding other kinds of knowledge.
7. They view research as an equal partnership between researchers and study participants.

Drawing on these assumptions, feminists who focus on organizations such as schools assert that traditional theories have limited ability to comprehend and account for differing perspectives about what's going on. But feminist approaches—because they are both critical and receptive to multiple views of reality—help people who work in organizations uncover dynamics that might otherwise remain hidden. Of course, these theories are particularly helpful for unpacking issues related to differences in the opportunities, status, and rewards available to males and females in a particular society (ours, for instance).

Extensions Into Queer Theory

Just as feminist theories emerged from the identification and disclosure of the limitations of theory in the masculine tradition, a new set of theories—under the umbrella of *queer theory*—emerged from consideration of the limitations in feminist theory. Unlike feminist theory's rejection of masculine assumptions, however, queer theory accepts many of the assumptions of feminism. In fact, it represents a logical extension of feminism—a more complete stage of development for ideas first developed in the feminist tradition.

"Queer theory" is a term that may be unfamiliar to readers of this book, and it is certainly a term that will not be found in most texts on school leadership. That's part of the problem. As discussion throughout this book emphasizes, examining and understanding organizations from as many different perspectives as possible is important work. Queer theory represents another perspective. In fact, the perspective provided by queer theory offers a model for approaching individual perspectives as themselves multifaceted, grounded in individual identities that are themselves multivalent.

The term *queer*, for much of its rhetorical history, served as a derogatory term for homosexuals. As academics working in the area of gay and lesbian studies began to push against their own disciplinary boundaries in the mid-1980s, however, the term queer was eventually appropriated for use in describing an approach to understanding sexuality that sought to transcend the limitations of defining individuals as gay, lesbian, bisexual, or straight. Queer theory, put simply, sets forth the idea that an individual's gender and sexuality are not fixed—either by biology or by socialization—but are simply the outward manifestations of decisions and acts by that individual. Terms like *gay*, *lesbian*, and so on are then replaced with the less restrictive term *queer*.

A later section of the chapter explores queer theory in a bit more detail, and particularly its applicability to schools and school leadership. First, however, the chapter considers some of the implications of traditional notions of gender by examining the roles that women have played in the educational enterprise and considering the roles they might play.

THE HISTORY OF WOMEN'S INVOLVEMENT IN EDUCATION

For the educational historian Joel Spring (1990), the schooling enterprise in 19th-century America is a story of the common school movement and its heroine, the schoolmarm. What emerges from Spring's examination is a narrative of how the expedient employment of women teachers led—ultimately and ironically—to the repositioning of women from the furthest margins of the colonial schooling enterprise to a point where, by 1890, 66% of the nation's nearly 400,000 public school teachers were women (Holmes & Weiss, 1995).

Spring contended that the realization of the "common school dream" was predicated, first and foremost, on the creation of a *stable, inexpensive, and moral teaching force*. Given this need, and the social and economic strictures under which women lived in the early 19th century, women teachers and the common school movement made a perfect match.

Beginning with the Troy Female Seminary, started in 1814, higher education for women was closely tied to preparation for teaching, the only occupation that was realistically open to women graduates. The curriculum at Troy was rigorous, however—including Latin and higher math—and afforded young women the opportunity to pursue academic work at levels that were unavailable to generations before them (Berkin & Norton, 1979).

The reason why women were drawn to teaching as a field of study and as a profession is self-evident: It was virtually the only choice they had. The reason why school boards and other hiring entities were drawn to women teachers merits consideration as well. Horace Mann's 1841 Boston School Board Annual Report asserted that women are better suited for teaching because they (a) possess natural childrearing skills, (b) are less distracted by worldly forces, and (c) are more morally upright than their male counterparts. It's easy to dismiss such stereotypes—that is, women had been given few, if any, opportunities to demonstrate skills in areas other than childrearing; women had little or no access to distracting worldly forces; and, owing to social and statutory norms, women's moral uprightness was under the direct control of their fathers or husbands. It's not so easy to dismiss the following statement from the report, however:

> As a class, they never look forward, as young men almost invariably do, to a period of legal emancipation from parental control, when they are to break away from the domestic circle and go abroad into the world, to build up a fortune for themselves; and hence, the sphere of hope and effort is narrower, and the whole forces of the mind are more readily concentrated upon the present. (Mann, as cited in Spring, 1990, p. 118)

Clearly, the educational, economic, and social constraints faced by women led to the creation of a captive labor market for schools.

Moreover, as mentioned earlier, the common school movement needed a teaching force that was not only stable and morally upright, but also *inexpensive*. Again, women fit the bill. Those who joined the ranks of the teaching profession could expect to earn as little as one-third of the salary that would be paid to a man in the same position.[2] No wonder the growing numbers of educated women

---

[2] In 1841, a rural male teacher could expect to earn $4.15 weekly, whereas a female rural teacher could expect only $2.51. In urban areas, the disparity was even greater; $11.93 weekly for men and $4.44 weekly for women. By 1864, wages had increased, but the disparity remained fairly constant—$7.86 versus $4.92 in rural areas, and $20.78 versus $7.67 in urban areas (Elsbree, 1939, as cited in Spring, 1990).

proved a boon to the common school movement. The "Littleton Plan" echoes Mann in even more explicit terms:

> God seems to have made women peculiarly suited to guide and develop the infant mind, and it seems to your committee very poor policy to pay a man 20 or 22 dollars a month, for teaching children their ABCs, when a female could do the work more successfully at one-third the price. (Stow, MA School Committee Annual Report, cited in Holmes & Weiss, 1995, p. 137)

Thus, in meeting the needs of girls and young women who sought higher education and an occupation, the teacher training programs also served the needs of the common school movement by providing communities with the inexpensive teaching force they required.

The 19th century saw vastly increased opportunities for women to further their education and to enter the professional ranks. As interpreted by some historians (e.g., Holmes & Weiss, 1995; Spring, 1990), however, the common school movement mirrored broader structures of oppression, reproducing an imbalance of power that made it extremely difficult for women to attain leadership roles in education (see Sidebar 8-1).

Sidebar 8-1: Leadership Roles in the Early 20th Century

As the 19th century came to a close, women dominated the ranks of the teaching profession. The percentage of the teaching workforce comprised of women rose steadily throughout the 1800s and into the 1900s, peaking in 1920 when 86% of 719,188 teachers were women (Holmes & Weiss, 1995). Moreover, this dominance by women occurred not only at the level of early childhood and elementary education (the levels for which they had long been stereotyped as well-suited), but at the high school level as well. By 1880, 60% of high school teachers in America were women (Biklen, 1987).

Despite their overwhelming numbers in the teaching ranks, however, the accession of women into leadership positions came slowly, and in the face of marked resistance. Of note, the accession did come about more readily in rural areas of the West and Midwest, where educated males were in short supply, and by the beginning of the 20th century, the position of county superintendent was frequently filled by a woman in these regions of the country (Holmes & Weiss, 1995).

In metropolitan areas, these changes came about much more slowly. There were, however, notable trailblazers who achieved leadership positions against almost overwhelming odds:

- Ella Flagg Young, who served as superintendent of Chicago City Schools from 1909–1915.
- Dr. Ethel Percy Andrus, who served as principal of Abraham Lincoln High School in Los Angeles from 1916–1944.
- Susan M. Dorsey, who served as superintendent of Los Angeles City Schools from 1920–1928.

These pioneers, noteworthy leaders in their own right, serve as exceptions rather than the rule. They met the challenges not only of attaining and exercising leadership in a male-dominated world, but of fending off hostile attempts to discredit and subordinate them (e.g., through accusations of lesbianism; see Blount, 1999).

To a certain extent, the division of labor within the field of education continues to reflect the more general social patterns of the nation—that is, in education as in society, a disproportionate number of men hold leadership positions. Nevertheless, women in the field of education have been more successful at assuming leadership roles than women in, say, the corporate world. In the next section, we look at just how successful.

Recent Levels and Types of Involvement

In 1999–2000, women made up 74.8% of the teaching force, but only 43.8% of principalships (NCES, 2004).[3] These numbers represent substantial gains over the last 30 years. Of particular note, the percentage of women principals in public schools increased from 35.8% to 43.8% from 1994 to 2000. Still, the representation of women in administration is clearly not proportional to their representation in schooling at large.

Moreover, the gains that have been made have come about mostly at the level of middle management (i.e., principal and assistant principal). Gains at the top (i.e., the superintendency) have not come about so readily. A recent sampling of 2,262 district superintendents revealed that only 13.1% were women (Glass et al., 2000). Figures from individual states paint a similar picture:

- A 1995 study revealed a total of 83 women superintendents in Illinois, over half of whom led small districts (i.e., with fewer than 1,000 students);

[3]Women did, however, make up 54.6% of *private school* K–12 principalships in 1993–1994 (NCES, 2004). Significantly, private school principals often supervise smaller schools with younger children (many private schools are elementary only) and for much lower pay; this perhaps suggests a more subtle bias against women who seek positions as educational leaders.

• In a 1988 Washington study, 14% (42 total) of 289 superintendents were women, and 43% (18) of the 42 women superintendents led districts with fewer than 245 students (Wolverton, 1999).

Clearly, gains at the level of the superintendency have lagged behind gains in middle management. Moreover, women's increased access to the superintendency has come about primarily in smaller districts with lower pay. This circumstance suggests that many hiring entities still question women's abilities as organizational leaders, particularly their ability to manage larger organizations. And for those women who do succeed at attaining superintendent positions, the costs are high: One multiple-state survey revealed that female superintendents are far more likely than their male counterparts to be single, divorced, widowed, or to have commuter marriages (McCreight, 1999). The future holds hope, however, according to some researchers (see Sidebar 8-2).

Sidebar 8-2: Looking Ahead

Some researchers predict that the future looks brighter for aspiring women administrators. Logan (1998) pointed to six changing conditions that, collectively, bode well for gender equity in hiring practices for school principals and superintendents:

1. School-site governance structures that emphasize local accountability for student achievement have changed the nature of who hires school leaders.

2. The increasing desire for leadership skills that promote collaboration, consensus-building, and empowerment of others has resulted in more opportunities for women.

3. An increasing number of vacancies and a dwindling applicant pool for positions of principal and superintendent have created high demand conditions for qualified aspirants, affording women candidates more opportunities.

4. Antidiscrimination legislation has fostered a more open environment for hiring women in nontraditional roles and has led more women to enter higher education.

5. Women have made up at least half of educational administration program enrollments since the mid-1980s, increasing their numbers in the hiring pool.

> 6. An increase in the percentage of women in the educational adminis-
> tration field means that more role models and support will be available
> to women.
>
> Other studies (Hill & Ragland, 1995; Scollay & Logan, 1999) have consid-
> ered the impacts of these conditions, and make similar arguments.

Certainly, women have made huge strides since the 19th century to secure their place in the leadership ranks of a profession they so clearly dominate in overall numbers. A division of labor still exists, however. In the next section, we examine the substantive difficulties that women administrators face as they attempt to retain their own identity while assuming a role that is socially designated (and socially constructed) as "man's work."

EQUALITY AND THE FEMINIST PLATFORM: WOMEN IN MEN'S CLOTHING

As noted earlier, feminist theorists have contended that not just the field, but the *construct* of school administration has been dominated by men:

> Educational theory and administrative practice have been dominated by men, who have acted as "gatekeepers" in setting the standards, producing the social knowledge and decreeing what is significant, relevant, and important in light of their own experience. (Blackmore, 1993, p. 27)

What Blackmore and others (e.g., Schmitt, 1994) have claimed is that there is a *masculinist hegemony* in educational administration. Operating in such a context, even those women who do succeed as administrators are succeeding in a "man's world." Although such success is an important achievement, it nevertheless "leaves unchallenged the hegemonic masculinity embodied in the principles and structures of administration" (Blackmore, 1993, p. 45). So working to increase the numbers of women administrators may be a worthy goal, but it is not enough. Theorists like Blackmore have argued that what is needed is a redefinition of leadership that is *inclusive* of multiple perspectives—including those grounded in gender and sexuality.

Articulating an inclusive leadership model is only the first step; widespread enactment of such models of leadership will be considerably more difficult. According to some writers, moreover, the way we prepare potential leaders for educational administration positions all too often contributes to the problem, perhaps unwittingly (Schmitt, 1994). Schmitt's work demonstrates how the research base that grounds much educational administration coursework is rooted in the experiences of men operating in male-dominated settings.[4] Put simply, the masculine perspective is the default setting.

Adapting to a "Man's World"

So, while women have gained significant ground in the field of educational administration, the enterprise itself is still dominated by men and its perspective is masculine. One might argue that this circumstance persists largely because of historical precedent and the resistance of organizations to change, but that argument may be too simplistic. According to some feminists in particular, that argument fails to account for the hegemonic power of the masculine culture. In fact, these theorists contend, men dominate the ranks precisely because they are inherently better suited for educational administration *as it has been traditionally understood and accepted.* There is a very important distinction to be made here. Men are not inherently better suited for leading schools; they are, however, better suited for occupying positions that have been defined (or *normalized*) in terms of the experiences of men previously serving in these positions (Hoyle & Skrla, 1999; Skrla, 2000).

So, the dynamic of *man as administrator and administrator as man* has operated cyclically to standardize a gendered definition of school leadership. In such a system, those with perspectives that differ from traditional male roles operate from outside the mainstream—a perspective that is inevitably critical. Marshall and Mitchell (1989), for example, built on Ferguson's (1984) analysis of women's place in a capitalist society to conceptualize women's careers as a critique of the administrative culture. Gender differences are present and important—in preferences, values, moral decision making. Moreover, women's characteristics are "deviant" in the face of male "defaults." These deviant values are discouraged and controlled by bureaucracies seeking to suppress opposition and propagate themselves through the succession of like successors. Rather than consider these deviant qualities of women as shortcomings or even simple misalignments, Marshall and Mitchell suggested that they are best understood and utilized as a means of highlighting deficiencies in the existing administrative culture.

In light of the normalization of a masculine hegemony and the resulting deviancy inherent in feminist approaches to leadership, women leaders inevitably

---

[4]There are, of course, exceptions. Schmitt also examined the impact of the Women in Leadership (WIL) Program at Eastern Michigan University, in which women's experiences and feminist theory are actively incorporated into thinking and learning about schools and school leadership.

face role conflict. One significant form of conflict exists when the coworkers of female leaders have conflicting expectations of (a) how a woman should behave, and (b) how a leader should behave (Tully, 1989). This type of conflict can create serious problems for the leader and for the organization. In moving toward a view of leadership that is inclusive of women's perspectives and qualities, then, it's important that we examine the perceptions of women leaders held by their coworkers.

Coworkers' Perceptions of Women Leaders.   Research on this issue suggests a paradox (Hudson & Rea, 1996; Irby & Brown, 1995). In general, coworkers—both men and women—recognize differences in the characteristics of male and female leaders, and share many of the same ideas about what characteristics define a good or effective leader. Moreover, the shared ideas about good or effective leadership are closely aligned with the perceived characteristics of women in leadership positions. Given these findings, it seems obvious that school people *ought* to prefer women leaders. But that's not the case. Despite a preference for the leadership characteristics that women are more likely to bring to administrative jobs, coworkers—again, both men and women—still indicate a preference for male leaders.[5]

Put simply and directly, the characteristics that are desired in leadership are characteristics that women appear to possess in ample supply—and more so than men. Because of the historical dominance of men in the field and the long-standing masculine ideology of leadership, however, women are less likely to be perceived as being right for the job. In contrast to the earlier image of "women in men's clothing" as a representation of the notion that women who join the ranks of school administrators must operate within a masculine hegemony, then, we might consider this a case of schools preferring "men in women's clothing."

RESEARCH FINDINGS ABOUT WOMEN'S LEADERSHIP

This section of the chapter provides a brief overview of some of the more significant research findings about women and their approaches to leadership. Although this evidence is useful for our description of some of the qualities and

---

[5]One other study examined the attitudes and perceptions of superintendents and school board presidents with regard to women in educational leadership (Shepard, 1997). A follow-up to a 1978 administration of the same survey, the 1996 respondents continued to perceive differences in the leadership characteristics of both women and men, but were more accepting of women leaders than were the 1978 respondents. Of note, in both survey years, superintendents were more accepting of women leaders than were school board presidents.

approaches that traditional leadership models exclude or downplay, a caveat is in order: In considering prototypically female approaches to leadership, we need to be careful not to "essentialize," ascribing specific characteristics separately to males or females and ignoring the complexities of individual identities (Capper, 1993; Grogan, 1996).

With this caveat in mind, the discussion turns to the evidence. Ozga (1993) provided a concise synthesis of research on leadership styles of women in school administration:

> Women's leadership styles are less hierarchical and more democratic. Women, for example, run more closely knit schools than do men, and communicate better with teachers. They use different, less dominating body language, and different language and procedures. Women appear more flexible and sensitive, and often more successful ... women spend less time on deskwork than men, visit more classrooms, keep up to date on curricular issues, spend more time with their peers and sponsor other women. Their language is more hesitant and tentative, their agendas more informal and flexible, and ... less distan[t] from subordinates ... Women emphasize cohesiveness. They are much less individualistic and spend time on fostering an integrative culture and climate ... women cope more readily with 'routine stress' and defuse conflict. They do not engage in displays of anger as control mechanisms and hence may be judged as weak ... group activities are much more highly valued by women than by men. (Blackmore, 1999, pp. 56–57)

In general, this research suggests that women leaders focus on relationships, use participatory approaches to management, and focus on tasks. In addition, women leaders tend to experience and respond to conflict in ways that differ from the experiences and responses of men.

Relationship Focus

In her groundbreaking text, *Women in Educational Administration* (1987), Carol Shakeshaft contended that "relationships with others are central to all actions of women administrators" (p. 197). Shakeshaft based this claim on literature indicating that women tend to display the following practices directed toward cultivating and sustaining relationships:

- Women administrators spend more of their time in meetings—both formal and informal—and in telephone conversations, and they spend more of their time engaged in contacts initiated by others (Berman, 1982).
- They exhibit a different *style* of interaction than their male counterparts—more informal, flexible, and casual (Pitner, 1981).

• They favor people-oriented projects (Palmer, 1983).

Shakeshaft noted that studies of female principals also suggest that they have more contact with subordinates than do male principals, and that they engage in interactions with male teachers much more often than male principals engage in interactions with female teachers (Gilbertson, 1981). Other research suggests that female superintendents interact more with other women, both within and outside the school system, as well as interacting more with teachers and students (Pitner, 1981). As part of their interaction with teachers, moreover, female superintendents visit schools much more often than do their male counterparts, and, when they visit, they spend more time in classrooms (Pitner, 1981).

More recent researchers (e.g., Blackmore, 1999; Curry, 2000) have questioned the usefulness of some of the earlier quantitative research cited by Shakeshaft and draw attention to contemporary qualitative approaches. These studies, using interview and case study methods, counter masculine discourse by examining the experiences, perspectives, and approaches of female leaders. In fact, one of the stated goals of such inquiry is to formulate a new discourse of feminist leadership. Findings from these studies tend to correspond closely to those reported in the earlier quantitative work, however.

Grogan (1996), for example, conducted interviews with women superintendents and found that her informants regarded "people skills" as their greatest strength. Others also viewed this characteristic as critical to the leadership that women provided. According to Grogan, the women superintendents in her study deployed care and interdependence as the basis for a distinctly moral approach to leadership (cf. Gilligan, 1993; Lyons, 1990).

In their analysis of case studies of female principals and superintendents, Regan and Brooks (1995) articulated a model of "relational leadership." Akin to "relational knowing" (Hollingsworth, 1992), this model construes interactions with others as central to the ways that women administrators create and process information and perform leadership responsibilities. According to Regan and Brooks, forming and maintaining relationships is not just something that women leaders do; it is, in fact, the way in which they do things.

Hurty (1995) found that female principals derive their power from relationships, rather than from traditional (hierarchical) authority structures. Acquiring power in this way, the women are able to exercise *power with* rather than *power over* (Brunner, 1994). The power they use focuses on collaboration, reciprocity, and mutuality, and it is grounded in what some theorists have termed "connectedness":

The vocabulary of connectedness symbolizes, perhaps most distinctly, the uniqueness of women's perspective on power. Connectedness refers to the importance of relationships and the web of human interaction that permeates and enriches any personal or organizational endeavor. Connectedness is illustrated by caring, interdependence, and the commitment to community. (Hurty, 1995, p. 395)

Participatory Management

Once again, Shakeshaft (1987) offers a useful review of early work. Her reading of the literature draws attention to key findings about women leaders and participatory management:

- Multiple studies (Berman, 1982; Hemphill, Griffiths, & Frederiksen, 1962, and Hines & Grobman, 1956) found that women's decision-making processes were perceived by subordinates as being more democratic, and were preferred by the subordinates.
- Fairholm and Fairholm (1984) found that the power tactics most often used by women principals—coalition building and cooptation—tended to support participation.
- Neuse (1978) found women leaders to be less committed to formal hierarchy and more willing to submerge personal power in order to encourage participation.
- Pitner (1981) reported that women superintendents were less likely to dominate meetings and more likely to use language that encouraged participation and the consideration of possibilities.
- Charters and Jovick (1981) found that women school leaders were more likely to engage in collegial decision making, an approach that actually served to enhance their power.

More recent qualitative studies also tend to confirm earlier findings while adding depth (see, e.g., Grogan, 1996; Regan & Brooks, 1995). Moreover, they demonstrate the collaborative approaches that women administrators use as they work to nurture community among school constituencies. For Regan and Brooks (1995), administrators' use of participatory management offers a school the opportunity to align a feminist vision with organizational and managerial substance: "rather than being the idiosyncratic decisions of one woman, [shared decisions] become solid examples of how implementation of the feminist attributes enrich school life for the entire community" (p. 54).

Task Focus

Research suggests that women leaders tend to focus attention on tasks as part of their commitment to community building. Tasks are, after all, what communities do in order to accomplish their most important aims, and even *traditional* leadership theory acknowledges that attention to both relationships *and* tasks is the key to effective leadership. Also of note, female leaders tend to direct more energy than men toward tasks that relate to instruction—that is, to the work that some researchers construe as schools' "core technology" (see, e.g., Petersen, 1999)—and they tend to derive more satisfaction than male leaders from those instructional tasks, including those related to supervision of instructional staff (Gross & Trask, 1964; Leonard, 1981; Young, 1984). Sidebar 8-3 provides a brief summary of one study of gender and leaders' focus on tasks.

Sidebar 8-3: Task Focus and Subordinates' Perceptions

Research by Forsyth and Forsyth (1984) offers insight into the complex relationships among task focus, gender, and subordinates' perceptions of feminist leadership. Their study examined the evaluative and perceptual biases (i.e., beliefs about what constitutes good leadership, and stereotyped beliefs about men and women) among organizational members. In the study, two separate groups (one with a stereotyped, conservative attitude toward women; the other with a nonstereotyped, liberal attitude) worked on a task under the direction of one of two women leaders (one fundamentally task oriented; the other fundamentally relationship oriented).

Results gathered from participant questionnaires and observations indicated that more conservative group members rejected the task-oriented female leaders, whereas liberal group members preferred the task-oriented female leaders. The study's findings suggest that biases against female leaders may be based on (a) subordinates' intuitive theories about leadership, and (b) their stereotyped expectations about how men and women will act when they serve as leaders (see also Tully, 1989).

Conflict

Female school leaders tend to manage conflict in ways that are closely related to their conceptualizations of power. One study (Hurty, 1995) explored women's perceptions about uses and misuses of power, concluding that "effective women principals use and talk about power in ways quite distinct from traditional power perspectives found in the literature of school administration and organizational theory" (p. 137). According to Hurty, for women, power is something to share—a perspective that shapes their typical reactions to conflict.

Other researchers (e.g., Bendelow, 1983; Hughes & Robertson, 1980) have claimed, moreover, that women's reactions to conflict tend to be more effective than traditional male reactions. They found, for instance, that (a) women are more likely to withdraw from conflict or to use collaborative strategies, whereas males are more likely to use authoritarian strategies and (b) women are more effective than men at resolving conflict among staff members and in using conflict reduction techniques.

Other research suggests a more complex interpretation. In one qualitative study involving female principals, Formisano (1987) explored the selection and use of specific strategies of conflict management in response to two types of conflict: (a) conflict thrust upon principals, and (b) conflict initiated by them. In response to both types of conflict, the actions of female principals were geared toward preserving interpersonal relationships. When another person initiated the conflict, the women principals tried to diffuse it by empathizing, asking questions and accommodating, using humor, giving the other person "a way out," and listening. When the principal herself initiated the conflict, she usually did so in order to stimulate productive collaboration on behalf of organizational change.

In addition to differences in approaches to managing conflict, research also suggests that the *frequency* and *kinds* of conflict are not the same for women and men (Shakeshaft, 1987). Hughes and Robertson (1980), for example, found that (a) women elementary school principals were more likely to have conflicts with male central office administrators than with parents, and (b) women elementary school principals reported no major conflicts with teachers. Several interpretations of the finding that women are more likely than men to have conflicts with central office administrators are possible. Hughes and Robertson favor an interpretation focusing on female principals' belief that they will never become the day-to-day colleagues of central office administrations. Shakeshaft, by contrast, suggested that the women principals may view the actions of male central office administrators (many with little or no elementary school experience) as direct challenges to their expertise and authority.

Studies comparing the conflict management styles and the task and relationship orientations of men and women as leaders rely on somewhat simplistic conceptions of gender, viewing it as a static demographic category. Research that might more properly be termed "feminist" does not principally inquire into the differences between men and women, as leaders or anything else. Instead, it seeks to explore the social world from the perspective of women. The insights made possible from this vantage point (i.e., from a feminist point of view) are explored in the next section.

THE FEMINIST PERSPECTIVE: POLITICS
OF DIFFERENCE AND THE ETHIC OF CARING

Over the past few decades, a growing number of academics (men and women) have applied feminist concerns to the examination of organizations, contributing to a broad and loosely constructed feminist critique of contemporary organizational theory. Wanca-Thibault and Tompkins (1998) have proposed a three-part typology for examining this perspective, consisting of (a) liberal feminism, (b) postmodern feminism, and (c) standpoint feminism.

Liberal feminism, which has provided the dominant perspective for feminism in America (Merchant, 1991), is derived from an examination of the central tenets of liberal democracy as viewed through the lens of women's experiences. Liberal democracy is predicated on *natural rights*, on participation in the processes of governing and of defining and sharing the common good. Liberal feminists have argued that women have been denied (namely, by men) the natural rights that all human beings should possess, and that the role of women in a capitalist democracy has been defined in ways that exclude them from substantive participation in the process of government and commerce.

Using liberal feminist theory as a critical lens, organizations can be evaluated on the extent to which women are treated equally. This line of inquiry focuses on questions such as "Are women paid the same as men for doing the same work?" and "Are women given equal access to promotion and other opportunities for advancement?" Put simply, the concerns of a critic operating from a liberal feminist perspective have to do with equality of opportunity. This perspective on organizations is important and even necessary, but it is also incomplete according to some feminists (e.g., Ashcraft, 1998).

Postmodern feminism operates from the assumption that discourse is what creates people's identities. "Male" and "female" are not "realities" in this conception; they are social constructs derived from patterns of discourse. Once these realities are deconstructed, language can be marshaled to pursue and posit other realities and to challenge the status quo via new patterns of discourse that construe women in ways that are empowering rather than marginalizing and subordinating.

Using postmodern feminism as a critical lens, researchers explore the ways that contemporary organizations produce discourse that creates and maintains individual and group identities. This discourse often results (via "teaching" and "learning") in power differentials—marginalization for some and power for others (Ashcraft, 1998). Postmodern feminist theory unpacks the discourse that has created and maintains inequities among men and women, and then offers new discourses.

Standpoint feminism evolved out of a Marxist consideration of the position of women with regard to the status quo. From this perspective, the politically and economically marginalized position of women serves as a useful platform from which to mount critique and transformation of the status quo. Whereas liberal feminism seeks "equality based on universal experiences, objective reality, order, and unity," standpoint feminism seeks "equality in terms of multiple realities and the complexity and richness that diversity brings" (Wanca-Thibault & Tompkins, 1998, p. 611). As it has evolved, this perspective has sought to account for the fact that experiences vary widely among women—most notably, along the lines of class, race, ethnicity, and nationality. This perspective then seeks to incorporate a diversity of voices aligned to challenge and transform the status quo; it doesn' seek a "unified voice" but rather a "unified order of diverse voices" (Bullis & Stout, 2000, p. 50).

Using feminist standpoint theory as a critical lens, scholars show how organizations mirror the status quo of society with its inequitable distributions of wealth and power. Women, in a Marxist sense, represent the *proletariat* of the organization because the role of women is to produce wealth for others who control the means of production. The unification and subsequent empowerment of women can then effect changes positioned to create a more equitable distribution of goods and power within the organization as a whole. The vantage point of the outsider is the position in an organization that allows for the clearest understanding of the inequities and strongest motivation for changing the organization. Standpoint feminism thus views the marginalized position of women in organizations as a viable leverage point from which to promote organizational change.

The Critical Vantage of the "Outsider"

As this discussion suggests, standpoint feminists contend that the institutional and cultural marginalization of women has resulted in the creation of an "outsider" vantage point that allows for and encourages critical insights into organizational structures and purposes. Harding (1991) offered a succinct statement on this vantage in her conceptualization of a feminist standpoint epistemology, which is premised on three assertions: (a) The experiences of women serve as a legitimate grounding for the construction of knowledge, (b) women must be allowed to speak from and about their gendered views of reality, and (c) women's everyday lives serve as criticisms of dominant ideologies grounded in male experiences.

Feminists like Harding aver that distinctly feminist lives and voices must share equally in the discourse that creates knowledge. They see this change as an imperative not only because it's an assertion of women's rights to be included, but because the outcomes are likely to be different when women play a substantive role in constructing knowledge (see Sidebar 8-4). Only with that repositioning, and the subsequent disclosure of multiple realities, can a more truthful and accurate representation of individuals, organizations, schools, and school leadership be rendered.

Sidebar 8-4: Do Women and Men Construct Knowledge Differently?

A 1986 study (Belenky, Clinchy, Goldberger, & Tarule) suggests that the processes through which men and women construct knowledge are appreciably different. Men tend to construct knowledge through processes of differentiation—differentiating ideas from one another, differentiating one's own perspectives from those of others—whereas women construct knowledge through processes of "connecting." Not only do women come to understand the world by seeking connections between their own experiences and those of others, they also seek connections among ideas. The differences in these approaches can be seen in classroom debates and discussion. In response to an initial claim, for example, males who participate might offer "no … but" responses. Women, by contrast, tend to offer "yes … and" responses.

Women's Special Propensity for Leadership in Contemporary Schools

Both the expectations for and the needs of the schooling enterprise in America have clearly changed from the common schools of the 19th century. The demands placed on leaders have changed as well. Today's schools appear to require leaders who bring to the table perspectives that are different from (and even opposite to) those supported by the bureaucratic and scientific management models that have been handed down. Feminist theorists contend that leadership grounded in the experiences of women can offer just such perspectives.

Grogan (1996, p. 161) provided examples of what contemporary school districts want in superintendency candidates, taken from job postings in four actual school districts:

- Skill[ed] in human relations and capable of working effectively with persons of differing personalities and viewpoints.
- Patient, caring, creative, respectful, and enthusiastic friend of the [district's] children.
- Accessible leaders with strong listening and communication skills, able to generate positive, trusting relationships.
- Leaders with outstanding human relationship skills.

The desired characteristics are quite clearly aligned with research findings about women's approaches to leadership.

In another work, Grogan (2000) explored the demands placed on superintendents in what she described as "the increasingly unpredictable environment" of K–12 schools (p. 117). Much of what is now demanded of superintendents[6] is related—directly and indirectly—to three definite and substantial shifts in the schooling enterprise: (a) a broadening of the definition of individuals who constitute the "stakeholders" in the schools, (b) an opening up of the schools to examination and input on the part of stakeholders, and (c) an ever-increasing supply of data for use (also misuse and abuse) in assessing the outcomes of schooling. The combination of these three shifts has, according to Grogan (pp. 117–118), produced key issues now confronted by school leaders:

- Varied stakeholders mean varied perspectives, needs, visions, and proposed solutions.
- Ambiguous messages from the varied stakeholders translate into pressure for continuous change.

The result is possible confusion for the school leader, particularly in *information management* and *human relations*. The combination of (a) vast amounts of information, (b) a diverse group of stakeholders, and (c) the need to share information widely requires that school leaders exercise considerable care over what to share, how to share it, and when to share it.

Someone deft at this work is unlikely to be a mere "manager." Being a woman, however, does not necessarily make an administrator deft at this work, either. Women can easily lead from the masculine perspectives—that is how many administrators are prepared, according to feminist theorists (see, e.g.,

---

[6]A growing movement toward school-based decision-making models (see Ziebarth, 1999) has resulted in principals leading and interacting with the public in ways that are quite similar to that of the superintendent; thus, much of what Grogan and others have to say about the superintendency is equally applicable to the concerns of school-level leaders.

Blackmore, 1989; Koll, et al, 1996). What might leadership from the feminist vantage look like? Strachan (1999) offered a reconceptualized leadership model in which leaders (a) work for improved social justice and equity for staff and students in schools, (b) challenge and resist injustices, (c) empower those with whom they work, and (d) establish a caring school community.

QUEER THEORY

Queer theory, in its short history, is related to both feminism and postmodernism. Although concerned most with social constructions of sexuality, queer theory is not "gay and lesbian theory," even if it is partly informed by the circumstances of gay and lesbian life. In its broadest formulations, it's about defining ways of being in the world that diverge sharply from "normal." One might observe that such divergence has been a prominent American project for some time (think about the icons of youth culture for the past 40 years). Such a position may strike some readers as peculiarly, or perversely, inapt for thinking about American schools. If some schools, however, are normally dysfunctional, then queer theory may have unexpected applicability. A final section of the chapter explores the concept of *queer leadership* to see what utility it might offer prospective principals and superintendents.

We do want to keep in mind, here, that perceptions about sexuality are considered adequate cause (especially among students) for belittlement, harassment, and abuse in far too many schools. From the standpoint of queer theory, this durable and widespread reality constitutes a sufficient provocation for its development and usefulness.

Difference and Identity

Difference is central to any conceptualization of identity:

> Identity gives us an idea of who we are and of how we relate to others and to the world in which we live. Identity marks the ways in which we are the same as others who share that position, and the ways in which we are different from those who do not. (Woodward, 1997, p. 2)

Feminism, initially, was about moving beyond a world defined through the perceptions and understandings of men. Women, feminism asserted, were not an incomplete or inferior form of man; they were *different* from men. As such, an identity needed to be constructed that would articulate (a) how women are different from men, and (b) how women are like other women.

Postmodern theorists viewed this two-part differentiation as too limited a construct through which to engage identity considerations. Traditional feminism construed women as one of only two possible collective identities, men and women, each with individual shared characteristics, interests, and commitments. Women, in this construct, were differentiated from men, as men were differentiated from women. Women were not differentiated from other women, however, nor were men differentiated from other men. This dichotomy left no opportunity for further differentiation, no way to further consider questions of identity beyond the two categories based on biological sex.

According to Butler (1990), feminists rejected the position that biology determines identity only to develop a narrative wherein the patriarchal culture imposes masculine and feminine genders, respectively, on men and women, thus ensuring the same result as the biological arguments they had dismissed.

Drawing largely on Foucault, Butler deconstructed the continuum of sex (male or female) causing gender (masculine or feminine) which in turn causes desire (for the other gender). What she posited instead is a notion of gender and desire as free floating and entirely independent of biology. Gender, in this construct, is something that one *performs*, not something that one *is*. This idea is central to queer theory—that is, the idea that one's identity (particularly in terms of gender or sexuality) is not the outward manifestation of an inner self, but a deliberate act, a choice that may well take different forms at differing times and places (see chap. 10, also, on "the coherent self.")

Sexual Hatred and Schooling

According to findings from a relevant national survey (Gay, Lesbian, and Straight Education Network, 2003), most lesbian, gay, bisexual, and transsexual students enter hostile environments each time they go through the schoolhouse doors. Verbal harassment was reported by 84% of student respondents, and 92% reported hearing homophobic remarks on a regular basis. Respondents viewed intervention by educators as poor, with 83% reporting that educators seldom or never intervened on their behalf. Just 3% of students reported that intervention by educators was consistent (i.e., always). Physical harassment and victimization were reportedly prevalent as well, with 39% reporting physical harassment and 58% reporting damage or theft related to sexual hatred. In fact, 64% felt unsafe at school because of their sexuality. (Sidebar 8-5 presents some alternatives.)

Other research has suggested that diminished academic performance may be the least harmful of negative impacts linked to hostile school environments. Others include higher rates of depression, higher rates of alcohol and drug abuse, higher rates of risky sexual behaviors, increased likelihood for running away and/or homelessness, and higher suicide rates (Human Rights Watch, 2001).

Sidebar 8-5: Schools, Teaching, and Homophobia

Are schools the only agents or institutions in a person's life to impose such burdens and threaten such injuries as those mentioned? Of course not. Schools are part of society and help create and recreate it through the socialization of young people. School leaders can, like most educators, turn a blind eye to the hostility prevailing in their schools, and by their blindness help produce the outcomes reported. Or they can see what's going on and work to reduce the hostility.

It seems unlikely that people are born fearing homosexuals. That's not to imply that the schools they attended are entirely responsible—a multitude of institutions are involved (e.g., families, communities, churches, the military). What's required to reduce hostility is not terribly challenging. GLSEN (2003), for example, suggests a three-part approach:

1. Institute policies that include "sexual orientation and gender identity" as protected categories parallel with existing categories of race, religion, and ability.
2. Provide training for teachers on how to support gay students.
3. Create and support student support programs such as Gay-Straight Student Alliances.

These provisions are fairly common in higher education. It takes courage and perspicacity to bring them to K–12 schooling, but the evidence suggests that they are needed.

Queer Leadership

The effects of sexual hatred in schools are not limited to the experiences of students. Faculty members who "come out" and publicly acknowledge their sexuality also face threats, harassment, and discrimination. Many teachers who keep their sexuality hidden say they do so out of fear of losing their jobs (Human Rights Watch, 2001). And it's a justifiable fear. Only 11 states and the District of Columbia prohibit discrimination in employment on the basis of sexual orientation, and only two of those—Minnesota and the District of Columbia—prohibit discrimination on the basis of gender identity.

Ironically, even the growth and acceptance of student support networks does not guarantee progress toward easing the pressures faced by teachers and staff. In Massachusetts, where state department officials estimate that two-thirds of all high schools have a Gay-Straight Alliance (GSA) student organization, there is still considerable pressure for teachers and staff to stay in the closet—in Boston, for instance, only about 20 of the system's 5,000 teachers are openly gay, according to the coordinator for the districts Safe Schools Initiative for GLBT Youth (Pappano, 2003).

What's lost by forcing scores of educators to stay in the closet? The points made by feminist theorists of leadership are relevant. Masculine ways of being predominate in the field of administration theory and practice; educators who practice a sexuality different from most of their peers also exist, whether men or women, outside the masculine territory. Their insights about finding a path in life will be missing from the conversation because of the prejudices of the field and of society—unless it is safer for them to talk.

Leadership informed by queer theory offers the potential for vision, thought, and action that is not restricted by dishonest, or overly prescriptive, conceptions of "normality." Queer leadership is, by definition, broadly emancipatory in purpose. That is, like leadership operating from the perspective of feminists, culturalists, and postmodernists, queer leadership emerges from an understanding and recognition of the dynamics of power and control. In the case of queer theory, that understanding emerges from insights about identity. Out of such insights, theorists contend, comes a general commitment to freedom and personal fulfillment (Strachan, 1999; Wislocki-Goin, 1993).

This kind of leadership has implications for everything from schoolwide governance structures to teachers' responsiveness to individual learning styles. Queer theorists have argued that gendered experiences are the catalyst and the vantage point for critical understanding, useful for helping all those (and not just homosexuals) who are poorly served by the status quo. It seems reasonable that prospective school leaders consider perspectives offered by the active and thoughtful consideration of difference grounded in gender and sexuality. It may seem strange to some readers that sexuality should be viewed as a key to human understanding, but such insights were the foundation of psychoanalysis and the work of Sigmund Freud and colleagues 100 years ago. The insight is not new, although it is still considered dangerous by many.

CASE STUDY

Background

Janice Morgan was a first-year principal at Welton Middle School in Jefferson Township District Schools. She was the first (and only) woman to serve as principal in this district of one high school, two middle schools, and three elementaries.

Janice was selected for the job by a panel of district principals and teachers from the middle school. The panel was especially impressed with Janice's experiences leading collaborative reform efforts, first in her role as union president in a neighboring district, and then in her role as elementary supervisor in Welton. With excellent interpersonal skills *and* a stringent work ethic, Janice seemed the perfect choice to guide the middle school faculty toward needed improvements in student attendance, behavior, and achievement.

As part of her graduate work in educational administration, Janice had taken a course on the history and foundations of leadership theory. Her research project for the class, an annotated bibliography covering a particular strand of leadership theory, focused on feminist theory. She'd chosen it largely because she was already fairly well acquainted with most of the other available choices (e.g., transformational leadership) and because she wanted to study something new and "alternative" to her past professional readings.

Through her research, Janice learned about the relationship between women's ways of leading and meeting the needs of contemporary organizations. The readings resonated with what she intuitively knew about school leadership, and strengthened her resolve to be the kind of school leader she had envisioned herself being.

The School Situation

Despite everyone's support for Janice's approach, she encountered roadblocks whenever she attempted in practice to promote change. For example, when she asked the faculty to increase the membership of the site-based decision-making council to include parent representatives from each of the neighborhood areas that the school served, not only did the faculty refuse, so did the superintendent. Arguing that membership on the site-based council was a board decision and that he was facing a divided board, the superintendent declined Janice's request to pursue this change.

Janice also had difficulty gaining support for school climate measures that she saw as crucial: an in-school timeout program to replace suspensions, a requirement that detailed lesson plans be prepared for substitutes, and a homework hotline. Expecting that faculty would embrace these measures, Janice was disappointed and depressed by their resistance. By the end of her first year, she was beginning to entertain fantasies about moving to a smaller elementary school in a more affluent district where her ideas might be more readily accepted.

The Problem

In mid-February, Janice received a call from the district office secretary requesting that she attend a meeting the following afternoon with the superintendent and assistant superintendent to discuss a "school improvement initiative." When she arrived, she found the high school principal and the three elementary principals waiting in the reception area. They, too, were involved in the meeting.

In the meeting, the superintendent shared his proposed school improvement initiative. He had just returned from attending (along with the school board members) the state's School Board Association conference, where one of the workshop topics at the conference had been strategic planning for school improvement. The board president and the superintendent had attended the session, and they both felt that this could be just the process that could "take the district to the next level." The assistant superintendent chimed in to inform the principals that a professional facilitator had been contracted to provide services to the district, and that he would be coming in 3 weeks for a preliminary meeting with representatives from each of the schools. In the meantime, they were to administer a questionnaire that was designed to elicit the goals, barriers, and core beliefs of staff, students, and parents. The questionnaires were distributed to the principals and they were sent back to their schools.

A week later, as Janice reviewed the questionnaires she was about to send to the district office, she was struck by the fact that people *really* did seem to want the kind of leadership approach she had tried to implement—shared decision making, developing a positive school climate. They just didn't seem to want it from her.

How Feminist Theory Helped

Janice recalled from her graduate work a body of research suggesting that members of organizations tend to desire leadership traits that are more closely associated with women (the very kinds of traits that characterize Janice's approach), yet also tend to prefer male supervisors in their organizations. The result, for many organizations, is a kind of disconnect between who they want to be as an organization and who they see getting them there.

Reflecting on the questionnaire results and her own experiences in her year at Welton, Janice believed that the school was experiencing this kind of disconnect. Janice had initially met the proposed strategic planning initiative with some indifference (she had read enough to know the limitations of this particular panacea, and she knew the superintendent and school board well enough to know that they would likely convert to some new religion at next year's meeting). As she pondered the activities planned by the facilitator, however, she saw the opportunity to disclose the "disconnect," and to better determine what the school as an organization actually did want of itself and of its leadership.

The Solution

Despite her initial indifference, then, Janice now saw the strategic planning process as a useful vehicle for the school community to determine what kind of organization they wanted to be and what kind of leadership they needed to get them there.

The day before the initial meetings with school leadership teams, the facilitator met with the principals and district administrators to review the process and to discuss questions and concerns. During the lunch break, Janice had the chance to talk one-on-one with Terry, the facilitator. Without going into a lot of detail (e.g., the theoretical basis for her ideas and beliefs), Janice confided to Terry that she saw in the school community a disconnect between (a) ideas about organizational culture and practices and (b) ideas about leadership style and traits. Terry listened, and told Janice he would give it some thought.

Later, just as the meeting was ending, Terry asked Janice if he could speak with her. He explained his idea to have the leadership team from the middle school develop a leadership strategy component, and suggested that the group use that component as addendums to the district's job description and evaluation instrument for school principals. The process would lead to a description of the kind of principal the school thought it *needed*, versus the kind it unconsciously seemed to *want*.

Terry asked Janice what she thought of the idea, and she told him she agreed completely with the approach. He then asked her if she had considered that the school might decide in a deliberate way that the kind of leadership they needed was *not* the kind Janice offered. Janice said that she was comfortable with that possibility—that she was interested in what was best for the school.

As the planning process proceeded at the middle school, Janice more than ever saw that she was capable of providing the kind of leadership the school re-

ally wanted and needed. As the work continued, moreover, the teachers, parents, and students began to see it too. After all, everyone's idea of who
principals are, what they do, and how they do it came exclusively from experiences with men. As they walked through the process of connecting ends (what
they wanted) with means (what kind of leadership was needed to get there),
they began to see the principal in a new light, and to view Janice as someone
who could work with them to be the kind of school they knew they could be.

CHAPTER SUMMARY

A critical reading of the history of American public education suggests a
gendered division of labor: women teach; men lead. The cumulative result of
this gendered division of labor has been the creation and normalization of an
administrative culture defined mostly in terms of men's experiences. Women
who enter the ranks of school administration are thus entering a culture that
historically has not accounted for their voices, and has often ignored them.

The theoretical and research base on women and leadership suggests that,
although there is no definitive "women's way of leading," there are, nevertheless, a set of characteristics that tend to more often evolve out of women's experiences: a focus on caring and building relationships, democratic processes of
management and decision making, a focus on tasks that are more directly related to teaching and learning, conflict management approaches that seek to
maintain the unity and stability of the organization rather than to assert personal power. These characteristics are valued for contemporary school leadership, but many if not most teachers—men and women—still say they prefer to
be supervised by men. From the perspective of feminist theory, such a finding
stands as evidence of the pervasive influence of a masculine administrative culture. Theoretically, however, the outlooks of women offer unique insights that
prospectively benefit the culture of education and the quality of school
leadership.

The discussion of queer theory considers the ways in which issues of sexuality
and gender identities play out in schools. Sexuality, theorists have argued, is a
central component in identity, but it is, in queer theory, a project of individual
self-construction and a realm of potential freedom traditionally ignored in
schools. Research results about abuse on the basis of sexual identity tend to support such theorizing. The chapter concludes with a consideration of queer theory as a grounding for leadership that regards the construct of "normal" as
negotiable.

9

Critical Theory and School Leadership

Jerry D. Johnson

Critical theory differs from the other theories in this book because it is an explicit theory of resistance to the neo-liberal ordering of economic and cultural life, particularly in Europe and the United States. It's concerned with class, and it offers perspectives different from those of cultural leadership and feminism. Skin color and sex are givens, whereas class structure, presumably, is perhaps more easily changeable and more widely contestable, at least on the view of much critical theory and its Marxist and neo-Marxian ancestors. The ERIC Thesaurus defines "critical theory" as follows:

> An evaluative approach to social science research, associated with Germany's neo-Marxist "Frankfurt School" (1923–1969) that aims to criticize as well as analyze society—opposing the political orthodoxy of modern communism, its goal is to promote human emancipatory forces and to expose ideas and systems that impede them. (Houston, 2001, ¶ 1)

Social class is the fundamental concept behind critical theory—the one that generates much of its interest, analysis, and forcefulness. Class, in this theoretical tradition, has to do with the distribution of wealth and not with social status.

Some readers may be familiar with statistics that describe how wealth is distributed across American society. Most people, however, are not so familiar with these data; income distribution receives a lot more coverage than does wealth distribution in mainstream media. Income is like cash flow (we need it to live); wealth, on the other hand, represents resources well beyond the requirements for living. Wealth is capital—resources used for investment in a

233

capitalist society, and not merely hoarded against future insecurity. Wealth is also, notably, a source of power in a way that even phenomenal incomes aren't. The statistics about wealth inequality might be considered worrisome. As recently as 2001,

- The wealthiest 1% of U.S. households controlled 33% of all net worth wealth and 40% of all financial wealth (i.e., monetary holdings such as stocks, bonds, bank accounts, and so on).
- The next wealthiest 19% of U.S. households controlled 51% of all net worth wealth and 52% of all financial wealth.
- The bottom 80% of U.S. households controlled 16% of all net worth wealth and 9% of all financial wealth. (Wolff, 2004)

One could go further back in time and see a very durable story: A small segment of the population exercises power and amasses wealth, and their exercise of power creates and maintains conditions that reinforce their wealth, privileges, and prerogatives. Critical theorists see many issues relevant to schooling in this old story. Their views are the subject of this chapter, which considers how critical theory can inform the work of school leaders.

Schools have long been regarded as the primary means by which individuals can improve their station in life; this view is perhaps the most persistent aspect of the American Dream. Yet despite all the efforts to offer this transformative public schooling experience, sharp inequities persist (and have recently worsened, according to government sources). Why? What's going on? The perspectives and interpretations developed by critical theorists offer ways of understanding why schools have not succeeded in redressing social imbalances, how they have contributed to maintaining those imbalances, and how they might operate differently.

Critical theory emphasizes analysis of social issues, not from the vantage of science and pretense to impartiality, but from the vantage of opposition to the dominant order, which is taken as unjust on face value (see Sidebar 9-1). The ideas of critical theory are located in significant changes made to Marx's theory of revolution, changes made partly in response to the rise of fascism, in the 1930s, and both then and later partly out of disgust with Stalin's totalitarianism. In a more general sense, critical theory is simply a form of critique that challenges conventional beliefs and social arrangements from a contemporary radical leftist position. This chapter doesn't aim to make radical leftists out of school principals, but aims instead to disclose options for thinking about the class issues that school administrators encounter in their schools and in the world into which those schools fit.

Sidebar 9-1: What Is Critical Theory? Who Are "Critical Theorists"?

Historically, critical theory is associated with the Institute for Social Research, founded in Germany in 1923 and known as the Frankfurt School. During the Nazi era, it migrated first to Switzerland and then to the United States. It was reestablished in Frankfurt in 1951. The Institute exists to this day (you can Google the historical description that the Institute provides), but the brilliance of the "Frankfurt School" has seemingly waned at the Institute. Nevertheless, the worldwide influence of the "Frankfurt School" scholars persists, including in education in the United States.

The approach of the founding scholars was multidisciplinary, drawing on sociology, psychology, philosophy, and political theory, with a strong basis in Marxist thought. Major figures in critical theory include Carl Grünberg (first director of the Institute), Theodor W. Adorno, Walter Benjamin, Erich Fromm, Max Horkheimer, Herbert Marcuse, and Jürgen Habermas. These thinkers had a profound influence on the emergence of the New Left in the 1960s, and the New Left and its concerns influenced a group of American educators including Henry Giroux, Peter McLaren, Marilyn Frankenstein, and Jean Anyon, whose works are commonly cited. In addition, the Italian theorist Antonio Gramsci [Italian, pronounced GRAM'–SHEE], writing about the same time as the Frankfurt thinkers, but dying much earlier, has exerted powerful influence.

Of the many books about critical theory (as opposed to books of critical theory), there is one whose short title offers a concise summation of the critical theorist perspective. The title is *Contested Knowledge* (Phillips, 2000). Critical theorists are not objective and disinterested analyzers of information and beliefs. Rather, they maintain a *critical interest*, questioning and contesting existing knowledge and the institutional mechanisms that disseminate it, with a particular interest in determining whose interests they serve. "Who benefits?" is a key question for critical theorists. It's a question educational leaders could well ask when policy proposals are made or evaluated.

Perhaps the most important educational insight to be had with critical theory is that the distribution of economic and cultural assets is grossly unfair and does much mischief among teachers and students in schools. Many educators can probably sympathize with this insight based on experience. This chapter aims to elaborate from this perspective.

SOCIAL REPRODUCTION AND RESISTANCE THEORIES

In this section, we consider some theoretical constructs that undergird critical theory and its implications for schools and school leadership: social stratification, social reproduction, legitimation, and resistance. To evaluate the impact of these constructs, it's important to keep in mind that a central tenet of critical theory is the obligation not just to disclose and understand the forces that create and reinforce inequities, but to challenge them once disclosed. Karl Marx once famously wrote in his thesis on Feuerbach: "The philosophers have only interpreted the world, in various ways; the point is to change it," which is a sentiment many Americans could agree with (while perhaps disagreeing with many of Marx's other values). In any case, these constructs describe issues useful to school leaders if they are to work in the interests of social justice.

Social Stratification Versus Social Reproduction

Social stratification refers to a system of unequal access to social and economic opportunities and rewards through the division of a society into layers (or *strata*). People in higher strata enjoy privileges and benefits that members of lower strata do not, and people in lower strata face obstacles and endure penalties that members of higher strata do not. The film *Layer Cake* (Vaughn, 2004) vividly illustrates this concept within the social and economic context of organized crime in contemporary London, England. A character uses the metaphor of the layer cake to explain the concept.

In a highly stratified society, inequality is an everyday reality built into the social structure (i.e., it is institutionalized), and the structure of inequality is maintained from one generation to the next. Although families can change strata, the strata themselves remain in place. The point is that people accept social stratification as natural—that's what "institutionalization" means.

Slavery is a form of social stratification with two strata: free and enslaved. A caste system is another form of stratification, one that typically comprises multiple levels. Although India's is probably the world's most well-known caste system, there are others, including Apartheid-era South Africa and the United States after the Civil War and during segregation. For the individual born into a caste system, content and quality of life are *predetermined* and enforced by both law and custom: One's caste determines occupation, educational opportunities, social interaction, housing, prospects for marriage—nearly every aspect of life.

American schools of today seem not to contend with a caste system (although the legacy of slavery persists, and some ethnic groups have been called "castelike"; see Ogbu, 1974, 1978, and Duncan, 1996). The schools do, however, contend with a class system, or a system of stratification built around socioeconomic status. Probably all of us are familiar with the standard categories of social class—lower class, middle class, upper class, upper middle, lower middle, middle middle, and so forth. Social class, however conceived, is part of everyday life, and for this reason it might be useful to take a step back to reconsider the concept of social class more carefully.

In principle, the class system in the United States is an open form of social ranking based primarily on economic criteria—for instance, based on how much money and property that an individual or family controls. Boundaries between classes are not as rigid as they are within a caste system, and there is opportunity for social mobility. For instance, a "Black" born into South African apartheid could not work his or her way into being a "coloured," nor could a "coloured" work his or her way into being a "White" (the terms within quotation marks were caste categories in South Africa); in a social class system, by contrast, a poor kid can rise into the middle class in various ways involving effort and luck. As opposed to status that is permanently given at birth under slavery or a caste system, then, the social class to which one belongs depends in some part on characteristics that the individual can control.

So—and again, in principle—the United States is supposed to be a society that, although comprised of varying levels of wealth, nevertheless offers opportunities for dictating one's own fate—for using one's talents to accumulate wealth and thereby to "move up" the social ladder. Despite the presumption that U.S. society offers such "meritocratic" possibilities, however, the division of wealth in American society has remained largely unchanged from generation to generation. In recent decades, moreover, it seems to be growing increasingly inequitable (Aronowitz & DiFazio, 1994; Harrison & Bluestone, 1988; Reich, 1991).

Why? Why does the rich class remain rich (and get richer, in comparison with the poor class), and why does the poor class remain poor (and get poorer, in comparison with the rich class)? These are very important questions for critical theorists, and for educators who would work in the interests of social justice, or, for that matter, the interests of *leaving no child behind* (the idea, not the Act). There are two primary and opposing responses to these sorts of questions—one answer offered by equilibrium theory and another offered by conflict theory (see Sidebar 9-2).

Sidebar 9-2: Explanations From Equilibrium Theory and Conflict Theory

As developed by Davis and Moore (1960), the *structural-functional theory of social stratification* argues that social inequality is the result of differentiations of marketable individual talents, and is both functional (maintaining society's state of equilibrium) and inevitable. In this construct, class structure ensures that the most qualified people do the most important work, and class structure is the result of fair competition (equal opportunity) where the biggest rewards go to the biggest winners. Given an adequate system of incentives (money, possessions, status, power) the cream will, according to equilibrium theorists, rise to the top. Poverty, in a functionalist mode of thinking, results from a combination of lack of talent, lack of effort, and (it's increasingly argued) bad genes.

Conflict theory offers a different view. Whereas functionalists see society as continually working toward a state of equilibrium, conflict theorists focus on describing the tensions in society. Marxists and neo-Marxists, in particular, have argued that history is an ongoing struggle between (a) those who possess wealth and who control the means by which to generate more wealth, and (b) those who generate wealth for others. The fact that the membership roster for these two groups looks pretty much the same from generation to generation and even century to century suggests to conflict theorists that some process or processes have occurred and are still occurring to reproduce the social order over and over. Critical theorists come to their work from this perspective, and most people who identify themselves as such find the explanations of poverty offered by equilibrium theories misleading at best.

Of course, there have been efforts—some of them quite extensive, many calling on schools—to promote greater equity in the United States. But they have made almost no difference. A sweeping program during the presidency of Lyndon Johnson, "The Great Society," did not end poverty, as it had promised, based on its commitments to equal opportunity. The Great Society's promises were exaggerations, and considerable disappointment and cynicism ensued. In the 1970s, some educators turned to social reproduction theory to explain the failure of education reform to reduce poverty.

Put simply, social reproduction theory argues that schooling has not only been unsuccessful in countering economic inequities, it operates in ways that maintain those inequities by reproducing the existing social class structure.

Schooling, on this view, is *supposed* to create inequalities. Here, we consider social reproduction theory in terms of two of its primary manifestations: economic reproduction and cultural reproduction.

The most influential work in terms of economic reproduction (a predecessor of American critical theorists working in the field of education) is *Schooling in Capitalist America* (1976) by Samuel Bowles and Herbert Gintis. Central to their argument is the idea that schools are organized and operate in ways that correspond to the organization and operation of a capitalist economy. As such, schools sort students into different strata based on their family's social class, resulting in a stratified student body prepared to assume stratified positions in a stratified economy and stratified social structure.

The sorting is not overt. It doesn't often happen that a student is told "Johnny, your father is a laborer, so you will join the vocational track at school," although something a lot like it happens routinely in many high schools. Instead, sorting takes place through interest, aptitude, and achievement testing that works to structure curricular tracking: "Johnny, your sixth-grade verbal aptitude test suggests that your placement in the general track at the high school is most appropriate and will be most beneficial to you, and you seem to enjoy working with your hands." To generations of educators, such judgments have seemed reasonable. Bowles and Gintis thought otherwise.

Economic reproduction has always been of first-rank importance to traditional Marxists, but the critical theorists are not traditional Marxists. Whereas Bowles and Gintis argued principally from the perspective of economics, for critical theorists, cultural issues assume first-rank importance, schools, certainly, but also the mass media, and ideology more generally. Economic matters remain important, but for critical theorists, cultural reproduction (including ideology) is more influential. Traditional Marxists believed that economics determined culture; critical theorists, by contrast, believe that culture determines economics. (This is a bit too simple, but basically accurate.)

In terms of cultural reproduction, the work of the critical theorists Bourdieu and Passeron (1990) is paramount for educators. Their argument understands culture as a form of capital or currency. For Bourdieu and Passeron, the transference of social stratification is more complex and more subtle than it was for Bowles and Gintis, who come from a more traditional Marxian perspective.

For Bourdieu and Passeron, schools *privilege* the language, interests, behaviors, values, and tastes of the dominant class (their "cultural capital"), while simultaneously devaluing the cultural capital of the working class. Indeed, the working class is hardly thought of as having a genuine culture.

Think of it this way: A kid from a devalued origin wants to buy a drink from a U.S. vending machine with a foreign currency (Mexican centavos or Turkish lira). The kid has some currency, but it's not the currency that the machine accepts. Unfortunately, the kid can't simply exchange the foreign currency for U.S. dollars at the schoolhouse door. The kid has to learn a host of hidden rules, make surprising and disturbing bargains, and enter a long period of negotiation, adjustment, accommodation, and assimilation. The full course is more than most kids can bear. The net result, as with economic reproduction, is the sorting of students into social strata—not just sorting them into strata, however, but *forming them* as strata for society's dominant order. What enters their minds in this process is as important—perhaps more important, most critical theorists would argue—than the occupations to which they are steered (e.g., pizza parlor, shop floor, or street corner) and how much debt they are allocated.

Schooling and the Legitimation of the Social Order

Because of their interest in cultural reproduction, critical theorists contend society maintains forms of schooling that reproduce the existing social structure from one generation to the next. This form of reproduction is particularly insidious because it is so well hidden from casual observers, and especially from casual observers who have been educated not to observe it. According to critical theorists, however, this education is only partly delivered in schools; much of the "education" takes place via the mass, mainstream media, as a form of marketing. This process involves both economic reproduction and cultural reproduction.

Schools, however, contribute to a stratified society in another very important way—or, more specifically, on another level—by *legitimating* the social order. The term *legitimate* (a verb, long "a" in the last syllable) is a key process for critical theorists. It's different from "legitimize." The difference has to do with embeddedness. Schools don't legitimize the social order, which would entail a specific, overt program to convince students that the social order was proper. Instead, by their ordinary operation and organization (e.g., testing, tracking, avoidance of controversy, patriotism, support for particular aspirations, and disciplinary practices) they validate the status quo. Moreover, according to critical theorists, most schools display very strong tendencies of this sort (e.g., Apple, 1993; Aronowitz, 1973; Giroux, 1988a). Schools, in their organizational behavior, continually reinforce the existing social order as in fact the only one that *does, can, and should* exist. They convey the message that the existing social order is normal, right, correct, to be expected—that it is a given reality not to be questioned very deeply and not to be seriously challenged. From the perspective of critical theorists, nearly everything schools do legitimates this status quo, with rare exceptions. Any educator who shares this insight about legitimation, of course, encounters certain obligations (more about this shortly).

Legitimation as an aspect of critical theory can be traced back at least to the sociologist Max Weber (1922/1968), who contended that the legitimacy of a social order is derived from and dependent on individuals' widespread acceptance of and obedience to the norms of society. Our particular social order is premised on an interconnected set of beliefs that, collectively, tell us that it is normal, natural, and inevitable for wealth and power to be concentrated in the hands of a very small dominant class. Schools, then, in addition to forming students for their "natural" place in the social order, also reinforce the idea that this is *the way life is supposed to be*. The lesson is that the existing social order and its schools are the ones we should expect and support. Weber (1922/1968) posited forms of authority that contribute to legitimation of traditional authority and legal-rational authority.

Traditional authority is built on the idea that "things have always been done this way." Repeated ways of doing schooling—say, ability tracking, or the idea that a K–12 education means participating in exactly 13 consecutive years of education, regardless of the pace at which learning occurs—are institutionalized as the way things are done in schooling. As a result, these practices (along with their implications—pedagogical, sociological, and ideological) remain unquestioned by most people. The durability of these practices conveys not only their own validity, but also, from the vantage of critical theory, the legitimacy of the social order these practices embody and support.

Schools, moreover, are government institutions. The government requires and enforces regular school attendance, and it supports schools with tax revenues. Attendance is a matter of lawfulness; truancy is a crime. This legal regime reinforces the belief that participation is valid and necessary. In fact, the decision not to continue one's education beyond a certain level even resembles a criminal offense like, say, drunk driving. When the decision of whether or not to go to school and earn passing grades is commensurate with the decision of whether or not to "knock back some shots" and "go for a spin," it's easy to see that participation in schooling becomes both an issue of compliance with legal authority, and, more significantly, a matter of good morals.

Jürgen Habermas (1987) also considered the function and process of legitimation, and developed the concept of a *crisis of legitimation*. This crisis occurs when the justification for the authority of a government is called into question by society at large or by a powerful group within society. Crisis of legitimation is obviously a very dangerous moments for a society. When it occurs, two outcomes are possible: (a) modest change sufficient to legitimate the old order or (b) fundamental change that legitimates a new order. Reformism has generally succeeded in U.S. politics, and is the preference of vested interests whose affairs are doing reasonably well. Option A represents reformism.

Crises of legitimation, not surprisingly, can also apply to particular institutions within a society—the military, the judiciary, the church—or the schools. Sometimes the most powerful vested interests can, in a democracy, instigate a crisis of legitimation on their own behalf. This happens when they are concerned that an institution may not be serving their interests well (see Sidebar 9-3).

Sidebar 9-3: Crisis of Legitimation: An Institutional Example

The 1983 report of the National Commission on Excellence, *A Nation at Risk*, is a good example. The Commission made the argument that schools were not effective in preparing students to compete with students from other parts of the world, thereby undermining the U.S. economy and the future well-being of all Americans. Who were the members of the Commission? The 18 members included 9 who had no direct connection to K–12 education; four higher-education presidents, two professors (chemistry and physics), a governor, a major corporate executive, and a former governor. Among the other 9 were 5 K–12 educators: two city superintendents (Albuquerque and San Diego), two principals (Detroit and Cleveland), and a national teacher-of-the-year. One other member was the former president of the Foundation for Teaching Economics, an organization whose mission is instruction about the benefits of market economies. It's fair to say that the commission included moderate liberals and moderate conservatives and was not, as some have charged, a mere conservative conspiracy.

This report's alarming language got widespread attention, as its Chair, David Gardner, intended (Kreisler, 1998). Journalists loved it, according to Gardner. It entered popular consciousness, where it was intended to do the most damage (or help the most, depending on one's view of the issue). What's more certain is that the report substantially shaped the school reform movements of the past 20 years.

The logic of the report, and of the process of having and establishing such a commission, was that because schools and school people were not getting the job done, those outside the school needed to hold them accountable. Increased testing, increased legislative oversight, and increased intervention by SEAs have shifted authority away from local schools and local educators. What's been legitimated, however, is not the schools, but the authority of state and federal governments to control local schools.

Here, then, is a possible example of an elite reform that induced, or perhaps sharpened, a crisis of legitimation and, in Max Weber's formulation, shifted the system of legitimation from traditional authority (local educators and local communities) to legal-rational authority (state and national governmental entities).

Legitimation and the Hidden Curriculum. The hidden curriculum legitimates the dominant social order, according to critical theorists. They believe, therefore, that teaching is one process through which the class structure is reproduced and, more specifically, continually legitimated (Saha, 1997)—but they also believe that teaching can create resistance to the agenda of the hidden curriculum. Two closely related concepts are relevant: (a) working-class *false consciousness* (see Aronowitz, 1973, for a U.S. application) and (b) ruling-class *hegemony* (Gramsci, 1971).

False consciousness is what the varied lessons of the hidden curriculum implant in students. It was described by Georg Lukács (1968) as a condition in which members of the working class have internalized beliefs that are contrary to their own interests, and thereby assist in their continued oppression and marginalization. John Gaventa (1980) used such a theory to explain the alleged fatalism, or passivity, of Appalachians in the face of long-standing mistreatment by coal companies. Paolo Freire [Portuguese, pronounced FRY-ray] applied the concept to adult education, with a curriculum that centered on the everyday concerns of working-class students (Freire, 1970, 1973). Using this method, he taught illiterate workers to read very quickly, and his work and ideas about education are now famous worldwide. (He was subsequently imprisoned by the military dictators of Brazil, then exiled, but returned to Brazil in 1980 and eventually became minister of education for São Paolo.)

Of course, the point of critical theorists is not that the poor are kept poor and powerless by a conspiracy among rich people per se, but by a cultural and economic system that gets into the heads of poor people and strongly shapes their behavior. Schools, according to this theory, help to put dangerous nonsense into the heads of the poor, and do a good job of it.

Hegemony is, in the system of domination, the obverse of false consciousness. Hegemony enables the system to install false consciousness efficiently and effectively into the heads of everyone (ruling class and poor alike). The term "hegemony" was introduced most prominently by Gramsci, leader of the Italian Communist Party during the rise of fascism, and later, a prisoner of Mussolini's government. Writing from prison, Gramsci broke with Marx's belief that culture was merely a by-product of capitalism. For Gramsci, control of cultural development was the source of the fascists' power—not control of the means of industrial production. Gramsci was among the first to predict the power of "the media." In our day, this slippery term includes advertising, infomercials, shopping channels, news, sports, music, movies, DVDs, CDs, music videos, computer games, internet shopping, email "spam," strip towns, malls, big-box stores, and on and on. All of these phenomena are seen—"read"—by critical theorists as laden with messages about what is right, proper, just, and possible.

Arguably, Gramsci realized that new developments in communication (e.g., radio in his day) extended their reach into every home, offering the ruling classes the chance to put their message in front of everyone. Today, it's more than a "chance," critical theorists would argue; it's a guaranteed certainty wherever one turns (in home, school, street, and store). Hegemony is practically a household word for critical theorists (who tend to over-use it), and they see it clearly at work in the institution of schooling.

One more point. This monopoly of economic activity, of culture, and of cultural production is self-replicating in the view of critical theorists. That's because ordinary people get their ideas of the possible from those in charge. It's not a recipe for liberation or social justice, according to the perspectives of critical theory.

The Ironies of Resistance

Reproduction theorists (e.g., Bowles & Gintis, 1976) considered the sorting mechanism of schools to operate in a rather direct fashion, with students as passive recipients, but critical theorists (e.g., Giroux, 1988a) contend that students play a more active role. Students can resist the lessons being taught.

The classic treatment of this idea comes out of Willis' (1977) long-term study of a group of male high school students in England. This group didn't do well academically, and they were frequently in trouble with school officials. According to Willis, however, the students' behavior wasn't unintelligent or merely chaotic. Significantly, for Willis, students were *not* rebelling against individual teachers and administrators, nor were they lashing out against authority in general. Instead, they had a project, the overt rejection of middle class-values and morality, industry, responsibility, conscientiousness, reliability, thoroughness, self-control, efficiency, and emotional stability. What's more, Willis concluded that their behaviors exhibited (a) a deep and sophisticated understanding of the workings of social reproduction, stratification, and class hegemony; and (b) a deliberate decision to resist those circumstances.

Many of us know students like this; how many of us can agree, however, that such students know what they're doing at such a level? Willis claimed they did and presented evidence to that effect.

Willis's story, of course, is British, but similar analyses have examined African American students who avoid "acting White" (see, e.g., Bergin & Cooks, 2002; Harpalani, 2002; Wilson, 2003). In the United States, many scholars have noted, race issues take the spotlight that is shone on social class in Britain. But in both countries, the two issues are most certainly in play.

Like reproduction theory, resistance theory has been criticized for being simplistic. Resistance theory has also been charged with not suggesting opportunities for school improvement that build on other insights of critical theory. Some theorists have, in fact, put a more positive spin on the concept by offering strategic approaches to resistance that can be explicitly taught (Paolo Freire, previously mentioned, was one of them). More about what critical pedagogues do momentarily, in the next section. That discussion is first placed in the context of the long tradition of American attempts to use schooling to effect changes in distributions of wealth and power in society.

SCHOOLS ' ROLE IN SOCIAL RECONSTRUCTION

In considering the application of critical theory to schools, it's important to recognize that school leaders and policymakers are generally not *deliberate* in organizing and operating schools so that they foster inequity. This point is very important, not because it gets everyone off the hook, but because it highlights the need to understand the structures within which (and through which) actions are played out. Individuals, in a sense, are actors in a play, and we've got to "read" the script to understand what the play is all about.

Throughout the history of American schooling, there have been educators and theorists who have sought to enlist schools in the service of redistributing power, status, and wealth in society. Arguably, the reason for their failure in this attempt is a failure to grasp the big picture—the script in which the actors move, and, further, the biography and intentions of the author. There's a lot, in this view, to see.

Historical Bases

The birth of the movement to have schools reconstruct society is a 1932 speech, given by George Counts at the annual meeting of the Progressive Education Association (Spring, 2001). Counts offered a scathing critique of the inequitable distributions of wealth and power in American society, and called on progressive educators to play a primary role in creating a new economic system that would release people from poverty. His speech was published later that same year with the title, *Dare the Schools Build a New Social Order?* This slim volume (Counts, 1932/1978) is still in print 75 years later, in an era when the ideals of socialism are so often presented as "unworkable."

Counts was a critic of capitalism, and he objected to the control of institutions like schooling by interests that serve capitalism. According to Spring (2001), Counts first showed up on the radar screen as a critic of the control of school boards by business interests. Counts reasoned that businessmen were incapable of leading schools in the sort of work needed to sustain a just and democratic society; he believed that teachers were, instead, the right leaders. George Counts, incidentally, served as president of the American Federation of Teachers from 1939 to 1942. He was not only an activist, but an astute scholar, a key colleague of John Dewey. His book, *The American Road to Culture*, is an accessible classic well worth reading.

Rather than pretending that the schooling process is doctrine-free, and devoting themselves to pedagogy that was contrary to democratic interests, Counts would have had teachers instead embrace the vision for a new, more socialist society, and openly teach that vision to students. This sort of work would have involved not only raising social awareness, but also teaching the knowledge and skills that are needed to create a new social order. In short, he called for teachers to abandon the practice of preparing students for participation in, as he saw it, a flawed and unjust capitalist economy and society in favor of preparing students to create a postcapitalist society that was just and that provided equal sharing of societal goods.

It's important to keep in mind that the context of this call (in 1932) was the Great Depression, when nearly 25% of Americans were out of work and the excesses of laissez faire capitalism were widely blamed for the prevalent misery. Some readers may, in fact, be surprised to learn that the organization to which they now belong, and to which they pay dues, once voted to accept a resolution that called on teachers to lead the way in consigning capitalism to a place in the past, along with slavery and feudalism. Counts' agenda was actually embraced by the National Education Association at its 1932 convention. The NEA issued a report affirming its central tenets, and calling on the organization to take a leadership role in creating, maintaining, and supporting this corps of teacher-activists who would indoctrinate students and build a new social order. The NEA's commitments were, of course, temporary. The Second World War ended the Great Depression and unified the nation; and internal debate over the nature of democracy and control of the economy ceased, never actually to be resumed at such a level by a major teachers' union.

In retrospect, we see that Counts' call stood little chance in the face of a society and a culture built around the tenets of capitalism. The seeds planted by this historical movement were later embraced and cultivated, however, and reappear—albeit in different forms—in the critical pedagogy work of later theorists.

The Contradictory Role of Schooling

Social reconstruction is not simply a radical idea, however. Its roots go back considerably further than Counts. In a sense, Americans have always thought that schooling ought to make and remake society. Considering these roots sheds light on the contradictory role of schooling (the tension between compliance and liberation), and the account suggests to us a valuable lesson: It's futile to try to change schools without understanding the institution's contradictory role with respect to society's class issues.

As far back as 1848, Horace Mann first offered the suggestion that mass public education could and should challenge the forces of class conflict described by Karl Marx:

> According to the European theory, men are divided into classes—some to toil and earn, others to seize and enjoy. According to the Massachusetts theory, all are to have an equal chance for earning and equal security in the enjoyment of what they earn. The latter [theory] tends to equality of condition; the former to the grossest of inequalities. Education ... beyond all other devices of human origin, is the great equalizer of the conditions of men—the balance-wheel of the social machinery ... it gives each man the independence and the means by which he can resist the selfishness of other men ... (Mann, as cited in Reitman, 1992, p. 34)

Although Mann was not a social reconstructionist as the idea is currently understood, he did see schooling as intervening in the way society worked. He hoped that common school education would improve the conditions of all, thereby providing all with the means to avoid poverty and contribute to the wealth of the nation. Mann was perhaps among the first to articulate the meritocratic scheme founded on "equal opportunity." The European idea that the game itself might be unfair didn't seem reasonable to him. The game, of course, was a very, very different one in 1848 in the United States: The nation was not yet industrialized, but Britain and Germany were (Hobsbawm, 1962).

Nevertheless, Mann's belief that (a) a stratified society is undesirable, and (b) schooling can undo the forces that create and maintain a stratified society, positions him as a predecessor of social reconstructionism. The significant difference is partly historical. America was still a thoroughly agrarian and mercantile society in 1848, and the emergence of industrial capitalism was still in its future (after the Civil War provoked industrial output), but in Counts' depression-era America, capitalism was well established and widely challenged.

This brief review shows that generations of American educators have considered the issue of how schooling should influence society. The relevant questions are difficult, and no cookbook or rulebook can help school leaders arrive at answers appropriate to their own circumstances: Should schools prepare students to take their place in the existing order? Or should preparation aim at something else? If the existing order is unjust, what then? Should schools prepare students to create a new social order that *is* just? *Can* they?

Possibilities for Transformation

Can schools create a new social order? Counts thought they might, if teachers dared. Mann thought they might, if schooling were systematically sponsored and managed by the government. Both visions ended in disappointment. What do critical theorists have to offer? Informed by ideas about the interconnectedness of institutions and culture in supporting and reinforcing the social order, and by the constructs of reproduction and resistance, recent theorists posit approaches to transformation that are both more cautious and more specific. Opportunities for social transformation are most recently seen by critical theorists in two primary forms: (a) a more subtle and more circumspect approach to the kinds of ideological teaching that Counts had advocated in the 1930, and (b) group-specific approaches that have evolved from the perceived limitations of critical theory's focus on social class.

The first, a more subtle and circumspect version of social reconstruction theory, is evidenced in the work of contemporary theorists of critical pedagogy like Paulo Freire, Michael Apple, Henry Giroux, and Peter McLaren. Reitman (1992) described work in this vein as "micro counter hegemonic." As opposed to the earlier notion that teachers challenge existing social structures by directly and openly criticizing those structures and teaching a new ideology, the recent approach of critical pedagogy avoids simple indoctrination and gives much more authority to students. Teachers (in the vein of critical pedagogy) work to facilitate students' development of a "critical consciousness" through which they fashion a new understanding of society and of their place in it. Working like this, then, teachers do not deliver lectures on the shortcomings of capitalism and the virtues of socialism. Critical pedagogues see such abstractions as less than useful, and quite possibly damaging. Instead, they embed in their daily practice (see Sidebar 9-4) a variety of values and actions intended to unpack real-life issues bearing on the use and misuse—and the constructions and misconstructions—of power.

Sidebar 9-4: What Do Critical-Theory Teachers Actually *Do*?

So what does the toolkit of a "critical pedagogue" look like? Fundamentally, it's the attitude of critique that motivates critical theory—*critique* at the ready and equipped with a particular value system (participatory democracy and hostility toward schooling that reproduces the prevailing class structure). This isn't much of an answer, however.

Based in part on Lakes and Burns's (2001) interesting article about "Mr. R." and his resistant students, here's what teachers working from an attitude of critique do:

1. *They say that resistance is justified.* They don't necessarily shout it, but they say it often enough that people know what they think.
2. *They listen to what students have to say,* even if they don't like what's said.
3. *They act as if kids have "agency"*—because they believe that kids not only react purposively to events in the school, but that kids base their actions on views, thoughts, and plans (compare to Sidebar 3-1).
4. *They ask kids to articulate their views, thoughts, and plans.* Such questioning makes classroom dialog possible—and more democratic. It enables critique.
5. *They reward honesty and reciprocate.* Reciprocating honesty is difficult and dangerous for teachers working in an institution whose purposes they doubt.

Critical pedagogues like reading and writing and thinking (there are critical pedagogues in math, too). But they don't fetishize the curriculum as comprised of "what every child should know and be able to do." They are understandably concerned about the interests that make this determination, and they are apt to see such educational prescription as a cultural and political disaster.

Additional possibilities for transformation have been suggested by feminists and culturalists, who understand the critical theorists' focus on class as insufficiently sensitive to sexism and racism. Marxist movements, indeed, have had a tendency to trivialize such matters. Feminist and culturalist critics of critical theory do seem to have a point worth considering (see chaps. 6 and 8).

DEMOCRACY AND SCHOOLING

Perhaps it's obvious that a democratic nation should have a democratic system of schooling, and that the two should support and reinforce each other. Perhaps it's *too* obvious. Linking schooling with democracy, "like most other truths, has become a very trite one" (Horace Mann, over 150 years ago, as cited in Cremin, 1957, pp. 89–90).

Critical theorists do indeed believe that schooling and the social order work to prop each other up. The pressing question then becomes: What kind of democracy is it they are supporting? Democracy seems to be an important idea for all the varieties of reformers considered here, from Mann to McLaren. So, what's democracy? In one familiar formulation—democracy versus Communism—democracy is the same as capitalism. This may seem self-evident to members of the generations raised from 1950 to 1980. We learned then that democracy was what "we" had, and Communism what "they" had.

That association was so tight and simplistic it couldn't possibly have captured much in the way of reality. Marxists, for instance, have always debated whether or not the Soviet Union was a communist state, with some Marxist critics saying it wasn't, especially many in the New Left. Some charged, instead, that the Soviet Union operated as a form of "state capitalism": Capitalism was what both nations had, in this view!

Such reflections indicate that the meaning of "democracy" is hardly self-evident. Fraser (1997, p. 57) put it like this:

> At one level, democracy refers to a government based on the consent of the governed as opposed to dictatorship or oligarchy based on birth, wealth, or simple power. There are, however, a number of variables which appear along the spectrum of the differing definitions of democracy. The consent of the governed can be a fairly passive acceptance of the rule of a leadership class. On the other hand, it can mean active involvement in the business of government by citizens at every level, not merely through voting but through the development of communities of active and equal citizens.

Is democracy (a) the active voice of citizens in exercising power (e.g., the town meeting) or (b) the passive endorsement by citizens of a ruling class (voting Republican or Democrat every 4 years)? It's a disturbing question because even the passive form of democracy prevails rather weakly in the United States, where barely a majority of eligible voters routinely vote. To think about this disturbing question, we turn to a comparison of consensus and conflict views of democracy (cf. Sidebar 9-2). The accounts are, of course, quite different.

Democracy: Competing Roles for Consensus and Conflict

Equilibrium theorists view the various parts of society as mutually accommodating one another, achieving, in the process, social balance, order, and the better functioning of society. When some parts endanger the whole, the dangers are "adjusted" out of the system, and society returns to stability as it continuously adjusts its various parts to the well-being of the whole. Consensus is the natural result of these processes of adjustment, emerging as a sort of dialog among institutions, corporations, and special interest groups.

Critical theorists, by contrast, view the apparent consensus as a manufactured one, a covering up of the fundamental conflicts that characterize the social structure. The appearance of consensus is achieved through power, particularly the power of a ruling class, which determines the way society works—who benefits and who loses out. Critical theorists observe that the role of citizens is marginal; they vote (or not), but they don't otherwise have much voice.

And here's the paradox: Any social order *is* predicated on legitimation and acceptance, but it continually engenders conflict. One resolution of the paradox, one favored by critical theorists, is that *consensus is manufactured through socialization* (or indoctrination). Schooling principally serves this purpose, in their view.

Democracy, in the view of critical theorists, is not a matter of constitutional forms, the rule of law, or political parties. These are still important features of governance, but critical theorists view democracy as a matter of voice, as in the first of Fraser's alternatives, *participatory democracy*. Hence, critical theorists often write (like the postmodernists) of "marginalized voices." They regard American democracy as an elite form of the idea of democracy because only members of elites end up having voice.

Critical theorists are also apt to judge the success of any form of democracy (neo-liberal, socialist, participatory, and so forth) by its outcomes. A society claiming to be a democracy and exhibiting a tremendously lopsided distribution of wealth presents evidence that its democratic institutions (constitutions, laws, courts, ideas, and dispositions of citizens) are flawed. For critical theorists, a real democracy is inclusive, and schools are the key institutions for teaching—for instilling—democratic values.

Inclusiveness and the Challenge for School Leadership

Let's consider three questions about school governance relevant to democracy and inclusive leadership: (a) Who is affected by a community's schools? (b) Who participates in decision making and school governance? (c) What are the differences that distinguish who participates from who doesn't? The answers provide some potentially useful insights.

The answer to the first question is, "nearly everyone." It would be difficult to find someone in a community who is not in some way or other affected by the organization and operation of schools. Even people who don't have school-age kids more than likely pay taxes, or are the recipient of services or benefits that compete in government budgets with schools and education-related programs.

The answer to the second question is "hardly anyone." Governance is the province of school board members and superintendents, with other entities (legislatures, SEAs) sharply structuring local options. School governance, in fact, relies less and less on democratic control and more and more on expert control. Successful superintendents are understood to be those in control of their boards, and proposals to eliminate school boards altogether are not uncommon (Land, 2002).

The answer to the third question is not so clear. What does distinguish those who get to participate from those who don't? Civic-mindedness? Successful campaigning? Politics? Connections? Voter apathy? These are among the usual answers. Critical theorists (e.g., Bourdieu), however, might rephrase the question as, "What kinds of capital are so valued by schooling that they constitute grounds for substantive participation?"

And mainstream research actually does address this question. Education level and family income have a strong influence on the extent to which parents participate in their children's schools (Muller & Kerbow, 1993). Further, schools have many routines for ensuring that this remains the case (Horvat, Weininger, & Lareau, 2003; Lareau, 1989). The answer for critical theorists, then, is that those with the most to gain are the ones most likely to participate in making decisions about what schools should be and do.

In this view, it's no surprise that the way schooling works remains unchanged. According to the critical theorists who write about school leadership, those with the power to make changes are the ones who benefit from the way things are. This arrangement doesn't rule out reform, but it does rule out transformation because most leaders remain blind to what's going on.

LEADING "AGAINST THE GRAIN"

What exactly are the implications of critical theory for prospective school administrators? Teachers, perhaps, can get away with "teaching against the grain" or "teaching as a subversive activity" (Postman & Weingartner, 1969; Simon, 1992); but principals and superintendents? You've got to be kidding!

We're not: All of the theories in this book distinguish themselves from the traditional administrative theories as being more "subversive." Indeed, critical theorists roundly condemn all "bourgeois" theories (i.e., what we call "traditional" theories) of leadership. Henry Giroux, in the preface to Spencer Maxcy's *Educational Leadership: A Critical Pragmatic Perspective* (1991) put the critical view in typically blunt language:

> The meaning of leadership has been narrowly defined by neo-conservatives as a practice that emulates the style and ideology of leading corporate executives *and* legitimates training students for the work world as the primary objective of schooling... the business of leadership [in schools] becomes the leadership of business as industry is increasingly called upon to intervene in local schools... draw[ing] upon a sector of society that has ... made leadership synonymous with greed. (Giroux, 1991, p. xi)

Critical theory is so subversive because, with its historical roots in Marxist thought, its ideas have been characterized as the enemy of the American way of life. Giroux and others, however, think otherwise. In their view, schools must reclaim democracy from the erosion sponsored by big business, and this is to be done by making schools more democratic. Again, resistance in their view is justified.

The Outlook of Critical Leadership

The sorts of actions taken by teachers working from the insights of critical theory appear in the previous Sidebar. The outlook for administrators follows a similar logic, but it is one that operates more publicly, with a greater variety of people, and with arguably deeper dilemmas and additional danger. This administrative outlook situates leadership quite differently from most other theories, and it also approaches its work philosophically.

The Location of Leadership   Critical theorists of school administration (e.g., Foster, 2004; Maxcy, 1991) make the unusual (but not unheard of) argument that leadership is not actually the province of the administrator. Instead, leadership is the directive force of a group. Leadership emerges as part of the deliberations of the group, and, most importantly, in the form of *collective action*. From this vantage, leadership isn't about a person, but about the group's self-knowledge and aspirations.

A school administrator working from a grounding in critical theory, therefore, is simply a person knowledgeable enough to facilitate the deliberation and collective action of a group of people associated with the school (teachers, parents, kids, community people). Calling the principal or superintendent "the leader" is an outlook that critical theorists find shortsighted and foolish. For them, such a focus is an illusion invoked by the dominant ideology. In reality, according to critical theorists, a traditional sort of "leader" (so-called) gets the consent of those led in various illegitimate ways: positional power, an attribution of expertise, disciplinary force, and so on. Teachers predictably resist such leadership, especially if they think the administrator in question is unreliable, misguided, or has a hidden agenda hurtful to their interests.

Like critical pedagogues in the classroom, critical pedagogues in the principal's office or the superintendent's office can work with this resistance to help teachers discover the real origins of their frustrations. Critical theorists would find that there's a lot to talk about:

1. Who says working-class parents won't show up for parent–teacher meetings?
2. Who says poor kids "drop out" of school?
3. Why does the district tell us to use this curriculum? Who says we have to?
4. Why do we have professional development that tells teachers what to think?
5. Who says we have to post the teaching schedule on the door?
6. Who says we have to listen to the superintendent about this?
7. Why are advisory boards stacked with members of the local elite?
8. Who benefits from the way school disciplinary practices are (not) working?
9. Who says what discipline means?
10. Who says this school needs to close?

This list of 10 items is the tip of an iceberg, in the view of critical theorists. There's a lot of anger and frustration among teachers generally, and it's often intense in schools that enroll lots of working-class kids. Which conversations to select is part of the art of working this opportunity—the opportunity of occupying the administrator's office. There's no cookbook for this sort of work because critical pedagogues *aren't doing a cookbook sort of work*, not in the classroom and not in the principal's office. By the way, the critical theorist of school administration, William Foster, reminded us that "Who says?" is sometimes a more important question than "Why?" It's the question that shows who exercises power and puts answers to "Why?" in proper context (see Foster, 2004, p. 179).

Philosophic Mindedness

Fundamentally, critical theory is an oppositional outlook on economic and cultural life. It understands that things are not as they seem, and that they are certainly not as they are said to be by the powers that be. In this particular view, there's a hidden agenda that turns on class issues and the rigging of an economic, cultural, and—most importantly for critical educators—an *intellectual* game.

The intellectual game aims to keep students—even members of the elite— from thinking too much for themselves. The children of the elite play the game (usually) and win at it (usually); but the point is that a genuine education will help all kids to see through the game, and to learn a great deal about thinking for themselves in the process. The view is different from "critical thinking" because of its insistence that social class and power relations become a key part of the critical thinking to be done.

Giroux (1988a) likes to call people who undertake this sort of education "transformative intellectuals." The two words are equally important— transformation and intellect—precisely because such people are *educators* and not just "school-ers." They use their minds and want students to learn to use theirs; they don't want to waste kids' time in the name of compelling their attendance at a building called "school." The transformation part of this idea concerns its economic, political, and cultural content: the guide for a vision of a more decent world, in the terms of critical theory. Teachers and administrators working in the mode of critical theory share such commitments, but principals arguably need to be better informed about the "transformative" work of critical pedagogy.

A school administrator might, under color of critical theory, simply drop out of education and become a revolutionary—but not a critical—pedagogue, whose work *is* education. This insight suggests that a critical administrator's approach to leadership needs to be measured, wise, restrained, forbearing, and logically tough. Otherwise great damage can be done (and this danger is part of the role, not part of critical pedagogy).

Spencer Maxcy (1991), a philosopher of education with an appreciation of critical theory, revived the idea of "philosophic mindedness" as a requisite for school leaders. It's an old idea, and is part of the reason why theory is regarded as so important in the curriculum for school administrators (see Sidebar 9-5).

Sidebar 9-5: Philosophic-Mindedness and Critical Administration

Spencer Maxcy, writing about critical school administration, judged Philip Smith's conception of philosophic mindedenss as particularly compatible with the commitments of critical theory (Smith, 1954). As part of a traditional outlook, Smith's presentation is value-free. We've abridged Maxcy's presentation of it and incorporated, in square brackets, logical extensions to the values of a critical outlook on school administration. For Smith and Maxcy, comprehensiveness, penetration, and flexibility are the overarching components of philosophic mindedness:

Comprehensiveness

- Viewing particularity in relation to a large field [e.g., critical theory].
- Maintaining tolerance for theoretical considerations [e.g., asking why instead of how].

Penetration

- Questioning what is taken for granted or what is self-evident [e.g., asking "who says?" and "who benefits?"].
- Seeking for and formulating fundamentals [e.g., asking why and discovering how class prejudice operates in the school or district].

Flexibility

- Being free from psychological rigidity [e.g., not being a leftist ideologue].
- Valuating ideas apart from their source [e.g., not thinking an idea is great just because Henry Grioux – or Spencer Maxcy, or Philip Smith— said so].

This adaptation shouldn't be read as a list of things to do, nor even as a list of things to be. It's provided as an illustration of the wide perspective needed, and the tint of the glasses worn by critical theorists.

Of course, if administration is merely processing paper and putting out fires, then maybe it's right to see critical theory as irrelevant. In this case, though, so is every theory. Theory isn't needed when the questions are easy and the answers certain.

Nevertheless, even a principal mired in petty management issues (perhaps especially such a one) can take useful insights from critical theory.

These insights need not bring the local establishment down unhappily and uncomfortably on the school, but perhaps they can help the school's educators find ways to give poor and working-class kids a better shake than they currently get.

Getting the People Through the Door

One way to get that better shake is to help the school take the side of poor and working-class parents. This is seldom done in schools, for all the reasons previously enumerated. And even if one knows the reasons, the work remains difficult.

Critical educators in the principal's or superintendent's office don't believe that an "open-door policy" and a wide invitation to participate in meetings would be enough to foster a democratic school culture. Poor and working-class students and parents and other community members know exactly who has the cultural capital needed for a place at the table and a voice in the conversation. They don't have it; and they know this fact because they went to school and learned the lessons of the hidden curriculum; they watch television and go to the movies. Poor and working-class people know their place, even if they resent some of the features of their exclusion.

Administrators can fashion many initiatives to bring poor and working-class community members into the life and the work of the school, but from a critical perspective, "programs" need to be grounded in a faculty's acknowledgment of class issues and sponsored by at least a vanguard of faculty members with a viable critique of the dominant order. Otherwise, the programs will fail—just as the open-door and various invitational tactics typically do.

Critical educators who take on an administrative role require philosophic mindedness in order to remain vigilant about evaluating their schools' efforts to cultivate wide and equitable participation. Because these efforts work "against the grain," they are extremely demanding. And, as a result, the tendency for administrators is to convince themselves that getting the initiative underway is all that's needed. Such initiatives, however, must be tended carefully and evaluated rigorously. Otherwise they will slowly turn "toward the grain," which is, after all, the course of least resistance. Because it's such hard work, the knowledge that there are school administrators who actually do take it on and scholars who write about it is encouraging (see Sidebar 9-6).

Sidebar 9-6: Reports From the Field of Critical Administration

Vignette No. 1. Nancy Kraft (1995), working as a staff developer, wrote a short article that offered an answer to one of the questions posed earlier: "Why do we have professional development that tells teachers what to think?" Teachers are supposed to execute the curriculum, not conceive it. Critical theorists (and Kraft) call this "deskilling." Professionalization, incidentally, is usually designed so that teachers strive to become more expert in executing the curriculum—so professionalization (as conceived) works hand-in-glove with deskilling.

Vignette No. 2. Sharon Lee and Kelly McKerrow (1991) observed (for 2 years) a principal's use of discipline in an elementary school. Their case study is titled *Two Pieces of Wood* and refers to (a) the paddle used for punishment and (b) the pencil given as a reward. The analysis uncovers a variety of blame-the-victim routines, including racism, and shows not only the inappropriateness of the principal's disciplinary regime, but its ineffectiveness.

What sort of responses might be more productive than those *critiqued*? Critical theory is about cultivating informed judgment, so prescriptions aren't in order. But speculation is; so we can speculate. A logical possibility in the first vignette would be to reestablish the link between curriculum conception and curriculum execution. Yes: It's a heresy in the religion of standards-based reform efforts. But it's fully compatible with the principles of constructivism. There are, moreover, many ways to approach such an aim, some of which might be self-destructive in some circumstances but not in others. Local judgment is essential: It's the point really, and that's why cookbooks of critical theory are illogical.

In the second vignette, the alternative would seem to be for a principal to think about discipline differently—not as control but (possibly) as the self-direction of students. This is not in line with "zero-tolerance" thinking, but it's a very, very familiar idea in the history of American schooling. Paddling wouldn't need to be renounced either—just used less and less, and eventually not at all.

Critical Administration and the Dilemma of Local Community

Traditional Marxism—the rootstock of critical theory—was very little concerned with the local. It equated localism with provincialism: ignorant, conservative, and hopelessly nostalgic (stuck on an illusion about the past). It sponsored a strongly internationalist perspective on the working class, whose interests were seen as transcending national borders. Indeed, once the Soviet Union was founded, its Communist Party established an international organization on the totalitarian principles of Stalin, doing (according to many reports from the political left, right, and center) wondrous damage around the world.

Critical theory, because it has rejected such misconceived orthodoxies, puts a much higher value on localities and on local developments. This is one reason for the interest in local "praxis" (customary practice). If, as claimed in Sidebar 9-6, local judgment, and not standardized prescriptions, is needed, and if, as also claimed, leadership is not a person, but the function of a comparatively inclusive open group, then it stands to reason that local community will surface as an important feature of school administration reconceived in this way. Foster (2004), in a brief article published after his death, arrived at this point exactly (in a path quite similar to the one followed in this book).

A similar focus is given to some conceptions (those that aren't nationalist or internationalist) of communitarianism. And some of the dilemmas for school administrators interested in either theory (or both) are quite similar, except for critical theory's insistence on the importance of class. The key dilemma, perhaps, for administrators in both cases is that the state says one thing, but the right thing to do is likely something else altogether. What should a principal do?

Some advise that local purposes can be reconciled with state and national purposes (e.g., Jennings, 2004) in part because they admire the fact that standards-based approaches purport to cultivate higher-order thinking. According to Jennings, for instance, reconciliation depends on rethinking, which involves a local sort of negotiation; and such negotiation gives communities the opportunity to create something that is both genuinely local and genuinely thoughtful. Jennings' analysis, unlike those of critical theorists, doesn't take class conflict and related ideological contests into account. A critical analysis, by contrast, would acknowledge the likelihood that members of a poor community would view state (or national) standards as inimical to their interests (see, e.g., Woodrum, 2004). Reconciliation on such a view would be tantamount to capitulation, and principals or superintendents acting from a base in critical theory would not countenance such reconciliation with the dominant order. A class-based analysis, in fact, requires a local response that would be *quite different* (Foster, 2004).

Richard Bates, a professor of educational administration at Deakin University in Australia, is one of the original translators of critical theory into the realm of school administration. His advice? Focus on community study, in the schools, of "capital formation" (Bates, 2000): financial, physical, human, and capital. What Bates has in mind, of course, is not the outlook of the dominant order on these forms of capital. Thus, such study would turn on local investigations about the formation, distribution, and control of wealth, infrastructure (e.g., transport), knowledge (e.g., who is permitted to know what), and social trust and responsibility (e.g., democracy, community itself). Bates concluded,

> By serving the needs of capital in the ways I have begun to suggest [schools] might empower students to take charge of their own formation and help them to act in a world that desperately needs their help. The local management of such schools requires the elaboration of a pedagogy which incorporates the four faces of capital into the activities of the school and its community in purposive and productive ways. (Bates, 2000, A Challenge Worth Accepting section ¶ 1)

Observe that Bates, as a critical theorist and heir of Marx, doesn't denounce capital, but *embraces* it—from a bottom-up rather than a top-down outlook. He's not worrying about whether or not such proposals can be reconciled with the demands of central authorities (as representatives of the dominant order). He might well acknowledge that they can be made to seem so, but the purpose of this sort of education cannot be value-free. It must be committed to social justice, and not as a matter of educational opportunities or even outcomes, but as a matter of educational process and content.

In truth, lots of community responses are possible. The point of critical theory, as Giroux likes to observe (e.g., Giroux, 1983, 1988a), is to sponsor a "language of possibility." For critical administrators, however, the nonnegotiable point of departure for theory and everyday practice is the understanding of false consciousness, hegemony, and the needs of advanced capitalism for continued legitimation.

CASE STUDY

Background

Kathy Thompson was in her first year as principal of T.R. Owens Elementary School in rural southeastern Missouri. Previously, she had been a social studies teacher at Williams County High School in the same district. Other than 4 years spent at the regional university earning her undergraduate degree, Kathy had lived in Williams County all her life. She had completed her master's degree through a combination of distance learning and compressed video courses and the 3-hour round-trip commute to the university.

As part of her master's degree in educational administration, Kathy had been introduced to the idea of critical theory as a lens for examining schools. Actually, it was partly a reintroduction, as Kathy had years earlier encountered many of the writers and philosophers categorized as "critical theorists" as part of her undergraduate study in political science and sociology. However, she had never before considered applying such radical interpretations to her work in schools.

Although she could see the logic in constructs like reproduction theory and cultural capital, it just didn't resonate with her own experiences. Take tracking, for instance: At the high school where she taught, separate basic English classes allowed teachers to focus on developing the kinds of skills useful to those students who had chosen to start working right after graduation. Students were not *forcibly* segregated into these basic classes; on the contrary, it was only after careful review of the student's transcript and individualized graduation plan, and following consultation with his or her parents, that appropriate placements were determined. Still, what she read and discussed in her graduate class remained as ideas floating around in the back of her mind.

The School Situation

In terms of accountability scores, T.R. Owens was the lowest performing school in the county. The students were ethnically homogenous; but in terms of social class, the school reflected its community with (a) a minority who owned small businesses and provided professional services, and (b) a majority who worked in service industries or commuted to low-skill manufacturing jobs in the river valley 40 miles away.

Kathy was considered by her supervisors and her peers at the high school to be a master teacher. In hiring Kathy for the principalship at the elementary school, the board and superintendent hoped she would be able to use her skills to "turn the test score situation around" at Owens. In conference with the superintendent, Kathy set as her central goal to get all students reading on grade level by the end of Grade 6 (Owens was a K–6 school). They each felt that the early grades were crucial, and that reading—both reading skill and a desire to read—were necessary for success in higher grades and other academic areas as Owens's kids moved on to other schools in the system.

The Problem

Over the summer, and drawing on some newly developed skills from her graduate program, she spent a great deal of time analyzing and interpreting student achievement data from previous years. Disaggregating the data according to eligibility for free and reduced-price meals, Kathy identified a substantial achievement gap between lower SES kids and higher SES kids at all grade levels tested.

It didn't surprise her a great deal that a gap existed at the second-grade level (the lowest grade tested), as she had always felt that families played a very important role in education and preparation for success in early primary grades. The fact that the gap did not narrow (in fact, it widened) through fourth grade and into sixth troubled her, however. Based on her analyses, she felt certain about two things: First, getting good test scores would not happen without raising the scores of the school's low-SES kids (at least half of the students—the other half—were doing well, with reading scores at or above grade level and comparable with state averages); second, whatever they had been doing to try to "close the gap" wasn't working.

In the course of developing her required professional growth plan, Kathy then refined her earlier goal of getting all kids to grade level in reading. Her new goal was focused on educational equity. Her activities would be to identify, share, implement, support, and monitor the use of best practices for raising the achievement of low-performing students (with an emphasis on low-SES kids); her measurable outcome would be a narrowing of the SES achievement gap over time.

In the last few weeks before school started, and in addition to the myriad tasks involved in getting ready for opening day, Kathy did a good deal of professional reading in preparation for her work on closing the achievement gap. The achievement gap literature was loaded with both explanations and solutions, some of them suspiciously simple. In any event, rather than jump in and accept these ideas as gospel—she was the kind of person who liked to get the "lay of the land" before drawing conclusions—Kathy intended to observe every classroom in the building at least once, and to compare what she learned that way with the theoretical work she had been reading.

How Critical Theory Helped

Kathy's observations confirmed some of what she had read in the achievement gap literature about teacher expectations for students and student work. Teachers *did* hold differing expectations for different students, and those differences *did* closely mirror socioeconomic differences. Significantly, though, the differentiation was not necessarily negative (i.e., oftentimes, the diminished expectations were conveyed in a sympathetic and even nurturing mode of interaction), nor was it deliberate (i.e., most teachers did not even realize they were differentiating expectations among students).

With several observations under her belt, Kathy first broached the subject of her findings with one especially conscientious and well-respected teacher, Susan Brown. Susan's initial response was denial and confusion. A few days later, however, Susan returned to Kathy's office and tearfully related that, after careful consideration and hours of soul searching, she had come to the realization that she had in fact been unwittingly sending messages to children about what they were capable of and what she expected of them.

Throughout the previous months of reading and teacher observations, Kathy had been reconsidering her own teaching career and the kinds of messages she sent to the high school kids she taught. Kathy shared this perspective with Susan, and together they resolved to work toward making use of this self-awareness as a grounding for their work with each other and with other teachers. Kathy also shared with Susan some of what she had learned about critical theory and schools—particularly, (a) how creating differing levels of expectations for students contributes to high-school tracking later on (informal tracking in elementary school contributes to formal tracking at the secondary level), (b) how all of this seems normal, natural, and proper because it is deeply ingrained in how we think and what we know, and (c) how some of the differentiation and "hidden curriculum" instructions operate so subtly because we don't know enough about the culture of impoverished students to even be able to know when or in what ways we're devaluing them.

The Solution

Working together, Susan and Kathy developed a schoolwide professional development plan geared toward helping teachers to both disclose and understand their personal beliefs about the academic potential of impoverished children, and to consider what those beliefs did to their teaching, and more importantly, how such teaching undercut the kids' learning now and, worse, in the future.

Realizing that this was slow, emotionally challenging work, Kathy decided to conduct miniworkshops in groups of no more than four teachers at a time, with time for personal reflection in between sessions. Initial workshops made use of materials developed by organizations like the NCCJ (National Conference for Community and Justice) for use in "People-to-People" seminars. Later, the workshops evolved into small reading groups sharing thoughts about books like Ruby Payne's *Framework for Understanding Poverty.*

What they learned working in these small groups led the whole faculty to request that their required 24 hours of annual professional development be tailored toward work in this area. In addition to changes in perceptions and changes in instructional methods, teachers also began to explore and obtain reading materials that spoke more directly to the culture their students knew. Kathy was hopeful that all of this would lead to some pretty interesting work on curriculum development in the near future.

CHAPTER SUMMARY

The society in which we live is one of sharp disparity between rich and poor, with current trends further separating the haves and have-nots. Critical theorists, operating from a neo-Marxist perspective, have examined the ways that institutions, knowledge, and beliefs contribute to and support the structures that define human existence within a social order. Schools, perhaps more than any other institution, disseminate formal knowledge and the ideology associated with what that knowledge is for and who gets access to it. This is one important way in which critical theorists understand "culture" differently from those who view culture from an ethnic, or anthropological, perspective.

Theories describing how schools interact with the social order are the subject of the first section of the chapter. Social stratification refers to the institutionalization of social ranking to create rigid structures (external and internal—i.e., both in society and in the individual's mind) that disrupt or deter actions that would allow for a fuller sharing of economic and social goods. Social reproduction is a theoretical construct suggesting that schools are organized and operated so as to ensure that existing wealth and power distributions will be passed on from one generation to the next. It's a complicated process, involving schools' organizational alignment with business and industry models (correspondence theory), schools' privileging of certain cultures over others (cultural capital theory), schools' teaching of one's place in the social order (hidden curriculum), and schools' role in reinforcing the status quo (legitimation).

In the second section, we consider attempts by school leaders to intervene in the social order to promote social justice from the perspective of critical theory. These attempts can be viewed historically as an evolving set of ideas about the forces with which schools contend, and of strategies and approaches for confronting economic structures and social dynamics. Throughout, attempts are limited most by the lack of understanding of the extensiveness, pervasiveness, and often the subtleness of the forces sustaining the status quo.

A third section examines the role of communication and consensus building in school leadership. Analyzing the perspectives of democratic consensus and conflict theorists points us toward questions of whose voices are heard and whose go unheard in what could (or should) be a participatory democracy of school visioning and leadership. According to the principles of critical theory, school administrators need to develop an understanding of the distribution of status, authority, and power in their decision-making community, and should attempt to expand the sphere to create a shared decision-making body and process that is representative of the entire community.

In the final section, we consider approaches under which school administrators, following the precepts of critical theory, might work for social justice, in the face of a schooling enterprise operated to affirm the dominant order—and its beliefs. Administrators confront, on this view, a comprehensive and well-organized adversary, one that is in the heads of almost everyone (including themselves). Significantly, hegemony plays out on both a microscopic and a macroscopic level, and so resistance and challenge must be enacted locally, and, from the outlook of critical *education* theory, the local arena may well be the most important. Finally, the chapter closes with a discussion of possibilities for action in terms of critical theory, providing two illustrative critiques and pointing readers to the works of the leading critical theorists of school administration.

10

Postmodernist Theories and School Leadership

Some writers represent our time in history as postmodern—the era following the modern period. They make this determination because they believe major economic, political, and cultural shifts have profoundly altered social relationships among human beings. Our world is different and, as a consequence, so too are we (e.g., Gergen, 1991; Hassard, 1993).

Postmodernist theory, while deeply cognizant of these historical shifts, does not primarily involve a description of them (but cf., Harvey, 1989; Jameson, 1991). Rather it makes claims about existence and knowledge that take historical changes into account (e.g., Foucault, 1971). Focusing on the fact that human beings are situated in a particular historical period as well as in particular cultural and social locations, postmodernist theory describes what it means that our experience of the world is contingent. It answers questions like these: "How does our historical, cultural, or social location determine what we think of as truth?" "What forces make us into who we are?" "Considering the influence of our location in place, time, and culture, how can we be free?"

Such questions seem deeply theoretical, but they actually concern how we live our lives on a daily basis. Take the question about truth: What are our assumptions when we ask a student, for example, to tell us the truth about an incident, perhaps a fight with another student? Do we believe that there is one version of what happened that represents a definitive truth about the incident? Or do we believe that each student involved will have a different—equally compelling—version of the truth about the incident? Or do we believe that,

266

while each will have a different version—one version will be better than another? Or do we believe that the truth about the fight will be constructed from many students' stories about it?

Although these questions do relate to practical matters, school principals probably don't stop to think about them very often, particularly in the midst of busy days in which real fights between real students are all too frequent. In this chapter, however, we take the time to examine such matters as self-hood, truth, power, and language using insights from postmodern theory. Then we apply a postmodern way of thinking to a consideration of organizations in general and schools in particular. Because our discussion draws on the writings of postmodern theorists, it inevitably uses some of the specialized (and often annoying) vocabulary that this theoretical tradition has spawned. A guide to postmodern vocabulary is provided in Sidebar 10-1.

Sidebar 10-1: Postmodern Glossary

Bricolage: the assemblage of ideas from different disciplines or traditions (or the leftovers from those disciplines or traditions) into one work of art or scholarship.

Discourse: language in all its forms (spoken, written, communicated through gesture) as well as other practices that create meaning.

Discursive practice: discourse that is connected to a particular social and cultural milieu from which it derives meaning and to which it contributes meaning.

Essentializing: seeking to characterize people or phenomena in terms of discrete sets of features that are thought to constitute them.

Fragmentation: the disconnection of parts of the self resulting from the complexity of economic and social life under late capitalism.

Grand narrative: a pervasive storyline (e.g., the story of technological progress) that claims to explain—and to impose—universal truths.

Incommensurable truths: ideas that cannot be compared and evaluated against one another because their assumptions are grounded in different discursive practices (e.g., the scientific and Judeo-Christian "truths" about the origins of life).

Language games: the structuring of social practices through rule-bound uses of language. For example, reporting of research claims follows a particular set of rules involving evidence, reference to previous related research, and so on.

Marginalized: belittled or dismissed by dominant groups, or according to dominant discursive practices.

Performative language: an utterance that takes direct action on the world; for example, when a superintendent declares "school is cancelled today because of snow," he or she is using that utterance to take action, not to make a statement about what's happening.

Rupture: a breech in an historical tradition or pattern, a sea-change or paradigm shift; also an effort to promote such a breech (e.g., the rupture dividing the modern from the postmodern era).

Simulacrum: a simulated (or artificial) process or product that comes to symbolize, coexist with, or replace a real process or product.

Surveillance: observation for the purpose of exerting control over behavior, thoughts, and self-definitions.

Text: anything that can be interpreted (e.g., discourse, social structures, social interactions, cultural practices, and so on).

Totalizing: attempting to offer a complete and definitive explanation.

Undecidable positions: ideas or ethical perspectives whose value in relationship to one another cannot be determined because objective criteria on which such judgments might be made do not (and cannot) exist.

Under erasure: a way to talk about a concept or worldview that is no longer adequate but that has not been superceded by another, better theorized, concept or worldview; saying that a concept is "under erasure" means that it needs to be critiqued but that the particulars of that critique are unknown, ambiguous, or varied.

The Critique of Modernism

According to many scholars, the Enlightenment represented the beginning of the "modern" period because it signaled a fundamental shift in how people thought about the natural world (e.g., Saul, 1992). Prior to the Enlightenment—with its focus on science and progress—people tended to view the natural world as God's immutable creation and therefore knowable primarily through its wholeness and mystery. This attitude toward the natural world did not keep people from observing it closely or from reflecting about it, but it did keep them from regarding it with doubt.

The Enlightenment attitude of skepticism, epitomized in the work of David Hume (1711–1776), enabled thinkers to look below the surface of the natural world in order to find universal laws governing its functioning. Knowledge of such laws, moreover, gave humans the basis for diagnosing problems and making improvements. Empirical science and technology were thus born hand-in-hand from a view of the world (i.e., humanism) that placed human beings at the center of creation. From this privileged position also came the insight that human beings were not just subjects—investigators and improvers—but also the objects of investigation and improvement. The belief that people can find out the truth about the natural and social worlds and can use those truths to promote progress, sometimes goes by the name "technical rationality."

But what if the assumptions of technical rationality are wrong or misguided? What if the quest for universal truth is arrogant and ethnocentric? What if there are multiple versions of truth with no basis for determining which is best? What if so-called progress produces more harm than good? And—worst of all—what if human beings aren't really in charge of nature?

The relevance of these "what ifs" to the human condition under late capitalism provides justification for a critique of the technical rationality of modernism (see, e.g., Kochan, 2002). This critique and the various intellectual camps and methodological approaches that constitute it go by a variety of names, many beginning with the prefix "post": postmodernism, poststructuralism, postindustrialism, posthumanism, postpositivism. But other "isms" are sometimes also used to describe this emerging tradition: constructivism, social constructionism, deconstructionism, and symbolic interactionism. In this chapter, we primarily explore the commonalities of these theoretical perspectives and sets of methodological assumptions, but an understanding of their differences can also be useful. Sidebar 10-2 provides some definitions that help to distinguish these critiques of (and alternatives to) modernist thinking.

Sidebar 10-2: Definitions for Terms Describing Various Critiques of Modernism

Term	Disciplinary Origins	Definition
Post-modernism	Aesthetics, literary criticism, art criticism, sociology	A stance on intellectual work (e.g., scholarship, art) that provides a critique of modernist premises such as absolute truth, scientific objectivity, and essential meaning and that makes use of alternative premises such as contingency, relativism, and irony (see, e.g., Bauman, 1987).

Post-structuralism	Sociology, philosophy, political theory	An approach to inquiry that explores difference and localism in contrast to structuralism, which seeks to identify uniform underlying processes that apply universally (see, e.g., Sim, 2001).
Post-humanism	Philosophy, literary criticism, environmentalism	Critical engagement with and critique of "humanism," a philosophical tradition that views human beings as the purpose of creation or as the pinnacle of evolution (see, e.g., Badmington, 2003).
Post-positivism	Sociology	Approach to inquiry that focuses on contingent, probabilistic, and multiple "truths" rather than on unitary and universal truth (see, e.g., Lincoln & Guba, 2000).
Post-industrialism	Economics, sociology	The economic shift away from the manufacture of goods to the delivery of information-based services; also changes in personal identity and social relationships resulting from this economic shift (see, e.g., Bell, 1973).
Constructivism	Psychology, philosophy	In psychology, constructivism represents the view that "each individual mentally constructs the world of experience through cognitive processes" (Young & Collin, 2004, p. 375).
Social constructionism	Philosophy, anthropology, sociology	The belief that knowledge is socially constructed and therefore does not map back to an objectively knowable reality (see, e.g., Garfinkel, 1967).
Symbolic interactionism	Anthropology, sociology	A way to study human groups premised on the beliefs that "human conduct involves transactions of meaning, a measure of uncertainty and change is ubiquitous in human social arrangements, and persons and their social groupings are always fused" (Maines, 2003, p. 6).
Deconstructionism	Literary criticism, cultural studies	A way to analyze ideas in relationship to the web of meanings that make those ideas possible and thereby opening up additional possibilities that support different meanings (see, e.g., Norris & Benjamin, 1988).

Rationality.   Although postmodern theorists offer a critique of rationality, they do not really abandon it. These theorists, after all, often use rational argumentation in order to present their critique of rationality. What they call for, however, is the removal of rationality from its pedestal—a project requiring us to view rationality in context. Contextualizing rationality reveals that (a) there are other important ways of knowing besides rational ones, (b) rational ways of knowing—and the technological manipulations of the natural and social world they support—have contributed to greed and injustice, (c) no single way of knowing leads to one unitary version of the truth, and (d) multiple perspectives support a variety of incommensurable truths and undecidable positions.

Even though educators may find these ideas hard to accept "in theory," this perspective actually does help us make sense of everyday life in schools. First, we frequently observe that truth is contested: For example, in some communities, citizens object to the constructivist curriculum in mathematics that many educators endorse. Sidebar 10-3 provides more detail about what some people call "The Math Wars." Second, we recognize that our "truths" about schooling are shaped by participation in the "discursive practices" associated with teaching and school leadership: For instance, we talk about things such as IEPs (individualized education plans), PDAs (public displays of affection), and block scheduling that noneducators do not understand in the same ways we do. Third, we trust intuition: For instance, even when experts specify a teaching method that is supposedly best to use, we sometimes feel that another approach would be better with a particular student or group of students. Finally, we have the experience of dealing with "undecidable" claims whenever we disagree with colleagues over critical issues (e.g., whether intelligence is inherited or acquired, whether accountability tests are a good or bad thing) about which we cannot reach resolution.

Sidebar 10-3: The Math Wars

Mathematics seems like such a well-defined body of knowledge that it is hard to imagine there would be contention about what it is and how it should be taught (see, e.g., Schoenfeld, 2004). Nevertheless, many school administrators now encounter such contention. Battle lines may even be drawn by the math teachers in a school. For example, "traditionalists" among the teaching staff may believe that students need to learn facts and processes, whereas devotees of "standards-based" mathematics, with its constructivist grounding, may believe they need to draw on experiences with numerical concepts in order to solve "messy" problems.

And teachers are not the only ones with a stake in the battle: Parents, community members, and college professors of mathematics often join the "traditionalist" camp, whereas teacher educators, including mathematics education professors, often join the constructivist camp.

A curious twist on the math wars, however, seems to be the anticonstructivist position that the constructivists seem to be taking. Because constructivist views of mathematics have made their way into national and state standards, they have come to represent the received wisdom. Many mathematics educators now view the standards as the "truth" and treat standards-based mathematics as "best practice." This perspective has strong modernist overtones.

If the constructivists want to "get postmodern," they'll arguably need to accept the ambiguity of the math wars, recognizing that each side offers a worthwhile perspective and that mathematics knowledge can be constructed in many ways, including through traditional curriculum and methods of instruction.

Grand Narratives.   According to postmodern theorists, modernist culture (primarily through the products of valorized sciences and technologies) perpetuates stories about reality, human knowledge of reality, and freedom. These stories influence assumptions that are so deeply embedded in our thinking that we have a hard time identifying them, let alone challenging them. Postmodernists call these stories "grand narratives," "master narratives," or "meta-narratives," because they believe these stories function to organize thinking within and across disciplines as well as to exclude alternative ways of viewing the world (see, e.g., Lyotard, 1984).

One of the most pervasive of these stories concerns the existence of universal laws and principles that transcend time, culture, and locale. Moreover, because these laws and principles are purported to represent proven "truths," scientists and technologists believe they have the right to impose them on everyone, universally. Such impositions are sometimes codified in policy, but often they are merely enacted in routine practice. In education, the NCLB requirement that schools adopt "scientifically based" teaching methods offers an illustration of the imposition of universal principles through explicit policy. The routine assignment of homework in an effort to reinforce skills taught in the classroom exemplifies the enactment in practice of a so-called "universal" truth, namely that repetition improves learning. Nevertheless, our experiences as educators suggest that scientifically based teaching methods sometimes do not work. They also remind us that, in many cases, learning happens instantaneously, without requiring repetitive homework exercises, or else it fails to happen despite intensive and extensive drill.

Also pervasive is a story about how accumulating knowledge contributes to progress. According to this story, scientific studies produce knowledge that not only advances human understanding but also improves the material and social conditions of human life. Postmodern theorists note, however, that there is no vantage point from which human beings—who are inevitably situated at particular places and times—can judge progress. People cannot experience times and places other than their own, so they are unable to gauge progress from the vantage of the past. Nor can they evaluate it from the vantage of the future because they cannot know the future. In fact, their projections about what the future might bring simply reflect their situatedness in a particular circumstance in the present. "Progress," it turns out, is culturally defined—defined moreover by the very same people—scientists and technologists—who claim to be producing it. A critique of the grand narrative of progress leads to the possibility that "progress" is a self-serving myth perpetuated by those who benefit most from it.

Coherent Selfhood. Postmodernism also offers some surprising insights about our individual identities. Not only does it debunk the idea that we each possess a discrete and coherent identity that characterizes our "essence," it also challenges the assumption that individual selves exist apart from the network of relationships that define them. This interpretation suggests that identity is mostly determined by forces external to each of us. In fact, because we exist within so many different networks, our selfhood becomes increasingly cluttered with different, often contradictory beliefs and values—a circumstance that results in what Kenneth Gergen (1991) called the "saturated self."

At the same time, because we can relate to ourselves and interrupt our relationships with others, we can structure experiences to promote greater freedom (Foucault, 1990). Our work to differentiate ourselves from the cultural expectations perpetuated by networks of other people is viewed by postmodern theorists as a transgression. This characterization may seem odd. We are routinely told, after all, that we have complete freedom to construct a unique identity: We can be anything we want to be. From the perspective of postmodernism, this story is, of course, a myth: Our "complete" freedom primarily turns out to be the normative control exerted by others. Perhaps a "thought experiment" will help to make this paradox easier to understand. Sidebar 10-4 poses a challenge that reveals the extent to which our behavior is constrained by how we see the "norm."

Sidebar 10-4: Imaginary Transgressions

Imagine taking a harmless action that nevertheless pushes you beyond the boundaries of what feels normal and acceptable. If you are religious, perhaps that action might involve using a swear word in public, perhaps even in church. Or, if you are fashion conscious, it might involve going to a party dressed in dirty and torn clothes. As you picture yourself taking this action, how do you feel? Would the word "shame" come to mind, or possibly the word "guilt?" You might say to yourself, "Well, I'd never do that." And you might also notice that the contemplated action makes you worry about what important people in your life (or even strangers) would think about you.

One thing that's clear is that the imagined action is indeed a transgression; it violates some set of expectations or norms. You may locate the source of those expectations in persons outside of yourself, but the anticipated feelings of shame or guilt suggest that they are also internalized. The feelings engendered by imagining the transgression keep you from taking the action you imagine.

The fact that the action you've conjured up makes you uncomfortable and, as a result, that you would not really do it shows the extent to which you lack freedom. Of course, you might argue that you wouldn't want to take the action you imagine, for example wearing dirty and torn clothes or swearing in church, so lacking the freedom to take that action hardly matters. Postmodern theorists have argued, though, that it's important to understand the extent to which unexamined norms control our actions and, sometimes, to fight against them. After all, norms of this type constrain not only trivial actions, but also important ones such as speaking out against oppression, befriending people who are quite different from us, and defying unfair rules and regulations. For example, how many educators that you know believe that the testing requirements of NCLB are unfair and oppressive? Yet, how many of them resist participation either actively (by refusing to give the tests) or passively (by choosing not to treat the tests seriously)?

Because transgression is necessary in order to expand freedom, some postmodern theorists focus attention on the insights made available through the experiences of those who are considered deviant, such as prisoners, mental patients, and homosexuals (e.g., Foucault, 1977). Foucault in particular took this approach—unearthing the knowledge of subjugated and marginalized groups, helping them give voice to their ideas, and joining their protests (Halperin, 1995). Foucault also advocated and engaged in intentional transgression (e.g., extreme sexual practices, drug use) as a means to expand personal freedom and to explore the realm beyond reason (see, e.g., Halperin, 1995).

Activities such as these allow each person to explore aspects of the self that exist outside of the normalizing scrutiny of others such as parents, teachers, doctors, and ministers. For Foucault (1990), this project of self-exploration represents the moral realm, in part because moral action requires freedom. For other postmodern theorists, however, intentional regard for "the other" provides the foundation for moral action because the self is constituted by a nonrational relationship to other people (e.g., Levinas, 1998). In both versions of postmodern morality, construction of the self through nonrational processes is central.

POSTMODERN BUILDING BLOCKS

Thus far, the discussion has considered the conditions of modernism that postmodern theorists critique, examining the character of their quarrels with rationality, grand narratives, and normalization. Important as such critiques are to postmodernism, they are not the only contribution of this theoretical approach. Postmodern writers have also made important additions to the literature in semiotics (i.e., the study of signs and their cultural relevance), cultural studies (see chap. 6), and anti-colonial studies (see chap. 7). Three major ideas undergird these contributions: discourse, power, and difference. We call these "building blocks" because they figure so prominently in postmodern theory.

Discourse

Bringing together insights from two quite different philosophical traditions—structural Marxism and analytic philosophy—postmodern theorists explore the idea that social relationships are created out of discourse. To understand the depth of this theme in postmodern theory, it's useful to look at its two different sources.

For Marx, social relationships resulted from people's location in the economy—as peasants or landowners under feudalism and as workers or owners of the workplace under capitalism. The structure holding the economy together and the relationships engendered by that structure represented what Marx thought of as the "economic base" (Marx, 1967/1867). Helping to sustain the relationships required by the economic base were other social institutions—the law, schools, the government—that formed a "superstructure."

Although Marx did not theorize extensively about the superstructure, later Marxist theorists, most notably Louis Althusser, built on Marx's insight, suggesting that the superstructure served the economic base but also had a life of its own (Althusser, 1969). This principle served as a beginning point for critical theory (see chap. 9), but it also influenced postmodernism through Foucault, who was a student of Althusser. Whereas critical theorists emphasized the mechanisms linking the structure with the superstructure (e.g., social reproduction, hegemony), postmodern theorists concentrated on the conditions that enabled the superstructure to exist. For Foucault in particular, practices—for instance, the professional practices associated with teaching—constituted the superstructure, and discourse constituted practices (Foucault, 1972).

The later work of the analytic philosopher, Wittgenstein (1960) also emphasized the link between cultural practice and language. But for Wittgenstein, the primary question was "How is language constituted?" and the answer, "through practice." (Note that for Foucault, the primary question was "How is practice constituted?" and the answer, "Through language.") Wittgenstein used the term "language games" to describe the practices that enabled language learning and that linked utterances to actions within a culture. In addition, however, he saw that language games constituted cultural practice by defining and limiting what members of a culture would be able to perceive about their world. With this insight, his thinking about language games came very close to Foucault's (e.g., 1972) conception of "discursive practices."

In some of Foucault's work (e.g., Foucault, 1971, 1972), discursive practices—and the networks of relationships they make possible—seem to represent the basis for most of what goes on among human beings. But in other work (e.g., Foucault, 1977) additional practices, which act directly on the body (e.g., seating schoolchildren in rows), also receive attention. Because these practices connect so closely to discourse, however, many postmodern theorists extend the use of that term to cover these nonlanguage practices as well. As Iedema (2003, p. 1) explained,

> The notion of "discourse" is not restricted to linguistic phenomena. It encompasses meaning making in general. Thus, discourse has many manifestations, ranging from ephemeral materialities such as spoken language (produced by vocal and air vibrations), to more resource-intensive materialities, such as writing and print, technologies, architectures, and infra-structures.

Power

Power is a critical consideration for school leaders, and some of the postmodern theorists have a useful interpretation of it. According to these theorists, power is a "constitutive condition" of human life. What this means is that power contributes to forming who we are, how we see ourselves, and the options we believe are available to us. Construed in this way, power rarely involves domination (Foucault, 1980). In fact, as we move through our lives, we increasingly internalize power to such an extent that, as adults, most of us police ourselves quite effectively.

This view of power differs considerably from the views put forth by other theories. Sidebar 10-5 presents several conceptions of power that are supported by theories other than postmodernism (e.g., structural functionism, critical theory, and so on).

Sidebar 10-5: Different Theoretical Formulations of "Power"

Structural-Functionalist Theories of Power

- Zero-sum views of power typically embody the idea that one person gets what he or she wants (has his or her interests met) from others. This also means that the person who responds to power gives something up (e.g., freedom). So if one person or group gains power, another person or group necessarily gives up or loses power.

- Elite theories of power focus on its concentration in the hands of a few.

- Pluralistic theories talk about the ways power is disbursed across a range of interest groups, who negotiate and compete for influence.

- Exchange theories view power as a medium of exchange in which those with more resources cultivate the dependence of those with fewer resources.

Conflict and Structural Theories of Power

- Marxists view power as patterns of economic relationships. All societies, they note, have had ruling classes and subordinate classes. The differing class interests rest on a sharply inequitable division of wealth— and this means that differences in power have a material basis (and not, as with the postmodernists, a basis simply or mostly in discourse).

- Neo-Marxists interpret power as ideology (significant ideas held by an influential group) in the context of dominant and oppressed groups. When a dominant group is able to control the ideas of those who are oppressed such that the oppressed contribute to their own oppression, the dominant group is successful in exercising a kind of power called "hegemony."

- Marx himself believed that scientific laws of history would bring the working class to power in a world order that was better for everyone. The belief in universal laws makes Marx a modernist according to many postmodernists.

Although theories of power are implicit in most postmodern writing, only some theorists engage in extensive theorizing about power. Foucault provides the most complete treatment of the issue, and his theories have direct implications for the way we "do" school.

Disciplinary Power. For Foucault, power relations are historically situated, but they are also localized. This apparent contradiction is best explained in *Discipline and Punish* (1977) in which Foucault contrasts the power of the monarch to inflict punishment on the body of the offender with the power of the modern state to control the prisoner through an apparatus of surveillance. In fact, according to Foucault, the modern state maintains various institutions in which surveillance works to create compliant subjects—people who will monitor their own behavior to such an extent that surveillance by external authorities eventually becomes unnecessary.

Schools are among the most important institutions in which surveillance, coupled with strict regulation of students' actions, produces, first, compliance and, then, self-control. Although schools certainly maintain formalized punishment rituals (e.g., detention, in-school suspension), the disciplinary regimens that schools establish—seating charts, recitations, bells, examinations—are far more effective in exerting control over each individual student. These regimens work so well because they assign each student to specific locations on what Foucault calls "the grid." By knowing where each student is on the grid and where he or she is supposed to be—that is, the child's location in relationship to spatial, temporal, and developmental benchmarks—teachers can distinguish between appropriate and inappropriate behavior and between adequate and inadequate progress. Such comparisons enable teachers to claim accurate knowledge of each student. (The claimed accuracy may be an overstatement, but that's not the point—the point is the effect of this regime of power, not the validity of its details.)

This technique for gaining knowledge about students became particularly important with the development of mass schooling. When schools in the United States began to process large numbers of students (in the mid-1800s), for example, educators began to be use rosters to identify students who were in attendance and those who were truant or late. But the system of surveillance was extended far beyond scrutiny of individual students' attendance. For more than 100 years in the United States, teachers have used marks on exams and homework, and even on practice papers, to keep track of each student's position in relation to other class members.

Now, state-mandated standards have become an important benchmark for constructing the grid that helps teachers observe and regulate students. Moreover, standardized accountability tests represent an increasingly important technology of surveillance. Not only is the disciplinary power of the accountability test directed at the child, it is also directed at the teacher and the school.

Interestingly, schools' and districts' frequent response to accountability testing—namely the deployment of self-monitoring and self-imposed reform—matches up with what Foucault's theory of disciplinary power would predict. Because states cannot possibly maintain constant oversight, they need school personnel to keep watch over themselves and increasingly to shape their own practices to fit the expected norm.

Pastoral Power.   According to Foucault, disciplinary power is neither the only, nor the most effective way to achieve widespread normalization of behavior. An even subtler technique involves what he refers to as "pastoral" or "confessional" power (Foucault, 1980, 1990). Using this technique, parents and people employed in the "helping" professions work to connect children's aspirations to socially appropriate roles. Guidance counselors use this technique, for example, when they interview students about their interests in order to steer them toward suitable colleges or roles in the workforce. The objective for both the counselor and the students is to arrive at a good fit. From Foucault's perspective, normalization is accomplished more readily when everyone involved perceives the fit to be good.

To illustrate, consider two students: Susan is an academically talented student from a middle-class family, and Suzette is an academically talented student from an impoverished family. For Susan, the guidance counselor's recommendation that she attend a well-respected state college is likely to resonate with the way she has learned to think about herself. Because there is a good "fit" between her view of what's normal and the counselor's, Susan is likely to take the counselor's advice, completing whatever high school courses and engaging in whatever other academic preparations the high school counselor prescribes. The pastoral power exerted by the guidance counselor is hardly visible in this case.

With Suzette, it's likely to be a different matter. If home and school conspire to convince her that college is not an option, Suzette's awareness of her own talents might cause her to rebel. If the school tries to convince her that college is a good choice, it may put her at odds with her family. Again, rebellion is a possible outcome. If her family holds aspirations for her college attendance but the school doesn't provide appropriate support, once again there's an uncomfortable mismatch. In order to "normalize" Suzette—that is, to prepare her for a socially acceptable role that she also sees as fitting, educators will need to deploy pastoral power over an extended period of time. Such power will work directly on Suzette's self-concept, helping her to imagine herself in an adult role that corresponds to one of the many "normal" roles available in our society.

According to Foucault, one of the most useful techniques of pastoral power is the confession. Because rituals associated with confession require us to tell the truth about ourselves, they give the person hearing our confession power over us. That person has the power to punish or forgive us, or to redirect our behavior. And our desire to get back into the good graces of the person to whom we make a confession renders us particularly compliant. This is the sense, for Foucault, in which knowledge becomes power (the knowledge of the one hearing the confession, in particular, but also the confessed knowledge of the one making the confession). Sidebar 10-6 presents examples showing how various professionals exercise confessional power over us in everyday life.

Sidebar 10-6: Confessional Power in the Hands of Professionals

Professional	Method of Confession	Outcomes of Confession
Doctor	The physical examination	Control of our bodies through medication, surgery, or health-promoting regimens
Therapist	The counseling session	Control of our thoughts and emotions through medication, behavioral routines, or cognitive scripts
Priest, minister, or rabbi	The confession or counseling session	Control of our behaviors through penance and prayer
Judge	The confession	Control of our behaviors through confinement, retribution, and penance
Teacher	The examination	Control of our opportunities through grading, calculation of scores, and tracking
Assistant principal	The confession	Control of our behaviors through exclusion or confinement

---

Resistance.   For Foucault, the exercise of power typically does not involve domination. Instead, power strategies are accessible to most people, most of the time. As a result, the exercise of power—even the power that advances the interests of the state—takes place locally. This circumstance opens up possibilities for resistance—both the passive kind that Foucault referred to as "recalcitrance" as well as more active "countermoves." Moreover, unlike Marxists, neo-Marxists, and critical theorists, Foucault sees resistance as an opportunity available to individuals, not as an organizing principle galvanizing groups with shared interests.

Construed in this way, resistance primarily involves the actions we take to change ourselves, not actions we explicitly take in order to change others. A couple of examples will clarify this distinction.

- Many teachers work in schools where principals are insisting on standards-based reform. Good teachers are now defined as those who base all of their lessons on specified standards. Teachers and others who have observed schools for awhile understand that this definition does not capture two important parts of school reality: the case of good teachers who don't bother with the standards and the case of bad teachers who are highly attentive to standards. Because there are other possibilities than the one insisted on by principals, teachers can resist. By choosing to base their practice on different idiosyncratic definitions of "the good teacher," they can expand the scope of their own freedom as well as augmenting the power moves available to others in the school. Defining teaching practice idiosyncratically takes a lot of work; it's easier simply to comply. But teachers who put in the effort extend the freedom available to students, especially to those students whose difficult circumstances typically restrict their options (see, e.g., Haberman, 1995).
- Many of us are raised with prejudices that limit our understanding of others and may even cause us to act badly toward them. Such prejudices, however, probably serve broader interests than our own, perhaps by reinforcing particular social and political hierarchies. Maintaining these prejudices (and their harmful effects) is something such hierarchies might want. We can, however, work on ourselves to get rid of these prejudices. Doing so, however, takes concerted effort because it involves erasing a picture of ourselves that feels familiar and normal. Nevertheless, by ridding ourselves of prejudice, we expand our freedom and reduce our contribution to dynamics that limit others' freedom.

As these examples suggest, individuals use resistance to keep organizations, communities, or even nations from exercising domination. Social change results from this circulation of power, although its trajectory is neither predictable nor directed toward a particular version of "improvement." In fact, because we cannot know where the circulation of power will lead, resistance to whatever oppression we encounter in our personal lives is the best we can do to work on behalf of freedom, at least according to some of the postmodernists.

Difference

One of the most important dualisms in modernist thinking is between "self" and "other" (Seth, 2001). That which is not the self is other. If the self is male, for example, the other is female. If the self is white skinned, the other is dark skinned. If the self is cosmopolitan, the other is rural. If the self is the colonizer, the other is the colonized.

Exploring these simple dualisms, postmodern theorists (e.g., Said, 1978) and postmodern feminists (e.g., Cornell, 1993) offer some useful insights: (a) The other represents what is not the self, and therefore it is not merely the opposite of the self; (b) if the other contains all that is not the self, then it determines the conditions under which the self can come into being; (c) in a sense, then, the self is contained within the other and vice versa; and (d) as a result of these conditions of self and other, it is useful to view the other as a set of multiplicities to which the self belongs.

This all sounds quite abstract. After all, in everyday life we don't typically think in terms of self and other, even though we tend to appreciate dualisms such as Men are From Mars, Women are From Venus (Gray, 1992). To make these ideas more concrete, therefore, it's helpful to choose an important characteristic of self-ness and to work it through the logic of the four points previously described.

Let's try this with race, perhaps "whiteness," a difficult concept for many White people. First, all races that are different from White, not just the Black race, represent, for White people, the other. Second, if we did not have other races to contrast with the White race, we would not see whiteness as relevant; in other words, without other races, whiteness would cease to be—the existence of whiteness, therefore, depends on other races. Third, whiteness is contained within nonwhiteness, and nonwhiteness is contained within whiteness. Finally, whiteness and all other races represent multiple sources of difference.

This way of thinking may seem roundabout, but it helps us "deconstruct" an important social condition that characterizes the daily experience of race, namely that White people do not typically see themselves in terms of race. This, in fact, explains why White people find the concept of whiteness so difficult: Race is understood by White people as a property of the other. Dyer (1997, p. 3), for example, described the condition in this way: "At the level of racial representation ... whites are not of a certain race, they're just of the human race." Perry (2001, p. 60) explained, "White culture is 'invisible' because it is constructed as 'normal'." Moreover, both of these authors and numerous other writers on "whiteness" discuss how the normalization of whiteness contributes to the oppression of people of other races.

A conscious engagement with racialized concepts of self and other, moreover, enables us to "interrupt" racial oppression in our own lives. When we come to see difference as a feature of our own identities, not just as something that applies to those whose differences are readily visible, we are less likely to "marginalize" others. At the same time, an appreciation of difference and all that it contributes to the social landscape greatly enriches our own experience. These insights are further elaborated in a branch of postmodern theory known as "queer theory" (see chap. 8).

The concept of difference also figures prominently in postmodern literary criticism (often called "deconstructionism"). In the writings of Derrida (e.g., 1974), difference provides a more general account of the "self–other" relationship we described earlier. For Derrida, however, language and meanings—rather than identities—are the topics of primary interest. Focusing on the multiplicities of meaning that are present in any utterance or written text, he explores the possibilities that are opened up when we think of reading and writing as a form of play.

This view of language frees us from the oppression of seeing text as a privileged way for one author to cause one meaning to become evident to every reader. From the postmodern perspective, the traditional formulation of how language works (an author causing a single meaning to form in all readers) is not only wrong, more importantly, it is tyrannical. By playing with language, however, we, as authors and readers, not only invite different interpretations but create a much richer and more accessible engagement with text. This approach gives each of us greater freedom and also extends freedom to a wider audience.

It also increases the complexity of language and of the ideas that language enables us to consider. Many people, however, see this complexity as unnecessarily arcane (esoteric and elitist), and they fault postmodern writers for their tendency to use big words, jargon, long and complicated sentences, and difficult if not impenetrable language. From the perspective of real-time, real-life teachers and principals, the criticism seems largely justified—even though postmodernist ideas are quite useful to educators. In Sidebar 10-7, we include excerpts from a send-up of postmodern jargon that was published in the *New York Times*.

Sidebar 10-7: Richard Bernstein on Postmodern Jargon

The following comments are excerpted from an editorial written for the *New York Times* by Richard Bernstein (1990):

"Rewriting the (Post)modern: (Post)colonialism / Feminism / Late Capitalism'" read the brochure advertising a conference that I attended at the University of Utah in March. The program was full of fashionable academic jargon—phrases like "reified theory," "(post)structuralist tropics" and "the racial subject"—all of it standard lexical fare in the arcane world of literary criticism.

The parentheses were placed not only around words but also around parts of words. There was one paper titled "Locating Un(re)presentable Desire: Narrational Transformations and Posmodern Man." Another was "It's Not (Post) Until it's Post(ed): (Post)modernism and the Terminological Endgames of Terrorism."

Trendy academic language has always kept me mindful of certain phrases from George Orwell's "Politics and the English Language," particularly the one in which he likens the users of prefabricated jargon to "cuttlefish squirting out ink." Yesterday, the cult terms were "intertexuality" and "the signifier." Today, it's parentheses carving up words like scimitars.

But a few months before the Utah meeting, my skepticism was challenged. At the convention of the Modern Language Association, the major professional body for academic literary critics, I ran into Philip Auslander, a professor of English at the Georgia Institute of Technology. "Why shouldn't literary critics have a technical language to express their ideas, in the same way that physicists or engineers do?" he asked.

Why indeed? What the lit crits argue is that they are looking at the world in a new way, a way that requires the invention of a new language. Nobody objects to the linguistic innovations of Freud or Einstein, necessary to express meanings that nobody else had expressed before. Why should the acolytes of the great French post-structuralists, like Roland Barthes, Jacques Derrida and Michel Foucault, be any different? ...

And so, the big question: Was this lingo squirted out by Orwell's cuttlefish or is it really useful? I contend that positionality is as inky as a word can get. And yet there is a seductive quality to some of this terminology: [I]t has a cultish sensuousness to it. As the lit crits might put it, you become part of the transgressive, rather than the dominant, discourse. You are a member of the club.

THEORETICAL POSSIBILITIES

The discussion in the previous section focuses on major concepts that distinguish postmodernist theories from other ways of thinking. Now it's time to take a look at some of the important theoretical "camps" that postmodernism encompasses. Two of these—constructivism and cultural pluralism—are now having a direct impact on schools. The impact of the other two camps is evident, but less direct.

Constructivism

Forming the basis these days for curriculum and instruction in most academic subjects, constructivist learning theory takes its inspiration from the work of French psychologist Jean Piaget and early Soviet psychologist Lev Vygotsky. Although the contributions of these innovative thinkers is widely acknowledged, the pedagogical version of constructivism represents a rich tradition in its own right, with a host of competing claims and a few consensus positions. For our purposes, the shared perspectives are more important to review than the academic debates among constructivists. The points of agreement include the following:

- Learners actively construct meaning.
- New learning connects to prior knowledge, sometimes adding to it, sometimes revising it.
- Social interaction contributes in important ways to learners' construction of meaning.

Understanding constructivism is critical for principals, who obviously need to participate in discussions about curriculum and instructional methods. And constructivist ideas also help principals think about how professional development might (or might not) promote teachers' learning and, therefore, which types of professional development would be most meaningful. In addition, some writers have claimed that leadership itself can be founded on constructivist premises.

Constructivist Curriculum and Instruction.   Standards from professional organizations at the national level are increasingly adopting a constructivist perspective, and many states base their curriculum standards on those from the national organizations. For example, the standards developed by the National Council for the Social Studies (1994, pp. 11–12) include five principles of teaching and learning, three of which clearly draw on constructivist ideas:

1. Social studies teaching and learning are powerful when they are meaningful.
2. Social studies teaching and learning are powerful when they are integrative.
3. Social studies teaching and learning are powerful when they are active.

Principles such as these encourage teachers to use content and teaching methods that differ considerably from traditional pedagogy, and change along these lines would have clear implications for school leadership. Some parents, for example, may not understand or approve of the content or the instructional techniques that constructivist teachers use. Teachers themselves disagree about the advisability of such changes. And the organizational structures and routines of schools probably would need to be altered in order to accommodate the integrated, active, and socially mediated learning experiences called for by constructivism.

Constructivist Professional Development. Adherents believe that the preparation and continuing education of educators ought to be grounded in constructivist principles. After all, they ask, how can educators make use of this method if they have never seen it used (see, e.g., Chicoine, 2004; Phelps & Cherin, 2003)? Despite the views of advocates, only a few reports of constructivist teacher education and professional development are available (e.g., Grossman & Williston, 2002; Mintrop, 2001; Osterman, 1998).

Constructivist Leadership. Some authors have also maintained that it is important to base school leadership on constructivist premises. For example, Prawat and Peterson (1999, p. 223) described the implications of constructivism for administrative practice:

> Constructivist learning theory points away from the notion of administrator as a person who smoothes the way, who helps ensure that the organization operates efficiently … Instead it points … toward the importance of encouraging members of an organization to learn and develop realizing that that goal is apt to be met when members of the organization work together to make it happen.

Lambert (1995, p. 29) offered a similar perspective:

> The function of leadership must be to engage people in the processes that create the conditions for learning and form common ground about teaching and learning. Schooling must be organized and led in such a way that these learning processes provide direction and momentum to human and educational development.

This view of administration emphasizes the need to engage teachers in organizational learning and to foster team work. These bland aims hardly seem unique to constructivism: They are also shared by advocates of transformational leadership (see chap. 2), dynamic systems theory (see chap. 4), and other contemporary theories.

Cultural Pluralism

Another theoretical approach with direct bearing on educational practice is cultural pluralism, which acknowledges and gives voice to multiple perspectives, especially those that have been marginalized by the dominant culture. As Safstrom (1999, p. 225) explained, this alternative to hegemony "opens itself to those who are excluded, to silenced voices, and to a politics of resistance."

Arguably, multicultural education belongs in the pluralist camp, but not all multiculturalists are postmodern pluralists (see chap. 6). Multicultural education, after all, came into existence before anyone was talking about postmodernism (see, e.g., Powers, 2002). It's important, therefore, to distinguish the kind of cultural pluralism that has postmodern connections from its other varieties.

Powers (2002) drew such distinctions in his analysis of the postmodern themes in the work of noted multiculturalist, James A. Banks. As Powers explained, "It would appear that Banks, trained originally in the methods and categories of modern social science, underwent something of a transformation, at least in his epistemological views" (p. 212). This means that Banks changed how he thought about knowledge, and what it takes to know something (and therefore to teach something so that a student knows it). Quotes assembled from his opus reveal the postmodern concepts that Banks found applicable to multiculturalism. These include (a) the existence of multiple truths, (b) the influence of values on knowledge claims, and (c) the effect of power relations on the construction of knowledge.

Postmodern pluralism also embraces a radical view of democracy in which critique of mainstream discourse and social practice helps to provide a complex, "antiessentialist" understanding of difference (Giroux, 1988b; Jacobs, 2002). Educators who see pluralism in this way tend to reiterate recommendations from critical pedagogy (see chap. 9), calling for the examination ("interrogation") of popular culture and renewed engagement with local democracy. Certain postmodernist thinkers might criticize the conception of improvement implicit in the emancipatory and humanist discourse of some pluralists, even those claiming to be postmodern.

Social Constructionism (a.k.a. "Radical Constructivism")

The previous discussion considers constructivism as it is elaborated by psychologists and educators influenced by psychologists, but another branch of constructivism (often called "social constructionism") is supported by the work of philosophers, anthropologists, and sociologists (see, e.g., Phillips, 1997). Although there is agreement across the disciplines about the major ideas contributed by the constructivist perspective, the application of ideas differs by discipline.

Whereas psychologists use the ideas to account for the working of individual minds, philosophers use them to critique the assertions underlying the modernist conception of science, and anthropologists and sociologists use them to explain the sources and internal logic of cultural practices. Common to these theorists is the claim that because knowledge is a human invention, truth is both relative and value laden. Constructivist psychologists challenge the behaviorist notion that the mind is an unknowable "black box," but for philosophers of science, this perspective challenges the belief that we can know the real world apart from our social constructions of it. Although constructionist philosophers differ on the question of whether or not there actually is a real world apart from our social constructions, they agree that human beings cannot develop conceptions of the real world that directly reveal its features. Knowledge in this view is always mediated by the human construction of meaning (see, e.g., Nagel, 1986). For scientists, those meanings come not only from culture but also from the communities of practice that determine legitimacy within each discipline and subdiscipline to which they belong (e.g., Suppes, 1993). This is one condition, for instance, that makes theories necessarily tentative.

In anthropology and sociology, by contrast, social constructionism supports analysis of cultural practices along two lines: (a) the conditions that enable those practices to arise and (b) the rules—either of action or discourse—by which they operate (see, e.g., Berger & Luckmann, 1966). A cursory review of recent publications in the social sciences revealed studies of the social construction of the underage drinker, workplace diversity, virginity, gambling, headaches, Valentine's Day, sexual dysfunction, victims, lesbianism, and kidney disease. The great variety of these topics suggests that the social constructionist approach has achieved considerable popularity. An example from education might illustrate why.

Schools' treatment of children with learning disabilities typically rests on the belief that "LD is a pathology that resides in the heads of individual students" (Dudley-Marling, 2004, p. 482). This perspective takes little account of the conditions under which children are identified as learning disabled, and as a result, it contributes to a deficit view of certain children. Nevertheless, as Dudley-Marling (p. 485) argued,

> The construction of LD, like any identity, depends on the complex interaction of people, places, and activities. Like other identities, the identity of LD is not only produced in a social context; it is itself part of the context that gives meaning to participants' actions.

If we take seriously the idea that LD is a social construction, however, we not only free children from the constraints of a disability label, we also give ourselves greater room to take action. As Dudley-Marling (pp. 488–489) explained,

> Teachers working from a social constructivist orientation begin by assessing the various factors that make up the social context in which students' learning identities are constructed so they can contemplate moves that might disrupt the performance of a learning problem. This stance does not obviate appropriate and explicit instructional support and direction, but it does recognize that even a small change in the patterns of interaction … can have a significant effect on students' learning identities.

The example illustrates the way that social constructionism contributes to new and potentially liberating insights about school practices. This interpretive stance might be usefully applied to some of schools' most ingrained, yet perplexing features. All of us have our own lists of such features, of course. The following features of schooling might appear on many of those lists, however: (a) discipline practices, (b) grouping arrangements, (c) teacher competence and incompetence, (d) school–community relations, and (e) athletics.

Deconstruction

Deconstruction is to text what social constructionist analysis is to cultural practices. Although this analogy isn't exact, it provides a useful starting point for considering an approach that many find particularly esoteric and perhaps even elitist. Let's see where it takes us.

Social constuctionist interpretation promotes understanding of practices by situating them in context. Interestingly, of course, an analogy is already in play when we use the word "context," whose first meaning in the American Heritage Dictionary (2002, p. 309) is "the part of a text or statement that surrounds a particular word or passage and determines its meaning." Drawing on the rationalist tradition of narrative analysis, which focuses on precise meanings, this dictionary definition embeds two assumptions: (a) that context is nearby to the text to which it contributes meaning and (b) that there is an agreed-upon "true" meaning that text reveals when properly situated in its context—one correct reading, in other words.

If we decide to engage in contextual interpretation that makes the opposite assumptions, then we're doing deconstruction (see, e.g., Derrida, 1978). Interpretation along these lines assumes that (a) context is everything that is and is not the particular text (e.g., all of the experiences of readers, the entire opus of written work, every possible utterance in any language) and (b) agreed-upon, true meanings are logically impossible given the nature of context. These assumptions render interpretation quite strange, directing attention away from what a narrative means to the conditions under which it acquires a particular meaning and the alternative meanings that it might acquire under different conditions. This method of interpretation provides support for multiple readings of any text, thereby democratizing the analysis of texts. It also invites everyone to play with text, thereby stripping power from the text itself. And it permits critics to analyze the strategies by which text privileges certain readings and marginalizes others—an approach that enables readers and writers to deal with text in ways that they find liberating or aesthetically pleasing..

Beyond its possible implications for the English literature curriculum, deconstruction may not seem particularly useful to educators. Nevertheless, it does offer a way to unpack and gain control over the stories that influence and often constrain educational practice.

Gary Anderson (1998), for example, undertook a deconstruction of the rhetoric of democratic participation that appears prominently in the school reform literature. One of his concerns is that rhetoric about democratic participation may represent a defensive maneuver intended to deal with public education's "crisis of legitimacy" (p. 576). Another of Anderson's concerns is that instead of promoting greater freedom, it may actually contribute to greater regulatory control over schools. Despite the pessimism of this analysis, it allows educators who want to promote democratic participation within their school communities to see what they're up against. School leaders might find it more useful to invent their own stories of democratic participation than to buy into one or another group's existing program. This way, they can frame ideas on their own terms, possibly responding better to the circumstances facing their schools.

POSTMODERNIST ORGANIZATIONS INCLUDING SCHOOLS

With a fuller understanding of the assumptions and variations of postmodernist theory, it's now time to turn attention to hopeful visions of what postmodernist organizations might be like. Gergen and Thatchenkery

(2004, p. 242) used the word "generative" to describe this type of theorizing. Examining such generative possibilities with an eye to their context (i.e., a postmodern world increasingly dominated by transnational corporations, a reduction in cultural variability, and so on), we can see how difficult and complex it would be to transform our present modernist organizations into postmodernist ones. Whereas some have argued that this transformation is already underway, others have offered reminders about the resilience of the modernist project and the organizational structures that support it (see, e.g., Gergen & Thatchenkery, 2004).

The Organic Organization

Those postmodernists who present generative organizational visions sound a lot like dynamic systems theorists (see chap, 4) in that they place learning at the center of organizational life. These theorists are concerned not only with the learning of each of the members of the organization, but also with the learning of the organization itself. For this reason, the organizations they imagine are not like machines (i.e., the modernist vision); they are more like living entities. In other words, they're organic.

Gergen and Thatchenkery (2004), for example, imply that participants in organic organizations will no longer put much faith in the sort of problem solving that makes use of rational choice methods. Instead, they will use dialog as a basis for critical reflection. Moreover, they will widen access to dialog, thereby enriching the conversations that lead to new ideas and productive decisions. As they seek to make changes in accordance with these insights, members of such organizations will focus on cultural and discursive practices rather than on technical procedures. Organizations, in this view, will cease to be structures (i.e., physical and hierarchical spaces) and instead will become knowledge systems—what Tsoukas (2005, p. 100) referred to as a "collective mind."

Iedema (2003, p. 3) offers a similar vision: "Post-bureaucratic organization is a complex dialectic that seeks to balance interactive participation, self-steering and self-fashioned workers, and the formalization of aspects of work ... " He suggests that members of postbureaucratic organizations will use language as the primary basis for negotiating worklife: "Workers no longer just do their work: they increasingly talk their work" (Iedema, 2003, p. 7). In addition, although he uses trendier language, he describes processes that resemble Senge's (1990) conception of team learning: "Textualization is a process of subjectification where, through the enunciation of knowledge about work, worker's self is organizationalized, and the organization is 'self-ed'" (Iedema, 2003, p. 3).

These speculations may strike most readers as somewhat contrived. Perhaps it's because the organizations we now work in have so little in common with the ones that these postmodernists imagine. Or perhaps, the modernist project still has a dominant influence on organizational aims irrespective of changes in the cultural and discursive practices that constitute worklife. Changing the material world through discourse, which is the sort of agency that many postmodern theorists have recommended, may prove to be less promising than these theorists wish. In fact, postmodernist theory may turn out to be a lot more useful as a method of critique than as the basis for futuristic visions. Arguably, postmodernists' skepticism about progress ought to warn them away from making normative claims on behalf of organizational improvement.

There is one body of empirically grounded theorizing that might be categorized as postmodernist because it combines ideas from constructivism and social constructionism. It examines the way social networks (i.e., communities that are both narrowly and widely dispersed) operate to cultivate the expertise of their members. Rather than focusing on organizations per se, this body of work looks at the "communities of practice" in which organizations are situated and to which they contribute. For example, teachers are employed by particular school districts, but their learning takes place in a wider community, which includes the faculty from their teacher preparation programs, colleagues from their own and other school districts, the educational researchers whose articles they read (or which are interpreted to them by others), and various additional sources. The literature on "communities of practice," moreover, seems also to have been an inspiration for the "professional learning communities" that are now gaining such popularity in some schools.

Communities of Practice

Reflecting on ethnographic observations of apprenticeships in various areas of endeavor (e.g., midwifery, meat-cutting, tailoring), Jean Lave and Etienne Wenger (1991) developed principles of social learning to explain how people acquire expertise (see also Wenger, 1998). Suggesting that both social and individual construction of knowledge is implicated, Wenger (2000, p. 227) writes:

> Whether we are apprentices or pioneers, newcomers or oldtimers, knowing always involves ... two components: the competence that our communities have established over time (i.e., what it takes to act and be recognized as a competent member), and our ongoing experience of the world as a member (in the context of a given community and beyond).

Learning, according to Lave and Wenger, is "situated" in "communities of practice." Participation in such communities, moreover, has a direct influence on how we see ourselves. In this view, education transforms us by inviting us to develop "new trajectories of participation" in groups that we value (p. 267). These communities of practice help us make meaning and acquire power. True education, according to Wenger, can never be planned, although planned experiences influence the meaning constructed in communities of practice. This perspective seems to give a rather positive spin to Foucault's (e.g., 1977) ideas about "normalization."

Professional Learning Communities. One approach to professional development brings a school's teachers together to reflect on practice. This approach is premised on several key beliefs: (a) that the teachers share responsibility for the success of all students, (b) that everyone in the school is a learner, not just the students, and (c) that ongoing critical inquiry will lead to improvement (e.g., Hord, 1997, 1998). Because this approach is so often used in the familiar school improvement efforts (to align schools' curriculum and instruction with state standards, to shape teachers' practice according to a particular version of "the norm"), it seems far more modernist than postmodernist. That the state is so often able to coopt practices that contribute to identity formation (in this case, the formation of teachers' identities) may be a testament to the resilience of the modernist project, suggesting again the value of a critique that doesn't accept modernism as a perpetual end state of human society.

Postmodernist Schools

Postmodernist ideas have influenced the views of educators who are disenchanted with mainstream school reform but who also believe that direct confrontation in the political arena is likely to be unproductive. Starrat (2001, p. 346), for example, suggests:

> The reconstruction of schooling involves both a deconstruction of meanings, values, and assumptions, the analysis of their negatives and their positives, of what is to be rejected and what kept, and a reconstruction, an invention of new meanings, new metaphors, new organizational dynamics, new institutional processes that will carry the playing of school into a more humanly satisfying and morally fulfilling story.

Toll (2001, pp. 364–365) provides specific guidance for using postmodernist ideas to sponsor change in school practice:

- *Recognize difference*: Replace the quest for sameness in school practices, values, and beliefs with a recognition that difference cannot be eliminated.
- *Pay attention to the margins*: Look beyond sites of power and commonly accepted discourse in schools (represented, for example, by the principal's office, middle-class parents of European decent, and classroom teachers) to find the "spaces" of individuals and ideas that are underrepresented.
- *Heed postmodern voices*: Hear that the voices of difference, the voices at the margins, will include knowledges, sources of authority, and ways-of-doing that are unfamiliar to and unrecognized by the mainstream.
- *Resist metanarratives [and] seek the local and contextual*: Challenge assumptions about how all schools work, what all teachers do, or what every parent wants, recognizing that in the multiplicity of voices and spaces found in any school situation there are myriad ways to conceptualize problems and solutions.
- *Recognize discursiveness*: Perceive that discourse—how individuals talk, act, and represent themselves in any situation—determines what is considered "normal" and who has power in schools; helps others to see that "how things are" in schools is a creation of discourse and not a statement of the only reality possible.
- *Consider power*: Develop awareness that the preceding strategies will challenge existing power relations in schools and school districts, and keep using these very strategies to confront and overcome this resistance.

These perspectives, as well as the views of postmodernists whose focus on schooling is less direct, help us rethink school practices relating to curriculum, disciplinary methods, and governance. "Rethinking," however, differs considerably from "reforming" in that it implies a range of possibilities, not just a few, preordained outcomes. Moreover, from a postmodernist vantage, one can never know what will turn out to be an improvement in the long term. Providing increased freedom in the here and now seems like the best an educational leader working from a postmodernist perspective can do.

The Curriculum.   For a variety of reasons, postmodern theorists would have a hard time with prescribed curricula, such as those put forth in state standards. They would be concerned, for example, that such curricula would contribute to a regime of truth, essentializing (see Sidebar 10-1) particular knowledge, excluding other knowledge, and misrepresenting knowledge as a form of consumption. In particular, they would question the motivation of policymakers who seek to mandate "what all children should know and be able to do" because such efforts look to them like inappropriate constraints on freedom.

Instead, they would ask educators to consider the value of local and previously disqualified knowledge. Doll (1993), for example, reminds us that there is not just one truth that should constitute the curriculum; the contribution of many diverse voices is needed in order to enrich and animate our understanding. At the same time, the inclusion of many voices adds to the complexity and ambiguity of knowledge, a circumstance that requires intellectual openness and sophistication.

Tolerance for ambiguity, moreover, requires that we allow power struggles over the curriculum to take place locally, trusting that the regimes of truth that prevail will be no worse in the long run than any other regime of truth. As Wells, Lopez, Scott, and Holme (1999, p. 175) note, a postmodernist perspective on diversity enables us to accept the fact that "the goals and purposes of education in some communities may be more about creating schools that reflect a particular cultural heritage than about improved test scores." For this reason, educators working from a postmodernist outlook might view local complaints about curriculum—including complaints from fundamentalist parents—more as temporary, if dangerous, opportunities than as disasters.

In some communities, local struggles might result in a curriculum that was, itself, informed by postmodernist ideas. Although few schools have such a curriculum, we can imagine what one might be like. For example, such a curriculum probably would encourage students to play with language and ideas, to consider various worldviews without seeking to judge them against one standard, to participate in dialog, and to see their identities as a project of self-discovery. In addition, a postmodernist curriculum would probably devote attention to examining ideas in historical and cultural context, interrogating power relations, and listening to the voices of those whose perspectives tend to be marginalized or excluded from mainstream discourse. It would also give free reign to students' imaginations.

Arguing against the requirement that curriculum be constrained by children's prior knowledge, social constructionist Keiran Egan (2003, p. 445) offered a comment that seems germane to speculations about postmodernist curriculum:

> For teaching, we need not be constrained by trying to make content associations with knowledge students already have, for there are other ways of expanding knowledge. For the curriculum, we need no longer be constrained to tie knowledge to the everyday experience of students, which can be very dreary for them, but can recognize that their imaginations allow much freedom in how they can go about grasping the universe of knowledge.

Discipline.   Considering their interest in freedom and their critique of technologies that limit freedom, many postmodern theorists would probably have concerns about the way discipline is handled in most schools. They also might interpret the constraints that schools impose—over the curriculum, the activities available to students, and the discourses that are permissible—as likely causes of misbehavior. Perhaps they'd conclude that there's an association between students' resistance and the meaninglessness that so many students ascribe to their school experience.

With these concerns in mind, postmodernist school leaders might work to examine and perhaps change a variety of disciplinary strategies, not just the ones that are presented explicitly in the student handbook for dealing with misbehavior, but also those that are implicit in everyday practice. Educators might, for instance, explore the disciplinary effects of practices such as testing, grading, assigned seating, bell schedules, and student grouping. The aim of such critical reflection would not, of course, be to encourage lawlessness or disorder! Instead, critical reflection would be seen as providing a basis for altering the most restrictive practices, the ones that are educationally disabling.

With respect to behavior, for example, short-lived punishments, such as time out or paddling, might actually be understood by postmodernists as less constraining than "therapeutic" interventions. So too might heterogeneous grouping, removal of tests and letter grades, and optional class attendance. Arguably, however, the whole enterprise of schooling might be viewed as a disciplinary technology, and postmodernist theory might suggest the need to abandon schooling altogether in favor of a diverse set of alternative practices. If this sounds unlikely or impossible, think again. Virtual schooling, home schooling, and various forms of competency certification (like the GED) are perhaps already moving the system of schooling in such a direction.

Governance.   Whereas postmodernists are skeptical about what can be accomplished in official political forums, they nonetheless support efforts to give voice to diverse individuals and groups. This combination of beliefs fits in with a view of governance as informal, open, and distributed. A school organized along these lines would promote extensive dialog among its participants, encouraging, in particular, the contributions of those whose voices are typically excluded—students and many parents.

Governance of such a school would also need to be positioned carefully with respect to official policies of democratization. As Spencer (2001) demonstrates, the state version of open participation in school governance embeds the liberal democratic coupling of rights and responsibilities. This combination seeks to ensure that the dialog taking place in local school governance bodies focuses on "improving the quality of education for the benefits of students" (Spencer, 2001, p. 9). And although this language seems harmless enough, official discourse about "improvement" embeds a host of troubling assumptions (e.g., that higher test scores indicate that a benefit has been conferred). As a result, this discourse is likely to be misaligned with and perhaps destructive of local interests.

Local school governance, if it is to take a postmodern turn, needs to invent itself and then continually to reinvent itself. What this might look like at any particular school is uncertain because invention opens up so many possibilities. One partially realized example is described by Deb Meier (2002) in her recollection of how her mentor, Lillian Weber, constructed schools as "interesting places for teachers to learn" (p. 26):

> Her wedge into the big schools was called the "open corridor." She found principals willing to put three, four, or five interested teachers, often of different grade levels, next to each other along one corridor—and then added student teachers .... She ensconced herself in the corridor and began to demonstrate, play, talk, discuss—while ostensibly supervising her student teachers. She created communities of adults and kids where their respective work was public and visible to families, colleagues, and peers.

As Meier notes, however, these arrangement were "fragile, rarely lasting more than a few years" (p. 26). A postmodernist perspective views such fluidity as inevitable—both reflective and productive of the ongoing negotiation of the social and discursive space that any school occupies. In an institutional sense, this perspective frees us from worries about getting things wrong because it shows us that rational arrangements and complex differences render universal standards of "goodness" problematic, if not impossible. There's something else, though, and that is the postmodernists' sense of the mutual responsibility of humans for one another's well-being, especially those living near us. According to Bauman (1993), this responsibility is a requirement imposed by (a) the ambiguities of social life and (b) human fascination with the other. From the postmodernist vantage, we are both free and obligated to take care of one another, and this means that the conditions of human life require that we embrace the project of education. It can't be abandoned just because it's difficult.

CASE STUDY: HERMAN UTTICK AND THE EXCUSED ABSENCE POLICY

Located in a quiet suburb in a southern state, Peach-Navy Base High School primarily serves the upper middle class community of Peach. Because of a district annexation that took place about 30 years ago, the school also serves the small town of Navy Base, which ironically no longer has a navy base. It is, however, home to a remarkably diverse population: low-income families moving in from rural areas, immigrants from South America and the Pacific Rim, and African American residents whose families have been there for generations. On the outskirts of Navy Base is a small community of religious fundamentalists, most of whom do not send their children to the local schools.

For years Peach-Navy Base has boasted well-behaved and academically focused students. But lately there have been disturbing changes. For the first time in 10 years, the school lost a point on the state report card for its below-standard attendance rates. And scores on accountability tests are also declining. Principal Herman Uttick has some theories about what's going on—overly indulgent parents, too many video games, not enough discipline at home—but he doesn't know anything for sure.

Recently, though, he recommended to the school council that a new attendance policy be put in place. The five teachers and four parents on the council saw the benefits of having a stricter policy and accepted Herman's recommendation unanimously. Under the new policy, a doctor's (or psychologist's) note is now required for all excused absences, except for those resulting from a death in the student's immediate family. Notes from parents are no longer accepted as evidence of students' sickness or medical appointments. Absences for family emergencies, travel, and educational outings are no longer permitted.

The Problem

Almost as soon as the new attendance policy was adopted, Uttick began receiving requests for exemptions. One family wanted their daughter's appointments for acupuncture to count as a medical exam; but the acupuncturist wasn't a doctor. One of the few students from the fundamentalist "commune" saw a faith healer on a regular basis. When Uttick made it clear that the acupuncturist and the faith healer didn't count as doctors, a small group of parents from Navy Base began to meet to discuss options.

As tensions were beginning to mount, Uttick made a judgment call that added fuel to the fire. He suspended Marty Boswell, the son of a prominent Peach businessman, for skipping school. Marty had brought in what looked like a doctor's note; but when the counselor, Mindy French, read it, she knew it was a hoax. Uttick certainly didn't want to be seen as playing favorites. He wanted to enforce the same standards of conduct for the affluent Peach students whose overall conduct helped to keep the "lid on" with the low-income Navy Base students.

Sitting across his desk from Mr. Boswell and Mr. Boswell's attorney, Uttick realized his mistake. Apparently (as the lawyer explained), bloodletting with leeches was now an accepted medical practice, and Marty's doctor had written the note. Of course Uttick backed off immediately, apologizing to Mr. Boswell and Marty.

But Marty didn't leave it there. Instead, he did what he could to let everyone in the school know what had happened. He didn't like Uttick, and neither did his friends. This was a way to get even.

Of course, once word got out that leech treatments were an excused absence, other students—those who thought acupuncture, consultation with faith healers, and visits to sweat lodges represented legitimate forms of healing—also demanded equal treatment. And so did their parents.

Uttick was in a terrible predicament. The policy was cutting down on absences; there was no doubt of that. But it was also precipitating a rebellion among a small, but increasingly vocal minority. Uttick did not want to be responsible for "silencing voices," but he did wish the group of parents from Navy Base would just leave him alone.

He was beginning to feel stress himself. "Pretty soon, I'll need a faith healer," he quipped to his wife. But he turned on the TV instead and began watching a special on unified field theory. "If the physicists can figure out the nature of the whole universe," he said to himself, "why can't I figure out a high school attendance policy?" And with that thought, an idea came to him.

The next day, Uttick called together the three most experienced science teachers at Peach-Navy Base and explained his predicament. Then he made a request. "Fellows," he said, "I need you to help me out by serving on a review panel to decide on these 'gray-area' absences. It won't take that much work, but it will give us all an objective way to tell the difference between real medicine and quackery. I'll make decisions about the clear-cut cases, and I'll refer the questionable ones to you."

Get Postmodern, Herman

It was fortunate for Uttick that one of his science teachers, Mr. Rivers, had been thinking about postmodernism. He was taking a course on the philosophy of science at the local university, and the class was reading some postmodernist critiques of modernism. Rivers wasn't sure he understood deconstruction and he hated the word "discourse," but he did understand what the authors meant when they said that science was a language game.

"Look," he said to Uttick, "what if I asked you to prove that science always led to the truth? You could try to do that, but I would always be able to show you a case where science had been wrong. Or, think about this—you're religious, right? Is there any way that science could prove the existence of God? Of course, you'd answer 'no,' but you still think God's existence is the truth."

"I think I see where you're heading with this," replied Uttick, "but what does truth have to do with who's a doctor and who isn't?"

"It's all about power," responded Rivers, "which 'doctor' has the power to find out the truth about a kid's problems. The MDs have official power; their knowledge fits in with our ideas—yours and mine— about what's a real illness, but maybe the official power—the finding out of the truth—does damage as often as it does good. It's like our discipline policy—we make kids tell us the 'truth' before we forgive them. But what if there is no single 'truth'?"

"Ok, I think I see what you're getting at," said Uttick, "but it's not very practical. I have a problem here, and I need to know what I should do."

"Well," laughed Rivers, "you know what Lewin said: 'there's nothing so practical as a good theory.'"

Although his discussion with Rivers didn't tell Uttick what to do, it gave him a lot to think about. He also did some reading—enough to suggest that he should be more aware of how power was working at Peach-Navy Base and to make him want to take steps to encourage wide conversation about matters that were important to the local community.

Open House

Herman Uttick decided not to dig in his heels. He suspended the attendance policy temporarily, explaining to students and families—to whomever would listen—that a policy was premature. "First they would need to figure out what made sense for local kids," he said.

One way to make sense of things was to talk about them, and Uttick thought it would be a good idea to get people talking. So he sent out invitations to an "open house." He didn't call it a debate because that seemed too formal; it clearly wasn't a presentation. "Open house" sounded about right for a get together with food and discussion.

When the appointed evening arrived, Uttick started things off by telling his story. "Here's what happened," he began. Lots of people had lots of things to say about the story and about other things. In fact, the discussion was just getting started when it was time for everyone to go home. "Let's keep this going," offered Uttick. And so they did.

CHAPTER SUMMARY

The body of postmodern theory fits well with many of its own tenets: It's complex, diverse, multivoiced, ironic, and paradoxical. Works in the postmodernist genre are often difficult to read—perhaps reminding us that the very act of sense making is difficult and its outcomes indeterminate. We can make provisional sense of things and, at the same time, there's always room for another, different reading.

Despite its difficulties, postmodernist theory provides signs suggesting the things about modernism that might be worth worrying about and the alternatives that might be worth considering. "You are in trouble," says the signpost in L.A. Story, and lots in the postmodern opus gives the same message.

We should worry, for example, about people and writings that claim to tell us the truth. And although we should understand that power is ubiquitous, we should be particularly worried about domination. As educators, we should also worry about the ways our practices shape—and especially limit—the identities of the students in our care.

But there's also lots of room within discourse and social practice to do things differently—to encourage diversity, explorations of personal freedom, interesting interpretations and appropriations, critique, and wonder. Not everything, we should be glad to hear, is known. And even what we know, we can know again differently. "There's more things in heaven and earth than are dreamt of in your philosophy," says the sign.

11

School Administration and Globalization

The word "globalization" first appeared at the end of the Second World War, but its usage became much more common following the end of the Cold War. Although most of us have probably paid very little attention to the rather sudden infiltration of this word into our minds, the connections between globalization and school leadership are nonetheless momentous. That's the reason for this chapter.

The sudden infiltration and accompanying lack of attention given this word are part of the danger the concept poses for educators. In fact, we may all be implicated in glossing over some troubling realities associated with this positive-sounding word. Whether or not the word stays with us, the phenomenon it signals will remain an influence on educational thinking and in schools and communities well into the future (Spring, 1998).

Globalization is about economics, in large measure, and economics is a perpetual concern of school administrators. Levies of various sorts and the business administration of schools and districts (not to mention state systems of schooling) are constantly in the news and constantly occupy the attention of school officials. But the local economic events (levies, changes in the funding formula, equity litigation) that impact schools and communities are not isolated from the economics of the "big picture."

Today, however, the big picture in economics extends not just to the nation as a whole but to nations across the globe. Both the volume of international trade and its speed have increased radically in the past decade (Bauman, 1998; Tilly, 2004). More deals made on a worldwide scale, and made more rapidly, spell faster and more intense changes for local communities worldwide, but perhaps most particularly in "developed nations" like the United States (see Sidebar 11-1).

Sidebar 11-1: Globalization Comes to West Virginia

For a long time, the tiny rural community of Buffalo, West Virginia, for instance, maintained a small but excellent high school enrolling just 250 or 300 students. The state capital was just barely within commuting distance, and the community was stable, although isolated from the population center of the country-wide school district.

Then a prominent U.S. Senator brokered a deal with Toyota motors. The deal established an engine assembly plant at Buffalo, and the community was subsequently and rapidly remade in many ways. One of the results of this development, perhaps ironically, was the planned closing of the excellent little school. Was this a boon or disaster for the school? For the district? For the community? The answers depend on how one sees the issues and where one's commitments lie. The governor and the senator of course announced a grand victory.

Beginning to understand the world economic system is tremendously important for local school administrators. Globalization—that is, the world economic system the term represents—exerts influence in local communities throughout the United States, sometimes for good and sometimes for ill. Sometimes, as when a manufacturing plant relocates to another nation, hundreds or thousands of jobs *vanish*, and the effect translates rapidly and disastrously to local schools. But, sometimes, as the vignette in Sidebar 11-1 suggests, even the acquisition of more jobs than there are adult workers available locally can subvert the integrity of a community. And the closure of its school might be one feature of that subversion.

The relevant questions for school administrators might include the following: "Who will live here?" "Who will pay taxes?" "Will the local economy improve or get worse?" "Will community 'improvement' mean a greater disparity between rich and poor or will it mean greater equity?" "What sorts of people and organizations will be exerting power locally?" "What role will I play in a changing community?" "What are my positions on changes affecting the school community?" "What are the possible risks and benefits of these positions?"

It is, of course, important that superintendents ponder these questions, but the questions are equally important to school principals. As Dennis Dunklee advised, principals need to look to district-level concerns in order to understand sources of support and challenge: "Effective principals start by looking at the bigger picture" (Dunklee, 2000, p. 22).

This chapter examines globalization, one of the biggest pictures of all that right now impact local schools, districts, and communities. But what is globalization? Is it a "theory," like feminism or critical theory, or is it a concept that describes a phenomenon happening in the world? Are there different versions of globalization? Which do we hear most often? Why? What do those different versions mean about how we think about schooling and school administration? What choices can we make? Which ones should we make?

This chapter aims to help prospective administrators *think* critically about these questions and the ensuing choices. Like the other chapters in the book, it doesn't prescribe what to think or what to do, but helps readers ask questions and formulate their own answers. However we currently view globalization—as an important worldwide improvement or as an expansion of corporate power—it's easy to see that the results of radically changing political, economic, and cultural institutions could make the 21st century much less secure for the developed world than has been the case in the past.

WHAT IS "GLOBALIZATION"?

In the typical account, globalization is something inevitable that is transforming national economies and world cultures to bring people into closer contact—particularly into closer trading contact. For instance, former president Bill Clinton, addressing the World Trade Organization in 1999, spoke for many business leaders when he said,

> [Globalization] will be about jobs, development and broadly shared prosperity; and about improving the quality of life, as well as the quality of work around the world; an expanded system of rule-based trade that keeps pace with the changing global economy and the changing global society. ("Rise of Globalism" section, ¶ 1)

But this isn't necessarily or inevitably so. Zygmunt Bauman, a Polish sociologist, claimed that in common usage, the word globalization has turned into "a no-questions-asked canon" (Bauman, 1998, p. 1). He means that *globalization* is a word that's used to shut people up, not to help them think.

The problem, according to Bauman, is that "what appears as globalization for some means localization for others ... [and] being local in a globalized world is a sign of social deprivation and degradation" (p. 2). This sobering assessment contrasts with the rosy images and strong imperatives issued in praise of globalization by international corporate and political leaders. But whom should we believe? Bauman advised that it's more important to ask lots of questions about globalization than to settle on *any* premature answers.

Defining "Globalization"

Clearly, globalization indicates many things—different things to different people. In this chapter, which focuses on the views of theorists who examine the relationship between globalization and public schooling, the focus is on globalization as *the postindustrial worldwide manifestation of free trade under neo-liberal economic rules*. Thinkers as different as Bill Clinton, George W. Bush, and Zygmunt Bauman would likely find this formulation acceptable. Let's start by unpacking the definition.

First, we're talking about a way of doing business. The phrase, "neo-liberal economic rules" refers simply to contemporary capitalism: the rights, privileges, expectations, and conventions of trade conducted so as to maximize private profit (see, e.g., Owen-Vandersluis, 2003). Profit is surplus capital, some of which is retained by owners (stockholders) and some of which is returned to expand a company's operations. Originally, liberal economic principles focused on individual rights, but in the contemporary world *corporate* rights seem more germane.

Second, we're talking about *advanced* capitalism. In some accounts (e.g., Hobsbawm, 1962), the birth of capitalism took place in Britain about 1700, as the capital accumulations of wealthy merchants met the emerging industrial era. At that time, wealth became something more than a hoard of valuable items ("riches"); it began to have implications for the economic development of nations. Unlimited *growth of capital* was the vision and method of capitalism, as compared to earlier economic systems (i.e., mercantilism, feudalism) in which use of wealth meant *using it up*. By contrast to mere wealth, "capital" indicates a resource that *increases itself without limit* (Heilbroner & Thurow, 1985).

From a corporate perspective, however, *advanced capitalism*, by contrast with early capitalism, is not just a national, but a *transnational* phenomenon. "*Trans*national" differs from "*inter*national" in that corporations operate not just between national borders—from one nation into another, but across all national borders, and in and out of national boundaries from moment to moment. The identities of transnational corporations conducting business in this way (as they do by definition), are not bound to any particular nation (see, e.g., Habermas, 2001). In the era of globalization, the new work of *national* governments is to guarantee transnational corporate rights through transnational laws and agreements, and to maintain order within their own borders (where transnational firms, after all, must eventually conduct business; Sassen, 1996). Saltman (2000, p. xv), drawing on work by Frederic Jameson, used the term "antifederalism" to refer to this shift in the role of nations.

Third, advanced capitalism is *postindustrial*. Capitalism created industry; so it was initially a postagrarian phenomenon, although, of course, agricultural production actually continued after the advent of industry. Similarly, a postindustrial capitalism hasn't done away with industry, although it has transformed it. Notably, as was the case with agriculture in the industrial period, postindustrial industry employs fewer and fewer people and does so with a declining profit margin. Computer-based enterprises arguably lead economic growth (and market volatility) today, but the real engines of transnational corporate growth lie within the infrastructure of international finance, including the telecommunications services that support it (Saltman, 2000; Sassen, 1996).

Fourth, and last, the part of the definition people usually grasp intuitively is "worldwide manifestation." Globalization indicates a planetary phenomenon. We all "get the point." Let's rephrase it, however, in light of the previous discussion: This postindustrial, digitally speeded transnational corporate capitalism is at constant work throughout the world, effectively remaking it. The worldwide manifestation of capitalism is part of a long history, but many observers have concluded that the events of the past several decades mark a point of qualitative difference (Bauman, 1998; Sassen, 1996).

Schooling and Remaking the World

Momentous economic and political events *remake the world*. In the era of globalization, answers to the questions, "who remakes the world?" and "to what ends?" are critically important to educators. They lead to other questions: "Who's in charge?" "What kind of world are they creating?" "Who benefits from the new world order?" "Who loses?" "What roles do schools play?" "What roles should they play?" If educators fail to ask such questions, others—powerful people representing powerful institutions—will supply answers (see Sidebar 11-2). And their answers, according to numerous commentators on globalization, will inevitably reflect the interests of global capitalism (e.g., Bauman, 1998; Giroux, 2000; Saltman, 2000; Sassen, 1996). Notably, such interests do not necessarily coincide (and often in fact conflict) with educators' interest in preparing citizens for participation in a democracy (Giroux, 2000).

Sidebar 11-2: The New Continental Order

Imagine that you are living in the country of Meer. A brutal regime—rulers of the nation of FiX—has occupied the country after an invasion. Your nation is not the first, nor will it be the last, to fall to the imperial ambitions of the FiXers.

Now, the leaders of your country have not merely declared a cease-fire, or given an outright surrender, but they have instead negotiated an armistice that removes them from the ranks of nations hostile to the FiXers. Other nations are being attacked, just like Meer, but the armistice between Meer and the FiXers voids the mutual defense pacts that your country, Meer, had signed with these other nations.

You're an ordinary person, not a scholar, not a wide reader, and you're a patriot. You're also a school principal. You accept national authority, and the newly appointed leader in Meer really is a national hero, well respected, and well liked. He saved the nation before and he can do it again, you believe. He's at least worth listening to very carefully.

The new and revered leader of Meer promises that the errors that led to Meer's defeat can be blamed on a certain class of people. They will be properly dealt with. Moreover, the future will be better. Beginning right now, new youth programs will be organized to instill the virtues of discipline, order, and respect for authority. Workers will be sent to FiX to establish "fraternal relations"—to get "FiXed." Improvements will take time, the great leader says, but when the revitalized Meer emerges from the rubble, it will stand as "a full partner of the new cross-continental union" being established by the FiXers. The schools have a special role to play in preparing workers for the new cross-continental economy. "We must prepare our youth to compete in a cross-continental economy!"

This educational message is repeated in many ways from day to day, and month to month. It's all you see on television, all you hear on the radio, and all you read in the educational magazines and journals. You're skeptical, of course. Although you don't like the FiXers, they are very polite and give seats on buses to old people and pregnant women. In the end, you believe that Meer's great leader knows what he's doing. Besides, politics is not really your concern. A new continental order is coming, so why not prepare kids to be part of it? It just makes sense, you think, to prepare kids for the real world.

The fable presented in Sidebar 11-2 is the thinly disguised story of France un-der Nazi occupation in the Second World War, as told by Marcel Ophuls (1971) in his classic documentary, *The Sorrow and the Pity*. As in the United States circa 1940, "National Socialism" (the Nazi organization and ideal) had supporters in France. According to Ophuls, most average French people *easily* entertained the idea that the Third Reich might dominate Europe and even the world. Many—perhaps most—were content to let their leaders articulate a postwar place for them in the empire to be established by Hitler's military industrial complex.

Ophuls's documentary makes a very critical point about French resistance to the Nazi regime: Members of the resistance (a small minority of the French people) tended not to have much to lose; they were most often workers or, in the words of one interviewee, "failures and maladjusted people." The middle classes (teachers, shopkeepers, professionals) did not usually take the risk of active resistance. They had too much to lose. The deepest inference to be made from Ophuls's film, however, is that most citizens in most nations would react much as the French did in 1940–1945. Their story is not in fact excep-tional, but *typical*.

What's the point for us in our role as educational leaders? Like most people, we *believe* the stories we hear *most often*. After all, life is difficult, our days make us bone-tired in the best of circumstances, and it's easy not to question too much. When the stories all around us paint a world for us in bold colors, we tend to accept it at face value. Every repetition makes that world seem more accept-able, more certain, and indeed, at last, *inevitable*.

If school leaders do not think about matters like educational purpose, diver-sity, the role of nations, and the mischief done by propaganda in everyday life, they're apt to treat mention of globalization with the same attention accorded to "fluoridation": *It's in the water and doing good things for us.* Watching Ophuls's film, though, can help us better appreciate the fact that passive acceptance of official stories is always a mistake. Listen, for instance, to this "official story" from the New Jersey Department of Education:

> We live in an age of exploding knowledge and rapid change in technology, infor-mation exchange, and communications. The changes which are taking place in our society have increased the demand for internationally competitive workers and for an educational system designed to meet that demand … To gain and re-tain high-wage employment that provides job satisfaction, they will also need to continue to learn throughout their lives. To compete in a global, informa-tion-based economy, the students we prepare must be able to solve real problems, reason effectively, and make logical connections. The world of work they enter will feature products and factories that are designed by mathematical models and computer simulations, computers that control production processes and plants,

and robots. Our state and country need people with the skills to develop and manage these new technologies. (New Jersey Department of Education, 1996, "The Need" ¶ 1–2)

What are people for in this view? They are competitors in a globalized economy, rather than citizens exercising political rights and making choices about democratic institutions (see also Saltman, 2000). Schools, it seems, should help redesign people to "manage new technologies." If diversity counts in this picture, it comes into play only as teachers and administrators contrive to make sure that all children (whatever their ethnicity, place of residence, or social class) conform to this intended redesign (Saltman, 2000). According to Saltman:

> Public education as a training ground for [global] corporate workers is now being framed as an issue of national security suggesting that the well-being of the nation depends on the well-being of the corporation. Such an understanding of public education openly envisions the state in the service of the private interest and profit. (Saltman, 2000, p. xvii)

Teaching the Commons (a Policy Vignette)

According to interpreters of globalization, the world is being remade according to perceptions about the "economic need" of the coming century, and educators are being told that preparing *individuals* to be maximally competitive in the workplace should be their primary aim (see, e.g., Giroux, 2000; Saltman, 2000). But is this the only thing schools can do? Is it the best thing for them to do?

Some commentators are concerned that, when the economic purposes of schooling are placed front and center, *public* purposes disappear (Giroux, 2000; Molnar, 1996). Some of these writers have argued that, instead of teaching competitiveness, schools should teach service to "the commons" (Theobald, 1997).

"The commons" may be an unfamiliar phrase to readers (see also chap. 5), but the idea it references fits well with what educators typically think of as their mission. Originally, the commons referred to physical space outdoors, namely the public land shared by the residents of a community (e.g., the land on which everyone grazed their sheep). Now the term is sometimes used to refer to space indoors such as an area accessible to all students, for sitting, eating, or socializing. It is also sometimes used to refer to those services, such as public education, that support and sustain the common good. In a related meaning, the phrase, however, also refers to a body of knowledge that advances the common interest of the public. For instance, in the language of recent reform efforts, the commons might be "what all children must know and be able to do."

Of course, language such as this inevitably leads to the question, "Who ought to determine the knowledge and skills that all children should possess?" And that question leads to the deeper questions: "What is the common good?" and "Who gets to define it?"

One set of answers—the one that may resonate best with business' aspirations for globalization—equates the common good with the corporate good (Giroux, 2000; Molnar, 1996; Saltman, 2000). This idea is embedded in the oft-cited paraphrase of a statement made by a former General Motors' CEO, "What's good for General Motors is good for the nation." And it tends to support schooling that focuses primarily on the development of workforce skills, tying what children should know and be able to do directly to job requirements.

Another set of answers fits better with the conception of democracy held by the founders of our nation. Viewing the common good in terms of broad-based participation in democratic institutions, it supports schooling on behalf of an educated citizenry (Theobald, 1997). Schooling with this aim entails an expanding, contingent, and even contested definition of what students should "know and be able to do," because it isn't clear exactly which knowledge and skills best support informed citizenship. Generally speaking, however, we might see citizenship requiring more knowledge rather than less knowledge, and more diverse knowledge rather than more uniform knowledge. This reasoning suggests that the commons might best be sustained when students gain the kinds of knowledge that inform debate, promote deliberation, and ultimately guide wise judgment. As Giroux (2000, p. 83) explained,

> One of the most important legacies of American public education has been providing students with the critical capacities, knowledge, and values that enable them to become active citizens striving to build a stronger democratic society. Within this tradition, Americans have defined schooling as a public good. Such a definition rightfully asserts the primacy of democratic values over corporate culture and commercial values.

POWER AND SCHOOL CULTURE VIEWED INTERNATIONALLY

The networking of the world as an economic unit is not so radically new a development as all the recent talk about globalization implies. It actually continues a line of global economic development that runs from the 15th century to the present (Tilly, 2004). Before globalization, we had "imperialism," and before that "colonialism." All three advance the same project, according to Joel Spring (1998).

In order to understand the role of education under imperialism and colonialism, we need briefly to consider the nature of traditional cultures and traditional education. What we in the United States recognize today as "education" is quite different from the education available to ordinary people throughout the world for past centuries.

Traditional Culture, Traditional Education

What we think of as education in the developed world, that is, formal schooling, is nothing like the sorts of education practiced before the emergence of capitalism in Western Europe around 1700. In fact, formal schooling has really achieved universality in the *developed* world only since 1960 or so. In 1900, almost no one went to high school in the United States, for instance. And many people who reached adulthood in the United States in the 1930s and 1940s left school well before completing the eighth grade.

In many parts of the developing world, high school attendance is still uncommon. Spring (1998) reported that in colonial Cambodia—in the developing world—the first high school opened its doors in 1933, and by 1954 had graduated just 100 students. Dongping Han (2001) reported that in a Chinese county of 800,000 inhabitants, the sole high school operating between 1933 and 1966 had graduated only about 1,000 students during all those 33 years.

Nevertheless, human beings cannot survive socially or communally without education, whether or not they sponsor much schooling. Humans have an astounding set of tricks for keeping alive and living well, in fortunate and in unfortunate circumstances, and this set of tricks is taught and learned, mostly outside of schools, even today, right here in the United States. The "tricks" vary rather widely among human cultures, and they change over time as the young innovate. Writing was certainly a good new trick, and it has seemed to require formal schooling, but humans were doubtless weaving, building, plowing, and *problem solving* at high levels long before schools were possible or mass schooling even dreamt of.

Education cannot, then, be synonymous with formal schooling. Even book learning doesn't require school attendance, and many of the West's cultural heroes (like William Faulkner and Albert Einstein) attended school less than one might suspect. Traditional cultures were, in fact, constituted educationally: The old taught the young. The young learned and often innovated, and taught their children. In the preliterate world, children probably learned most often as part of the work routines of household and community. They had to learn, because they had to work, and vice versa. Among others, John Dewey, the great progressive educator, called this "learning by doing," and, about

1900, it seemed like a shocking and radical new idea to use in schools. Although practiced for millennia in traditional cultures worldwide, its practice in classrooms was uncommon.

In fact, the invention of schooling was required in order to separate education from work. Formal schooling was a leisuretime activity[1] (not work) devoted to considering the world at arm's length. This separation is not bad, per se, but it does characterize the difference between formal education and traditional education. Formal education is associated with individual leisure, traditional education with communal and family work.

Is this separation necessary today? Tom Tiller is a professor of education in Norway. Tiller (2000) reported that as a child in Northern Norway (not so long ago) he attended school only on alternate days. Every other day was a "day off." Tiller's day off was not like *Ferris Buehler's Day Off* (a popular teen caper film of the 1980s):

> We weren't just out of school, we were immersed in life. The day off gave us rich experiences. That day insured that holistic learning occurred in our lives. We were involved in many informal apprentice–master relationships. We young people were invited into important, legitimate learning positions … The other day provided clear space for creativity and excitement. (Tiller, 2000, p. 223)

So, what we (mistakenly!) imagine to be real "education" (formal schooling, preferably for many long years) is an extremely recent development, even in the developed world. Tiller, with savvy irony, observed,

> The "other" day, that is the day we were off from school, was far more important for our lives after graduation than we then realized. *That day off meant that even our school, which seemed only minimally relevant, was comparatively good.* Today, however, school totally dominates the life of our children. This places great demands on the school to provide students with fulfilling life experiences, and it requires new organizational structures. We're approaching an either-or situation: either give back to youth that "other" day, that day off, *or school will lose its meaning and legitimacy* [emphasis added]. (Tiller, 2000, p. 218)

Moreover, when people talk or write about the importance of education for the developing world—in South America, Asia, and Africa—they often fail to honor the education provided by traditional culture. Instead, the typical recommendation is that these places should adopt a system that imitates formal schooling as practiced in the developed world (the very plan that Tiller understood as threatening to the legitimacy of formal schooling itself!).

---

[1]The word *school* comes from the ancient Greek word *schōle* (*leisure*).

This vignette about "the day off" is meant to suggest to readers that the assumption that formal schooling is necessarily a good thing *can* be questioned thoughtfully. What seems self-evident and obvious, in fact, is exactly the thing to question.

In the United States, American Indians are especially concerned that their schooling honor traditional educational purposes. Indians struggled for most of the 20th century *against* the kind of formal schooling imposed by missionaries and by federal and state governments (Lomawaima, 1999). Since about 1960, however, American Indians have been increasingly successful in pressing their rights to determine their own forms of education. Notable elements of schooling as devised by Indian leaders now emphasize traditional culture and traditional education as well as the subjects needed for negotiating in and with U.S. society. Indian schooling moves forward with its struggle to become bicultural.

Tacit views of what is correct for formal schooling, however, continue to threaten prospects for biculturalism in Indian education. The threats are compounded when schools serving Indians are not tribally controlled (Tippeconnic, 1997). Indeed, the effects of high-stakes testing and national demands for accountability tend to push issues such as language preservation (a critical mission in Indian education) and local knowledge (important also in rural education) into the deep shadows of curriculum work—in Indian schools and in most other U.S. schools as well (see, e.g., Theobald, 1997; Strike, 1997).

Pluralism in Contrast to Globalization

When European and American colonialism were the schemes that dominated international development—roughly from 1500 to 1900—most of the world was thought, in European and American centers of power, to be populated by largely unknown and certainly outlandish peoples. Their habits, customs, and beliefs confused and intrigued intellectuals in the colonial "mother" countries. Jonathan Swift's *Gulliver's Travels* (Swift, 1726/1940) captured, in political satire, the sense of wonder at the variety of possible human (or, as was often thought, quasi-human) arrangements lurking in the wide, and largely unknown, world of the time. For progressive thinkers like Swift and Jean-Jacques Rousseau (famous for constructing the image of "the noble savage"), this diversity seems to have held potential for advancing human wisdom and justice. For many more, like the Englishmen Cecil Rhodes (African "empire builder") and Sir Francis Galton (father of both statistics and gifted education), the world's "savages" needed the civilizing force of European laws and conceptions of individual rights (Spring, 1998), not to mention corporate discipline.

As colonialism advanced its grasp of the nonindustrial world, Western intellectuals' fascination continued, although with an increasing pessimism. In the novels of Herman Melville and Joseph Conrad, exotic cultures are settings for European and American misery and confusion. For instance, in Conrad's famous story, *The Heart of Darkness*, written in the early 20th century, Europeans arriving in remote parts of Africa discovered their own emptiness, not a realm of new insight and enlightenment. See Sidebar 11-3.

Sidebar 11-3: Globalization and the Emptiness of Home

Globalization seems to push the emptiness discovered by Conrad's hero in *The Heart of Darkness* to planetary proportions. How does this happen?

A small proportion of the planet's population become "globalized" elites, often traveling back and forth across the planet. Sometimes, these elites have no single home base, but may maintain apartments in several global cities (London, Singapore, and New York or Paris, for instance). The rest of the world's population—practically all of us, in other words—is not so much globalized as localized, wrote Zygmunt Bauman. Our lives will not be flashy and successful, but increasingly dreary and meaningless, and we will experience sharply and with great envy the contrast between ourselves and the globalized elite. Bauman argued,

> If the new exterritoriality of the elite feels like intoxicating freedom, the territoriality of the rest feels less like home ground, and ever more like prison—all the more humiliating for the obtrusive sight of the others' freedom to move … The "locality" in the new world of high speed is not what the locality used to be at a time when information moved only together with the bodies of its carriers; neither the locality, nor the localized population has much in common with the "local community" [of former times]. (Bauman, 1998, pp. 23–24)

Localization, thus viewed, is the dark side of globalization—the side not taken seriously by world leaders in the developed West, nor, in fact by prominent educational leaders. It's important to note, as Bauman does, that this new "localization" is very different from a beloved town or city or countryside, which we might call "home," or in which we might feel that we are in touch with the best life has to offer while at the same time living modestly.

The rising pessimism in modernist novels may have stemmed in part from the increasing knowledge (and declining diversity) of world cultures. World culture theorists, such as Meyer, Boli, Thomas, and Ramirez (1997), for example, have examined the diffusion of cultural practices from the developed world and the resulting demise of practices from diverse indigenous cultures. These theorists have argued that, as "strange and outlandish" cultures have acquired not only snowmobiles and microwave ovens, but recycled American sitcoms, the seeming mystery and variety of human social forms has contracted into an increasingly common—though hardly universal or ubiquitous—set of experiences worldwide.

Western Education and Colonialism

It's true that cultures have been colliding and mixing for many millennia, of course; the Persians, the Bantus, the Jews, and the Sikhs have roamed continents and the world (Appiah, 1998). All existing languages, including English, are living testimony to this mixing. But during practically all previous eras, the time line of this mixing was long—spanning many generations, so that the formerly plural cultures of the planet remained identifiably separate in most people's lifetimes. Even knowing of one another's existence was at one time unlikely.

This separation, which seemed nearly absolute before about 1700, has since nearly disappeared. Colonialism, that is, the maintenance of colonies throughout the world by European powers (e.g., Spain, the Netherlands, Belgium, France, and most particularly, Britain) ended that separation and in the course of a few centuries remade local economies to serve the "mother" countries (Tilly, 2004). The Industrial Revolution accelerated matters, as colonies were converted from remote sources of valuable imports and into connected markets for manufactured goods.

It's important to realize that this history produced *colonial administrations* that endured and grew increasingly strong, maintaining links with Europe and, starting in the 19th century, the United States. Those administrations and the elite class of people who staffed them *survived* colonial rule. Colonies achieved independence from the European countries that ruled them, but colonial administrations endured.

Try to imagine the English ruling India, a section of one tiny island (England) ruling a continental territory (India) many times its size in territory and population, one with a longer and perhaps arguably complex civilization, and with many more languages and cultures. Initially, force of arms helped subdue native populations, but over the course of many decades and centuries, the suppression and allegiance of populations had to be secured by far more effective means than murder and pillage (which provoke counterproductive instability and resistance).

Western education—schooling on the model developed in Europe—constituted those more effective means. The schools that colonial powers established for native elites, moreover, were almost always conducted in the language of the occupying nation. England, of course, was the leading colonial empire of the 19th century, and that is how English became the language of global commerce.

At the start of the 19th century, Charles Grant (as quoted in Spring, 1998, p. 15) insisted on the importance of using English as the language of instruction in India: "To introduce the language of the conquerors, seems to be an obvious means of assimilating a conquered people to them." This policy is the same as that followed in boarding schools for American Indians through the 1950s, where use of native languages was severely and consistently *punished*.

Later in the 19th century, Thomas Macaulay (subsequently British Prime Minister) noted the special role for education in helping to administer a vast empire:

> We must at present do our best to form a class who may be interpreters between us and the millions whom we govern; a class of persons, Indian in blood and colour, but English in taste, in opinions, in morals, and in intellect. (as quoted in Spring, 1998, p. 16)

It is good to remember the obvious in this case: Only already powerful countries colonize, and the interests of native people predictably have almost no influence on the empire builders (see, e.g., Russell, 2002). Schooling, under these circumstances, is a technology to produce workers who can help the empire builders achieve their objectives.

Although some might argue that a Western education would not be so bad for Africans or Asians, others explain that the select few to receive Western-style schooling formed an elite class of administrators who were sympathetic to the aims of the empire builders (see, e.g., Tupas, 2003). At base, the issues were economic, not educational; schooling in the colonies served not native interests, but those of the colonizers:

> The land at present available in our colony is suitable for European settlement. We cannot carry out this settlement, however, without additional labor. This must be provided by the natives and we shall train them for it … We shall make people realize that we Germans are masters of the country and the natives are servants. (Carl Sclettwein, 1905, as quoted in Cohen, 1994, p. 93)

Such educational purposes and the regimes to realize them were common throughout Asia and Africa until the official dissolution of European colonial empires that set in after 1945 (i.e., the end of the Second World War).

The largest empire, of course, left the legacy of English as the birthright of local ruling elites. In Singapore, in India, and in large parts of Africa, schools, and especially universities, still employ English as the language of instruction. As Grant and Macaulay predicted, however, language use also entails commitments and dispositions that link minds together with the prerogatives of the former colonial regimes. Education, in short, is the institution that allowed colonial, and later imperial, regimes to function profitably for the long term. It has also enabled and facilitated globalization. As Bgoya (2001) explained, "English is the language of this globalisation and English serves fundamentally the interests of those for whom it is both an export commodity and a language of conquest and domination" (p. 286).

Globalization as Power

Globalization is the kind of phenomenon that can occur only as the result of *immense* economic, cultural, political, and military power. This power extends the achievements of colonialism (colonies as sources of exotic products) and imperialism (colonies as markets for manufactured goods) more insistently and with greater coordination than ever before. According to Bgoya (2001, p. 286),

> Using the immense financial resources at their disposal [the masters of the global economy and cultural industries] install and remove politicians so that, both at home and abroad, governments do what they want. This alliance of business and government is the pillar of the strategy to strengthen the political and economic power centres in Western capitals for global exploitation.

Moreover, like its predecessors (i.e., colonialism and imperialism) globalization uses educational institutions to give it legitimacy and long-term viability. In the United States, for example, globalization is positioned as a challenge that educators need to address. International comparisons of educational performance provide a tangible gauge of how well educators are meeting the challenge. Often this challenge is expressed in terms of the competition among nations (Saltman, 2000).

Sometimes the insistence on competition turns ridiculous. For instance, the description of a session at a recent American Association for the Advancement of Science (AAAS) meeting on "educating scientists, engineers, and technicians for the 21st century" included the peculiar statement:

> The very existence of open markets means that we are all in competition … [with] foreign workers who may have a better education or demand lower wages or both. The real choice is not whether to compete globally, but how to do it. (as cited in Howley, Harmon, & Carter, 1998, p. 5)

Such quotes convey the impression that everyone accepts the advent, prerogatives, and social and cultural effects of globalization, and that they are willing to act contrary to their own logical interests (like "*demanding* lower wages") in order to help nations (or perhaps) transnational corporations compete with one another.

This uncritical mind set, widely propagated, helps disguise the problems that many analysts associate with globalization. Although world leaders speak hopefully of a "rising tide that floats all boats," globalization seems to be creating a world economy that is increasingly more unequal (e.g, Tilly, 2004). Major U.S. cities like New York and Chicago share the control of planetary wealth with global cities in Japan, Germany, England, and a handful of other developed nations. This concentration of wealth and power, however, is associated with a decline in even the meager share of global wealth falling to the poorest 20% of nations, down from 2.3% in 1961 to just 1.4% in 1991 (Bauman, 1998, p. 71). Tony Clarke of The International Forum on Globalization observed,

> The real power to rule is being exercised not by governments and their agencies, but by transnational corporations (TNCs) … Today, 50 of the top 100 economies in the world are [those of] TNCs, 70% of global trade is controlled by just 500 corporations, and a mere 1% of the TNCs on this planet own half the total stock of foreign direct investment … Transnational corporations have effectively secured a system of rule and domination in the new world order. (Clarke, 2001, "Introduction," ¶ 2)

EDUCATIONAL REFORM IN THE GLOBAL CONTEXT

"Educational reform" is a short phrase with a long history. The contemporary mass education system in the United States is itself a result of reform efforts that began well before the beginning of the 20th century. In 1905, for another example, the National Association of Manufacturers pressed for the massive reform of American schools on the basis of the German threat to American competitiveness (Cremin, 1962). And the current reform movement—the standards movement—represents the culmination of efforts over the past 20 or so years to address *A Nation at Risk,* the 1983 indictment of the U.S. system of schooling. Arguably, this most recent reform movement is intended not only to serve U.S. interests by improving our position in the global economy but also to serve the interests of the transnational corporations that are coming to dominate economic relations globally.[2]

---

[2]According to some commentators (e.g., Tilly, 2004), these sets of interests (i.e., those of the United States and those of transnational corporations) are in conflict to some extent.

At the same time, because knowledge of school reform traverses the globe, there is also a process of "borrowing" and "lending" that characterizes such reform worldwide (Steiner-Khamsi, 2004). For example, outcomes-based education, which was a temporary way station toward standards-based reform in the United States, has been picked up enthusiastically by some countries in Africa (e.g., Spreen, 2004). School choice—also a product of the standards movement—has found a home in places as disparate as the United Kingdom and Tanzania (e.g., Stambach, 2003). The degree to which borrowing and lending of school reforms represent natural processes of diffusion or impositions of a dominant perspective by powerful transnational organizations (e.g., the World Bank, UNESCO) is debated by scholars of comparative and international education (Anderson-Levitt, 2003; Angus, 2004; Steiner-Khamsi, 2004). So too are questions about how local communities translate reforms—adopt, modify, or subvert them—based on their own values and interests (Anderson-Levitt, 2003). Furthermore, the question of whose interests are served by these dynamics is certainly germane, but is rarely addressed.

Interestingly, a major question facing reformers across the world concerns the proper way to govern schools. On the surface, we might assume that a particular governance method would advance one purpose, whereas other governance methods would advance quite different purposes. For example, we might imagine that decentralized schooling would advance local democratic participation whereas centralized schooling would advance "nation building." The actual case, however, is more complex and contradictory, as the following discussion shows.

Comparative Modes of Educational Governance

The interplay of centralization and decentralization is an important concern in the era of globalization (Anderson-Levitt, 2003). Ironically, both governance strategies can be used simultaneously to narrow the public purposes of formal schooling in ways that conform better to the requirements of globalization (Saltman, 2000). And, of course, theoretically, either might be used to expand the public purposes of schooling, whether those purposes are construed primarily in local, national, or international terms. Nonetheless, as commentators have argued, whichever governance approach—or combination of approaches—nations adopt, the trend in educational policy has primarily been in one direction. In general, such policy equates individual interests with the economic interests of corporations and more or less drops the public interest—concern for the commons—from the equation (Giroux, 2000; Molnar, 1996).

The ongoing privatization of schooling in the United States certainly constitutes a form of decentralization (breaking up the "monopoly" of public schooling). This form of decentralization—privatization—contracts the "public space" that exists in society (Giroux, 2000; Molnar, 1996). At the same time that such decentralizing efforts are underway, initiatives such as the *No Child Left Behind Act* are centralizing the content of schooling (see Anderson-Levitt, 2003), in line (as we saw in official statements earlier) with the globalization agenda. The fact that both tendencies not only coexist but also support one another hinges on the changing role of the citizen and the nation state, to be considered shortly.

Centralizing Within Decentralization. If educational reform is a matter of *national* security, greater centralization of schooling might seem advisable. After all, one might reason, reform that addresses national security in the 21st century cannot be responsibly organized at the level of grassroots variability. Already, with its 50-plus systems of schooling, the United States is at some disadvantage compared to nations like Japan, France, Korea, and Singapore, and even nations like Egypt, where national ministries establish and regulate the single system of schooling that prevails.

Historically, however, American schools were local institutions, with vigorous involement by local people in their establishment and operation (Theobald, 1997). In the ideal, which varied predictably from reality, schools were subsidiary to the local community, much as they still are among the Amish, who aim to practice an agrarian way of life that is attuned to divine purposes, as they interpret them.

As industry came to dominate the U.S. economy, agrarian localism gave way to an industrial plan for schooling. This reform did not just *separate* schools from communities, it physically removed them. In rural areas as in city wards, schools and districts grew in size, consolidated into larger—often *much larger*—professionally managed administrative units. This process of removing schools from communities is still going on, according to the National Trust for Historic Preservation, which recently published a booklet about "school sprawl" (Beaumont & Pianca, 2000).

School consolidation and school sprawl are features of *centralization*, but they focus on centralization within states, rather than on centralization nationally. Teachers in the United States, for example, are not certified nationally nor are they hired by a national ministry of education, as happens, for instance, in Australia and many other nations. One might suspect, then, that quite a bit of variability would exist in the schooling systems operated by different states.

This is not the case, however. Ironically, even though the powers of individual state education agencies are at an all-time high, state systems are probably more alike than ever. High-stakes testing and accountability have, for instance, been deployed in nearly all the states as of this writing, with similar (although hardly identical) intentions and provisions (Educational Commission of the States, 2005). Moreover, national reform efforts, such as those incorporated in the *No Child Left Behind Act* rapidly reach and exert substantial influence on every district in the nation, irrespective of the state in which it is located.

Decentralizing From Within Centralization.   Because flexibility and innovation serve the requirements of the postindustrial economy, a new kind of decentralization ("privatization") is touted by some reformers (see, e.g., Chubb & Moe, 1990). The argument is made, with some evidence to support it, that *bureaucratic* approaches to professional school governance (a major achievement of earlier reforms) now stymie or altogether suppress the flexibility and innovation that should characterize effective education in the present century (Rosen, 2003). Indeed, the argument in favor of this sort of decentralization suggests that the competition that makes businesses excellent will naturally help schools improve. The disenchantment of the public with its schools (Mathews, 1996), moreover, gives these proposals natural supporters.

Globalization and Citizens of the Nation State

Commentators on globalization worry that citizenship, which was once grounded in the local governance of local places within nation states, is now in jeopardy (e.g., Giroux, 2000; Saltman, 2000). In the agrarian age, citizenship was in fact the ultimate grounding for the legitimacy of the nation. The United States (1776) and the French Republic (1789) were founded on this principle. Citizens had natural rights, which empowered them, individually and jointly, to form or dissolve nations and to found or overturn governments. Citizens (actual people) were to control the political organization of nations. This was once the meaning of "democracy."

How could this startling aim be realized in a world, circa 1776, thoroughly dominated by the power of a divinely ordained nobility? The answer was that education needed to prepare ordinary people for the role of citizen. To sponsor such an education, mass schooling had to be invented, a form of schooling that had to reach more and more children as the franchise[3] became more and more inclusive.

---

[3]The right to vote defined who would be considered an active citizen—and this right was slowly widened in the United States from just White male property owners to all adults beginning at age 18 (with legal rights not always ensuring access to the polling booth).

In an important way, then, education actually constituted the nation state, both in terms of its legitimacy (it made the citizens whose existence justified the nation) and in terms of the nation's political actors (it made the citizens who secured the fate of the nation). This is how education, the nation, and the citizen were conceived in an agrarian age, and this is really the image most people retain when they consider the role of schooling in a democracy. Today, citizens need to wonder how apt this image is to the emerging ("postindustrial") global order. Interestingly but not surprisingly, the U.S. Constitution is silent about the role of corporations in politics, since they barely existed in 1789.

Whereas the purpose of education in the nationalist era was to create an informed citizenry, that purpose changed in the industrial era. Notably, in service of industrial expansion, education became a *system* of scientifically managed career selection and preparation. Despite this change in purpose, the sentiment about citizenship was left in place. Thus, in the 1950s and 1960s, "citizenship" (or "civics") became institutionalized as a specialized social studies course that principally considered the mechanisms of government, but not the very difficult and troubling issues of corporate power. The emphasis was on creating "good" citizens, individuals who exercised the right to vote but most likely remained aloof from heated political contest, unless they became professional politicians (see, e.g., Spring, 1998; Zinn, 1999).

The real political power, however, increasingly devolved to large corporations. Corporations had a great deal at stake and the funds to protect and advance their interests through the political process (often via trade associations), whereas mere citizens lacked comparable resources to articulate or advance public interests in the political sphere (Molnar, 1996; Saltman, 2000). According to some observers (e.g., Spring, 1998), schooling had also failed many individuals, denying them the intellectual tools needed for effective citizenship.

The postindustrial era (the era of globalization) is bringing additional changes. Saskia Sassen, a leading scholar of globalization, believes that multinational firms are the true citizens of "the new world order." Further, she questions whether globalization truly represents a benefit to the citizens of democracies. She asks,

> Do we want the global capital market to exercise this discipline over our governments: and to do so at all costs— jobs, wages, safety, health—and without a public debate? While it is true that these markets are the result of multiple decisions by multiple investors and thus have a certain democratic aura, all the "voters" have to own capital, and small investors typically operate through institutional investors, such as pension funds, banks, and hedge funds. This leaves the vast majority of a country's citizens without any say. (1996, p. 51)

Some educational commentators (e.g., Giroux, 2000; Saltman, 2000), more-over, have suggested that if the historical role of the individual citizen is in de-cline, so too is the role of public education. The reasoning goes like this: (a) If the public purpose of education no longer really exists (because the individual citizen has been supplanted by the corporate citizen), then (b) public schools are really no longer needed, or they are needed for much more limited purposes.

LOCATING THE UNITED STATES
IN THE LARGER WORLD

The United States has a special role in globalization, a role to which we have paid scant attention so far. The role is this: The United States is so far the domi-nant player. When politicians talk about securing a grand destiny for the United States in this century, they are not speaking as representatives of a country of underdogs seeking finally to make good in the world. They are talking about a national economy that consumes a disproportionate share of the world's re-sources, and one that maintains a standard of living so high that the poor of the United States "enjoy" resources that make them seem rich by the standards that prevail throughout the developing world.

In the context of this degree of wealth and worldwide influence, the lan-guage of competitiveness seems to some observers to reflect thoughtlessness and greed (see, e.g., Orr, 1995). Moreover, such observers worry that this out-look on the world has a determining influence on contemporary American schooling (see, e.g., Howley et al., 1995; Molnar, 1996; Orr, 1995; Purpel, 1999; Spring, 1998).

Still, we need to ponder why it seems so easy for Americans, who are in reality a generous people, to accept a system of schooling reformed so explicitly in the service of greed. There are several possible answers.

The first concerns the interaction of capitalist and protestant worldviews (Spring, 1998; Weber, 1904/1958). In some denominations particularly, wealth is a sign of God's grace. The logic for this position is this: (a) If such qualities as individual industry, thrift, and responsibility are among Christian *virtues*, then, (b) their reward (as virtues) in the form of wealth might well be anticipated, es-pecially (c) under a capitalist economic system. The absence of such virtues might also be expected to produce poverty. Thus, from one vantage on Chris-tianity, economic well-being proceeds directly from right living.

Other interpretations of Christianity, of course, don't emphasize so rigid a view of sin and virtue, but stress forgiveness, charity, and the holiness of the poor. In the New Testament, Christ Himself harbors contempt for the rich and compassion for the poor. "The meek shall inherit the earth," He said. He was probably thinking of the poor and those who take their side. So the interaction of Christianity and capitalist ideology is hardly a full answer to our question.

Another answer is patriotism. Many Americans believe that the United States is the best nation on earth. Some people might think this is the result of its citizens' high level of aggregate virtue, although international statistics on crime might be understood as providing contradictory evidence. If this is the case in reality, for whatever reason, then a reasonable conclusion might be that the American Way should become the way of the whole world. Struggling nations, in this view, need to learn our ways, and doing business with them is perhaps one of the best means of helping them learn. Spring (1998), among others, blames the U.S. history curriculum for reinforcing a thoughtless kind of "U.S. Number One" patriotism.

There is another, less prideful, view of patriotism, however—one that stresses the values of liberty, equality, and the common good. Acted upon, this view would permit other nations to forge different paths (liberty on an international and national scale), and it would treat the varying cultures within different nations, not as naïve, but as valuable because of the unique integrity they possess. Furthermore, this view would acknowledge that construction of the common good here at home, as well as in other nations, is incomplete—a critical project still in need of a great deal of attention.

Ironically, another possible answer relates to the failure of Americans to *think* globally. Doing so would mean examining the implications of increasing global disparities in wealth and income (both across nations and within nations), global threats to the environment, and intensifying geopolitical instability resulting from competition for limited resources. One commentator with strong views about what such an honest appraisal of globalization entails is David Korten. We turn next to a consideration of his arguments as well as those of others who have come to similar conclusions.

Diversity—Internal and External

David Korten (1998) characterizes globalization as an extremist ideology. He argued that the ideology of the global free market has displaced the traditional pluralism that, in his estimation, has sustained the United States for generations.

The extremist ideology, according to Korten, includes the myth that the success of developed nations in the post-World War II period was due to free-market traditions. Korten claimed that, on the contrary, the success stemmed from "rejection of ideological extremism in favor of a system of governance based on a pragmatic, nonideological, institutional balance among the forces of government, market, and civil society" (p. 184).

In other words, in Korten's view, the strength of the United States lay in the respect its institutions accorded diversity: the necessity of competing views (e.g., many of those articulated in this book), the productivity of well-informed debate, the experimentation with radically different social and political arrangements, and the cross-fertilization arising from the clash of different cultures. In Korten's view, America needs both socialists and capitalists; those who believe in schooling mostly for jobs and those who believe in schooling mostly for the life of the mind; the pious and the free thinkers; sinners and saints. America, in this view, needs people of all races, cultures, and creeds. From this perspective, the more alike we become, the weaker become our economics, politics, cultures, and ethics.

Korten's view is really a traditional American view, generous toward newcomers, and grounded in toleration and democratic hopefulness. For this reason, his accusation that globalization represents an "extremist" position is quite compelling. Korten prescribed internal diversity as the healthy alternative for American society.

In *Short Route to Chaos*, Stephen Arons (1997) gave much the same prescription for schooling in the United States. According to Arons, American schools, shaped by programs that seek to standardize education and also by professional educational bureaucracies, suffer because they are so dramatically out of step with the actual and traditional diversity of American society. Arons, like famed New York City educator Deborah Meier, supported public school choice: Schools operated in the public interest, but on commitments and methods that vary substantially from school to school. Arons and Meier believed that a vigorous democracy is served best by this traditional diversity. On these terms, the standards movement with its "systemic reforms" based on standards and accountability is fatally wrong. If it succeeds, according to these authors, it will further injure an already imperiled democracy (see also, Strike, 1997).

A similar argument pertains to diversity throughout the world. Commentators like Bauman (1998) and Spring (1998) are troubled by globalization for reasons that accord with Korten's observations about pluralism. Both authors portray the operation of globalization as suppressing or eliminating cultural, economic, and political practices across the world. In place of diverse indigenous cultures, global capitalism introduces mass culture with its constellation of Western cultural products, values, and expectations. And the vastly superior economic power of Western nations ensures that Western-style mass culture will have a degree of success nearly everywhere on earth.

If this analysis sounds too abstract or remote to merit consideration by school administrators, consider that this sort of cultural colonialism also operates within the *developed* world, and within subcultures of single nations in the developed world (including the United States). The analogy provided in Sidebar 11-4 illustrates the way cultural colonialism works at the "micro" level within school systems.

Sidebar 11-4: Constructivist "Tyranny"

Consider the choice of Melissa Freeport, a principal concerned with improving mathematics learning in an inner-city school that enrolls a large minority population. Melissa is a former math teacher—a really good one. She knows that math is about ideas and patterns and relationships among numbers rather than just about getting right answers and remembering the "correct" steps to solve routine problems. She also knows that most of the kids in her elementary school are likely not to complete high school.

Melissa has been advised by the curriculum specialists in her large district to adopt one of the NSF-funded curriculum systems. She understands the materials are well designed and represent, through their constructivist approach, a lot of what she believes to be true about teaching and learning. At the same time, she knows that her faculty is not by any means ready to accept the program; there is horrendous staff turnover at the school, and expectations are consistently low. Melissa thinks that a direct-instruction approach will probably serve students better at this time, but she's afraid to voice her concern because it seems like an insult to the district's curriculum experts. She doesn't want to be seen as a heretic or a loser.

Melissa's dilemma is a common one, and it has something in common with cultural colonization. Very influential forces are trying to shape her professional judgments, but, like most of us, Melissa retains her doubts and her capacity to think for herself. In the end though, again like most of us, she'll probably capitulate and adopt the reformist program. New administrators and teachers preparing to become administrators are not likely to realize that 30 years ago *behaviorism* (now all but discredited as an approach to teaching and learning) was the dominant ideology of instruction. Direct instruction relies on the insights of behaviorism, which, although widely discredited at present, retain their relevance to some settings, possibly including Melissa's.

Even on the terms of neo-liberal economics, the functioning of the global economy would seem to benefit—via the strong participation of Eastern nations like China, Japan, Korea, and Singapore—from diversity. The Eastern approach, which stresses loyalty to the collectivity over individualism (whether the State is capitalist, like Japan, or free-market socialist, like Singapore, or communist, like China), remains the chief threat (via economic and political competition) to Western dominion over the globe. If competition is good for the system, it would seem logical to conclude that very different national characters would strengthen, not subvert, the global economy.

Arguably, the same degree of pluralism that sustains the U.S. democracy is needed globally. If a single economic regime—the neo-liberal economics of advanced capitalism—dominates the world, it will work to reduce cultural, political, and economic diversity worldwide. These losses are intellectual, cultural, and spiritual, and they could prove to be immensely harmful or ultimately fatal to the well-being of the planet (Orr, 1995). The end result of such losses may be the erosion of the very traditions that were once thought to constitute a true and powerful education (see, e.g., Howley et al., 1995).

"International" Children in American Schools

In the 19th century, immigrants to the United States were expected to "Americanize." It's difficult, however, for us to imagine today what our nation was like in, say, 1850 or 1890. Who were the Americans, at that time? What did it mean to "Americanize?"

America in the 19th century was rural and agrarian. Thus, part of what made the United States appealing to immigrants was the prospect of obtaining land. After 1890, however, the agrarian ideal, together with the prominence of agricultural livelihoods, declined precipitously. Industrialization in the 20th century meant the growth of big business. Corporations dwarfed individuals as political actors, especially in the last half of the 20th century. These two changes—the closing of the frontier and the rise of corporations as political actors—also meant the decline of the democratic project as it had been known from 1776 through the early 1900s, according to some writers (Kemmis, 1990; Theobald, 1997). Whereas immigrants always faced challenges, difficulties intensified as a result of industrialization and World War I xenophobia (e.g., Katz, 2001). Certainly by the middle of the 20th century, immigrants arriving in the United States confronted a different America and a different project of "Americanization" as compared to their predecessors.

What then does it mean for contemporary immigrant students to "Americanize"? First it means confronting an economic system in which monetary success is valorized. At the same time, the jobs that immigrants are able to obtain typically do not offer success on these terms.

Second, it means confronting the mass culture of the United States and inevitably abandoning, subverting, or submerging cultural practices from home. Language is, perhaps, the most significant of these cultural practices. The United States has never been particularly hospitable to languages other than English; and in recent years, policies have become even less accepting of language differences. Enacted and proposed "English-only" policies (e.g., California's Proposition 227) suggest that, far from wishing to cultivate bilingualism, U.S. policymakers hope to eliminate language diversity (e.g., Wiley & Wright, 2004).

Third, people of color who come to the United States confront complex racial prejudices and discriminatory policies and practices. Not only does the White mainstream view them as inferior, so too do other people of color with longer histories in the United States (see, e.g. Perlmutter, 2002). Moreover, as immigrant populations move into sections of the country where they compete for jobs with long-time residents, struggles over limited resources (e.g., jobs, housing) often become ethnically or racially charged.

Curiously, the proportion of "international children" in U.S. schools is increasing as a share of the total student population. In the conventional view, these children, who often live in marginal circumstances, need to be converted into productive workers and eager consumers—a job that multinational business interests assign to the schools (Giroux, 2000; Molnar, 1996). Otherwise, as the argument goes, they will grow up to have children who will also experience difficulty "Americanizing" (see Michie, 1999). Hypothetically, people in such circumstances could one day outnumber those who believe they represent the "true" America. Nevertheless, if current patterns persist, most immigrants will join the ranks of the poor, and the rich cultural diversity they offer will be overlooked (e.g., Portes, 2002).

Alternatives to Colonialism

The tenets of globalization—corporate expansion and the declining role of democratic citizenship—do not augur well for success in achieving worldwide social equity or planetary sustainability. But there are alternatives, and we briefly discuss two important ones.

For lack of a better term, we'll call the first alternative "environmentalism." This approach focuses on the earth as a potentially sustainable resource for peoples across the globe (see, e.g., Orr, 1994). Viewing corporate expansion as a threat to the earth itself, environmentalism of this sort, which is sometimes called "deep ecology," joins diverse peoples in the project of finding earthfriendly ways to produce, consume, and conserve resources (Weber, 1994). Because environmental issues concern everyone and because environmentalists value diversity (both biological and cultural), this approach represents a global option. The phrase "think globally, act locally" embodies the sentiment of environmentalists who seek peaceful and sustainable approaches to world citizenship.

A second alternative sometimes is referred to as "internationalism." This approach focuses on linkages among peoples from various nations in order to create greater appreciation and understanding as well as the achievement of common aims (e.g., Cambridge & Thompson, 2004; Jones, 1998). Marxism perhaps represents the earliest internationalist movement. As Gilbert (1978) argued, Marx believed that the interests of workers transcended national borders: "Common enemies created a common interest in unity among proletarians of different countries" (p. 348). According to some commentators, the expansion of capitalism worldwide represents just the sort of enemy about which Marx was concerned (e.g., Harrod & O'Brien, 2002; Munck, 2002). Harrod and O'Brien (2002) contend, for example, that an important response to globalization is the establishment of worldwide trade unions. Although there are still internationalists in the Marxist tradition, many contemporary internationalists focus on the civic, rather than social-class, interests that unite people across nations. McGrew (1999) and Habermas (2001), for example, argued that the expansion of transnational corporations signals the need for democratic processes that also extend beyond national borders.

GLOBALIZATION AND LOCALIZATION IN CARTER SCHOOLS: CASE STUDY

The principals of the four high schools in Carter School District, a small-town district in the Southwest, are about to take part in their monthly meeting with the superintendent. The main item on this month's agenda concerns what to do about math and science scores on the state accountability tests. A special effort to clear the agenda for consideration of this topic has been in the works for months, but one crisis after another has kept the agenda booked.

Now that the issue is actually going to be addressed, Brad Wilson is getting nervous. He's the veteran principal at Carter South—the school in the part of town that serves the Mexican-American families. Most are new to the country and are employed by a local furniture factory. They earn low wages, and their English is minimal. Predictably, the kids at South have the lowest scores—not just in math and science, but in everything. When talk of accountability scores gets underway, Brad wishes he could hide under the table.

The Meeting

The meeting starts in the usual way, with informal conversation among the principals, the curriculum director, and the assistant superintendent while they wait for Superintendent Marjorie Harrelson to arrive. Her calendar is so booked up that she's a few minutes late for every meeting; but once she arrives, the pace always picks up dramatically, and everyone in the room comes to attention. Harrelson has the hard-boiled demeanor of a seasoned admiral—no-nonsense, abrasive, and always attentive to keeping things ship-shape. She and Brad, for example, have never gotten along. He sees it as a matter of style: She throws punches, and he rolls with them.

The leadership team is used to Marjorie, so this morning they quiet down and "listen up" as soon as she walks into the room. "Here's what we're going to do," she announces immediately. "It won't be easy, but it seems like the best thing."

Brad takes a deep breath, because he knows his school is going to take the hit. Maybe it's time to consider early retirement, he thinks.

"We're going to convert South to a vocational school. It won't change enrollment much. Those kids don't go to college anyway. They might as well get some practical skills. And it's the kids at the other schools that need to carry this district. They're the ones who are going to go to college and get the high-tech jobs. And the good news is, if South goes vocational, we can give those kids the *Work-Steps* test rather than the academic diploma test. They won't be pulling down our scores any more."

Brad is surprised by the proposal, but not displeased. He expected to be asked to find a way to draw blood from a stone—to get his kids to do better on the academic diploma test. Instead, the proposal asks him to turn gold into lead. It will be a lot of work, but it seems like a winning proposition. "I guess I'll stay a few more years and see this through," Brad says to himself.

Just as Brad is beginning to think about how to break the news to his teachers and which teachers he might be able to RIF, the silence following Marjorie's announcement is interrupted by the quiet voice of Ramona Mandel, the newest member of the leadership team. Ramona is the first-year principal at Carter East, the smallest of the four schools. Everyone says she's capable, and her background as a long-time Peace Corp volunteer gives her an interesting perspective.

"This sounds just like Malawi," she says, "and it makes me very uncomfortable."

Shocked but intrigued, Marjorie nods her head indicating that Ramona can go on.

"You see," Ramona continues, "in Malawi, there's one kind of education for poor rural students and a totally different kind of education for urban students who are headed for jobs in corporations or in the government. It's almost like a caste system: Most rural kids don't even have a chance. Or, if they're really ambitious, they have to leave their families and villages in order to get an education."

"I don't get it. This isn't Africa." Marjorie's slight sarcasm reveals her momentary annoyance.

"Well, what we'd be doing if we turn South into a vocational school is to take away the option for the Mexican-American kids to get a solid academic education. And how can we expect them to be good citizens and to contribute to the community if they don't have a decent academic education? How many of them, do you think, would leave their part of town in order to take a rigorous literature or American history class at one of the other high schools?"

"And why exactly would they need to?" Brad decides to enter the discussion: It is *his* school after all. "They'll be able to read and do simple math by the time they're in high school. Most of them already hate the literature and history classes we're making them take now. Getting something practical will at least keep them off of welfare."

Marjorie listens intently as the two principals argue the point. Although Ramona's position seemed off target at first, she now wonders if Ramona might have a point. How much of what she's heard about the global economy actually applies to the people in Carter, anyway? Will pushing South to become vocational actually hurt Carter in the long-term? She's read some things about the way globalization can harm local economies, and she's a bit worried.

"Ok, I've listened to you both," she says. "It's time for us to think some more about this before we *do* anything."

CHAPTER SUMMARY

We addressed globalization in this chapter for several reasons—partly because it's the economic basis of "the information age" and partly because school administrators are continually bombarded by (perhaps misguided) directives to lead schools into the globalized 21st century. These two reasons are, of course, related.

The chapter defines globalization as *the postindustrial worldwide manifestation of free trade under neo-liberal economic rules.* In plain English, this means "advanced capitalism taken to worldwide scale on the back of the digital revolution." The key concepts related to globalization are localization, colonialism, imperialism, transnational corporations, centralization–decentralization, democracy, the nature of citizenship, and the relationship between diversity and pluralism.

As the chapter explains, the developmental line represented by colonialism, imperialism, and globalization entails the rise beginning in the 19th century of mass education, in part as an instrument to pacify, or "civilize," the masses of people drawn into industrial employment worldwide. This effort didn't just take place in the industrial nations, but was also used in colonies to establish native administrative elites who could help colonial powers rule their territories. Often, the Western language became the language of instruction, and this is how—by the end of the 20th century— English became the planetary common language of commerce, diplomacy, and emerging transnational culture. Later, under imperialism, native elites were able to help the former colonial powers establish strong markets for their industrial goods among their former colonies.

As imperialism turned into globalization, school systems here and elsewhere in the world were increasingly used to bolster the interests and prerogatives of transnational corporations. Sometimes the influence has been subtle, and sometimes heavy-handed. According to many commentators, the chief practical problem with this educational influence is that it remakes students as future global economic warriors, and the history of colonialism and imperialism suggests that such a preparation can lead to catastrophic ends.

More fundamentally, critics worry, the influence of transnational corporations in the world economy seems to be creating new forms of political governance that subvert the long-settled power of nation states. As these critics noted, the fundamental justification for the very existence of nation states is the citizen: Under democratic forms of government, schools exist to create citizens capable of sustaining nations. Without citizens, public schooling would be needed only to the extent necessary to create workers and consumers.

At the same time, those who analyze and interpret globalization express concern about the way it works to restrict diversity both in the United States and across the world. According to world culture theorists, in fact, the process of educational "borrowing" and "lending" is reducing differences in educational practices in nations as different as Tanzania and the United Kingdom, and everywhere else in between.

Although current communication technologies make it easy to see that all nations are part of a world community, that insight does not necessarily provide support for globalization via the growth of enormously powerful transnational corporations. Some commentators have proposed alternatives. The chapter considers two: environmentalism and internationalism. Whereas environmentalism seeks to unite people in order to sustain the earth and its resources, internationalism joins peoples of the world in support of common interests (e.g., the interests shared by workers across nations, the interests of citizens for global peace).

12

Thinking About Making Schools Better

STABILITY AND CHANGE IN SCHOOLS

If this book accomplishes what we hoped it would, readers would now be able to use a variety of theoretical lenses to examine their schools. And they will also be able to use different theories to think about alternative versions of what schools might be like. Knowledge of formal theoretical work, moreover, illustrates how theories are made and their connection to our experiences of the world. Such knowledge also provides a basis for examining our tacit theories—bringing them to the surface, articulating and evaluating their claims, and revising them—in other words, for turning our tacit theories into explicit, intentional ones.

These tacit-made-explicit theories are extremely useful because they help us answer important questions such as "Are our school's aims important, and to whom?" "What other aims might our school community find equally or even more important?" "In what ways do our practices fit in with our most worthy aims, and in what ways do they ignore or subvert them?"

In seeking answers to these and other related questions, it's important to recognize that schools support both stability and change—neither of which is good in itself. Sidebar 12-1 shows how the issues implied by these questions—issues concerning educational ends (i.e., aims) and means—might fit in with the need to maintain stability or seek change.

Sidebar 12-1:

Ends and Means—Conditions Favoring Stability and Change

	Stability	Change
Ends	The community judges the school's aims to be worthy.	The community sees a need for different aims.
Means	The educators judge that the educational strategies are likely to accomplish the school's aims.	The educators judge that the educational strategies are not likely to accomplish the school's aims.

In any society, the institution of education, which includes informal practices as well as formal ones, inevitably plays a role in transmitting cultural knowledge. And despite the bad rap it sometimes gets, transmission of knowledge is critical for the survival of a culture. So too is change: Cultural survival depends on adaptation just as much as it depends on the perpetuation of durable practices. The issue (for any culture) is not *whether* education should be used for stability or change, but *how* education can support a proper combination of stability and change.

Of course, deciding what represents a "proper" combination is typically not an intentional process; a workable (not necessarily "proper") combination simply comes into being. For example, in many U.S. communities, people are quick to embrace new technologies (e.g., mobile phones, computer technologies), but comparatively slow in changing attitudes about family structure. Few would argue that the speed with which we accept technological change coupled with the relative slowness with which we accept social change represents a "proper combination." And some would argue that this combination serves us badly (e.g., Mander & Goldsmith, 1996; Skolnick, 2004).

There are, however, social groups that strive to make intentional decisions about stability and change. For example, elders in Amish communities routinely consider the ramifications of new technologies for the spiritual well-being of community members. And the planning processes adopted by some organizations encourage strategic thinking about organizational strengths (i.e., the organizational conditions that should remain the same) and pressing challenges (i.e., the provocations for organizational change). Arguably, initiatives for local school improvement should involve strategic thinking of this sort, but in practice, such initiatives often rely on external determinations (e.g., those of policymakers or education bureaucrats) about what ought to change and what ought to remain the same. Such external determinations, however, do not necessarily support a balance between stability and change that promotes the well-being of a school community.

This circumstance reflects the fact that culture is local and contingent, whereas educational policy tends to be distant and universal. We continually hear, for example, about "best practice," which is supposed to accomplish widely valued aims with scientifically verified methods. The idea of "best practice," however, rests on two questionable assumptions: (a) that the same specific set of educational aims is valued in every community and (b) that educational methods primarily involve technical rather than cultural practices. These assumptions are challenged by the postpositivist theories explored in this book.

In contrast to improvement efforts that attempt to impose "best practice," those that take a postpositivist stance acknowledge that education is embedded in culture. As a cultural product, moreover, education belongs to the communities that are raising the children of the next generation. It doesn't "belong" to the state in quite the same way.

Who Should Decide?

As the discussion thus far has suggested, decisions about education focus on ends and means, and they concern the question, "What ought to persist and what ought to change?" Principals confront such decisions head-on when they undertake improvement planning—an increasingly popular activity in this era of mandated "reforms." But they also confront such decisions whenever they engage in less formal planning, even short-term planning of curriculum, professional development, resource allocation, or behavior management.

A principal, however, cannot make such decisions alone. In fact, the theories presented in this book—even when they don't speak explicitly to the issue—support the view that a principal *ought not to* make such decisions alone. Despite considerable differences among the theories, they all support leadership practices that are egalitarian, democratic, empowering, and culturally responsive. The theories differ somewhat in focus, which leads to a difference in perspective about the groups that need to be included in organizational decision making. Dynamic systems theory, for example, focuses attention on means (i.e., how an organization accomplishes its aims), whereas communitarian theory focuses attention on ends (i.e., what constitutes the common good). Of course, ends and means are not all that easy to separate. In a sense, for instance, communitarians value democratic engagement as an end, but they believe that democratic engagement (the end) can be realized only through processes of democratic engagement (the means).

It may be useful, however, to think differently about the scope of engagement when we consider educational ends, on the one hand, and educational means, on the other. As a function of culture, formal education is situated in communities. Communitarians, cultural theorists, and postmodern theorists would probably agree that, as a consequence of how formal education is situated, community members ought to be the ones to determine educational ends. On this view, professional educators and state policymakers ought to play a limited role in such determinations.

In contrast, professional educators possess "expert" knowledge that gives them a special place in decision making about educational means—practices relating to instruction and schooling processes. Dynamic systems theory and social constructionism, in particular, support an approach that places decisions about educational means primarily within the jurisdiction of groups of educators. Much of what's written about critical pedagogy also implies that educators ought to play a decisive role in selecting instructional methods, specifically those that engage and ultimately empower students.

So far the discussion of educational deliberation expands on the ideas presented in Sidebar 12-1, which locates primary responsibility for decisions about educational ends with community members and primary responsibility for decisions about educational means with a school or district's educators. There are two situations, however, that call for the involvement of participants from outside a community.

The first situation occurs when a community uses its schools to accomplish educational ends that are unjust or inhumane. In this situation, the state has a reason to intervene. In order to protect the community's children from an intolerant or toxic community, somebody with the authority to do so needs to step in. For example, a racist community might want to adopt a curriculum in which African Americans are taught basic skills only, whereas Whites are taught advanced academic subject matter. In this case, state regulations requiring that students of all races be assured access to the same curriculum might be needed in order to restrain injustices resulting from power relations at the local level. Multicultural theorists, some critical theorists and feminists, and a few communitarians believe that state intervention on behalf of equity and social justice is sometimes necessary.

The second situation occurs when the educators in a school fail—either because they lack the will or the ability—to accomplish the educational aims set forth by a community. When this happens, someone needs to take action. In this case, however, state intervention is problematic. Because the state is too far removed from the community to set relevant educational aims, it also may be too far removed to regulate the practices used to realize those aims. Community oversight, informed by professional expertise, might be a workable alternative. For example, if a local school board suspected that the teachers in a school were not competent to deliver the curriculum, they might employ external evaluators and consultants to help the school get on the right track.

Of course, there are no "rules of thumb" showing exactly when a state or community ought to intervene. In fact, as previous discussion has suggested, states have extended their regulatory power into all communities, not just toxic ones. Nevertheless, principals who are committed to democratic governance understand when state intervention gets in the way, and they take action to shield their schools and communities from unwarranted state intrusion. Sidebar 12-2 tells the story of one such principal.

Sidebar 12-2: The Case of "Mr. G."

In his 1994 article, Ulrich Reitzug described Mr. G., a principal who promoted the empowerment and democratic engagement of the teachers in his school.

- First, Mr. G. provided a "supportive environment for critique" (p. 292). In order to do so, he communicated trust, encouraged risk-taking, and allowed teachers and students to solve their own problems. In order to encourage critique, moreover, Mr. G. had to "counteract the effects of policy initiatives promoting standardization and reliance on external criteria for the determination of appropriate practice" (p. 292).

- Second, he fostered critique by "asking questions that stimulated examination of teaching practice, requiring justification of practice based on personal practical knowledge, practicing critique by wandering around, and providing alternative frameworks for thinking about teaching and learning" (p. 296).

- Finally, Mr. G. created a climate of "possibility" by providing tangible and intangible resources, which enabled teachers to put their ideas into action (p. 301).

The Role of Theory

As the story of Mr. G. showed, principals who wish to involve others in democratic decision making need to ask challenging questions and offer provocative commentary in order to stimulate critique. Although principals can formulate such provocations on the basis of their own experiences and insights, they also may find that formal theories are helpful. Such theories connect to wider intellectual traditions and therefore open up rich avenues for dialog among members of the school community. An example will show how a principal's insights coupled with formal theory can provide useful challenges to the thinking of teachers, parents, and other community members.

At Middleboro High School, student engagement is decreasing while the number of student discipline referrals is rising. Principal Mike Warner spent his first year at the school watching and listening, and he has some "theories" about what's going on. But before settling on one explanation or on a course of action, he makes a mental inventory of the insights that some formal theories offer. Here's his list:

- Communitarian theory draws attention to the breakdown between the communities served by Middleboro and the school. Most teachers are White and live outside the community; whereas most families are Puerto Rican and have multigenerational ties to the community.
- Dynamic systems theory brings up the possibility that the teachers at Middleboro have mental models that interfere with effective teaching. These mental models may come from teachers' backgrounds in middle-class White America. Expectations for student behavior and performance may arise from these mental models, and such expectations may actually support a self-fulfilling prophesy—sustaining rather than changing patterns of undesirable behavior and low performance.
- One theory of comparative culture—that of Hofstede—suggests that there might be a mismatch between the cultural preferences of teachers and students. The Puerto Rican culture from which the students come may be more egalitarian (i.e., have lower tolerance for power distance), more masculine, and more risk-avoiding than the cultures of the White teachers. Some student behaviors, which teachers have been interpreting as insolent, may reflect the discomfort that students feel when they are expected to view the world in ways that do not accord with their cultural preferences.
- Some critical and postmodern theories illustrate possible dynamics. For example, security measures recently adopted by the school may be causing students to exhibit resistant behavior. State-mandated testing may be having the same effect. Students may not see the school as a place where they can explore their own identities but rather as a place that imposes unwanted identities on them.

Because Mike hopes to use theories productively for the benefit of the school, his goal is not to choose among the different perspectives. In other words, he doesn't need to decide if he's a critical theorist or a communitarian in order to use insights from those theories as a way to get a handle on what's going on. He does, however, need to assess the degree to which the insights offered by each of the theories matches the evidence: The theories provide leads that Mike ought to pursue. And once he has a handle on what's going on, he can use theories in another way. They can help him imagine alternatives—cultural practices that are likely to improve the health and productivity of the school organization.

Of course, somewhere along the way, Mike needs to invite others to join him in this process of critical interrogation. He can use the ends and means distinction as a way to decide who should be involved. If aims are at stake—as most of the theoretical insights seem to imply—then opening up the process broadly to the community makes sense. Questions like "What is this school for?", "How can the culture of the school connect to students' home cultures?", and "How can the school make relevant linkages to the local community?" can provide the starting points for dialog involving teachers, students, parents, and other community members.

Matters relating to professional practice (i.e., those concerning educational means)—such as the way teachers' mental models work to limit opportunities for students—can be addressed in more restricted forums. Groups of teachers and administrators—not parents and students—need to investigate such matters. Opening up discussions of teaching practice to a wider audience would, in many cases, frighten and discourage teachers. At the same time, failure to improve the effectiveness and cultural responsiveness of teaching practices would most likely interfere with the school's efforts to cultivate the trust of students and community members. Mike cannot afford to let discussions among teachers end with promises and plans. Considering what's going on at Middleboro, some things actually *do* need to change.

As it turns out, Mike Warner's second year on the job will involve organizing and facilitating a series of ongoing discussions. And his primary responsibility as a leader will be to find ways to translate what's decided as a result of those discussions into actions that sustain or change schooling practices.

SCHOOL BETTERMENT IN THE HERE AND NOW

Most of the theories discussed in this book cast doubt on simple views of social progress. At the same time, most of them imply that social arrangements across the globe embed serious faults: structural inequalities, ideological tyranny, and day-to-day injustices. But doesn't the contradiction between these two insights put us in a terrible bind? The world needs to improve, but improvement efforts are suspect. How can we proceed?

One way, of course, is to ignore the cautions raised by these theories and proceed with improvement initiatives, as prescribed by state and national policymakers. The track record for such initiatives has not been good, however (see, e.g., Scott, 1998; Tyack & Cuban, 1995). Moreover, the theory behind them is questionable. Does the distant state really know what's best for every community? Is there one set of "best practices" that works to promote learning of all types, under all circumstances, in all contexts? Do policymakers really understand the teaching–learning process better than do educators? Should the economic interests of global capitalism exert the major influence on education everywhere?

Another way to proceed is to reframe "improvement initiatives" as local efforts to make things better. *School betterment*, unlike systemic improvement, focuses on the actions that local educators and community members take in order to heighten schools' responsiveness to worthy educational aims and to increase their capacity to achieve those ends. Many schools that we all know have lost their sense of common purpose. They have simply adopted as their own the educational aims put forth by state and national policymakers. In contrast, some schools seem to know where they want to go, but have found few effective strategies for getting there. School betterment efforts can address either circumstance or both.

The next sections of the chapter provide extended examples, cases in which principals use various theories to lead their schools toward betterment. In two of the cases, educational ends (or aims) are at stake, and in the other two, educational means are of greater concern. And two of the cases (one concerning ends and one concerning means) focus on stability, whereas the other two focus on change. Common to all four cases is a "theory of action" that rests on the following assumptions: (a) Thinking about school betterment needs to be an ongoing and intentional process, (b) theories help us think about school betterment, (c) processes for thinking and making decisions about school betterment need to involve as many members of the school community as possible, (d) betterment is contingent on the sense making of a particular group of people at a particular place and time, and (e) provocations that lead to discussions about school betterment can come from various sources, including state and national policymakers.

CASE STUDIES: EDUCATIONAL ENDS

Although they seem to focus on immediate problems encountered by schools, the two case studies in this section turn out to concern fundamental educational aims. In the first case study, the school community decides that existing educational aims need to be preserved and supported. In the second, the principal realizes that messages coming from a variety of sources point to serious flaws with the educational aims that are influencing school practices. Both cases show how principals can use formal theories to help them think about complicated issues, even dilemmas that implicate decisions about educational stability and change.

Bilingual No Matter What

Serving Spanish-speaking families in a large urban center, Parks Middle School has maintained a bilingual program for the last 10 years. Educators at the school believe in the program, and the community strongly endorses it. Not surprisingly, however, the program has weathered some serious political storms. The worst storm thus far occurred when the state passed a law limiting support for bilingual approaches to instruction. The law threatened the program's funding, and it challenged the school's requirement that all of its teachers be fluent in both English and Spanish. Since the passage of the law, the school has managed to continue its bilingual program by obtaining grant funds to pay for materials and by using citywide guidelines for magnet schools to justify its personnel policies.

A new threat, however, is on the horizon. And as a result, it's time once again for the school community to evaluate the relevance of the school's vision: "communication for all; language competence as a tool, not a barrier" and its mission: "to provide high-quality academic instruction in English and Spanish."

The Threat. The state legislature has just passed a new education bill, with more stringent requirements for school accountability. Schools that do not meet accountability targets have 3 years to improve, or else they face outside audits that may result in their take over by the state or even their closure.

Parks students have not performed well—although not badly either—on state accountability tests. Whereas a pass rate of 83% is expected by the state, sixth- and eighth-grade pass rates at Parks hover around 70%. Consultants from the state have intimated on more than one occasion that the bilingual program—which involves instruction in English in the mornings and in Spanish in the afternoons—may be interfering with students' mastery of the knowledge and skills specified in the state department of education's standards.

Although the teachers at the school and their long-time principal, Marcia Prieto, disagree with these assessments, they understand that the new accountability requirements provide a provocation for examining the direction the school has been taking. Marcia has used public forums in the past in order to gauge community sentiment, and she has been thinking that it's time to arrange such a forum again.

The Forum.   Because she wants as many people as possible to attend the forum, Marcia advertises it widely, sending home messages with students, posting notices in various stores and in local churches, calling her contacts among community activists, and making personal visits to each classroom to discuss the forum with students. She understands also that if she gets the kind of turnout she's looking for, she will need to guide the discussion carefully. Although she does not want to give the impression that there's a crisis, she does want to communicate the seriousness of the issue. And she wants to give everyone a chance to express their views.

Perhaps she'll ask people to sit in groups at tables and talk about what they like and don't like about the school. Each group can arrive at a list of questions that they'd like the school staff to consider. Then, at a follow-up meeting, the teachers can share responses to the community's questions. Those responses and community members' reactions to them will provide a starting point for framing possible courses of action.

Theories Help.   As the teachers work to answer the community member's questions, Marcia helps them think about the issues. Because she understands a variety of theories, she can frame the school's situation in different ways. Her understanding of critical theory and globalization theory, for example, supports a cautious (even skeptical) view of the state's accountability requirements. Her knowledge of culturalist and comparative views about education as well as her knowledge of constructivism reminds her of the value of linking the curriculum to students' "lived experiences." And her recent reading of articles by postmodernist educators reassures her that the school's practice of giving students a lot of freedom provides benefits that are not likely to show up on standardized achievement tests.

At the same time, Marcia's familiarity with more traditional positivist theories helps her think about some of the organizational dynamics at Parks. In particular, she is concerned that, too often lately, members of the administrative team have been engaging in unproductive negotiations with teachers over small matters (i.e., authorizations of field trips, completion of lesson plans) rather than treating teachers as competent colleagues. Somehow (Marcia's not sure exactly how), dynamics of "command and control" have gained a foothold at Parks. She understands, however, that changing her own practice and discussing the issue with the assistant principal and guidance counselor will likely be all that's needed to turn things around.

What the Community Wants and What They Decide.   After the community forum, Marcia and the teachers read the comments and questions from parents and community members. Mostly, the comments reveal strong support for the school and its bilingual curriculum. A few parents actually question why some teachers have started to give assignments that focus specifically on the content covered on the state tests. Although their comments indicate that they think teachers probably know what's best, they report that their children are bored by test drills and worksheets.

As Marcia and the teachers consider the community queries, they begin to realize that state testing has been pushing them in a direction that is not consistent with their mission. Just as the teachers have been trying to "sneak in" a little bit of test preparation, Marcia and the other administrators have been trying to "sneak in" a little too much "top-down" control. The result seems to be a mismatch between the values they espouse and their actual practices. Neither Marcia nor the teachers think the mismatch is healthy.

In the follow-up meeting with parents and community members, Marcia and the teachers share their insights and misgivings. Marcia explains how tempting it would be to abandon their special mission in favor of a narrow focus on state standards, but she also explains that neither she nor the staff wants to yield to that temptation. Rather, their preference is to continue to pursue—with renewed vigor—the mission that has been in place for the past 10 years. Nevertheless, Marcia shares the view that she and the teachers would be open to another option, if the community favors it strongly.

Parents and community members, for their part, explain how little the state tests mean to them and how important it is to them that their children enjoy school. They offer strong praise for the bilingual program, reporting that their children's bilingualism is also helping other family members feel more comfortable about moving back and forth from Spanish to English. Like the educators, they prefer the option of sticking with the original mission.

The Hidden Agenda

Willow Glen High School, located in a suburb of a major east-coast city, serves 2,700 students in Grades 9 though 12. Since its construction in 1968, the school has offered a comprehensive curriculum, with five distinct tracks: advanced placement, honors, college preparatory, general, and vocational. Guidance counselors at the three "feeder" middle schools work with students and their parents to decide the track that is appropriate for each student.

Although it certainly isn't intentional, this process seems to result in tracking that matches up with socioeconomic divisions in the community. Low-income students typically wind up in the general and vocational tracks, middle-class students in the college-prep track, and affluent students in the honors and advanced placement tracks. As a result, the school sends its most affluent students to Ivy League colleges and most of its middle class students to state colleges. Few of its low-income students, however, pursue postsecondary schooling. In fact, among low-income students, there is a high dropout rate. School personnel, moreover, do not engage in follow-up activities to find out about the employment experiences of graduates. Teachers hear stories occasionally about general track students who go into the military or wind up on welfare, but no one knows for sure what happens to graduates of the school's general and vocational programs.

This situation didn't seem to distress anyone until recently. Two changes, however, are now prompting citizens and educators from Willow Glen to take a closer look at tracking. The first change relates to community demographics. Whereas in the past Willow Glen was primarily an affluent community, it is now primarily a low- and middle-income community. The majority of its students are now placed in the college prep, general, and vocational tracks, with the other tracks reserved for a small elite. Nevertheless, budgeting for the honors and advanced placement classes is still extremely generous, class sizes are tiny, and the school's best teachers are assigned to teach the school's few high-performing students.

A second change is the arrival of a new principal, Matt Norton, an African American educator from New Jersey with a doctorate from a highly respected state university. Matt has worked primarily in large urban systems, as an assistant principal, curriculum director, and assistant superintendent. The job at Willow Glen is his first principalship. Matt is well versed in the education literature, and he is passionately committed to social justice.

The Visit and the Strategic Planning Event.   Sometime in the middle of his first year at Willow Glen, Matt receives a visit from a group of community organizers. They talk about their interest in getting Willow Glen involved in an initiative to improve the chances of low-income youth in the entire metropolitan area. It's an ambitious undertaking, requiring collaboration among a number of agencies and offering the possibility of initial grant support and eventual line-item funding from the state.

Matt is enthusiastic and agrees to take the first step, which involves participation in communitywide strategic planning. Because Matt is new to the community, however, he thinks it's best for a leader from another agency—Willow Glen Community Action—to organize the event.

When he arrives at the Community Center on the appointed evening, Matt is surprised by the turnout—hundreds of local citizens. And he's also surprised by what he hears. The facilitator starts the session with an agenda-setting activity in which she asks the audience to brainstorm agenda items and then to provide a show of hands to indicate which are the most important. Problems with the school are at the top of the list: too few opportunities for students to participate in extracurricular activities, unsupportive teachers and counselors, an unacceptably high dropout rate.

Matt is taken aback at first by the forcefulness with which local citizens criticize the school. From his observations so far, the school has seemed functional, with students focused on their schoolwork, few serious discipline problems, and a reasonable level of "school spirit." Matt wonders if he's hearing just one side of the story. After all, the people who come to an event billed as "communitywide strategic planning" might be the ones with an axe to grind.

Student and Teacher Meetings.   Matt decides that he needs to hear from other groups in order to find out how well the community members' criticisms match up with others' perceptions of the school. He hires a facilitator to conduct five meetings—one with all students at each grade level and one with all teachers—to identify their views of the school's strengths and weaknesses. It's a shotgun approach, but he thinks it might be a good starting point.

When Matt reviews the videotapes of the four grade-level meetings with students, he's shocked. Not only are the students critical, they are remarkably articulate about the nature of their concerns. And although extracurricular opportunities are on the list, the curriculum comes in for the biggest hit. Most of the students talk about boring, watered-down classes that don't seem to prepare them for anything in the future—not for college, not for technical school, not for jobs.

The videotape of the meeting with teachers is equally shocking, but only in light of what Matt has heard from the students and community members. The teachers generally agree it's a good school that operates smoothly, with only a few glitches. They do complain that the large size of the school makes it difficult for them to get together for departmental meetings, and they think hiring more support staff to help them with class preparations and noninstructional duties would be a good idea. Although they don't have many concerns about the school, the teachers seem quite worried about its students. Teachers say the students lack the motivation—and even the basic intelligence—of the students they used to work with just a few years ago. And most of the teachers wish there were a separate vocational school to send the students for whom college is not an option.

Matt Takes a Look at Theory.   Extremely distressed by the mismatch between students' and teachers' perceptions, Matt decides to go back to some theoretical works that he read in graduate school. In particular, he recalls the salience of critical theory and rereads some books and articles suggesting that schooling practices often reproduce dominant economic and power relations. Some of these works also explain why low-income kids don't see schooling as a vehicle for pulling themselves out of poverty.

In the course of his reading, Matt becomes reacquainted with the theoretical (and empirical) relationship between curriculum tracking and social inequality. And in the bibliographies of some of the works he reads, he also finds out about positivist studies linking educational attainment with income, social class and race with dropout rates, and so on.

Selecting the most powerful excerpts from what he's been reading, Matt pulls together a packet of materials to share with teachers. He knows, though, that most of the teachers are not going to be interested and that simply distributing materials may turn out to be useless or even counterproductive.

So Matt returns to another body of theory—this time the somewhat more traditional theories on social and organizational change. From his reading in this literature, he decides on a strategy that incorporates some top-down actions, namely requiring that all departments conduct thorough self-studies of their curricula and requiring that all teachers view the tapes of the student and teacher forums. But the strategy also supports a range of bottom-up provisions—release time for a group of teachers (those most committed to social justice) to study the literature on tracking; empowerment of a school improvement council including teachers, parents, and students; and selection of two "opinion leaders" from the teaching staff to serve on the interagency team that is writing the initial grant to provide special programs for low-income youth.

From all he's learned about his school and much of what he's read, Matt is now convinced that curriculum tracking provides a way for the school to achieve an unstated, but nonetheless very real educational aim—sorting students into economic strata on the basis of their social-class backgrounds. Moreover, once he acknowledges that this unworthy aim is what sustains tracking at Willow Glen, Matt realizes that other school practices—from staffing to extracurricular tryouts—are also working toward this end.

The insight disturbs him profoundly, but it leads to a turning point in his thinking. Now he understands that changing the curriculum tracks won't be enough. Matt sees how important it will be in the near future to bring together the entire school community in an effort to identify educational aims that everyone agrees are worthy. Although the actions he's already taken might be helpful, they might also backfire unless he can find a way to connect them to a change initiative that is truly radical—one that really goes to the root of what's happening at Willow Glen.

Debriefing

Principals probably have less occasion to deal with deliberations about educational ends, such as those considered in the two case studies in this section, than with deliberations about educational means. For one thing, the means of education—teaching practices, discipline plans, staffing arrangements, and so on—can always be refined and readjusted, whereas the aims of education seem to be more durable. At the same time, principals should be alert to circumstances in which deliberations seem to concern educational means, but really implicate educational ends.

In the second case study, for example, Matt Norton might have concluded that the question of whether or not the curriculum should be tracked was primarily a matter of pedagogy. If he had done so, he probably would have chosen to work primarily with the teachers and not to undertake a thorough investigation of the perspectives of students, parents, and community members. Of course, approaching the question in this way, Matt would have been likely to overlook the issue that really was at stake—a deeper issue concerning educational aims. This circumstance, moreover, probably would have jeopardized the long-term efficacy of *any* solution that resulted from deliberations focusing only on educational means.

Perhaps the confusion of issues involving means and ends happens in education more often than we usually acknowledge. In the absence of worthy and widely endorsed aims, methods that might otherwise be adequate to the task can fail miserably. And if we tell ourselves that such failures result only from the use of ineffective methods, we might find that we're engaged in a never-ending but fruitless search for a "magic bullet"—the sort of search that has arguably characterized the history of school reform in the United States for the last 100 or so years.

CASE STUDIES: EDUCATIONAL MEANS

The previous discussion does not, of course, imply that issues concerning educational means are trivial or occur infrequently. In fact, they take place so often that, in many instances, they go unrecognized. For example, teachers frequently try out different teaching methods, schools often revise their behavior management plans, and districts periodically adopt new textbooks.

Some of these decisions are made with almost no discussion—sometimes with almost no thought.

In some cases, in fact, it seems completely reasonable that educators should make such decisions "on automatic pilot." After all, the craft that educators practice—of teaching or of administration—requires that they respond intuitively to a host of choices relating to daily experience in schools.

Of course, intuitive, automatic decisions obviously do not provide opportunities for reflection, collaboration, or planning. And with complicated or weighty issues, these processes are extremely important. The two case studies included in this section demonstrate how theoretical considerations help educators think about difficult issues relating to educational means.

Traditional Math Works for Us

At the end of a busy day, Beth Pettry sits at her desk idly looking out of the window toward the school parking lot. Beth has been principal at Green High School for 15 years, and she knows that not all days are as exhausting as this one has been. The kids seemed to be testing everybody's patience. And, of course, it didn't help that all four math teachers were off in Spring City at an in-service session.

Just as she is thinking about the math faculty, all four of them drive up to the building and get out of their cars. They immediately huddle together in the parking lot, obviously talking heatedly about something. Beth watches for a while, but then packs up her briefcase and heads for home.

Green is located in a Midwestern farm community, about 50 miles from the state capital. Although Beth grew up on a farm, she now lives in the capital, where her husband works and her children go to school. The 100-mile commute each day gives Beth lots of time to reflect on what's happening at the high school.

The Math Teachers Complain.   The next afternoon Seymour Morton, the chair of the math department, stops by the office to talk with Beth. He says he's disgusted with what the state consultants are saying about how math ought to be taught. As far as he's concerned, they're way off base. He explains to Beth that the consultants are saying more or less the same things he's been reading in his association journal and newsletters, but he thinks the new constructivist approach is cumbersome and misguided.

Over the course of the next couple of days, Beth hears from the other three math teachers, who basically tell the same story as Seymour. They are displeased to be receiving pressure from the state consultants to teach math in ways they think are wrong-headed. They want Beth to agree to support them in the decision to use the same teaching methods they've always used and to tell the state consultants to back off.

Reflection.   For the past couple of days Beth has been using her time in the car to think about the teachers' reactions to the expectation that they use "reform math." Her own preference for constructivism and especially its view of students as active constructors of knowledge disposes her to favor the reform approach. But constructivism itself—particularly the social constructionist version—talks about the way knowledge is situated in cultural practice. The mathematics that's being taught at Green seems to fit in with what everyone—the community, the teachers, and the students—expect math to be. "Reform math" is what's out of synch, but is it better, nonetheless?

This question prompts Beth to think about the articles she read in the online class she completed last semester to fulfill her professional development requirement. At the time the readings seemed a bit far-fetched to Beth, but some of the points keep coming to mind. For example, one article talked about the way "modernist" educational reforms seek to increase the uniformity and predictability of schools, thereby reducing their variability. The article used data from case studies to demonstrate that high-performing schools actually use very different instructional practices—ranging from quite traditional to extremely progressive. The authors argued that there is not just "one best way" to teach, but many different good ways. Another one of the readings made a similar point, but focused on agricultural and infrastructure "reforms" in developing nations.

As a result of her reflections, Beth decides that it might not make sense to insist that the teachers change over to "reform math." But she wants to hear how they're thinking about the issue.

The Conversation.   Beth arranges an after-school meeting with the math teachers. She brews a pot of coffee and sets out bakery cookies. She hopes to encourage the teachers to let down their defenses and talk about the math reforms openly, exploring what the reforms might offer as well as the problems they might cause. She expects the teachers to vent their frustrations and then to get into more substantive matters.

Because she knows her teachers well, Beth is not at all surprised by the tenor of the discussion. It starts off with Veronica Blessing whining, "Well, if that's what the state department wants, we just have no choice," and with Seymour Morton retorting, "The state department doesn't know what it wants; those folks haven't taught math for years—almost as bad as those math ed professors that keep talking about constructivism." And it goes on in the same vein for about an hour, at which point the teachers start to look at their watches.

Beth looks at her watch too and says, "Gee, time flies when we're having fun, but where are we?" Seymour replies, "Well, we've just trashed the state department, and I guess that's for good." "No we didn't," announced Veronica, "We just decided to do what we're told."

Beth sums things up by explaining that Seymour's and Veronica's points characterize the choice that the math department faces, but that there really hasn't been any resolution. She asks them to think some more about the issues and to meet again in a week to talk about what the math department is going to do.

What They Decide.   In the end it takes four meetings for the group to come to a decision. In the process, though, they've had a chance to do a lot of talking about what they think math is, how kids learn math, which teaching practices they prefer and why, how their students respond to various teaching approaches, and a number of other related issues. It's been a good conversation.

Their decision, though, is to keep the math program pretty much intact. Their conversation has shown, however, that they are all comfortable providing practical examples of math concepts; in fact all of them have done so for years. It's a part of the reform math they can accept. The rest—an integrated curriculum, math journals, lots of small-group work—just doesn't seem to fit with their ideas about math or math teaching. The students seem to be learning math just fine the "old way," so they're going to stick with it.

Beth agrees to support the teachers' decision, and thinks it might be a good idea to request a waiver from the state department. Although it's a lot of paper work, she thinks a waiver will give the math teachers protection from state intervention and therefore greater freedom to do what they think is best.

Zero Tolerance

Langford Elementary School is located in the heart of a once thriving midwestern city that has been in decline for about two decades. At this point, the neighborhood of Langford is a slum, with low-rent and subsidized housing, a street-corner drug trade, and a high crime rate. Moreover, the school—a century-old stone structure with a cinder block gymnasium added on in the 1950s—hardly seems like a haven in this depressed community. In fact, the school appears to be anything but inviting. Recently, in an effort to keep vandals from defacing the building, the school board approved the installation of a 7 ft. fence topped with razor wire. Despite this intimidating addition, gang members still have been getting into the schoolyard, leaving their painted insignias on the walls of the gymnasium.

Because it's a small school (around 250 students) serving younger children (Grades K–5), the school does not have an armed security guard. Limited resources have forced some cutbacks in the district, and now only larger elementary schools—and of course middle and high schools—are allowed to hire security personnel. For this reason, about 2 years ago the school staff agreed to adopt an extremely strict zero-tolerance policy. Under the policy, students receive automatic 5-day out-of-school suspensions for verbal abuse toward teachers or other students and for fighting, and automatic one-year expulsions for making explicit threats, instigating fights in which someone is injured, and bringing weapons to school. Last year, 140 students were suspended at least once, and 30 were expelled.

A New Beginning.   Two years ago, Langford Elementary experienced major staffing changes. Seventeen of the school's 20 professional employees left; 6 teachers and a principal retired, and the rest took other positions in the district. The teachers who were employed as replacements are all new to the profession, just one or 2 years out of college. And the new principal, Alverna Williams, is also inexperienced, with just 4 years as a teacher and no experience as a principal.

Alverna grew up in Langford and knows many of the families that live in the neighborhood. She's energetic, funny, and dedicated to the community. In fact, Alverna herself attended Langford Elementary and is keenly aware of its decline in recent years. She's determined, though, to make it a good school once again—one where all the students feel welcome and experience success.

Looking Around and Thinking About Things.   As soon as she accepts the job, Alverna tells herself that the first thing to do is to spend some time watching what's going on at the school. Although she's quite sure that the school needs to improve, she's not sure what its problems really are. Nevertheless, there are a few teachers on the staff who have been at Langford for a number of years, and it is these educators to whom Alverna turns.

"Just tell me everything you can about the school," she inquires. "Tell me everything you know about what's happened here in the last 10 years."

The story she pieces together from their answers is a typical one, particularly for distressed urban places. With the decline of the city, the funding base for the schools has diminished, the families in the neighborhood are struggling, and the school has been targeted again and again for improvement. The staff, which has had high turnover every year for the last 10, has tried one reform package after another. But test scores are still going down, and discipline incidents are on the rise. In fact, ever since the school implemented its new zero-tolerance policy, students' behavior seems to have gotten worse. Of course, it isn't clear if there's really an association; perhaps it's just a coincidence.

Whatever the actual relationship between the behavior policy and the incidences of misbehavior, Alverna finds the discipline issue quite troubling. Her intuitive sense of the matter is that the attitude of mistrust that the policy helps to sustain may be keeping teachers and students from forming meaningful relationships. She remembers Deb Meier's book, *In Schools We Trust,* and thinks that maybe with a small school and a new staff, something else besides "zero-tolerance" would be possible. Of course, she knows the school will need to have some sort of policy that's called "zero-tolerance," but it could be less extensive and certainly less punitive.

The Study Group.   At the January teachers' meeting, Alverna asks for volunteers to investigate discipline options. She's pleased when five teachers agree to form a group to study the issue. Two are new teachers who attended preparation programs that encouraged the use of "evidence-based" practices. The other three are "old-timers"—teachers with a long-term professional commitment to Langford.

Throughout the winter, the group meets once a week to discuss the insights offered by two books. Although both books seem to be well regarded, they present conflicting perspectives. Whereas one book focuses on a behavior modification approach with a proven track record, the other casts doubt on the ethics and ultimate effectiveness of that same approach. After arguing back and forth about which book makes the stronger case, the members of the group finally come to the conclusion that they really can't decide. In fact, with compelling evidence on both sides of the debate, they realize that evidence alone cannot be the basis for determining what to do.

During the spring months, the members of the group use a different method of investigation. Rather than reading about "what works" in a narrow sense, they decide to explore various broad conceptions of "the good school." As part of this investigation, they do some additional reading of published works. But the group actually devises another approach that turns out to be more illuminating. Inspired by the journal entry of one of the teachers, the group members decide they all will write about their views of the good school and share their writings with one another.

The activity supports a surprising conclusion. Although there are differences in their perspectives, with some teachers focusing a bit more on community than others and some emphasizing academics a bit more than others, the similarities are clear-cut. For all five teachers, care forms the centerpiece of the good school, and what the teachers mean by "care" has far more to do with nurture, trust, and responsibility than with rules, sanctions, and rewards. Their theory about what *should be* bears very little resemblance to what actually *is* going on at Langford.

The Consensus. Just before the end of the school year, the teachers in the study group ask Alverna if they can meet with the rest of the teaching staff to discuss what they've learned about school discipline. Alverna decides that the issue is sufficiently important to serve as the focus for the last professional development day of the year. She believes a full-day agenda is a good idea, particularly if the aim of the meeting is to arrive at a new behavior policy.

Alverna suggests that the study group members take the lead in organizing and facilitating the teachers' meeting, and she is pleasantly surprised by their approach. Rather than presenting the teachers with a draft policy or with evidence supporting one or another method of behavior management, as Alverna expected, they ask their colleagues to spend the morning writing about and then discussing the good school. This activity provides a basis for a more focused discussion of policy options in the afternoon.

Although there are some tense moments throughout the day as teachers explore the differences in their views of the good school, they seem to reach consensus by midafternoon. The themes of care, responsibility, trust, family spirit, and nurture are so prevalent in their written comments and discussion points that the wrong-headedness of the current "zero-tolerance" policy seems self-evident. When one of the study group members asks all of the teachers to give a thumbs-up or thumbs-down vote on the current policy, it fails overwhelmingly.

Although the meeting does not end with the adoption of a new policy, it does lead to agreement about the principles that should guide the development of a new policy. Those principles—things like, "Children's mistakes provide an opportunity for learning"—also turn out to have implications for practices beyond those used to improve students' behavior—instructional practices, grouping practices, parent involvement, and so on. The teachers realize there's more work to be done, and they're excited to find themselves at the beginning of a change process that feels right to them.

Debriefing

In this section of the chapter, stories about two schools show the importance of context and sense making to determinations about "what will work." In these stories, as in real life, such determinations primarily depend on how educators connect views about educational methods to wider views of the world; and they depend far less on evidence about the technical properties of particular interventions. "What works," turns out to be every bit as much a question about what we believe in, as it is a question about what we know. That's because we can't put our hearts into practices we don't believe in, even if those practices "work" for other educators or in other schools and communities. Fortunately, lots of different practices "work" when we devote our energies to using them well.

These insights shed light on the distinction between "best practices"—methods that purport to work effectively everywhere—and "betterment practices"—those we invent to work well in our own local circumstances. As discussion throughout this book has suggested, the search for "best practices" is the project of positivist social science with its mechanistic view of the social world and its restricted comprehension of progress. Although the term "betterment practices" is coined here as shorthand for the contrasting view, the ideas it embeds gain support from a variety of theories that challenge positivist assumptions. In fact, almost all of the postpositivist theories discussed in this book offer a version of betterment that acknowledges complexity and contingency, accepts and encourages diversity, and supports local engagement with the important issues confronting all human communities.

PARTING SHOTS

Just about every theory book in education—this one included—seems to present an array of conflicting ideas whose practical relevance to the day-to-day struggles of teachers and school leaders isn't immediately apparent. One temptation, as a result, is to dismiss all of the ideas summarily, concluding that theoretical work is generally too arcane and impractical to be of much use. Another temptation is to look for the single theory that seems to confirm our preexisting beliefs, using this one set of ideas as protection against other competing theoretical formulations. For example, the claim, "I'm a communitarian," sometimes keeps an educator from exploring feminism or critical theory or even from looking deeply into communitarianism. These reactions to theory, while understandable, seem unfortunate.

This book presents theory as a way to help educators—particularly those who want to provide leadership to schools—think about schooling and education. Moreover, its treatment of theory implies that a rich understanding of various descriptive and normative theories prepares educators to think more deeply and more fully about what they encounter in classrooms, schools, and communities. On these terms, the more theory an educator understands the better.

Of course, everyone knows of cases in which educators use the thinking process as a way to keep from having to take action. The phrase "paralysis by analysis" captures this idea. Far more often in schools, however, actions and reactions crowd out thinking. In fact, "shooting from the hip" is such a common occurrence that some writers on business leadership have actually codified it as the "ready, fire, aim" method.

But good leaders neither keep action at bay nor act rashly. Rather, they act with perspicacity, drawing on insights that come from their ongoing intellectual engagement with important ideas and their continual reflection about practical matters. In fact, for good leaders, the two types of thinking are mutually reinforcing to such an extent that they become indistinguishable. Everything these leaders read, every idea they encounter adds to their leadership toolkit. At the same time, wide reading and deep thinking rarely obscure their commitments. Instead, these practices—and the habits of mind these practices engender—help good leaders clarify their commitments, understand them more fully, and act on them with greater assurance. What some might criticize as the eclecticism of this approach, we defend as intellectual openness. Certainly among the good leaders we know, the combination of wide understanding and deep commitment contributes to purposeful action, sensitivity to context, and genuine humility in the face of a work that is at once daunting and transcendent.

References

Abalos, D. (1996). *Strategies of transformation toward a multicultural society: Fulfilling the story of democracy*. Westport, CT: Praeger.

Alaska Native Knowledge Network. (1998). *Alaska standards for culturally responsive schools*. Fairbanks, AK: University of Alaska. (ERIC Document Reproduction Service No. ED425035)

Althusser, L. (1969). *For Marx* (B. Brewster, Trans.). London: Allen Lane.

American Association of University Women Educational Foundation. (1993). *Hostile hallways: The AAUW survey on sexual harassment in America's schools*. Washington, DC: Author.

American Heritage Dictionary of the English Language. (2000). New York: Houghton Mifflin.

Anderson, G. L. (1998). Toward authentic participation: Deconstructing the discourses of participatory reforms in education. *American Educational Research Journal, 35*(4), 571–603.

Anderson, J. (1995). *Who's in charge? State differences in public school teachers' perceptions of their control over determining curriculum, texts, and course content*. Washington, DC: Office of Educational Research and Improvement. (ERIC Document Reproduction Service No. ED 387 860)

Anderson, R. S. (1962). *Japan: Three epochs of modern education*. Washington, DC: Department of Health, Education, and Welfare; Office of Education.

Anderson-Levitt, K. (Ed.). (2003). *Local meanings, global schooling: Anthropology and world culture theory*. New York: Palgrave Macmillan.

Angus, L. (2004). Globalization and educational change: Bringing about the reshaping and re-norming of practice. *Journal of Education Policy, 19*(1), 23–41.

Appiah, K. (1998). Foreword. In S. Sassen (Ed.), *Globalization and its discontents* (pp. xi–xv). New York: The New Press.

Apple, M. (1993). The politics of official knowledge: Does a national curriculum make sense? *Teachers College Record, 95*(2), 222–241.

Apple, M. (2000). *Official knowledge: Democratic education in a conservative age* (2nd ed.). New York: Routledge.

Argyris, C., Putman, R., & Smith, D. M. (1985). *Action science: Concepts, methods, and skills for research and intervention*. San Francisco: Jossey-Bass.

Argyris, C., & Schon, D. (1974). *Theory in practice: Increasing professional effectiveness.* San Francisco: Jossey-Bass.

Aronowitz, S. (1973). *False promises: The shaping of American working class consciousness.* New York: McGraw-Hill.

Aronowitz, S., & DiFazio, W. (1994). *The jobless future: Sci-tech and the dogma of work.* Minneapolis: University of Minnesota Press.

Arons, S. (1997). *Short route to chaos: Conscience, community, and the re-constitution of American schooling.* Amherst, MA: University of Massachusetts Press.

Ashcraft, K. (1998). I wouldn't say I'm a feminist, but ...: Organizational micropractice and gender identity. *Management Communication Quarterly, 11*(4), 587–597.

Astley, W. G. (1985). Organizational size and bureaucratic structure. *Organization Studies, 6*(3), 201–228.

Axline, V. M. (1964). *Dibs: In search of self; personality development in play therapy.* Boston, MA: Houghton Mifflin.

Ayalon, H., & Gamoran, A. (2000). Stratification in academic secondary programs and educational inequality: Comparison of Israel and the United States. *Comparative Education Review, 44,* 54–80.

Ayers, W. (1994). Can city schools be saved? *Educational Leadership, 51*(8), 60–63.

Badmington, N. (2003). Theorizing posthumanism. *Cultural Critique, 53,* 10–27.

Baker, R. S. (2001). The paradoxes of desegregation: Race, class, and education, 1935–1975. *American Journal of Education, 109*(3), 320–343.

Bass, B. M. (1990). *Bass and Stogdill's handbook of leadership: Theory, research, and managerial applications* (3rd ed.). New York: Free Press.

Bass, B. M., & Avolio, B. J. (Eds.). (1994). *Improving organizational effectiveness through transformational leadership.* Thousand Oaks, CA: Sage.

Bates, R. (2000). *How do local school managers adapt to an increasingly globalised environment?* [online]. Hindmarsh, Australia: Australian Principals Associations Professional Development Council. Retrieved December 20, 2005, from http://www.apapdc.edu.au/archive/ASPA/conference2000/papers/art_4_28.htm

Batioukova, Z. I., & Shaposhnikova, T. D. (Eds.). (1997). *Innovation in Russian schools* (M. Korolov, Trans.). Bloomington, IN: Phi Delta Kappa Educational Foundation.

Battista, M. (1999). The mathematical miseducation of America's youth: Ignoring research and scientific study in education. *Phi Delta Kappan, 80*(6), 424–433.

Baudrillard, J. (1983). *Simulations* (P. Foss, P. Paul, & P. Beitchman, Trans.). New York: Semiotext(e).

Bauman, Z. (1987). *Legislators and interpreters: On modernity, post-modernity, and intellectuals.* Ithaca, NY: Cornell University Press.

Bauman, Z. (1993). *Postmodern ethics.* London, England: Blackwell.

Bauman, Z. (1998). *Globalization: The human consequences.* New York: Columbia University Press.

Beaumont, C., & Pianca, E. (2000). *Historic neighborhood schools in the age of sprawl: Why Johnny can't walk to school.* Washington, DC: National Trust for Historic Preservation.

Belenky, M. F., Clinchy, N., Goldberger, N., & Tarule, J. (1986). *Women's ways of knowing: The development of self, voice, and mind.* New York: Basic Books.

Bell, D. (1973). *The coming of post-industrial society: A venture in social forecasting.* New York: Basic Books.

Bellah, R .N., Madsen, R., Sullivan, W .M., & Tipton, S. M. (1985). *Habits of the heart: Individualism and commitment in American life.* Berkeley, CA: University of California Press.

Bellamy, C. (2004). *State of the world's children 2004.* New York: United Nations Children's Fund.

Bendelow, M. (1983). Managerial women's approaches to organizational conflict: A qualitative study. *Dissertations Abstracts International, 44*(9), 2620-A.

Bender, T. (1978). *Community and social change in America*. New Brunswick, NJ: Rutgers University Press.

Bennett, M. J. (1986). A developmental approach to training for intercultural sensitivity. *International Journal of Intercultural Relations, 10*(2), 179–195.

Bennett, M. J. (1993). Towards ethnorelativism: A developmental model of intercultural sensitivity. In M. Paige (Ed.), *Education for the intercultural experience* (pp. 21–71). Yarmouth, ME: Intercultural Press.

Berger, P. L., & Luckmann, T. (1989). *The social construction of reality: A treatise in the sociology of knowledge*. New York: Doubleday.

Bergin, D, & Cooks, H. (2002). High school students of color talk about accusations of "acting white." *Urban Review, 34*(2), 113–134.

Berkin, C., & Norton, M. (1979). *Women of America: A history*. Boston: Houghton Mifflin.

Berliner, D. C., & Biddle, B. J. (1995). *The manufactured crisis: Myths, fraud, and the attack on America's public schools*. Redding, MA: Addison-Wesley.

Berman, J. (1982, March). *The managerial behavior of female high school principals: Implications for training*. Paper presented at the American Educational Research Association annual meeting, New York, NY.

Bernstein, R. (1990, July 28). On language: When parentheses are transgressive. *New York Times*, p. 16.

Bernstein, R. (2005, August 11). *Texas becomes nation's newest "majority-minority" state, census bureau announces*. Washington, DC: United States Bureau of Census. Retrieved October 22, 2005, from http://www.census.gov/Press-Release/www/releases/archives/population/005514.html.

Bertalanffy, L. v. (1968). *General system theory: Foundation, development, applications*. New York: G. Braziller.

Betton, K. (2004, September 23). Gullahs struggle to keep heritage and land. *blAcknews*. Retrieved September 12, 2005, from http://blackamericaweb.com/site.aspx/bawnews/gullah922

Bgoya, W. (2001). The effect of globalisation in Africa and the choice of language in publishing. *International Review of Education, 47*(3–4), 283–292.

Bickel, R., & Dufrene, R. (2001). Community, opportunity, and crime on school property: A quantitative case study. *Educational Foundations, 15*, 19–39.

Biklen, S. (1987). Women in American elementary school teaching: A case study. In P. Schmuck (Ed.), *Women educators: Employees of schools in western countries* (pp. 223–243). Albany: SUNY Press.

Blackmore, J. (1989). Changes from within: Feminist educators and administrative leadership. *Peabody Journal of Education, 66*(3), 19–40.

Blackmore, J. (1993). "In the shadow of men": The historical construction of educational administration as a masculinist enterprise. In J. Blackmore & J. Kenway (Eds.). *Gender matters in educational administration and policy: A feminist introduction* (pp. 27–45). Washington, DC: Falmer Press.

Blackmore, J. (1999). *Troubling women: Feminism, leadership, and educational change*. Buckingham, UK: Open University Press.

Blake, R. R., & Mouton, J. S. (1961). *Group dynamics: Key to decision making*, Houston: Gulf Publishing.

Blount, J. (1999). Turning out ladies: Elected women superintendents and the push for an appointive system, 1900–1935. In C. Brunner (Ed.), *Sacred dreams: Women and the superintendency* (pp. 9–18). Albany: SUNY Press.

Bolman, L. G., & Deal, T. E. (2003). *Reframing organizations: Artistry, choice, and leadership* (3rd ed.). San Francisco, CA: Jossey-Bass.

Bourdieu, P., & Passeron, J. (1990). *Reproduction in education, society, and culture*. (R. Nice, Trans.). Newbury Park, CA: Sage.

Bowen, S., & Wyatt, N. (1993). *Transforming visions: Feminist critiques in communications studies.* Cresskill, NJ: Hampton Press.

Bowles, S., & Gintis, H. (1976). *Schooling in capitalist America: Educational reform and the contradictions of economic life.* New York: Basic Books.

Bracey, G. W. (2002). *The war against America's public schools: Privatizing schools, commercializing education.* Boston: Allyn & Bacon.

Brady, J. (1995). *Schooling young children: A feminist pedagogy of liberatory learning.* Albany, NY: State University of New York Press.

Brint, S.G. (1998). *Schools and societies.* Thousand Oaks, CA: Pine Forge Press.

Brown, M. C., & Land, R. E. (2005). *The politics of curricular change: Race, hegemony, and power in education.* New York: P. Lang.

Brown, R. (1991). *Schools of thought: How the politics of literacy shape thinking in the classroom.* San Francisco, CA: Jossey-Bass.

Brown, R. H. (1989). *Social science as civic discourse: Essays on the invention, legitimation, and uses of social theory.* Chicago: University of Chicago Press.

Bruner, J. (1996). *The culture of education.* Cambridge, MA: Harvard University Press.

Brunner, C. (1994, April). *Emancipatory research: Support for women's access to power.* (Draft). Paper presented at the American Association of School Administrators Annual Meeting, New Orleans, LA.

Buber, M. (1949). *Paths in utopia* (R. F .C. Hull, Trans.) Boston: Beacon Press.

Bullis, C., & Stout, K. R. (2000). Organizational socialization: A feminist standpoint perspective. In P. M. Buzzanell (Ed.), *Rethinking organizational and managerial communication from feminist perspectives* (pp. 47–75). Thousand Oaks, CA: Sage.

Burbules, N. C., & Callister, T. A. (2000). Universities in transition: The promise and the challenge of new technologies. *Teachers College Record, 102*(2), 271–293.

Burns, J. M. (1978). *Leadership.* New York: Harper & Row.

Butler, J. (1990). *Gender trouble: Feminism and the subversion of identity.* New York: Routledge.

Callahan, R. (1962). *Education and the cult of efficiency: A study of the social forces that have shaped the administration of the public schools.* Chicago: University of Chicago Press.

Cambridge, J., & Thompson, J. (2004). Internationalism and globalization as contexts for international education. *Compare A Journal of Comparative Education, 34*(2), 161–175.

Canter, L., & Canter, M. (1992). *Assertive discipline: Positive behavior management for today's classroom.* Santa Monica, CA: Lee Canter and Associates.

Cantor, J., Kester, D., & Miller, A. (1997, August). *Amazing results! Teacher expectations and student achievement (TESA) follow-up survey of TESA-trained teachers in 45 states and the District of Columbia.* Paper presented at the Annual Meeting of the California Educational Research Association, Santa Barbara, CA. (ERIC Document Reproduction Service No. ED 443 801)

Capper, C. (1993). Educational administration in a pluralistic society: A multiparadigm approach. In C. Capper (Ed.), *Educational administration in a pluralistic society* (pp. 7–35). Albany, NY: SUNY Press.

Castermans, D., Wilquet, V., Steyaert, J., van de Ven, W., Fryns, J., & Devriendt, K. (2004). Chromosomal anomalies in individuals with autism: A strategy towards the identification of genes involved in autism. *Autism: The International Journal of Research and Practice, 8*(2), 141–161.

Chabbott, C., & Emerson, E. (Eds.). (2003). *Understanding others, educating ourselves: Getting more from international comparative studies in education.* Washington, DC: Board on International Comparative Studies in Education (BICSE), National Academy of Sciences.

Charters, W., & Jovick, T. (1981). The gender of principals and principal/teacher relations in elementary schools. In P. A. Schmuck, W. W. Charters, Jr., & R. O. Carlson (Eds.), *Educational policy and management: Sex differentials* (pp. 307–331). New York: Academic Press.

Chavéz Chavéz, R., & O'Donnell, J. (1998). *Speaking the unpleasant: The politics of [non] engagement in the multicultural education terrain.* Albany: State University of New York Press.

Chicoine, D. (2004). Ignoring the obvious: A constructivist critique of a traditional teacher education program. *Educational Studies Journal of the American Educational Studies Association, 36*(3), 245–263.

Christy, W. K., & McNeal, L. (1999, November). Implications of legislative policy development for public school districts, *Annual Meeting of the Southern Regional Council on Educational Administration.* Charlotte, NC. (ERIC Document Reproduction Service No. ED481628)

Chubb, J. E., & Moe, T. M. (1990). *Politics, markets, and America's schools.* Washington, DC: Brookings Institution.

Clarke, M. M., Madaus, G. F., Horn, C. L., & Ramos, M. A. (2000). Retrospective on educational testing and assessment in the 20th century. *Journal of Curriculum Studies, 32*(2), 159–181.

Clarke, T. (2001). *The emergence of corporate governance and what to do about it* [Electronic excerpt]. Retrieved July 1, 2001, from the International Forum on Globalization's web page: http://www.ifg.org/corprule.html

Clinton, W. (1999, December). *Clinton addresses the WTO.* Retrieved July 1, 2001, from the Public Broadcasting System Newshour web site: http://www.pbs.org/ newshour/bb/ international/wto/clinton_wto_12-1.html

Cohen, C. (1994). *Administering education in Namibia: The colonial period to the present.* Windhoek, Namibia: Namibian Scientific Society.

Cohen, D. (1988). *Teaching practice: Plus ça change.* East Lansing, MI: National Center for Research on Teacher Education.

Coleman, J. S., & Hoffer, T. (1987). *Public and private high schools: The impact of communities.* New York: Basic Books.

Conant, J. (1959). *The American high school today.* New York: McGraw-Hill.

Conger, J. A., & Kanungo, R. (1996). *Charismatic leadership in organizations.* Thousand Oaks, CA: Sage.

Connell, R. (1993). *Schools and social justice.* Philadelphia: Temple University Press.

Conway, J. A., & Calzi, F. (1996). The dark side of shared decision making. *Educational Leadership, 53*(4), 45–49.

Cooper, H. M., & Good, T. L. (1983). *Pygmalion grows up: Studies in the expectation communication process.* New York: Longman.

Cornell, D. (1991). *Beyond accommodation : Ethical feminism, deconstruction, and the law.* New York: Routledge.

Cornell, D. (1993). *Transformations.* New York: Routledge.

Costas, E. F. (1996). *The left-handed: Their "sinister" history.*(ERIC Document Reproduction Service No. ED 399519)

Counts, G. (1978). *Dare the school build a new social order?* Carbondale, IL: Southern Illinois Press. (Original work published 1932)

Cremin, L. (1957). *The republic and the school: Horace Mann on the education of free men.* New York: Teachers College Press.

Cremin, L. (1962). *The transformation of the school: Progressivism in American education, 1876–1957.* New York: Knopf.

Cremin, L. A. (1980). *American education, the national experience, 1783–1876.* New York: Harper & Row.

Cuban, L. (1990). Reforming again, again, and again. *Educational Researcher, 19*(1), 3–13.

Cuban, L. (1993). *How teachers taught: Constancy and change in American classrooms, 1890–1990* (2nd ed.). New York: Teachers College Press.

Cuban, L. (2001a). *How can I fix it? Finding solutions and managing dilemmas, an educator's road map.* New York: Teachers College Press.

Cuban, L. (2001b). *Leadership for student learning: Urban school leadership—different in kind and degree*. Washington, DC: Institute for Educational Leadership. (ERIC Document Reproduction Service No. ED459300)

Curry, B. (2000). *Women in power: Pathways to leadership in education*. New York: Teachers College Press.

Darling-Hammond, L. (1997). *The right to learn: A blueprint for creating schools that work*. San Francisco: Jossey-Bass.

Davis, K., & Moore, W. (1960). *Some principles of stratification*. Indianapolis: Bobbs-Merrill.

Deal, T. E., & Peterson, K. D. (1999). *Shaping school culture*. San Francisco: Jossey-Bass.

Dee, T. S. (2001). *Teachers, race and student achievement in a randomized experiment* (NBER Working Paper). Cambridge, MA: National Bureau of Economic Research. (ERIC Document Reproduction Service No. ED 464172)

Delannoy, F. (2000). *Education reforms in Chile: 1990–1998: A lesson in pragmatism*. (Country Studies Education Reform and Management Publication Series. Vol. 1, No. 1.) Washington, DC: World Bank.

Derrida, J. (1974). *Of grammatology*. (G. C. Spivak, Trans.). Baltimore, MD: The Johns Hopkins University Press.

Derrida, J. (1978). *Writing and difference* (A. Bass, Trans.). Chicago: University of Chicago Press.

DeYoung, A. (1995). *The life and death of a rural American high school: Farewell, Little Kanawha*. New York: Garland.

DeYoung, A., & Theobald, P. (1991). Community schools in the national context: The social and cultural impact of educational reform movements on American rural schools. *Journal of Research in Rural Education, 7*(3), 3–14.

Dickens, C. (1907). *Hard times*. New York: E. P. Dutton and Co. (Original work published 1854)

DiMaggio, P. J., & Powell, W. W. (1983). The iron cage revised: Institutional isomorphism and collective rationality in organizational fields. *American Sociological Review, 48*, 147–160.

Doll, W .E. (1993). Curriculum possibilities in a "post-"future. *Journal of Curriculum and Supervision, 8*(4), 277–292.

Dorn, S. (1998). The political legacy of school accountability systems. *Education Policy Analysis Archives, 6*(1). Retrieved November 15, 2005, from http://epaa.asu.edu/epaa/v6n1.html

Doyle, Denis P. (1997). Education and character: A conservative view. *Phi Delta Kappan, 78*(6), 440–443.

du Gay, P. (2000). *In praise of bureaucracy: Weber, organization, ethics*. Thousand Oaks, CA: Sage.

Dudley-Marling, C. (2004). The social construction of learning disabilities. *Journal of Learning Disabilities, 37*(6), 482–489.

Duncan, C. (1996). Understanding persistent poverty: Social class contexts in rural communities. *Rural Sociology, 61*(1), 103–124.

Dunklee, D. R. (2000). *If you want to lead, not just manage: A primer for principals*. Thousand Oaks, CA: Corwin Press.

Dyer, R. (1997). *White*. New York: Routledge.

Eagleton, T. (1991). *Ideology: An introduction*. London: Verso.

Educational Commission of the States. (2005). *State of the state* (State policy database). Retrieved September 17, 2005 from http://www.ecs.org/ecsmain.asp?page=/html/issuesK12.asp

Egan, K. (2003). Start with what the student knows or with what the student can imagine? *Phi Delta Kappan, 84*(6), 443–445.

Elliott, B., & MacLennan, D. (1994). Education, modernity, and neo-conservative school reform in Canada, Britain, and the U.S. *British Journal of Sociology of Education, 15*(2), 165–185.

Elsbree, W. (1939). *The America teacher: Evolution of a profession in a democracy*. New York: American Book Company.

Epstein, D., & Johnson, R. (1998). *Schooling sexualities*. Buckingham, England: Open University Press.

Everhart, R. B. E. (1982). *The public school monopoly: A critical analysis of education and the state in American society*. Cambridge, MA: Ballinger.

Executive Office of the President. (1990). *National goals for education*. Washington, DC: The White House. (ERIC Document Reproduction Service No. ED319143)

Fairholm, G., & Fairholm, B. (1984). Fifteen power tactics principals can use to improve management effectiveness. *NASSP Bulletin, 68*(142), 68–75.

Fallows, J. (1987). Gradgrind's heirs: Despite what the U.S. Department of Education says, you would not want your kids to go to a Japanese secondary school. *Atlantic Monthly, 259*(3), 16–24.

Fanning, J. (1995). *Rural school consolidation and student learning* (ERIC Digest). Charleston, WV: ERIC Clearinghouse on Rural Education and Small Schools. (ERIC Document Reproduction Service No. ED 384484)

Ferguson, K. (1984). *The feminist case against bureaucracy*. Philadelphia: Temple University Press.

Fiedler, F. E., & Chemers, M. M. (1984). *Improved leadership effectiveness: The leader match concept* (2nd ed.). New York: Wiley.

Fiscus, J. W. (2000). Zero tolerance: Effective policy or display of administrative machismo? *The Safety Zone, 2*(1), 1–2.

Fontaine, C. (1998). Democracy, schools, and communities. In V. Perrone (Ed.), *Toward place and community* (pp. 22–23). Cambridge, MA: Graduate School of Education, Harvard University. (ERIC Document Reproduction Service No. ED444791)

Formisano, J. (1987, April). *How women principals respond to conflict: A qualitative study*. Paper presented at the American Educational Research Association annual meeting, Washington, DC.

Forrester, J. W. (1975). *Collected papers*. Cambridge, MA: Wright-Allen Press.

Forsyth, D., & Forsyth, N. (1984, April). *Subordinates' reactions to female leaders*. Paper presented at the Eastern Psychological Association Annual Meeting, Baltimore, MD.

Foster, S., & Nicholls, J. (2003, April). *Portrayal of America's role during World War II: An analysis of school textbooks from England, Japan, Sweden, and the USA*. Paper presented at the Annual Meeting of the American Educational Research Association, Chicago, IL.

Foster, W. (2004). The decline of the local: A challenge to educational leadership. *Educational Administration Quarterly, 40*(2), 176–191.

Foucault, M. (1971). *The order of things: An archeology of the human sciences*. New York: Pantheon Books.

Foucault, M. (1972). *The archaeology of knowledge* (A. M. S. Smith, Trans.). New York: Pantheon Books.

Foucault, M. (1977). *Discipline and punish: The birth of the prison*. London: Penguin.

Foucault, M. (1980). Two lectures. In C. Gordon (Ed.), *Power/knowledge: Selected interviews and other writings 1972–1977* (pp. 78–108). New York: Pantheon Books

Foucault, M. (1990). *The history of sexuality* (R. Hurley, Trans.). New York: Vintage Books.

Fraser, J. (1997). *Reading, writing, and justice: School reform as if democracy matters*. Albany: SUNY Press.

Freire, P. (1970). *Pedagogy of the oppressed.* (M. B. Ramos, Trans.). New York: Penguin Books.

Freire, P. (1973). *Education for critical consciousness*. New York: Seabury Press.

Frost, R. (1921). The road not taken. In *Mountain interval* (p. 9). New York: Henry Holt.

Fullan, M. (2001). *The new meaning of educational change* (3rd ed.). New York: Teachers College Press.

Fullan, M., & Watson, N. (2000). School-based management: Reconceptualizing to improve learning outcomes. *School Effectiveness and School Improvement. 11*(4), 453–473.

Futrell, M. (1999). Recruiting minority teachers. *Educational Leadership, 56*(8), 30–33.

Gamoran, A. (1996). Curriculum standardization and equality of opportunity in Scottish secondary education, 1984–1990. *Sociology of Education, 29*, 1–21.

Garfinkel, H. (1967). *Studies in ethnomethodology.* Englewood Cliffs, NJ: Prentice-Hall.

Gatto, J. (1990). *Dumbing us down.* Philadelphia: New Society Publishers.

Gatto, J. T. (2002). *Dumbing us down: The hidden curriculum of compulsory schooling* (2nd ed.). Gabriola Island, BC: New Society Publishers.

Gauri, V. (1998). *School choice in Chile: Two decades of educational reform.* Pittsburgh, PA: University of Pittsburgh Press.

Gaventa, J. (1980). *Power and powerlessness: Quiescence and rebellion in an Appalachian valley.* Urbana: University of Illinois Press.

Gay, Lesbian, and Straight Education Network. (2003). *The 2003 national school climate survey.* New York: Author.

Geertz, C. (1973). *The interpretation of cultures: Selected essays.* New York: Basic Books.

Gergen, K .J. (1991). *The saturated self: Dilemmas of identity in contemporary life.* New York: Basic Books.

Gergen, K. J., & Thackenkery, T. J. (2004). Organization science as social construction: Postmodern potentials. *Journal of Applied Behavioral Science, 40*(2), 228–249.

Gibbons, M. (2002). *The self-directed learning handbook: Challenging adolescent students to excel.* San Francisco: Jossey-Bass.

Gibson, C., & Jung, K. (2002). *Historical census statistics on population totals by race, 1790 to 1990, and by Hispanic origin, 1970 to 1990, for the United States, regions, divisions, and states* (Working Paper series no. 56). Washington, DC: Population Division, United States Bureau of Census. Retrieved October 22, 2005, from http://www.census.gov/population/www/documentation/twps0056.html

Gilbert, A. (1978). Marx on internationalism and war. *Philosophy and Public Affairs, 7*(4), 346–369.

Gilbertson, M. (1981). The influence of gender on the verbal interactions among principals and staff members: An exploratory study. In P. Schmuck, W. W. Charters, Jr., & R. O. Carlson (Eds.) *Educational policy and management: Sex differentials* (pp. 297–306). New York: Academic Press.

Gilligan, C. (1993). *In a different voice.* Cambridge, MA: Harvard University Press.

Giroux, H. (1983a). *Theory and resistance in education: A pedagogy for the opposition.* South Hadley, MA: Bergin & Garvey.

Giroux, H. A. (1983b). *Theory and resistance in education: A pedagogy for the opposition.* South Hadley, MA: Bergin & Garvey.

Giroux, H. A. (1988a). *Teachers as intellectuals: Toward a critical pedagogy of learning.* South Hadley, MA: Bergin & Garvey.

Giroux, H. A. (1988b). Postmodernism and the discourse of educational criticism. *Journal of Education, 170*(3), 5–30.

Giroux, H. A. (1991). Series introduction: Toward a discourse of leadership and radical democracy. In S. Maxcy (Ed.), *Educational leadership: A critical pragmatic perspective* (pp. ix–xiii). New York: Bergin & Garvey.

Giroux, H. A. (2000). *Stealing innocence: Youth, corporate power, and the politics of culture.* New York: St. Martin's Press.

Glass, T., Bjork, L., & Brunner, C. (2000). *The study of the American school superintendency, 2000: A look at the superintendent of education of the new millennium.* Arlington, VA: American Association of School Administrators.

Gleick, J. (1987). *Chaos: Making a new science.* New York: Penguin.

Glickman, C. D. (1981). *Developmental supervision: Alternative practices for helping teachers improve instruction.* Alexandria, VA: Association for Supervision and Curriculum Development.

Goals 2000: Educate America Act of 1993, 20 U.S.C, § 5801 et seq. (USC, 1994, Supplement 1). (ERIC Document Reproduction Service No. ED369149)

Gooding, R., & Wagner, J. (1985). A meta-analytic review of the relationship between size and performance: The productivity and efficiency of organizations and their subunits. *Administrative Science Quarterly, 30,* 462–481.

Goodson, F. T. (1994). Culture wars and the rules of the English classroom. *The English Journal, (83)*5, 21–24.

Gordon, M. (1964). *Assimilation in American life: The role of race, religion, and national origins.* New York: Oxford University Press.

Gove, P. (Ed.). (1976). *Websters Third New International Dictionary.* Springfield, MA: G. & C. Merriam Co.

Gramsci, A. (1971). *Selections from the prison notebooks of Antonio Gramsci.* (Q. Hoare & G. N. Smith, Trans.). London: Lawrence & Wishart.

Gray, J. (1992). *Men are from Mars, women are from Venus: A practical guide for improving communication and getting what you want in your relationships.* New York: HarperCollins.

Greenleaf, R. K. (1977). *Servant leadership: A journey into the nature of legitimate power and greatness.* New York: Paulist Press.

Grogan, M. (1996). *Voices of women aspiring to the superintendency.* Albany, NY: SUNY Press.

Grogan, M. (2000). Laying the groundwork for a reconception of the superintendency from feminist postmodern perspectives. *Educational Administration Quarterly, 36*(1), 117–142.

Gross, N., & Trask, A. (1964). *Men and women as elementary school principals.* Cambridge, MA: Graduate School of Education, Harvard University. (ERIC Document Reproduction Service No. ED002949)

Grossman, S., & Williston, J. (2002). "I have a voice:" An analysis of a constructivist early childhood graduate program. Teaching Strategies. *Childhood Education, 78*(4), 248–250.

Gruenewald, D. A. (2003). The best of both worlds: A critical pedagogy of place. *Educational Researcher, 32*(4), 3–12.

Gulick, L. (1992). Notes on the theory of organization. In J. M. Shafritz & A. C. Hyde (Eds.), *Classics of public administration* (3rd ed., pp. 79–87). Pacific Grove: Brooks/Cole. (Original work published 1937)

Gutek, G. (1988). *Philosophical and ideological perspectives on education.* Englewood Cliffs, NJ: Prentice-Hall.

Haberman, M. (1995). *Star teachers of children in poverty.* West Lafayette, IN: Kappa Delta Pi.

Haberman, M. (2000). Urban schools: Day camps or custodial centers? *Phi Delta Kappan, 82*(3), 203–208.

Haberman, M. (2003). *Who benefits from failing urban school districts? An essay on equity and justice for diverse children in urban poverty.* (ERIC Document Reproduction Service No. ED 477538)

Habermas, J. (1987). Lifeworld and system: A critique of functionalist reason (vol. 2). *The Theory of communicative action* (T. McCarthy, Trans.). Boston: Beacon Press.

Habermas, J. (2001). *The postnational constellation: Political essays.* Cambridge, England: Polity Press.

Hall, E. T. (1963). *The silent language.* Greenwich, CT: Fawcett Publications.

Hall, E. T. (1976). *Beyond culture.* Garden City, NY: Anchor Press.

Hall, E. T. (1984). *The dance of life: The other dimension of time.* Garden City, NY: Anchor Press/Doubleday.

Hall, G. E., & Hord, S. M (2001). *Implementing change: Patterns, principles, and potholes.* Boston, MA: Allyn and Bacon.

Halperin, D. M. (1995). *Saint Foucault: Towards a gay hagiography*. New York: Oxford University Press.

Han, D. (2001). *The unknown cultural revolution: Educational reforms and their impact on China's rural development*. New York: Garland.

Handel, M. J. (Ed.). (2003). *The sociology of organizations: Classic, contemporary, and critical readings*. Thousand Oaks, CA: Sage.

Hanushek, E., & Raymond, M. (2002). *Sorting out accountability systems*. Stanford, CA: Hoover Institution.

Harding, S. (1991). *Whose science? Whose knowledge?: Thinking from women's lives*. Ithaca, NY: Cornell UP.

Harpalani, V. (2002). What does "acting white" really mean? Racial identity formation and academic achievement among black youth. *Perspectives on Urban Education, 1*(1). Retrieved April 16, 2006 from http://www.urbanedjournal.org/archive/Issue%201/commentaries/comment0001.html

Harrison, B., & Bluestone, B. (1988). *The great U-turn*. New York: Basic Books.

Harrod, J., & O'Brien, R. (Eds.). (2002). *Global unions? Theory and strategies of organized labour in the global political economy*. London: Routledge.

Harvey, D. (1989). *The condition of postmodernity: An enquiry into the origins of cultural change*. Cambridge, MA: Blackwell.

Harvey, M. J. (1991, September). *Strategy for the new principal: Negotiating the culture of the school*. Paper presented at the annual meeting of the Australian Council for Educational Administration, Gold Coast, Queensland, Australia. (ERIC Document Reproduction Service No. ED 359 670)

Hassard, J. (1993). *Sociology and organization theory: Positivism, paradigms, and postmodernity*. New York: Cambridge University Press.

Hauser, M. E., & Jipson, J. A. (Eds.) (1998). *Intersections: Feminisms/early childhoods*. New York: Peter Lang.

Hawkins, S. R., Campanaro, A., Pitts, T. B., & Steiner, H. (2002). Weapons in an affluent suburban school. *Journal of School Violence, 1*(1), 53–65.

Heilbroner, R., & Thurow, L. (1985). *Understanding macroeconomics* (8th ed.). Englewood Cliffs, NJ: Prentice-Hall.

Hemphill, J., Griffiths, D., & Frederiksen, N. (1962). *Administrative performance and personality*. New York: Teachers College Press.

Heraclitus. (1969). *Fragments* (G. Patrick, Trans.). Chicago: Argonaut. (Related materials available World Wide Web: http://plato.evansville.edu/public/burnet/ch3a.htm).

Hersey, P., & Blanchard, K. H. (1982). *Management of organizational behavior: Utilizing human resources* (4th ed.). Englewood Cliffs, NJ: Prentice-Hall.

Hill, M., & Ragland, J. (1995). *Women as educational leaders: Opening windows, pushing ceilings*. Thousand Oaks, CA: Corwin Press.

Hines, V., & Grobman, H. (1956). The weaker sex is losing out. *School Board Journal, 132*, 100–102.

Hing, B. (1997). *To be an American: Cultural pluralism and the rhetoric of assimilation*. New York: New York University Press.

Hobbs, F., & Stoops, N. (2002). *Demographic trends in the 20th century census* (2000 special reports, censr-4). Washington, DC: United States Census Bureau, United States Department of Commerce.

Hobsbawm, E. (1962). *The age of revolution, 1789–1848*. Cleveland, OH: World Publishing Company.

Hobsbawm, E. (1990). *Nations and nationalism since 1780: Programme, myth, reality*. New York: Cambridge University Press.

Hobsbawm, E. (1992). *Nations and nationalism since 1780: Programme, myth, reality* (2nd ed.). New York: Cambridge University Press.

Hofstede, G. (1986). Cultural differences in teaching and learning. *International Journal of Intercultural Relations, 10*(3), 301–320.

Hofstede, G. (1997). *Cultures and organizations: Software of the mind.* New York: McGraw-Hill.

Hofstede, G., & Bond, M. H. (1988). Confucius & economic growth: New trends in culture's consequences. *Organizational Dynamics, 16*(4), 4–21.

Hollingsworth, S. (1992, April). *Relational knowing, "gendered experience," and teaching urban schools.* Paper presented at the annual meeting of the American Educational Research Association Special Interest Group: Research on Women and Education.

Holmes, M., & Weiss, B. (1995). *Lives of women public schoolteachers: Scenes from American educational history.* New York: Garland.

hooks, b. (1994.) *Teaching to transgress: Education as the practice of freedom.* New York: Routledge.

hooks, b. (1996). *Bone black: Memories of girlhood.* New York: Henry Holt.

Hoover-Dempsey, K. V., Bassler, O. C., & Burow, R. (1995). Parents' reported involvement in students' homework: Strategies and practices. *The Elementary School Journal, 95*(5), 435–450.

Hord, S. M. (1997). *Professional learning communities: Communities of continuous inquiry and improvement.* Austin, TX: Southwest Educational Development Laboratory. (ERIC Document Reproduction Service No. ED 410 659)

Hord, S. M. (1998). Creating a professional learning community: Cottonwood Creek School. *Issues about Change, 6*(2), 1–8.

Horvat, E. M., Weininger, E. B., & Lareau, A. (2003). From social ties to social capital: Class differences in the relations between schools and parent networks. *American Educational Research Journal, 40*(2), 319–351.

House, R. J., Spangler, W. D., & Woycke, J. (1991). Personality and charisma in the US presidency: A psychological theory of leadership effectiveness. *Administrative Science Quarterly, 36,* 364–396.

Houston, J. (Ed.). (2001). *Thesaurus of ERIC descriptors* (14th ed.). Phoenix, AZ: Oryx Press. ("Critical Theory" retrieved December 15, 2005, from *Thesaurus* search at http://www.eric.ed.gov/)

Howard, G. (1999). *We can't teach what we don't know: White teachers, multiracial schools.* New York: Teachers College Press.

Howley, A. A., Pendarvis, E., & Woodrum, A. (2004). *The rural school principalship: Promises and challenges.* Charleston, WV: AEL, Inc.

Howley, A. & Spatig, L. (1998). When theory bumps into reality: The form and function of the popular culture of teaching. In T. Daspit & J. Weaver (Eds.), *Popular culture and critical pedagogy: Reading, constructing, connecting* (pp. 139–159). New York: Garland.

Howley, C. (1996a). Compounding disadvantage: The effects of school and district size on student achievement in West Virginia. *Journal of Research in Rural Education, 12*(1), 25–32.

Howley, C. (1996b). Sizing up schooling: A West Virginia analysis and critique. *Dissertation abstracts International(A), 57*(3), 940. (University Microfilms No. AAT9622575).

Howley, C., & Bickel, R. (2002). The influence of scale: Small schools make a big difference for children from poor families. *American School Board Journal, 189*(3), 28–30.

Howley, C., Harmon, H., & Carter, C. (1998, March). *Rural education as a framework for critiquing globalization; or, if you think globally, can you educate locally.* Paper presented at the the annual meeting of the American Educational Research Association, San Diego, CA.

Howley, C. B., & Howley, A. A. (2004, September 24). School size and the influence of socioeconomic status on student achievement: Confronting the threat of size bias in national data sets. *Education Policy Analysis Archives, 12*(52). Retrieved September 9, 2005 from http://epaa.asu.edu/epaa/v12n52/

Howley, C., Howley, A., & Pendarvis, E. (1995). *Out of our minds: Anti-intellectualism and talent development in American schooling.* New York: Teachers College Press.

Howley, C. B., Howley, A. A., & Shamblen, S. (2001). Riding the school bus: A comparison of the rural and suburban experience in five states. *Journal of Research in Rural Education, 17*(1), 1–22.

Hoy, W. K., & Miskel, C. G. (2001). *Educational administration: Theory, research, and practice* (6th ed.). New York: McGraw-Hill.

Hoyle, J., & Skrla, L. (1999). The politics of superintendent evaluation. *Journal of Personnel Evaluation in Education, 13*(4), 405–419.

Hudson, J., & Rea, D. (1996, September). *Teacher's perceptions of women in the principalship: A current perspective.* Paper presented at the Women in Educational Leadership annual conference, Lincoln, NE.

Hudson, M. J., & Holmes, B. J. (1994). Missing teachers, impaired communities: The unanticipated consequences of Brown v. Board of Education on the African American teaching force at the precollegiate level. *Journal of Negro Education, 63*(3), 388–393.

Hughes, L., & Robertson, T. (1980). Principals and the management of conflict. *Planning and Changing, 11*(1), 3–16.

Human Rights Watch. (2001). *Hatred in the hallways: Violence and discrimination against lesbian, gay, bisexual and transgender students in U.S. schools.* New York: Author.

Hunter, M. (1982). *Mastery teaching.* El Segundo, CA: TIP Publications.

Hunter, W., & Benson, G. (1997). Arrows in time: The misapplication of chaos theory to education. *Journal of Curriculum Studies, 29*(1), 87–100.

Hurty, K. (1995). Women principals: Leading with power. In D. Dunlap & P. Schmuck (Eds.), *Women leading in education* (pp. 380–406). Albany: SUNY Press.

Husen, T. (1985). The school in the achievement-oriented society: Crisis and reform. *Phi Delta Kappan, 66*(6), 398–402.

Hutchison, D. (2004). *A natural history of place in education.* NY: Teachers College Press.

Iedema, R. (2003). *Discourses of post-bureaucratic organization.* Philadelphia: John Benjamins Publishing Company.

Illich, I. (1971). *Deschooling society.* New York: Harper & Row.

Interstate School Leaders Licensure Consortium. (1996). *Standards for school leaders.* Denver, CO: Council of Chief State School Officers. Retrieved October 18, 2005, from http://www.ccsso.org/content/pdfs/isllcstd.pdf

Irby, B., & Brown, G. (1995, April). *Constructing a feminist inclusive theory of leadership.* Paper presented at the American Educational Research Association annual conference, San Francisco, CA.

Jackson, S., & Solis, J. (1995). *Beyond comfort zones in multiculturalism: Confronting the politics of privilege.* Westport, CT: Bergin & Garvey.

Jacobs, J. (1994). *Systems of survival: A dialogue on the moral foundations of politics and commerce.* New York: Vintage Books.

Jacobs, W. R. (2002). Learning and living difference that makes a difference: Postmodern theory and multicultural education. *Multicultural Education, 9*(4), 2–10.

Jameson, F. (1991). *Postmodernism, or, the cultural logic of late capitalism.* Durham, NC: Duke University Press.

Jaycox, R. R. (2004). *Redefining "school": A case study of an internet charter school* (DAI-A 65/09, p. 3265). Unpublished doctoral dissertation, Ohio University, Athens, OH.

Jennings, N. (2004). Standards and local curriculum: A zero-sum game? *Journal of Research in Rural Education, 16*(3), 193–201. Retrieved December 19, 2005, from: http://www.acclaim-math.org/docs/jrre_archives/v16,n3,p193–201,Jennings.pdf

Jollife, D. (2002). Rural poverty rate stayed under 15 percent in 1999. *Rural America, 16*(4), 39–41.

Jones, P. W. (1998). Globalisation and internationalism: Democratic Prospects for world education. *Comparative Education, 34*(2), 143–155.

Kalbacher, J., & DeAre, D. (1988). *Rural and rural farm population, 1987* (Current Population Reports series P-27, no. 61). Washington, DC: Economic Research Service, United States Department of Agriculture. (ERIC Document Reproduction Service No. ED301398)

Kannapel, P. J., Aagaard, L., Coe, P., & Reeves, C. A. (2000). *Elementary change: Moving toward systemic school reform in rural Kentucky.* Charleston, WV: AEL, Inc.

Katz, C. (1997). Private property versus markets: Democratic and communitarian critiques of capitalism. *The American Political Science Review, 91*(2), 277–289.

Katz, M. B. (1968). *The irony of early school reform: Educational innovation in mid-nineteenth century Massachusetts.* Cambridge, MA: Harvard University Press.

Katz, M. B. (1987). *Reconstructing American education.* Cambridge, MA: Harvard University Press.

Katz, M. B. (2001). *The irony of early school reform: Educational innovation in mid-nineteenth century Massachusetts* (Reissued edition). New York: Teachers College Press.

Kaufman, R. (1995). *Mapping educational success: Strategic thinking and planning for school administrators* (rev. ed.). Thousand Oaks, CA: Corwin Press.

Kellert, S. (1993). *In the wake of chaos: Unpredictable order in dynamical systems.* Chicago: University of Chicago Press.

Kemmis, D. (1990). *Community and the politics of place.* Norman, OK: University of Oklahoma Press.

Kemper, E. A., & Teddlie, C. (2000). Mandated site-based management in Texas: Exploring implementation in urban high schools. *Teaching and Change, 7*(2), 172–200.

Kentucky Department of Education. (2004). *Kentucky's learning goals and academic expectations.* Frankfort, KY: Author.

Kerckhoff, A. C. (1986). Effects of ability grouping. *American Sociological Review, 1,* 842–858.

King, S. (1993). The limited presence of African-American teachers. *Review of Educational Research, 63*(2), 115–149.

Kliebard, H. M. (2002). *Changing course: American curriculum reform in the 20th century.* New York: Teachers College Press.

Kluckhohn, C. (1949). *Mirror for man: The relation of anthropology to modern life.* New York: Whittlesey House.

Kochan, F. (2002). Hope and possibility: Advancing an argument for a Habermasian perspective in educational administration. *Studies in Philosophy and Education, 21,* 137–155.

Kohn, A. (1993). *Punished by rewards: The trouble with gold stars, incentive plans, A's, praise, and other bribes.* Boston: Houghton Mifflin.

Koll, P., Robertson, P., Lampe, S., & Hegedus, D. (1996). The practical side of research: Studying administrative leadership. *NASSP Bulletin, 80*(578), 102–109.

Korten, D. C. (1998). *Globalizing civil society: Reclaiming our right to power.* New York: Seven Stories Press.

Kozol, J. (1991). *Savage inequalities: Children in America's schools.* New York: Crown.

Kraft, N. (1995). The dilemmas of deskilling: Reflections of a staff developer. *Journal of Staff Development, 16*(3), 31–35.

Kreisler, H. (1998, October 21). *Leadership in education: Conversation with David Pierpont Gardner, President of the William and Flora Hewlett Foundation.* Retrieved December 12, 2005, from http://globetrotter.berkeley.edu/ conversations/Gardner/gardner-con0.html

Lakes, R., & Burns, J. (2001). "It's like their culture": Resistant boys in the new vocationalism. *Journal of Industrial Teacher Education, 38*(4), 25–40.

Lambert, L. (1995). Toward a theory of constructivist leadership. In L. Lambert, D. Walker, D. P. Zimmerman, & J. E. Cooper (Eds.), *The constructivist leader* (pp. 28–51). New York: Teachers College Press.

Land, D. (2002). Local school boards under review: Their role and effectiveness in relation to students' academic achievement. *Review of Educational Research, 72*(2), 229–278.

Lankford, H., Loeb, S., & Wyckoff, J. (2002). Teacher sorting and the plight of urban schools: A descriptive analysis. *Educational Evaluation and Policy Analysis, 24*(1), 37–62.

Lao Tzu. (1997). *Lao Tzu: Tao te ching: A book about the way and the power of the way* (U. K. Le Guin with J. Seaton, Trans.). Boston: Shambhala. (Other translations available World Wide Web; for instance: http://www.clas.ufl.edu/users/gthursby/taoism/ttcstan3.htm)

Lareau, A. (1989). *Home advantage: Social class and parental intervention in elementary education.* New York: The Falmer Press.

Lasch, C. (1977). *Haven in a heartless world: The family besieged.* New York: Basic Books.

Lasch, C. (1991). *The true and only heaven: Progress and its critics.* New York: Norton.

Lave, J., & Wenger, E. (1991). *Situated learning: Legitimate peripheral participation.* Cambridge, England: Cambridge University Press.

Lee, J. O. (2002). State vs. local control of educational standards: Effects on teaching. *Educational Forum, 67*(1), 36–46.

Lee, S., & McKerrow, K. (1991, April). *Two pieces of wood: Symbols of control.* Paper presented at the Annual Meeting of the American Educational Research Association, Chicago, IL. (ERIC Document Reproduction No. ED332368)

Leithwood, K. A. (1992). The move toward transformational leadership. *Educational Leadership, 49*(5), 8–12.

Leithwood, K., & Menzies, T. (1998). A review of research concerning the implementation of site-based management. *School Effectiveness and School Improvement, 9*(3), 233–285.

Leonard, R. (1981, April). *Managerial styles in academe: Do men and women differ?* Paper presented at the Southern Speech Communication Association Annual Meeting, Austin, TX.

Levin, H. (Ed.). (2001). *Privatizing education: Can the marketplace deliver choice, efficiency, equity, and social cohesion?* Boston: Allyn & Bacon.

Levinas, E. (1998). *Entre nous: On thinking of the other* (M. B. Smith & B. Harshav, Trans.). New York: Columbia University Press.

Lewin, K. (1951). *Field theory in social science.* New York: Harper & Row.

Lieberman, A. (Ed.). (1988). *Building a professional culture in schools.* New York: Teachers College Press.

Lieberman, A. (Ed.). (1995). *The work of restructuring schools: Building from the ground up.* New York: Teachers College Press.

Lima, E. & Lima, M. (1998). Identity, cultural diversity, and education: Notes toward a pedagogy of the excluded. In Y. Zou & E. Trueba (Eds.), *Ethnic identity and power: Cultural contexts of political action in school and society* (pp. 321–344). Albany, NY: State University of New York Press.

Lincoln, Y. S., & Guba, E. G. (2000). Paradigmatic controversies, contradictions, and emerging confluences. In N. K. Denzin & Y. S. Lincoln (Eds.), *Handbook of qualitative research* (pp. 163–188). Thousand Oaks, CA: Sage.

Lipman, P. (1998). *Race, class, and power in school restructuring.* Albany, NY: State University of New York Press.

Logan, J. (1998). School leadership of the 90s and beyond: A window of opportunity for women educators. *Advancing Women in Leadership Journal, 1*(3). [Online journal] available: www.advancingwomen.com

Lomawaima, K. (1999). The unnatural history of American Indian education. In K. Swisher & J. Tippeconnic (Eds.), *Next steps: Research and practice to advance Indian education* (pp. 1–32). Charleston, WV: ERIC Clearinghouse on Rural Education and Small Schools.

Lowe, J. (2002). Computer-based education: Is it a panacea? *Journal of Research on Technology in Education, 34*(2), 163–171.

Lubienski, C., & Lubienski, S. (2006). *Charter, private, and public schools and academic achievement: New evidence from NAEP mathematics data.* New York: National Center for the Study of Privatization in Education. Retrieved April 18, 2006 from http://www.ncspe.org/publications_files/op111.pdf

Lukács, G. (1968). *Historical consciousness: Or, the remembered past.* New York: Harper & Row.

Lutz, F. W., & Merz, C. (1992). *The politics of school/community relations.* New York: Teachers College Press.

Lyons, N. (1990). Visions and competencies: An educational agenda for exploring ethical and intellectual dimensions of decision and conflict negotiation. In J. Antler & S. Biklen (Eds.), *Changing education: Women as radicals and conservators* (pp. 277–294). Albany: SUNY Press.

Lyotard, J. (1984). *The postmodern condition: A report on knowledge* (G. Bennington & B. Massumi, Trans.). Minneapolis, MN: University of Minnesota Press.

Lyson, T. (2002). What does a school mean to a community? Assessing the social and economic benefits of schools to rural villages in New York. *Journal of Research in Rural Education, 17*(3), 131–137.

Ma, L. (1999). *Knowing and teaching elementary school mathematics.* Mahwah, NJ: Lawrence Erlbaum Associates.

Machiavelli, N. (1999). *The prince* (G. Bull, Trans.). New York: Penguin. (Original work published 1515, W. Marriott translation available World Wide Web: http://www.ilt.columbia.edu/academic/digitexts/machiavelli/the_prince/title.html)

Maines, D. R. (2003). Interactionism's place. *Symbolic Interaction, 26*(1), 5–18.

Majors, R. (Ed.). (2001). *Educating our black children: New directions and radical approaches.* Independence, KY: RoutledgeFalmer.

Mander, J., & Goldsmith, E. (Eds.). (1996). *The case against the global economy and a turn toward the local.* San Francisco: Sierra Club Books.

Maranto, R. (2005). A tale of two cities: School privatization in Philadelphia and Chester. *American Journal of Education, 111*(2), 151.

Marcoulides, G. A., & Heck, R. H. (1994). The changing role of educational assessment in the 1990s. *Education and Urban Society, 26*(4), 332–339.

Marris, P. (1975). *Loss and change.* New York: Anchor Press/Doubleday.

Marsh, D., & Codding, J. (1999). *The new American high school.* Thousand Oaks, CA: Corwin Press.

Marshall, C., & Mitchell, B. (1989, March). *Women's careers as a critique of the administrative culture.* Paper presented at the American Educational Research Association Annual Conference, San Francisco, CA.

Martin, K. (1997). Diversity orientations: Culture, ethnicity, and race. In L. Naylor (Ed.), *Cultural Diversity in the United States* (pp. 75–90). Westport, CT: Bergin & Garvey.

Marx, K. (1907). *Capital: A critique of political economy.* New York: International Publishers. (Original work published 1867)

Masini, D. E., & Edirisooriya, G. (2000, November). *Never a nation at risk: Exorcising the ghost of education past.* Paper presented at the Annual Meeting of the Mid-South Educational Research Association, Bowling Green, KY. (ERIC Document Reproduction Service No. ED448180)

Maslow, A. H. (1962). *Toward a psychology of being.* Princeton, NJ: Van Nostrand.

Mathews, D. (1996). *Is there a public for public education?* Dayton, OH: Kettering Foundation Press.

Maxcy, S. (1991). *Educational leadership: A critical pragmatic perspective.* New York: Bergin & Garvey.

Mayberry, M. (1999). Reproductive and resistant pedagogies: The comparative roles of collaborative learning and feminist pedagogy in science education. In M. Mayberry & E. C. Rose (Eds.), *Meeting the challenge: Innovative feminist pedagogies in action* (pp. 1–22). New York: Routledge.

Mazzeo, C. (2001). Frameworks of state: Assessment policy in historical perspective. *Teachers College Record, 103*(3), 367–397.

McCadden, B. M. (1998). Why is Michael always getting timed out? Race, class, and the disciplining of other people's children. In R. E. Butchart & B. McEwan (Eds.), *Classroom dis-*

cipline in American schools: Problems and possibilities for democratic education. Albany, NY: State University of New York Press.

McCreight, C. (1999). Female superintendents, barriers, and the struggle for equity. Eugene, OR: ERIC Clearinghouse on Educational Management. (ERIC Reproduction Service No. ED 432 041)

McCroskey, J., & Richmond, V. (1978). Community size as a predictor of development of communication apprehension: Replication and extension. *Communication Education, 27*(3), 12–19.

McGregor, D. (1960). *The human side of enterprise.* New York: McGraw-Hill.

McGrew, A. G. (1999). Democratizing global governance: Democratic theory and democracy beyond borders. *Theoria (Pietermaritzburg), 94,* 1–29.

McMeekin, R. (2004). *Understanding educational accountability and how it can be applied to the countries of Latin America.* (Background paper for a Conference on Educational Accountability, to be held in Santiago, Chile, March 2005).

McNeil, L. M. (2000). *Contradictions of school reform : Educational costs of standardized testing.* New York: Routledge.

McPherson, A. F., & Willms, J. D. (1986). Certification, class conflict, religion, and community: A socio-historical explanation of the effectiveness of contemporary schools. In A. C. Kerckhoff (Ed.), *Research in sociology of education and socialization* (Vol. 6, pp. 227–302). Greenwich, CT: JAI Press.

McSweeney, B. (2002). Hofstede's model of national cultural differences and consequences: A triumph of faith—A failure of analysis. *Human Relations, 55*(1), 89–118.

Mechanic, D. (1962). Sources of power of lower participants in complex organizations. *Administrative Science Quarterly, 7*(3), 349–364.

Meier, D. (1995). *The power of their ideas: Lessons for America from a small school in Harlem.* Boston: Beacon Press.

Meier, D. (2002). *In schools we trust: Creating communities of learning in an era of testing and standardization.* Boston: Beacon.

Merchant, C. (1991). Ecofeminism and feminist theory. In I. Diamond & G. Orienstein (Eds.), *Reweaving the world: The emergence of ecofeminism* (pp. 100–105). San Francisco: Sierra Club Books.

Merten, D. E. (1996). Burnout as cheerleader: The cultural basis for prestige and privilege in junior high school. *Anthropology & Education Quarterly, 27*(1), 51–70.

Meyer, J. W., Boli, J., Thomas, G., & Ramirez, F. O. (1997). World society and the nation state. *American Journal of Sociology, 1,* 144–181.

Meyer, J. W., & Scott, W. R., (with Rowan, B., & Deal, T. E.). (1983). *Organizational environments: Ritual and rationality.* Beverly Hills, CA: Sage.

Michie, G. (1999). *Holler if you hear me: The education of a teacher and his students.* New York: Teachers College Press.

Miller, R. L. (1990). Beyond contact theory: The impact of community affluence on integration efforts in five suburban high schools. *Youth and Society, 22*(1), 12–34.

Mintrop, H. (2001). Educating students to teach in a constructivist way—Can it all be done? *Teachers College Record, 103*(2), 207–239.

Mintzberg, H. (1994). *The rise and fall of strategic planning: Reconceiving roles for planning, plans, planners.* New York: Free Press.

Mish, F. C. (1984). *Webster's ninth new collegiate dictionary.* Springfield, MA: Merriam-Webster.

Molnar, A. (1996). *Giving kids the business: The commercialization of America's schools.* Boulder, CO: Westview Press.

Montessori, M. (1946). *Education for a new world.* Madras, India: Kalakshetra Press.

Moore, P. (1999). When persuasion fails: Coping with power struggles. *Technical Communication, 46*(3), 351–359.

Morgan, D., & Alwin, D. (1980). When less is more: School size and social participation. *Social Psychology Quarterly, 43,* 241–252.

Morton, D. (1992). On "hostile pedagogy," "supportive pedagogy," and "political correctness": Letter to a student complaining of his grade. *Journal of Urban and Cultural Studies, 2*(2), 79–94.

Moses, R. P., & Cobb, C. E., Jr. (2001). *Radical equations: Math literacy and civil rights.* Boston: Beacon Press.

Muijs, D., Harris, A., Chapman, C., Stoll, L., & Russ, J. (2004). Improving schools in socioeconomically disadvantaged areas—A review of research evidence. *School Effectiveness and School Improvement, 15*(2), 149–175.

Muller, C., & Kerbow, D. (1993). *Parent involvement in the home, school, and community.* In B. Schneider & J. S. Coleman (Eds.), *Parents, their children, and schools* (pp. 13–42). Boulder, CO: Westview Press.

Munck, R. (2002). *Globalisation and labour: The new "great transformation."* London: Zed.

Mungazi, D. A. (1999). *The evolution of educational theory in the United States.* Westport, CT: Praeger.

Munson, B. (1968). *Changing community dimensions: The interrelationships of social and economic variables.* Columbus, OH: College of Administrative Science, Ohio State University.

Nagel, E. (1964). *The structure of science.* New York: Harcourt Brace.

Nagel, T. (1986). *The view from nowhere.* New York: Oxford University Press.

Nash, G., & Dunn, R. (1995). History standards and culture wars. *Social Education, 59*(1), 5–7.

National Center for Education Statistics. (2002). *Common Core of Data.* Washington, DC: Author.

National Center for Education Statistics. (2004). *Digest of Education Statistics.* Washington, DC: Author.

National Commission on Excellence in Education. (1983). *A nation at risk: The imperative for educational reform.* Washington, DC: Author.

National Commission on Excellence in Educational Administration. (1987). *Leaders for America's schools.* Tempe, AZ: University Council for Educational Administration. (ERIC Document Reproduction Service No. ED286265)

National Commission on Excellence. (1983). *A nation at risk: The imperative for educational reform.* Washington, DC: United States Department of Education. Retrieved October 31, 2005, from http://www.ed.gov/pubs/NatAtRisk/index.html

National Council for the Social Studies. *Curriculum standards for social studies: Expectations of excellence.* Washington, DC: Author.

National Council of Teachers of Mathematics. (2000). *Principles and standards for school mathematics.* Reston, VA: Author.

National Policy Board for Educational Administration. (2002). *Standards for advanced programs in educational leadership: For principals, superintendents, curriculum directors, and supervisors.* Reston, VA: Educational Leadership Constituent Council. Retrieved November 18, 2005, from http://www.npbea.org/ELCC/ELCCStandards%20_5-02.pdf

Neuman, M. J., & Bennett, J. (2001). Starting strong: Policy implications for early childhood education and care in the U.S. *Phi Delta Kappan, 83*(3), 246–254.

Neuse, S. (1978). Professionalism and authority: Women in public service. *Public Administration Review, 38,* 436–441.

New Jersey Department of Education. (1996). *New Jersey core curriculum content standards: The need* [Electronic version]. Retrieved July 1, 2001, from http://www.state.nj.us/njded/CCC/01introneed.htm

Ng, R., Staton, P., & Scane, J. (Eds.). (1995). *Anti-racism, feminism, and critical approaches to education.* Westport, CT: Bergin & Garvey.

Noddings, N. (1984). *Caring, a feminine approach to ethics and moral education.* Berkeley, CA: University of California Press.

Norris, C., & Benjamin, A. (1988). *What is deconstruction?* New York: St. Martin's Press.

Oakes, J. (1985). *Keeping track: How schools structure inequality.* New Haven, CT: Yale University Press.

O'Brien, G., & Pearson, J. (2004). Autism and learning disability. *Autism: The International Journal of Research and Practice, 8*(2), 125–140.

Ogbu, J. (1974). *The next generation: An ethnography of education in an urban neighborhood.* New York: Academic Press.

Ogbu, J. (1978). *Minority education and caste: The American system in cross-cultural perspective.* New York: Academic Press.

Ohanian, S. (1999). *One size fits few: The folly of educational standards.* Portsmouth, NH: Heinemann.

Ophuls, M. (Director). (1971). *The sorrow and the pity* (Le chagrin et la pitié) [documentary film]. Released by Milestone Films, Harrington Park, NJ. Classic film available from a variety of retail outlets.

Orfield, G. (2001). *Schools more separate: Consequences of a decade of resegregation.* Cambridge, MA: The Civil Rights Project, Harvard University.

Orfield, G., & Yun, J. T. (1999). *Resegregation in American schools.* Cambridge, MA: The Civil Rights Project, Harvard University.

Orr, D. (1994). *Earth in mind: On education, environment, and the human prospect.* Washington, DC: Island Press.

Osborn, M., Broadfoot, P., Planel, C., & Pollard, A. (1997). Social class, educational opportunity and equal entitlement: Dilemmas of schooling in England and France. *Comparative Education, 33*(3), 375–393.

Osterman, K. (1998, April). *Using constructivism and reflective practice to bridge the theory/practice gap.* Paper presented at the Annual Meeting of the American Educational Research Association. (ERIC Document Reproduction Service No. ED425518)

Owen-Vandersluis, S. (2003). *Ethics and cultural policy in a global economy.* New York: Palgrave Macmillan.

Oxford English Dictionary. (1971). *A new English Dictionary on a historical basis* (Compact Edition). Oxford, England: Oxford University Press.

Ozga, J. (1993). Introduction: In a different mode. In J. Ozga (Ed.), *Women in educational management.* Buckingham, England: Open University Press.

Palmer, D. (1983). Personal values and managerial decisions: Are there differences between women and men? *College Student Journal, 17*(2). 124–131.

Pappano, L. (2003, November 9). Support no certainty for gay teachers. Retrieved April 21, 2004, from http://www.bostonglobe.com

Parkerson, D. H., & Parkerson, J. A. (1998). *The emergence of the common school in the US countryside.* Lewiston, NY: The Edwin Mellen Press.

Parry, T. R. (1997). Theory meets reality in the education voucher debate: Some evidence from Chile. *Education Economics, 5*(3), 307–331.

Paterson, F. M. S. (1989). *Out of place: Public policy and the emergence of truancy.* London: The Falmer Press.

Payne, R. (1998). *The framework for understanding poverty.* Highlands, TX: Aha! Processing, Inc.

Perkinson, H. J. (1971). *The possibilities of error: An approach to education.* New York: David McKay.

Perlmutter, P. (2002). Minority group prejudice. *Society, 39*(3), 59–65.

Perry, P. (2001). White means never having to say you're ethnic: White youth and the construction of "cultureless" identities. *Journal of Contemporary Ethnography, 30*(1), 56–91.

Perryman, J. (2005). School leadership and management after special measures: Discipline without the gaze? *School Leadership and Management, 25*(3), 281–297.

Peshkin, A. (1982). *The imperfect union.* Chicago: University of Chicago Press.

Peterson, G. (1999). Demonstrated actions of instructional leaders: An examination of five California superintendents. *Education Policy Analysis Archives, 7*(18). Retrieved April 17, 2006 from http://epaa.asu.edu/epaa/v7n18.html

Peterson, K. D. (2002). Positive or negative. *Journal of Staff Development, 23*(3), 10–15.

Phelps, A. J., & Cherin, L. (2003). The power of practice: What students learn from how we teach. *Journal of Chemical Education, 80*(7), 829–832.

Phillips, D. C. (1997). Coming to grips with radical social constructivisms. *Science & Education, 6*(1–2), 85–104.

Phillips, J. (2000). *Contested knowledge: A guide to critical theory.* New York: St. Martins.

Pierce v. Society of Sisters, 268 US 510 (U. S. Supreme Court 1925).

Pitner, N. (1981). Hormones and harems: Are the activities of superintending different for a women? In P. Schmuck, W. Charters, & R. Carlson (Eds.), *Educational policy and management: Sex differentials* (pp. 297–306). New York: Academic Press.

Plank, D. (2003, April). *The domestic policy impact of international evidence: The case of school choice.* Paper presented at the annual meeting of the American Educational Research Association, Chicago, IL.

Porter, M. K. (1995, October). *In the best interest of the children: Community engagement with education in Appalachian Kentucky.* Paper presented at the Annual Conference of the National Rural Education Association, Salt Lake City, UT. (ERIC Document Reproduction Service No. ED 411 102)

Portes, A. (2002). Immigration's aftermath. *American Prospect: A Journal for the Liberal Imagination, 13*(7), 1–3.

Postman, N. (1985). *Amusing ourselves to death: Public discourse in the age of show business.* New York: Viking.

Postman, N., & Weingartner, C. (1969). *Teaching as a subversive activity.* New York: Dell.

Powell, B., & Steelman, L. C. (1996). Bewitched, bothered, and bewildering: The use and misuse of state SAT and ACT scores. *Harvard Educational Review, 661*(1), 27–59.

Powers, T. F. (2002). Postmodernism and James A. Banks' multiculturalism: The limits of intellectual history. *Educational Theory, 52*(2), 209–221.

Prawat, R. S., & Peterson, P. L. (1999). Social constructivist views of learning. In J. Murphy & K. S. Louis (Eds.), *Handbook of research on educational administration: A project of the American Educational Research Association* (pp. 203–226). San Francisco: Jossey Bass.

Presthus, R. (1962). *The organizational society: An analysis and a theory.* New York: Vintage Books.

Purpel, D. (1999). *Moral outrage in education.* New York: Peter Lang.

Quigley, R. (2005, August 24). District narrows search for principal [Electronic version]. *Beaufort Gazette.* Retrieved September 12, 2005, from http://www.beaufortgazette.com/local_news/story/5125721p-4665227c.html

Raadschelders, J. (1997). Size and organizational differentiation in historical perspective. *Journal of Public Administration Research and Theory, 7*(3), 419–441.

Ravitch, D. (1995). *National standards in American education: A citizen's guide.* Washington, DC: Brookings Institution.

Ravitch, D. (2000). *Left back: A century of failed school reforms.* New York: Simon & Schuster.

Ravitch, D. (2003). The test of time. *Education Next, 3*(2), 32–38.

Raynor, A. (2005, Spring). Small learning communities: Putting power in the "C". *VUE: Voices in Urban Education,* 32–43.

Raywid, M. A. (1999). On the viability of the comprehensive high school. *Educational Administration Quarterly, 35*(2), 305–310.

Reagan, T. G. (1996). *Non-Western educational traditions: Alternative approaches to educational thought and practice.* Hillsdale, NJ: Lawrence Erlbaum Associates.

Reardon, S. F., & Yun, J. T. (2001). Suburban racial change and suburban school segregation, 1987-95. *Sociology of Education, 74*(2), 79–101.

Regan, H., & Brooks, G. (1995). *Out of women's experience: Creating relational leadership.* Thousand Oaks, CA: Corwin Press.

Reich, R. (1991). *The work of nations: Preparing ourselves for 21st Century capitalism.* New York: Knopf.

Reitman, S. (1992). *The educational messiah complex: American faith in the redemptive power of schooling.* Sacramento, CA: Caddo Gap Press.

Reitzug, U. C. (1994). A case study of empowering principal behavior. *American Educational Research Journal, 31*(2), 283–307.

Reynolds, D. R. (2001, May). *Rural school consolidation in early twentieth century Iowa: Lessons for the early twenty-first century.* Paper presented at the Annual Meeting of the Wallace Family Conference on Gifted Education in Rural Schools, Iowa City, IA. (ERIC Document Reproduction Service No. ED 464778)

Rice, J. M. (1893). *The public school system in the United States.* New York: The Century Company.

Rieley, J. B. (1997). Scenario planning in higher education. *Community College Journal, 68*(1), 23–26.

Riley, B. E. (1977). *Accountability in education: A recurring concept.* (ERIC Document Reproduction Service No. ED 214269)

Rimer, A. (1984). Elementary school secretary: Information decision makers. *Educational Horizons, 63*(1), 16–18.

Rogers, E. M. (1995). *Diffusion of innovations* (4th ed.). New York: The Free Press.

Rogoff, B. (2003). *The cultural nature of human development.* Oxford, England: Oxford University Press.

Rorty, R. (1999). *Philosophy and social hope.* New York: Penguin.

Rosen, L. (2003). The politics of identity and marketiation of US Schools: How local meanings mediate global struggles. In G. Steiner-Khamsi (Ed.), *The global politics of educational borrowing and lending* (pp. 161–182). New York: Teachers College Press.

Rosenthal, R., & Jacobson, L. (1992). *Pygmalion in the classroom: Teacher expectation and pupils' intellectual development* (expanded edition). New York: Irvington Publishers.

Ross, D. (2001). The math wars. *The New Individualist: An Objectivist Review of Politics and Culture, 5*(4). Retrieved September 20, 2005 from http://www.ios.org/navigator/issues/nav_5-2001.asp

Rotberg, I. (1998). Interpretation of international test score comparisons. *Science, 280*(15), 1030–1031.

Rousseau, J.-J. (1911). *Emile* (B. Foley, Trans.). New York: E. P. Dutton. (Original work published 1762)

Rule, J. B. (1997). *Theory and progress in social science.* New York: Cambridge University Press.

Rural School and Community Trust. (2000). *Standards in public schools.* Randolph, VT: The Rural School and Community Trust. (ERIC Document Reproduction Service No. ED456003)

Russell, C. (2002). Language, violence, and Indian mis-education. *American Indian Culture and Research Journal, 26*(4), 97–112.

Safstrom, C. (1999). On the way to a postmodern curriculum theory—moving from the question of unity to the question of difference. *Studies in Philosophy and Education, 18,* 221–233.

Saha, L. (1997). *International encyclopedia of the sociology of education.* New York: Pergamon.

Said, E. (1978). *Orientalism.* New York: Random House.

Saltman, K. (2000). *Collateral damage: Corporatizing public schools—A threat to democracy.* Lanham, MD: Rowman & Littlefield.

Sarason, S. (1971). *The culture of the school and the problem of change.* Boston: Allyn & Bacon.

Sassen, S. (1996). *Losing control? Sovereignty in an age of globalization*. New York: Columbia University Press.

Saul, J. R. (1992). *Voltaire's bastards: The dictatorship of reason in the West*. New York: Free Press.

Saunders, D. J. (1995). Did your mom eat your homework? Schools shift the blame for academic failure to parents. *Policy Review, 7*(2), 68–71.

Savage, C. J. (2001). "Because we did more with less": The agency of African American teachers in Franklin, Tennessee: 1890–1967. *Peabody Journal of Education, 76*(2), 170–203.

Schein, E. (1992). *Organizational culture and leadership*. San Francisco: Jossey-Bass.

Schmidt, W. H., Houang, R., & Cogan, L. (2002). A coherent curriculum: The case of mathematics. *American Educator, 26*(2), 10–26, 47–48.

Schmidt, W. H., McKnight, C. C., Houang, R. T., Wang, H., Wiley, D. E., Cogan, L. S., & Wolfe, R. G. (2001). *Why schools matter: A cross-national comparison of curriculum and learning*. San Francisco: Jossey-Bass.

Schmitt, D. (1994, February). *Integrating new theory and practice to prepare women for roles in educational administration*. Paper presented for the American Association of Colleges for Teacher Education Annual Conference, Chicago, IL.

Schoenfeld, A. H. (2004). The math wars. *Educational Policy, 18*(1), 253–286.

Schultz, E. A. (1990). *Dialog at the margins: Whorf, Bakhtin, and linguistic relativity*. Madison, WI: University of Wisconsin Press.

Scollay, S., & Logan, J. (1999). The gender equity role of educational administration: Where are we? Where do we want to go? *Journal of School Leadership, 9*(2), 97–124.

Scott, J. (1998). *Seeing like a state: How certain schemes to improve the human condition have failed*. New Haven, CT: Yale University Press.

Scott, W. R. (1995). Introduction: Institutional theory and organizations. In W. R. Scott & S. Christensen (Eds.), *The institutional construction of organizations: International and longitudinal studies* (pp. xi–xxiii). Thousand Oaks, CA: Sage.

Sedlak, M., Wheeler, C., Pullin, D., & Cusick, P. (1986). *Selling students short: Classroom bargains and academic reform in the American high school*. New York: Teachers College Press.

Senge, P. M. (1990). *The fifth discipline: The art and practice of the learning organization* (1st ed.). New York: Doubleday.

Serafin, A. (1998, April). *Outreach to future Hispanic educational leaders*. Paper presented at the National Student Success Conference, Kansas City, MO.

Sergiovanni, T. (1993). *Building community in schools*. San Francisco: Jossey-Bass.

Sergiovanni, T. (1994). Organizations or communities? Changing the metaphor changes the theory. *Educational Administration Quarterly, 30*(2), 214–226.

Sergiovanni, T. (2000). *The lifeworld of leadership: Creating culture, community, and personal meaning in our schools*. San Francisco: Jossey-Bass.

Seth, V. (2001). Self and similitude: Translating difference (modern colonialism and renaissance conquests). *Postcolonial Studies, 4*(3), 297–309.

Shakeshaft, C. (1987). *Women in educational administration*. Newbury Park, CA: Sage.

Shapiro, H., & Purpel, D. (1998). *Critical social issues in American education: Transformation in a postmodern world*. Mahwah, NJ: Lawrence Erlbaum Associates.

Shaughnessy, M. F. (2005, August 30). An interview with Ruby Payne: About teaching children in poverty. *EducationNews.org*. Retrieved October 18, 2005, from http://www.educationnews.org/an-interview-with-ruby-payne.htm

Shen, J. (2001). Teacher and principal empowerment: National, longitudinal, and comparative perspectives. *Educational Horizons, 79*(3), 124–129.

Shepard, S. (1997, October). *Differences in the perceived employment characteristics of men and women and employer/organizational policies toward men and women*. Paper presented at the Women in Educational Leadership Annual Conference, Lincoln, NE.

Sher, J. P. (1995). The battle for the soul of rural school reform. *Phi Delta Kappan, 77*(2), 143–148.

Sherwin, G., & Schmidt, S. (2003). Communication codes among African-American children and youth: The fast track from special education to prison. *Journal of Correctional Education, 54*(2), 45–52.

Siddle Walker, V. (1996). *Their highest potential: An African American school community in the segregated South.* Chapel Hill, NC: University of North Carolina Press.

Siegal, A. (1999). Despite growth, women, minorities still tiny portion of all U.S. superintendents. *AASA Leadership News* [On-line]: http://www.aasa.org/in/misc/4%2D14%2D99women.htm

Sim, S. (Ed.). (2001). *The Routledge companion to postmodernism.* New York: Routledge.

Simmons, A. (1999). *A safe place for dangerous truths: Using dialogue to overcome fear and distrust at work.* New York: American Management Association.

Simon, R. (1992). *Teaching against the grain: Texts for a pedagogy of possibility.* New York: Bergin & Garvey.

Skolnick, A. (2004). Rethinking the politics of the family. *Dissent, 51*(4), 45–47.

Skrla, L. (2000). The social construction of gender in the superintendency. *Journal of Education Policy, 15*(30), 293–316.

Smith, A., & Vaux, T. (2003). *Education, conflict and international development,* (Issues Paper). London: Department of International Development.

Smith, F. (2002). *The glass wall: Why mathematics can seem difficult.* New York: Teachers College Press.

Smith, G. A. (2002). Place-based education: Learning to be where we are. *Phi Delta Kappan, 83*(8), 584–594.

Smith, P. G. (1954). The role of philosophy in the preparation of school administrators. (Doctoral dissertation, Ohio State University, 1954). *Dissertation Abstracts International, 20*(8), 3166. (UMI No. AAT 6000117)

Smith, W. F., & Andrews, R. L. (1989). *Instructional leadership: How principals make a difference.* Alexandria, VA: Association for Supervision and Curriculum Development.

Snyder, T. D., & Hoffman, C. M. (2003). *Digest of education statistics, 2002.* Washington, DC: National Center for Education Statistics. (ERIC Document Reproduction Service No. ED 481156)

Snyder, T., Plisko, V., & Sonnenberg, W. (2004). *Digest of education statistics.* Washington, DC: U.S. Department of Education, National Center for Education Statistics. Retrieved October 15, 2005, from http://nces.ed.gov/programs/digest/d04/ch_2.asp

Sobel, D. (2004). *Place-based education: Connecting classrooms and communities.* Great Barrington, MA: The Orion Society.

Sokolof, H. (1996). A deliberative model for engaging the community. *School Administrator, 53*(10), 12–14, 16–18.

Spencer, B. L. (2001, April). *The seduction of the subject/citizen: Governmentality and school governance policy.* Paper presented at the Annual Meeting of the American Educational Research Association, Seattle, WA. (ERIC Document Reproduction Service No. ED 454585)

Spillane, J. P. (1996). School district matter: Local educational authorities and state instructional policy. *Educational Policy, 10*(1), 63–87.

Spindler, G. (Ed.). (1982). *Doing the ethnography of schooling.* New York: Holt, Rinehart, & Winston.

Spreen, C. A. (2004). Appropriating borrowed policies: Outcomes-based education in South Africa. In G. Steiner-Khamsi (Ed.), *The global politics of educational borrowing and lending* (pp. 101–113). New York: Teachers College Press.

Spring, J. (1990). *The American school, 1642–1990: Varieties of historical interpretation of the foundations and development of American Education.* New York: Longman.

Spring, J. (1994). *Deculturalization and the struggle for equality: A brief history of the education of dominated cultures in the United States.* New York: McGraw Hill.

Spring, J. (1998). *Education and the rise of the global economy.* Mahwah, NJ: Lawrence Erlbaum Associates.

Spring, J. (2001). *The American school, 1642–2000.* Boston: McGraw-Hill.

Stambach, A. (2003). World cultural and anthropological interpretations of "choice programming" in Tanzania. In K. Anderson-Levitt (Ed.), *Local meanings, global schooling: Anthropology and world culture theory* (pp. 141–160). New York: Palgrave Macmillan.

Starrat, R. (2001). Democratic leadership theory in late modernity: An oxymoron or ironic possibility? *International Journal of Leadership in Education, 4,* 333–352.

Steiner-Khamsi, G. (Ed.). (2004). *The global politics of educational borrowing and lending.* New York: Teachers College Press.

Stevenson, H. W., Chen, C., & Lee, S. Y. (1993). Mathematics achievement of Chinese, Japanese, and American children: Ten years later. *Science, 259,* 53–58.

Stigler, J. W., Gonzales, P. A., Kawanka, T., Knoll, S., & Serrano, A. (1999). *The TIMSS videotape classroom study: Methods and findings from an exploratory research project on eighth-grade mathematics instruction in Germany, Japan, and the United States.* Washington, DC: U.S. Department of Education, National Center for Educational Statistics.

Stigler, J. W., & Hiebert, J. (1999). *The teaching gap: Best ideas from the world's teachers for improving education in the classroom.* New York: The Free Press.

Strachan, J. (1997, March). *Resistance, agreement and appropriation: Practising feminist educational leadership in a "new right" context.* Paper presented at the Annual Meeting of the American Educational Research Association, Chicago, IL. (ERIC Document Reproduction Service No. ED 406 751)

Strachan, J. (1999). Feminist educational leadership: Locating the concepts in practice. *Gender and Education, 11*(3), 309–322.

Strang, D. (1987). The administrative transformation of American education: School district consolidation, 1938–1980. *Administrative Science Quarterly, 32*(3), 352–366.

Strike, K. A. (1997). Centralized goal formation and systemic reform: Reflections on liberty, localism, and pluralism. *Education Policy Analysis Archives, 5*(11), 1–37. Retrieved April 17, 2006 from http://epaa.asu.edu/epaa/v5n11.html

Strueber, C. (2004, June 9). St. Helena principal Davis appeals contract decision. *Beaufort Gazette* (online). Retrieved September 12, 2005, from http://www.beaufortgazette.com/local_news/story/364702p-3236411c.html

Sughrue, J. A. (2003). Zero tolerance for children: Two wrongs do not make a right. *Educational Administration Quarterly, 39*(2), 238–258.

Sungaila, H. (1990). The new science of chaos: Making a new science of leadership? *Journal of Educational Administration, 28*(2), 4–23.

Suppes, F. (1993) Credentialing scientific claims. *Perspectives on Science, 1*(2), 153–203.

Swift, J. (1940). *Gulliver's travels: An account of the four voyages into several remote nations of the world/now written down by Jonathan Swift.* New York: The Heritage Press. (Original work published 1726)

Tam, H. (1998). *Communitarianism: A new agenda for politics and citizenship.* New York: New York University Press.

Tasmanian Department of Education. (2005). [Equity standards: Discrimination/ bullying, harassment]. Retrieved September 10, 2005 from http://www.education.tas.gov.au/ equitystandards/discrimination/support/ rdefinitions.htm

Taylor, F. W. (1911). *The principles of scientific management.* New York: Harper & Brothers.

Terman, L. M. (1919). *The intelligence of school children, how children differ in ability, the use of mental tests in school grading and the proper education of exceptional children.* Boston: Houghton Mifflin.

Theobald, P. (1997). *Teaching the commons: Place, pride, and the renewal of community.* Boulder, CO: Westview.

Theobald, P., & Curtiss, J. (2000). Communities as curricula. *FORUM for Applied Research and Public Policy, 15* (1), 106–111.

Thompson, J. (1967). *Organizations in action: Social science bases of administrative theory.* New York: McGraw-Hill.

Thompson, T. (1992). Increasing opportunities for minorities in school administration. *NASSP Bulletin, 76*(546), 6–11.

Tiller, T. (2000, May). Every other day. In J. Montgomery & A. Kitchenham (Eds.), *Proceedings of the "Rural Communities and Identities in the Global Millennium" International Conference.* Namaimo, BC: Malaspina University-College (ERIC Document Reproduction Service No. ED 455064).

Tilly, C. (2004). Past, present, and future globalizations. In G. Steiner-Khamsi (Ed.), *The global politics of educational borrowing and lending* (pp. 13–28). New York: Teachers College Press.

Timar, T., & Tyack, D. (1999). *The invisible hand of ideology: Perspectives from the history of school governance.* Denver, CO: Education Commission of the States. (ERIC Document Reproduction Service No. ED433609)

Tippeconnic, J. (1997). Tribal control of American Indian education: Observations since the 1960s with implications for the future. In K. Swisher & J. Tippeconnic (Eds.), *Next steps: Research and practice to advance Indian education,* pp. 33–52. Charleston, WV: ERIC Clearinghouse on Rural Education and Small Schools.

Toll, C. (2001). Critical and postmodern perspectives on school change. *Journal of Curriculum and Supervision, 16,* 345–367.

Tsoukas, H. (2005). *Complex knowledge: Studies in organizational epistemology.* Oxford, England: Oxford University Press.

Tucker, K. (1999). Scenario planning. *Association Management, 51*(4), 70–75.

Tully, K. (1989). *A feminist redefinition of leadership.* Unpublished manuscript. (ERIC Document Reproduction Service No. ED315370)

Tupas, T. R. F. (2003). History, language planners, and strategies of forgetting: The problem of consciousness in the Philippines. *Language Problems & Language Planning, 27*(1), 1–25.

Tyack, D. B. (1974). *The one best system: A history of American urban education.* Cambridge, MA: Harvard University Press.

Tyack, D. B., & Cuban, L. (1995). *Tinkering toward utopia: A century of public school reform.* Cambridge, MA: Harvard University Press.

Tyack, D. B., & Hansot, E. (1982). *Managers of virtue: Public school leadership in America, 1820–1980.* New York: Basic Books.

U.S. Department of Education, National Center for Educational Statistics. (1998). *Pursuing excellence: A study of U.S. twelfth-grade mathematics and science achievement in international context* (NCES 98–049). Washington, DC: U.S. Government Printing Office.

Vaughn, M. (Director/Producer). (2004). *Layer cake* (Motion picture). [Distributed in the U.S. by Columbia Tristar Pictures.]

Vroom, V. H., & Jago, A. G. (1988). *The new leadership: Managing participation in organizations.* Englewood Cliffs, NJ: Prentice-Hall.

Walberg, H. J., & Bast, J. (1998). Understanding market-based school reform. *The CEIC Review, 8*(1). Retrieved October 1, 2005, from http://www.temple.edu/lss/htmlpublications/ceicreviews/ceic8-1.htm

Walzer, M. (1988). *The company of critics: Social criticism and political commitment in the twentieth century.* New York: Basic Books.

Walzer, M. (1995). The concept of civil society. In M. Walzer (Ed.), *Toward a global civil society* (pp. 1–28). Providence, RI: Berghahn Books.

Wanca-Thibault, M., & Tompkins, P. (1998). Speaking like a man (and a woman) about organizational communication: Feminization and feminism as a recognizable voice. *Management Communication Quarterly, 11*(4), 606–621.

Washington, S. M. (2005). Bringing traditional teachings to leadership. *American Indian Quarterly, 28*(3–4), 583–603.

Weber, M. (1947). *The theory of social and economic organization* (A. M. Henderson, Trans.). New York: Oxford University Press.

Weber, M. (1958). *The protestant ethic and the spirit of capitalism* (T. Parsons, Trans.). New York: Scribner's. (Original work published 1904)

Weber, M. (1968). *Basic concepts in sociology.* (H. P. Secher, Trans.). New York: Citadel Press. (Original work published 1922, first section of *Wirtschaft und Gesellschaft*, "Soziologische Grundbegriffe")

Weber, M. (1924/1968). *Economy and society: An outline of interpretive sociology.* Berkeley, CA: University of California Press.

Weber, S. (1994). Deep ecology: Beyond mere environmentalism. *Pathways: The Ontario Journal of Outdoor Education, 6*(2), 10–12.

Weiler, K. (1988). *Women teaching for change.* South Hadley, MA: Bergin & Garvey.

Wells, A., Lopez, A., Scott, J., & Holme, J. (1999). Charter schools as postmodern paradox: Rethinking social stratification in an age of deregulated school choice. *Harvard Educational Review, 69,* 172–204.

Wenger, E. (1998). *Communities of practice: Learning, meaning, and identity.* Cambridge, England: Cambridge University Press.

Wenger, E. (2000). Communities of practice and social learning systems. *Organization, 7*(2), 225–246.

West, C. (1999). The new cultural politics of difference. In C. West (Ed.), *The Cornel West Reader* (pp. 119–140). New York: Civitas.

Wheat, D. (2000). *Value-added accountability: A systems solution to the school accreditation problem.* Springfield, MA: Thomas Jefferson Institute for Public Policy. (Available on the World Wide Web: http://www.thomasjeffersoninst.org)

Wheatley, M. (1994). *Leadership and the new science: Learning about organization from an orderly universe.* San Francisco: Berrett-Koehler Publishers.

White, T. H. (1958). *The once and future king.* New York: Putnam.

Wiley, T. G., & Wright, W. E. (2004). Against the undertow: Language-minority education policy and politics in the "age of accountability." *Educational Policy, 18*(1), 142–168 .

Wilkinson, D. (1996).Integration dilemmas in a racist culture. *Society, 33*(3), 27–31.

Wilkinson, K. P. (1991). *The community in rural America.* New York: Greenwood Press.

Williams, J. H. (2003a). Why compare? *International Educator, 12*(4), 18–25.

Williams, J. H. (2003b, March). *Educational performance of the poor: An analysis of PISA data.* Paper presented at the Annual Meeting of the Comparative and International Education Society, New Orleans, LA.

Williams, R. (1961). *The long revolution.* Aylesbury, England: Watson and Viney.

Williams, R. (1973). *The country and the city.* New York: Oxford University Press.

Williams, R. (1983). *Keywords: A vocabulary of culture and society* [Rev. ed.]. New York: Oxford University Press.

Williams, R. (1989). *The politics of modernism.* London: Verso.

Williams, R. (2001). Culture is ordinary. In J. Higgins (Ed.), *The Raymond Williams reader* (pp. 10–24). Oxford, England: Blackwell. (Original work published 1958)

Willis, P. (1977). *Learning to labour: How working class kids get working class jobs.* Farnborough, England: Saxon House.

Willms, J. D. (1999). *Inequalities in literacy skills among youth in Canada and the United States.* (International Adult Literacy Survey No. 6). Ottawa, ON: Human Resources Development Canada and National Literacy Secretariat.

Willower, D. J. (1996). Postpositivist conceptions of science in educational administration: An introduction. *Educational Administration Quarterly, 32*(3), 344–365.

Wilson, J. (2003). James Q. Wilson on John Ogbu: Convincing black students that studying hard is not "acting white." *Journal of Blacks in Higher Education, 39*, 85–88.

Wiseman, A. W. (2003, April). *The expectation paradox in forty nations: A cross-national study of how school environments influence what principals do.* Paper presented at the Annual Meeting of the American Educational Research Association, Chicago, IL. (ERIC Document Reproduction Service No. ED479287)

Wislocki-Goin, M. (1993). *The Tantric proposition in leadership education: You make me feel like a natural woman.* Paper presented at the Women in Higher Education annual conference, El Paso, TX.

Wittgenstein, L. (1960). *Philosophical investigations* (G. E. M. Anscombe, Trans.). New York: Macmillan.

Wolff, E. (2000). *Recent Trends in wealth ownership, 1983–1998* (Working Paper No. 300). Blithewood, NY: Levy Economics Institute.

Wolverton, M. (1999). The school superintendency: Male bastion or equal opportunity? *Advancing Women in Leadership Journal, 2*(2), 7–14.

Woodrum, A. (2004, September 7). State-mandated testing and cultural resistance in Appalachian schools: Competing values and expectations. *Journal of Research in Rural Education, 19*(1). Retrieved December 22, 2005, from http://www.umaine.edu/jrre/19-1.htm.

Woodson, C. (1996). *The miseducation of the Negro.* Grand Rapids, MI: Candace Press. (Original work published 1933)

Woodward, K. (1997). *Identity and difference.* Newbury Park, CA: Sage.

Young, I. P. (1984). An examination of job satisfaction for female and male public school superintendents. *Planning and Changing, 15*(2), 114–24.

Young, R. A., & Collin, A. (2004). Introduction: Constructivism and social constructionism in the career field. *Journal of Vocational Behavior, 64*(3), 373–388.

Yukl, G. (2006). *Leadership in organizations* (6th ed.). Upper Saddle River, NJ: Prentice-Hall.

Ziebarth, T. (1999). *The changing landscape of education governance.* Denver, CO: Education Commission of the States.

Zinn, H. (1999). *A people's history of the United States: 1492–present.* New York: Harper Collins.

Zucker, L. (1977). The role of institutionalization in cultural persistence. *American Sociological Review, 42*(5), 726–743.

Author Index

Subject Index

A

Acceptance, 195–196
Accountability, 46–47, 65
   issues regarding, 68–71
   policies on, effects of, 97
   surveillance and, 278–279
Action, theories of, 4–6
Adaptation, 196
   by systems, 92–94
Administration, *see* School administration
African Americans, 54, *see also* People
      with darker skins
Agency, critical theory and, 249
Algebra, and racism, 165
Alternative theories, 6–10
   and school administration, 71–73
American Indians, and traditional educa-
      tion, 313
Andrus, Ethel Percy, 211
Anomie, mass society and, 116
Anthropology, 175
Antiracist curriculum, 164–167
Apathy, mass society and, 116
Aristotle, 109
Assertive discipline, 21
Assimilation
   behavioral, 155
   structural, 155–156
Assimilationist perspective, 197
Autism, theories on, 23

B

Bacon, Francis, 109
Banking model, of education, 46
Behavioral assimilation, 155
Behaviorism, 21
   hidden values in, 26–27
Beliefs, versus theory, 50
Best practice
   assumptions of, 335
   issues with, 24
Bilingualism, case study on, 341–343
Bricolage, definition of, 267
Bureaucracy
   and privatization, 321
   and schools, 21
   theories of, 6–7, 29–30, 31*t*
Busing, 27

C

Canada, quality of life in, 115
Capacity building, 103
Capitalism
   critical theory on, 246–247
   and democracy, 250
   and globalization, 305–306
   neo-liberalism and, 110
   and schools, 239
Case studies
   communitarianism and, 142–144

future of, 212–213
history of, 210–211
Working class, and school administration,
257–258

Y

Young, Ella Flagg, 211
Youth suicide rates, 58

Z

Zero-tolerance policies, 59–60
case study on, 350–353X